Learning Resources Center
Collin County Community College District
PRESTON RIDGE CAMPUS
Frisco, Texas 75035

Real Democracy

JS   Bryan, Frank M.
431
B79   Real democracy.
2004

    $19.00

American Politics and Political Economy
A series edited by Benjamin I. Page

REAL democracy

The New England Town Meeting and How It Works

Frank M. Bryan

The University of Chicago Press
Chicago and London

Frank M. Bryan is professor of political science at the University of Vermont. He is the author, coauthor, or editor of four books, including *Politics in the Rural States* and *The Vermont Papers: Recreating Democracy on a Human Scale*, as well as several books of Yankee humor such as the bestseller *Real Vermonters Don't Milk Goats*.

The University of Chicago Press, Chicago 60637
The University of Chicago Press, Ltd., London
© 2004 by The University of Chicago
All rights reserved. Published 2004
Printed in the United States of America

13 12 11 10 09 08 07 06 05 04   1 2 3 4 5
ISBN: 0-226-07796-9 (cloth)
ISBN: 0-226-07797-7 (paper)

Library of Congress Cataloging-in-Publication Data

Bryan, Frank M.
    Real democracy: the New England town meeting and how
it works/Frank M. Bryan.
        p.   cm.– (American politics and political economy)
    Includes bibliographical references and index.
    ISBN 0-226-07796-9 (alk. paper) –
    ISBN 0-226-07797-7 (pbk. : alk. paper)
        1. Local government–New England.   2. Democracy–New England.
    3. Political participation–New England. I. Title. II. Series.

JS431.B79 2004
320.8'5'0974–dc21   2003008362

⊗ The paper used in this publication meets the minimum requirements of the American National Standard for Information Sciences—Permanence of Paper for Printed Library Materials, ANSI Z39.48-1992.

For my children

Rebecca
Linda
Catherine
Jennifer
Jeffrey
Frank
Rachel

I'm going out to clean the pasture spring;
I'll only stop to rake the leaves away
(And wait to watch the water clear, I may):
I shan't be gone long—You come too.

Robert Frost, "The Pasture"

Contents

PRESTON RIDGE LIBRARY
COLLIN COLLEGE
FRISCO, TX 75035

There are several ways of crossing barbed-wire fences according to your inner differences.

Frances Frost

The epigraph is from Frances Frost, "Advice to a Trespasser," in *Hemlock Wall* (New Haven: Yale University Press, 1929), 32. Frances Frost, a Vermonter best known for her children's stories, was no relation to Robert Frost, although she was a prizewinning poet (the Yale Prize, the Golden Rose Award of the New England Poetry Club, and the Shelley Memorial Award). See Margaret Edwards, "Frances Frost, 1905–1959: Sketch of a Vermont Poet," *Vermont History* 56 (Spring 1988): 102–111.

It was the summer of 1972. Jane Mansbridge called, and we agreed to meet halfway. She was hard into the research for *Beyond Adversary Democracy*,[1] which contains the best treatment ever published of town meeting democracy in one place, and she was living in "Selby"—her fictitious name for the Vermont town she was studying. I was living in an abandoned deer camp on Big Hollow Road in Starksboro. Since we shared an interest in town meeting, where could we meet and swap what we knew? In the hundred or so miles of green mountains between Selby and Starksboro, "halfway" meeting places are hard to find. But there is a covered bridge across a river along the highway. I suggested it as much as a test as for any other reason. That would do, she said, without missing a beat.

We had never met before we parked our cars on the roadside by the bridge that June afternoon and headed down to a shady spot in the cow pasture beside the river. But there's something in crossing a barbed wire fence together that breaks the ice. Near the end of our conversation and our exchange of ideas, data, and various methodological conundrums, I made a mistake. I whined. Working grantless, without graduate students, and with a huge teaching load (four classes per semester in a small college, St. Michael's in Colchester, Vermont), how could I ever accomplish what it would take to write the definitive book on town meeting?

1. Jane Mansbridge, *Beyond Adversary Democracy* (New York: Basic Books, 1980).

The glint in her eyes danced between reproach and amusement. "Then it will become your life's work, Frank," she said.

And so it has.

The Anthropology of Making Do

My mother raised me a Democrat. Vermont raised me a democrat. This book springs from a life of fighting the dissonance between the two. From my earliest recollections I witnessed real democracy work itself out in the little town of Newbury, high on the fall line of the Connecticut River. My interest in social science, however, began with a teacher named Scott Mahoney, who despite being a socialist, a Democrat, and gay, managed to do passably well in a Republican farming town of 1,453 people and a high school with sixty students.[2] In my freshman "civics" course he sent us to town meeting. Most of us had been before, of course, but he insisted we record *data*, not just impressions. The next day in class was the first time I ever heard the term "political science." Later, as a college student, I noticed something. Nearly everyone who said or wrote anything about small-town life or town meeting got it wrong. They inflated the hell out of either the positives or the negatives.

Up front I'd better tell you this: I am a passionate believer in real democracy—where the people make decisions that matter, on the spot, in face-to-face assemblies that have the force of law. Before town meeting day the town taxes itself to fund a community library. The next day it does not. The people of the town have voted the expenditure down. Although I might not like the result, I'll live with it—and not because town meeting is filled with "the chosen people of God," as Jefferson said. If it were filled with all those chosen people, I'd probably be too bored to pay attention. I'll live with the result because, as former congressman Morris Udall put it, "Democracy is like sex. When it is good, it is very, very good. When it is bad, it is still better than anything else."[3]

---

2. My graduating class contained seven students. I finished in the top ten.

3. On the other hand, the harm done to town meeting by inflated romanticized accounts of its workings is incalculable. Over the past thirty-five years I have marked dozens of accounts like this: In 1977 the University of Vermont advertised itself as located in a state where "on the first Tuesday in March each year, residents gather at a town hall or school auditorium or church basement to vote on most of the matters of import affecting the town in the coming twelve months." "Being in Vermont," in *The University of Vermont 1977* (Burlington: University of Vermont, 1977, 2. Wrong. The residents vote on many matters of import, but most are decided somewhere else. In 1986 a major front-page piece in the *Hartford Current* led with the (correct)

A desire to put the record straight set the design of my work. I have been committed to creating a baseline for the empirical study of town meeting so that future scholars will be able to study its evolution and performance in a way forever lost for ancient Athens. To do this I mixed "thick description"[4] with thin. But the primary task was to increase the number of real democracies about which we have "thin" data. To be *sure* about the claim, for example, that women are less apt to attend town meeting than men requires an investigation of hundreds of meetings. To be as sure about an additional finding that this inequality is greater at night meetings than at day meetings requires an original sample at least twice as large. The more factors considered, the more cases needed.[5] And so it goes. This book is based on a detailed analysis of nearly fifteen hundred town meetings. Still, again and again I find myself cursing my lack of cases.

The great bulk of my evidentiary base for this book is found in what I call *The "Unexpurgated" Real Democracy*, an uncut version of the original volume.[6] More a lab report than a book, it can be found on my Web site, www.uvm.edu/~fbryan, and in the Special Collections section of the Bailey/Howe Library at the University of Vermont. There one will find over three hundred additional tables and figures, methodological addenda and appendixes, student essays, extended footnotes, additional findings, and other material that might be thought of as back roads off the main highway of a long journey. As the years go by I will also update the fundamental data on real democracy that directly support this volume for as long as I am able. Numbers fascinate me.

---

claim that a general store in Newfane, Vermont, was closed, with a sign on the door that read "Closed. Went to Town Meeting." Then followed: "The owner, like most other residents, was at the one-story Grange Hall down the road, voting for three selectmen, a second sheriff and a new budget." William Cockerham, "Small-Town Vermonters Cling to Town Meetings," *Hartford Current*, March 9, 1986, 1. Wrong. A simple majority of the residents could not even *fit inside* the Grange hall at Newfane. Robert Dahl emphasizes the physical limits of size in ancient Athens. If every citizen of Athens had attended the assembly, the meeting place on the hill of Pnyx could not have held them all. Robert A. Dahl, *Democracy and Its Critics* (New Haven: Yale University Press, 1989), 16.

4. This is Gilbert Ryle's term, popularized by Clifford Geertz in "Thick Description: Toward an Interpretive Theory of Culture," in Geertz's *The Interpretation of Culture* (New York: Basic Books, 1973), 3–32.

5. These kinds of questions are what David Easton called "second gauge" hypotheses, and they drive much of the analysis in the central chapters of the book. David Easton, *The Political System*, 2nd ed. (New York: Alfred A. Knopf, 1971).

6. One of the readers to whom the publishers sent this original volume made the following notation in the margin on page 643. "Help. I feel like I am at a party with people I don't like and I can't get away!" It was this reader (who thankfully was very supportive of the book) who suggested the word "unexpurgated."

A belief that the Republic cannot survive without democracy and (in turn) that democratic possibility is limited to small places set the prescription for my work. For those of us who labor at the science of governance (and is there a better calling beyond the cloth?), I believe it is time to look inward toward the heart of the polity. It is time for us to return to the towns, the villages, where pasture springs in the high hills of home feed the streams that fill the reservoirs of our national citizenship. Tiny places that govern themselves are both laboratories for the science of democracy and watersheds that sustain our liberal and continental politics.

In her presidential address before the American Political Science Association in 1997, Elinor Ostrom directed our attention to the theory of collective action, which she called "*the* central subject of political science." To investigate this theory, she argued, we need empirically grounded investigation of three "core" relationships—reciprocity, reputation, and trust. Where better to study these relationships than in the context of face-to-face decision making by citizens of whole communities? Except for some townships in Minnesota, the New England town is the only place in America where general-purpose governments render binding collective action decisions (laws) in small face-to-face assemblies of common citizens. Vermont is the best place in New England with enough small town meeting governments to make possible a long-term comparative study of town meeting.

Students, Time, and Self: An Odyssey

The only way to know what happens at a town meeting is to be there. In the town of South Hero[7] in 1999 the town meeting lasted five hours and twelve

---

7. Katherine Krebs, Kevin Sigmund, and Mike Hapwood were the students who actually did the counting in South Hero in 1999. At 9:40 a.m. they recorded 158 people in attendance, 82 women and 76 men. By 2:30 p.m., when they counted for the fourth time, only 43 men and 48 women remained at the Folsom Educational and Community Center where town meeting was held. In the place for notes beside the attendance counts, the students wrote, "lots of kids." The tradition of starting kids early in Vermont—whether it's driving trucks, handling shotguns, or doing democracy—is still intact in many places. Katherine Krebs, Kevin Sigmund, and Mike Hapwood, "The 1999 Comparative Town Meeting Study: Town of South Hero," Burlington, University of Vermont, Real Democracy Data Base, March 1999. Here in part is what Katherine Krebs (who grew up in South Hero) wrote in her essay. "Town meeting day in South Hero felt like a homecoming for me. I remember vividly having the day off from school but being babysat at town meeting anyway as my parents participated in the meeting. . . . I knew a great number of the people there and had formed impressions about them at a young age. . . . It was interesting watching these people congregate and participate with such vigor in the events of the town. There were people who had had numerous children go through the school system who argued, nevertheless, against the school budget. There were people who argued against everything, and it made one wonder, surely these people enjoy roads to drive on, a sheriff and fire squad protection.

minutes (not counting a short lunch break). In that time fifty-one different people spoke at least once. Twenty-three of these were women. The only way to collect data like these is to take the day off work, go to South Hero's town meeting on the first Tuesday in March, stay at the meeting from the time it begins until the time it ends, and record what happens. Town meetings are usually held only once a year. Most town meetings in Vermont are held on the same day, the first Tuesday after the first Monday in March. No one person could cover more than two or three a year, and grants to fund such coverage were out of the question. But I had two things aplenty: students and time. So I returned to an old formula substituting "professor, student, time" for "committee, grant, staff."[8]

Undergraduates can count. Undergraduates will go to strange places and count accurately if they are prepared and if they understand the *adventure* of it. They also need one more thing—a sense of mission. On the first day of any class I've ever taught over the past thirty-three years, I have told my students that I would treat them as young *political scientists*. I told them, because I believe it to be true, that political science is more intellectually challenging and more important than any other science. I've also worked hard to establish a sense of romance: "Take Bryan's course and you'll end up in one of those hayseed conventions under a foot of snow one hundred miles from nowhere." The "field trip" was from the beginning an integral part of the course. Without it this project could not have happened.

But I realized that for some people, attending Town Meeting is their form of involvement. It is their right.... While many of the people who argued and debated seemed infuriatingly ignorant or uninformed, it simply validated the need for open forums and the democratic process." Katherine Krebs, "South Hero Town Meeting Day 1999," Burlington, University of Vermont, March 1999. There you have it; lessons of tolerance and patience and respect for the commonweal learned at an early age. Fifteen years earlier, here in part is what Tracy Fitzgerald had to say about town meeting in South Hero. "What I did realize was that the town meeting of South Hero, Vermont, isn't that much different from my own town meeting in Marblehead, Massachusetts. The issues debated in South Hero are no different from what I have seen on the warrant in Marblehead. Granted, I did not hear one fight about who was going to put how many lobster pots where, and my town does have more than 2,500 people, but I was quite surprised at the modernness of a supposedly quintessential example of a real Vermont lifestyle." Tracy Fitzgerald, "Town Meeting of South Hero," Burlington, University of Vermont, March 1984.

8. When I was in graduate school at the University of Connecticut I took a seminar with the comparativist G. Lowell Field. He had continually involved his students in the work on *Comparative Political Development: The Precedent of the West* (Ithaca: Cornell University Press, 1967). In a review shortly afterward I wrote, "Field substituted for the 'committee-grant-staff' formula of scholarly research the nearly forgotten 'professor, student, time' approach once used extensively on the Continent." Frank Bryan, "*Comparative Political Development: The Precedent of the West,*" *Academic Reviewer* 3 (January 1969): 37–39. His example inspired the method that made this book possible.

Most important, I made sure the data these students produced involved no judgments on their part.[9] The numbers required only their attention. Each component of information was remarkably simple. Even a junior high school student could understand and record it accurately. Because so many students visited so many towns each year, I was able to exclude results that contained errors or were incomplete. For instance, if the data sheets indicated that the students got to the meeting late or left early, I did not include those data in the findings. Even excluding three or four cases for this reason, I usually compiled close to fifty complete town meetings each year.

But to describe town meeting without the context of its life, its feel, its nesting in the heart of the Vermont town would be like describing love without describing passion—damned misleading. So in my mixing of "thin" and "thick" I have tried to tell as best I can what life in Vermont's towns is like. It is one thing to know about a Vermont town that 21 percent of the voters attended town meeting in 1987. It is another to know that the man who made a fool of himself arguing against a $1,500 subsidy for a day-care center for low-income working women was a logger who two years earlier had watched his brother slide under a bulldozer and carried his crushed body out of the woods alone in a vain attempt to save his life. Put it this way. If a test group of one hundred political scientists were to read this book after having studied Frost's poems in *North of Boston* for a semester, they would have a far greater knowledge of and appreciation for town meeting than a group of one hundred who did not.

So from time to time in this book I interrupt the analysis with "Witnesses"—firsthand accounts of town meeting by people who were there, including myself. My witnesses range from Aleksandr Solzhenitsyn's farewell address to the people of Cavendish to excerpts from student essays. Now and then I will walk you step by step through parts of town meetings. We need to share the fascinating mix of liberal processes and communal ambiance that typifies what goes on inside a town hall. And I have not tried to reduce or rationalize the number of towns you will be introduced to. While you may become familiar with some towns, others will come and go. Let them. The senses are astounded more by the complication and variety of real democracy than by its symmetry.

Finally, to fill out the context in which I have studied real democracy I have included personal reminiscences, reflections, and observations about

9. I did, however, call for judgments in the essays the students were required to write. These ranged in length and quality depending on the course I was teaching. I have over four thousand essays on record with the data file for the meeting the student attended.

Vermont, its towns, and its people—flashbacks and mutterings from a boyhood and an adulthood of loving only one place, this feisty, cantankerous, liberal, cold, glorious little republic of Vermont. I have, in short, included autobiography in my methodology. Much of this is found in the footnotes. I expect you to read them, and I justify this unusual approach by claiming, shamelessly, that I have learned something of value by working for years on Vermont farms, living more with farmers and loggers than with academics, and by experiencing from childhood the satisfaction, frustration, irritation, anxiety, and hope that real democracy brings.

WITNESS

Aleksandr Solzhenitsyn Bids Farewell

[From] Minutes of the Cavendish Town Meeting—1994

Moderator led the assembly in the Pledge of Allegiance to the Flag of the United States of America.
The moderator asked those present to pause for a moment of silence in memory of the members of our community who died during the past year.
Moderator stated if there is no objection he would like to dispense with the rules for a moment and call a brief recess to allow a distinguished friend and resident to address the group assembled. There was no objection.
The following speech was given by Aleksandr Solzhenitsyn and interpreted by his son Stephan:

"Citizens of Cavendish, our dear neighbors,

At town meeting seventeen years ago I told you about my exile and explained the necessary steps which I took to ensure a calm working environment, without the burden of constant visitors.

You were very understanding; you forgave my unusual way of life, and even took it upon yourselves to protect my privacy. For this, I have been grateful throughout all these years and today, as my stay here comes to an end, I thank you. Your kindness and cooperation helped to create the best possible conditions for my work.

The eighteen years which I have spent here have been the most productive of my life. I have written absolutely everything I wanted to. I offer today those of my books that have been translated into English to the town library.

Our children grew up and went to school here, alongside your children. For them, Vermont is home. Indeed, our whole family has come to feel at home among you. Exile is always difficult, and yet I could not [have] imagined a better place to live, and wait, and wait for my return home than Cavendish, Vermont.

And so this spring in May, my wife and I are going back to Russia, which is going through one of the most difficult periods in its entire history—a period of rampant poverty, a period where standards of human decency have fallen, a period of lawlessness and economic chaos. That is the painful price we had to pay to rid ourselves of communism, during whose seventy-year reign of terror sixty million people died just from the regime's war on its own nation. I hope that I can be of at least some small help to my tortured nation, although it is impossible to predict how successful my efforts will be. Besides, I am not young.

I have observed here in Cavendish, and in the surrounding towns the sensible and sure process of grassroots democracy where the local population decides most of its problems on its own, not waiting for the decision of higher authorities. Alas, this we still do not have in Russia, and that is our greatest shortcoming.

Our sons will complete their education in America, and the house in Cavendish will remain their home.

Lately, while I have been walking on the nearby roads, taking in the surroundings with a farewell glance, I have found every meeting with many of you to be warm and friendly.

And so today, both to those of you whom I have met over these years, and to those whom I have not met I say: thank you and farewell. I wish all the very best to Cavendish and the area around it. God bless you all.

Aleksandr Solzhenitsyn[10]

10. Town of Cavendish, "Minutes of the Cavendish Town Meeting—1994," *Town Report,* year ending December 1994.

Acknowledgments

Given this book's gestation, it would be silly to attempt to list those who have helped along the way. Better to omit hundreds than to forget ten. Still, I need to thank my colleagues Alan Wertheimer and Bob Taylor at the University of Vermont for reading earlier drafts of the manuscript. William J. Smith's enthusiasm and capability in dealing with matters methodological was a comfort, as was Gene Laber's and Alan Howard's. It was through Benjamin Page's faith and patience that the manuscript found its way into his series on American politics and political economy at the University of Chicago Press. It was there that I came under the guidance of John Tryneski. I was told early on by another of the Press's authors that John was an "author's editor" and I would like him a lot. He is and I do.

Senior manuscript editor Alice Bennett was uncanny in her ability to be technically astute and insightful at the same time.

Most of all I want to thank Jane Mansbridge. She read every page of the original manuscript (all 850 of them), looked at every table and figure (all 338), and then with painstaking acuity (and even good humor) urged me to give up my tome and write a book instead. It was she who wrote in the margin of one of the pages in the middle of the manuscript: "Help! I feel like I'm at a party with people I don't like and can't get away!" But she stayed to the end anyway, and I pray I was able to live up to her high standards.

Beginning in 1969 at St. Michael's College in Colchester, Vermont, and continuing to this very day at the University of Vermont in Burlington, thousands of students have done the legwork that allowed me to establish the database that made this book possible. For over three decades, year in and year out, I have promised them that what they did could become a valuable contribution to what we know about democracy. If it does not turn out that way, the fault is not theirs. Thinking back over these thirty-four years, their collective effort continues to astound me, and the remembrances continue to bring me joy. How lucky I have been.

Finally, there is my friend Melissa Lee. In the spring of 1975 I wrote asking this long-legged city girl teaching school in Burlington, Vermont, if she would please hook up with a former student of mine at St. Michael's College (I was teaching in Bozeman, Montana, that winter) and go to the town meeting in my hometown of Newbury to collect data. It was only a hundred miles away. Foolishly, she did. We married in the fall. She's been going to town meetings with me ever since and has been intimately involved with every aspect of this book. She is a good citizen but cares as much for political science as I do for boiled turnip greens. Now and then I look at her as she sits working away at some town meeting in some faraway little town in the hills of Vermont and feel guilty. But then I think, hey, I warned her in 1975! Besides, words don't exist to thank her enough.

We shall not cease from exploration
And the end of all our exploring
Will be to arrive where we started
And know the place for the first time.

T. S. Eliot, *Four Quartets*

The epigraph is from T. S. Eliot, *Little Gidding*. Thanks to Daniel Kemmis, the former mayor of Missoula, Montana, for reminding me of Elliot's words in his exquisite book, *Community and the Politics of Place* (Norman: University of Oklahoma Press, 1990).

Introduction

The Methodology of Starting from Scratch

It is the spring of 1992. Twenty-five hundred years earlier in a place called Athens, a Greek named Cleisthenes took a risk for an idea. The idea took hold. Few others promised more happiness or provoked more anguish in the two and one-half millennia of Western civilization that were to follow. It was incandescent, this idea of democracy: coming and going, rising and falling, dodging in and out of the passions of history. It has been defined and redefined, cursed and cheered, understood and misunderstood, lived for and died for. Nations and regimes have been named in its honor. Tens of thousands of scholars have labored in its vineyard, and the fruits of their labor fill library shelves throughout the world. As a global enterprise, the principles of democracy rival even those of the planet's great religions. No other secular notion has so triggered the sanctimony and sincerity, the good and the evil, the despair and the hope.

Democracy.

Athens Is Where You Find It

On March 3, 1992, Stephen Fine, a citizen of Athens, Vermont, was unaware that he was marking the twenty-five hundredth anniversary of the birth of democracy when, at 10:01 a.m., he was first at town meeting to rise and address the assembly. Neither was Marjorie Walker, who, as tradition in Athens dictated, was next to speak. When Athens, Vermont, first began to practice open, face-to-face democracy, women were not allowed to participate. But by 1992 that had changed. Walker made several announcements and then read the list of items (the town warning) that the assembled polis would address. Nearly 60 percent of the citizens of Athens were present. Their deliberations would end in votes that they and every citizen of the town not present would have to obey under penalty of law.

After introducing a few guests (who addressed the assembly briefly), Mr. Fine gave way to David Bemis, whose job it was to ask the people if they would reaffirm Fine's right to conduct the meeting. If not, they could choose someone else to do the job. Another citizen, James Waryas, immediately nominated Fine, and a third, Philip Reeve, seconded the nomination. A fourth, David Kenny, asked that the nominations be closed and that the clerk cast one ballot for Fine. Carol Bingham seconded this motion, a vote was taken, and Fine was elected. This process took less than two minutes. It was now 10:50 a.m. Fine stepped forward to take his position before the assembly again, and the people of Athens got down to the business of governing themselves.

About this time a pair of the world's leading experts on democracy, Josiah Ober of Princeton and Charles Hedrick of the University of California at Santa Cruz, were preparing an international celebration to mark the birthday of what the people in another Athens, the Athens of ancient Greece, had created twenty-five hundred years earlier. Because of their efforts the government of the United States provided funding, conferences were held in Washington and Greece, a display was mounted at the Smithsonian Institution, and a six-week summer institute was held in California. The summer institute attracted the participation of Bernard Grofman, a political scientist at the University of California at Irvine. The result was a series of short essays on Athenian democracy for a small journal sent to every member of the American Political Science Association.[1]

The American Political Science Association consists of about 15,000 professionals whose business it is to know about governance.[2] They probably represent at any given time over 50,000 years of postgraduate education, committed (usually at a dear price) out of their highest-energy years, simply to *prepare* to ply their trade. They have accumulated in the aggregate over 250,000 years of teaching and research. The essays they published for themselves under Grofman's direction were written by a cadre of scholars of singular competence, led by Sheldon S. Wolin of Princeton.

---

1. Bernard Grofman, ed., "The 2500th Anniversary of Democracy: Lessons of Athenian Democracy," *Political Science and Politics 26* (September 1993): 471–494.

2. www.apsa.com. The membership of the American Political Science Association (unfortunately) represents less than half the number of practicing political scientists in the United States.

Here is the problem. While I doubt that any of the citizens of the Athens town meeting knew they were gathering to practice democracy on its twenty-five hundredth birthday, it is equally doubtful that any of these scholars writing about ancient Athens were aware of what was going on in Athens, Vermont. Worse, I suspect I could name—and count on one hand—all of the members of the American Political Association who knew there was an Athens, Vermont, and had some idea of the character of the action taking place there that day. Besides me, none of the twenty members of the political science department at the University of Vermont did. I'll bet Richard Winters and Denis Sullivan at Dartmouth did, and I'm sure Jane Mansbridge at Harvard's Kennedy School did. Joseph Zimmerman of SUNY Albany may have. That's about it.

Why is this so?

Real Democracy: Now and Then

I make two claims: First, what happened in Athens, Vermont, in 1992 was not strange, or random, or even a unique event. Second, it was real democracy. The first claim is easily supported. In America, town meeting predates representative government. It is stitched into the fabric of New England and dominates the patchwork of its public past. It occurs in each New England state at a set time and in a set place. It is accessible to every citizen, coded in law, and conducted regularly in over 1,000 towns. In my state of Vermont citizens in more than 230 towns meet at least once each year to pass laws governing the town. Since the dawn of modern political science[3] the people have come together to govern themselves in approximately 11,280 individual, properly "warned," town-based, democratic assemblies in Vermont alone.

The second claim is more tendentious. Certainly all polities that call themselves democracies are "real." But I say that nearly all representative structures that provide the frame of governance for the "democracies" of the world are substitutes for democracy, not approximations of democracy. This is *not* to say these "democracies" are less than they might be or that they are not better at what they do than town meeting is at what it does. It is to say that using the word "democracy" to cover representative systems is, as Robert Dahl observed, an "intellectual handicap."[4] Real democracy (for good or ill)

3. We all have our favorites, but I place the date at 1949 with V. O. Key's publication of *Southern Politics in State and Nation* (New York: Alfred A. Knopf, 1949).

4. Robert A. Dahl, "The City in the Future of Democracy," *American Political Science Review* 61 (December 1967): 953–969. In 1982 Dahl said: "The term democracy is like an ancient

occurs only when all eligible citizens of a general-purpose government are legislators; that is, called to meet in a deliberative, face-to-face assembly and to bind themselves under laws they fashion themselves.

Real democracies come in better and worse forms. They promote both good and bad policies. They make their participants both satisfied and frustrated. "Real" does not mean "good." Real democracy is better to the extent that all who live in a jurisdiction are citizens and all citizens are eligible to participate. It is better when attendance at meetings and participation in them are high and egalitarian. Real democracies are whole when they make all the laws that govern them. Otherwise they are to some degree partial. Nor is real democracy to be confused with direct, plebiscite democracy.[5] The bottom line is this: in a real democracy, the citizens—in person, in face-to-face meetings of the whole—make the laws that govern the actions of everyone within their geographic boundaries. This definition is strict. It means that only *governments* can be real democracies. Poker clubs and snowmobile associations may govern themselves democratically under this definition, of course. They may indeed be more "democratic" than a town. But they can never be democracies.

To what extent does democracy in Athens match democracy in Athens? Remarkably well, as it turns out. True, substantial (indeed, paradigm threatening) differences are present. But given the passage of time, the variations in geography and cultures, and the lack of any direct genetic linkage between the two, the similarities are compelling.[6] These similarities extend far

---

kitchen midden packed with assorted leftovers from 2500 years of nearly continuous usage." Robert A. Dahl, *Dilemmas of Pluralist Democracy* (New Haven: Yale University Press, 1982). 5. On the distinctions between real democracy and its other forms, see also Giovanni Sartori, *The Theory of Democracy Revisited* (Chatham, NJ: Chatham House, 1987), 282–284; Joseph A. Schumpeter, *Capitalism, Socialism and Democracy*, 3rd ed. (New York: Harper, 1950), 246; and Danilo Zolo, *Democracy and Complexity* (University Park: Pennsylvania State University Press, 1992), 58. Some scholars have paid serious attention to real democracy. Among them are Benjamin R. Barber, *The Death of Communal Liberty: A History of Freedom in a Swiss Mountain Canton* (Princeton: Princeton University Press, 1974); Robert A. Dahl, *Democracy and Its Critics* (New Haven: Yale University Press, 1989), 13–23; Jane Mansbridge, *Beyond Adversary Democracy* (New York: Basic Books, 1980), 1–23 and 270–289; and Carole Pateman, *Participation and Democratic Theory* (Cambridge: Cambridge University Press, 1970), 1–22.

5. Although authors of textbooks in American government nearly always make the distinction, now and then they equate the New England town meeting with such things as referendum voting in the Swiss cantons. See Beth Henschen and Edward Sidlow, *America at Odds: An Introduction to American Government* (Belmont, CA: West/Wadsworth, 1999), 9–10.

6. Comparisons of Athens with town meeting begin early in American history. Much of what we know about the first quarter century of postrevolutionary New England (especially its northern frontier) must be credited to the industry of one man, Timothy Dwight. On vacations from his job as president of Yale University he traipsed over a tough land and found the time to write about everything from government to horticulture. His take on town meeting:

beyond the single most obvious likeness that both were lawmaking assemblies of the whole. In town meetings, spectators, the press, and other "outsiders" are often asked to sit in places reserved for them.[7] When the assembly met in Athens (at the Pnyx), outsiders and spectators sat on the side of the hill behind the speaker's podium. The Athenian democracy made laws not only for Athenians but also for "metics"—residents who paid taxes but could not vote. Vermont towns make laws not only for their own registered voters but also for out-of-town, second-home, and "camp" residents who pay (often very high) local property taxes but cannot participate in town meeting.[8] Political manipulation appeared in both places as well. In Vermont, items that farmers might oppose were sometimes placed near the end of the agenda in the hope that they would have gone home to milk before the items were called up. In Greece more conservative proposals were often postponed until the navy, which required the rowing power of the more radical *thetes*, was out to sea and thus underrepresented in the assembly.[9]

"The Legislature of each town is, like that of Athens, composed of inhabitants, personally present; a majority of whom decides every question." His next comment, however, attempts to distinguish town meetings from Athens in a way that I will emphasize in later parts of this book. The first New Englanders were committed to rules of procedure. As Dwight put it, town meetings are "controlled by exact rules; and are under the direction of the proper officers. The confusion, incident to popular meetings, and so often disgraceful to those of Athens and Rome, is effectually prevented." Dwight shares the Americans' distaste for things Athenian that so troubled Madison and his colleagues. Timothy Dwight, *Travels in New England and New York*, vol. 1 (New Haven, CT: Timothy Dwight; A. Converse, Printer, 1821), 31. Dwight no doubt exaggerates in suggesting that all town meetings were "controlled by exact rules." It is easy to find accounts of the breakdown of what he called "very honorable decorum." See, for instance, David Syrett, "Town-Meeting Politics in Massachusetts, 1776–1786," *William and Mary Quarterly* 21 (July 1964): 352–366. Unfortunately, Syrett's piece extrapolates beyond a listing of transgressions, which by his own language happened now and then and here and there, to an unbelievable final claim that town meeting was "almost always characterized by the willingness of its officials to break or ignore the rules by which they professed to live."

7. The thousands of student accounts I have read over the past thirty-four years indicate that most students were allowed to sit pretty much where they wanted to and many times were given special places of advantage to watch and record data on the meetings.

8. Athens had a property tax as well, the *eisphorai*. It too was progressive in a sense, because only the richest paid it. Athens, Greece, had the equivalent of the Athens, Vermont, "listers"—those people who rated property for purposes of taxation—and it also had a match for the Athens, Vermont, "grand list," the *timema*. But tax collection in the city-state was delegated to the *symmoriai*, groups of the wealthiest property owners. The richest *symmorite* was required to put up all the tax payment for his group in advance and then reimburse himself from the group's membership later. Athens, Vermont, elects a tax collector. See Mogens Herman Hansen, *The Athenian Democracy in the Age of Demosthenes*, trans. J. A. Cook (Oxford: Basil Blackwell, 1991), 368, 370.

9. The Dutch classical scholar Herman Hansen credits the absence of the thetes with partial responsibility for the coming of the Oligarchy of the Four Hundred, since "the entire Athenian navy was stationed off Samos" at the time. Hansen, *Athenian Democracy*, 126.

Like the Athenian assembly twenty-five hundred years earlier, the Vermont town meeting jealously protects its participatory prerogatives. The Greeks guarded entry into their assembly with six *lexiarchoi*. Those caught trying to participate illegally could receive a death sentence.[10] Athens, Vermont, has never gone this far, but individual towns have often denied citizens of other jurisdictions the right to speak.[11] In 1844 the town of St. Albans, Vermont, refused to allow General Winfield Scott, a special emissary of President Martin Van Buren, to speak to them on the matter of the town's "flaunting" American neutrality laws by supporting anti-British forces in Canada. More recently the governor of Vermont found herself standing outside the Duxbury meeting hall while the citizens within voted on whether to allow her to speak to the town.[12]

The Board of Selectmen sets the agenda for town meeting in Athens, Vermont. In Athens, Greece, it was set by the *prytaneis* (an executive

---

10. In Demosthenes' time the *lexiarchoi* were replaced by a committee of thirty, three from each of the ten newly established tribes. Hansen, *Athenian Democracy*, 129.

11. I try to attend at least five regular town meetings every year, including the ones in my old hometown of Newbury (1943–1970) and my current hometown (1971–2001) of Starksboro. Sometimes I am forced to listen to the drone of some special-interest representative or politician "from away" who has been granted permission to speak. Sometimes I catch myself entertaining the notion that the Greeks' death penalty was not bereft of redeeming qualities. Of this I am certain: their willingness to indict someone who "proposed an inexpedient law" clearly has merit. See David Stockton, *The Classical Athenian Democracy* (Oxford: Oxford University Press, 1990), 81.

12. Madeleine Kunin was a brave governor. In the winter of 1987 she expended a large sum of her political capital establishing a controversial regional planning law in Vermont. While taking a fast tour of several town meetings in March, speaking briefly at each, she stopped at the town of Duxbury. The moderator announced her arrival, and she prepared to step forward to address the meeting. But before she could begin, a motion was raised from the floor to prevent her from doing so. A secret ballot on the question was requested and granted. The governor decided to wait out the balloting in the parking lot, suffering, in her own words, some "anger and humiliation." Had she been raised or experienced in the town meeting tradition (Kunin lived in the city of Burlington, which is governed by a council), she would not have taken it so hard. From the meeting in the tiny town of Belvidere in 1984: "When the election of a town auditor came up, a brave lady accepted a nomination for the post. Another was nominated, and they voted right there in front of everyone! The first lady was beaten, and I felt sorry it was in front of the townspeople, many her friends. To make matters worse, she accepted a second nomination for auditor and was defeated again. Twice in ten minutes. You knew she was hanging her head lower when she left than when she came in" (Sean P. Hart, "Town Meeting in Belvidere," Burlington, University of Vermont, March 1984). Political defeat in the open, among one's friends and enemies (neighbors all), happens not infrequently at town meeting. But in the end the governor acted admirably. Perhaps it was the light drifting snow outside the Duxbury town hall that day. When she returned after a positive vote allowed her to address the assembly, she applauded freedom of speech with "firm conviction" and commended the town for upholding it. See her political remembrances in Madeleine Kunin, *Living a Political Life* (New York: Alfred A. Knopf, 1994), 393–394.

committee of the Council).[13] The agenda in Vermont (the warning) must be published ("warned") at least thirty days before the meeting. In Greece it was posted four days before the meeting. In Vermont agenda articles may be open-ended proposals for discussion or more or less concrete ordinances to be voted up or down. In Greece proposals or *probouleuma* could similarly be open-ended or specific. In Vermont the meeting starts in the morning and can run all day. The same was true in Athens, although the meeting was often over by noon. So too in Vermont. In the Greek *ekklesia*, discussion began with the question "Who wishes to speak?" In the Vermont town meeting the phrase is often "What is your pleasure?"

The Vermont Athens of 1992 and the Greek Athens of antiquity shared other similarities. In neither could items not on the agenda be approved into law.[14] Both meetings might open with a prayer.[15] Most voting in both places was conducted by voice or a show of hands, and secret ballots were few. In a town meeting's secret ballot citizens walk forward and drop marked slips of paper into a box. In the assembly of Athens they dropped pebbles into an urn.[16] It appears that from time to time the process of voting was quite complicated in ancient Athens, as it is in Vermont when amendments to amendments are offered and so forth. Even the *rhétores* of the Athenian assembly (defined loosely as citizens who move articles, frame debates, or in other ways participate a lot) have their Yankee counterparts.[17]

13. Vermont towns have no structure analogous to the Athenian Council, which comprised fifty members from each of the ten tribes. Each tribe's contingent of representatives served as an executive committee for one-tenth of the ten-month "Council year," and its members were called *prytaneis*.

14. The Vermont town meeting has a "new business" article that is taken up at the end of the meeting. Some of the most interesting discussion often takes place at this time. However, no binding action may be taken.

15. The Athenians included a sacrifice, whereas Vermonters do not, unless we include allowing a representative from the state legislature to explain what is going on in Montpelier. Many Vermont towns have dispensed with an opening prayer in the past thirty years, but most have some opening ceremony like a salute to the (American) flag.

16. Voting "by ballot" was rare, however, in the Athens of Greece during the classical period (Hansen, *Athenian Democracy*, 147), and it may not ever have been as secret as the modern town meeting process. E. S. Staveley finds peeking going on in pictures of voting on vase paintings. E. S. Staveley, *Greek and Roman Voting and Elections* (Ithaca: Cornell University Press, 1972), 83–86.

17. Verbal participation in town meeting is the subject of chapters 6 and 7. On the matter of rhétores, the Vermont town meeting has citizens who have informally carved out a place for themselves in the life of the town and act as principal participators in the verbal activity of town meeting. I have never, of course, heard them referred to as *rhétores*, or for that matter, any other generic term, although a wide variety of sprightly (and often scatological) nouns have been developed to describe a small minority of such speakers. For an analysis of the Athenian rhétores, see Harvey Yunis, *Taming Democracy: Models of Political Rhetoric in Classical Athens* (Ithaca: Cornell University Press, 1996), 4–10.

The differences between the two meetings have more to do with structure. Athens, Vermont, usually has only one meeting a year. In Greece, Athens
had as many as forty. In Vermont town officers are never chosen by lot, although the practice of appointing those not present to office from the floor
of many town meetings might be considered extremely bad luck by some
of those so selected. In Greece selection by lot was the common practice.
Athens, Vermont, has no term limits for town officers. There were such limits in ancient Athens.[18]

But the most important differences between the Mediterranean Athens
of 500 BC and the Athens, Vermont, of AD 1992 involved size and power.
Athens, Greece, was a nation. It had an army and a navy. It fought wars in
which thousands died. Athens, Vermont, is a town within a state within a
nation. It has no army other than the town constable, unless one counts the
members of the road crew and local rescue squad who may own deer rifles.
No one knows for sure exactly how many citizens there were in Athens in
the fourth and fifth centuries BC when democracy flowered there, but most
agree that about 30,000 male citizens were eligible to attend the meeting at
the Pnyx in the year 500 BC.[19] In AD 1992 in Athens, Vermont, 183 citizens
of both sexes were eligible to attend town meeting at the schoolhouse. Do
these vast differences in size and power scuttle the comparison between Greek
and Vermont democracy?

Not necessarily. For most of the democracy in Attica (the geographical
expanse of the city-state, or polis, of Athens) did not take place, as Lewis
Mumford pointed out as early as 1961, in Athens proper.[20] Indeed, the

18. More general sources I found useful besides those cited earlier are J. A. O. Larsen,
Representative Government in Greek and Roman History (Berkeley: University of California Press,
1955), and Raphael Sealey, *A History of the Greek City States, ca. 700–388 B.C.* (Berkeley: University
of California Press, 1976). These were also particularly useful in their treatment of the demes (see
below). Even in their chicanery I find echoes of the Greeks in town meetings. Mansbridge
summarizes one set of claims for Greek adversarialism: evidence exists that the Greeks operated
political machines (for instance, to prepare ballots). Political clubs held preassembly meetings to
decide who was to speak about what and how. These schemers "also tried to influence voters before
the assembly meeting by persuasion, bribes, and threats." Sometimes they also "packed the
assembly, initiated applause and appropriate interruptions, and filibustered to postpone a vote."
Mansbridge, *Beyond Adversary Democracy*, 13–15, 335–338.

19. One of the better sources on the architecture (both physical and social) of Greek
democracy is R. E. Wycherley, *How the Greeks Built Cities* (New York: W. W. Norton, 1976).

20. Mumford was impressed with the village life of the Greeks and its impact on cities such
as Athens. "The democratic practices of the village," he writes, "without strong class or vocational
cleavages, fostered a habit of taking council together." Thus the "village measure prevailed in the
development of Greek cities." Lewis Mumford, *The City in History* (New York: Harcourt, Brace
and World, 1961), 128–129. Victor Davis Hanson claims that the small family farm (precisely the
institution that defined the socioeconomic culture of the Vermont town) provided the

fact that (from the founders to the present day) the comparative reference point of America's only example of real democracy, the New England town meeting, has been based on the Athenian *city* experience is an intellectual tragedy.[21] How different our understanding would have been had we known the dimensions of real democracy as it took place in the little Greek communities scattered over the countryside—communities that lack chronicles but that must have been in some degree analogous to Vermont's towns. For many Athenians these communities, called demes, were, says R. K. Sinclair, "the center of their lives."[22] According to David Whitehead, the scholar of record on the subject, not only did the demes provide the political and demographic infrastructure of Athens the city-state, they also contribute "one of the most obvious explanations [for the] success with which radical participatory democracy functioned in fifth and fourth century Athens."[23]

Pallenais, for example, was one of the 139 local governments (demes) of Attica. It was about halfway between the city of Athens and the deme of Marathon southeast of what is now the city of Kifissia and north of Amarousio.

---

circumstances and ideology to create and then support Greek constitutional government in the polis. See especially his chapter "Before Democracy," in *The Other Greeks: The Family Farm and the Agrarian Roots of Western Civilization* (New York: Free Press, 1995), 181–220.

21. I bear Athens no grudge. If this book does nothing else it should establish that, given the *limitations* size imposes on real democracy, Athens accomplished something just this side of miraculous.

22. R. K. Sinclair, *Democracy and Participation in Athens* (Cambridge: Cambridge University Press, 1988), 51. See also Frank Bryan and John McClaughry, *The Vermont Papers: Recreating Democracy on a Human Scale* (Chelsea, VT: Chelsea Green Press, 1989), 3.

23. David Whitehead, *The Demes of Attica, 508/7-ca. 250 B.C.* (Princeton: Princeton University Press, 1986), xvii. Classical scholar R. J. Hooper supports Whitehead. He further explicitly agrees with Pateman, Tocqueville, and others on the relation between small democracies and larger republics. Athens was possible, he argues, because the demes allowed for people to be trained in "an administrative and political apprenticeship at a lower parochial level" (R. J. Hooper, *The Basis of Athenian Democracy*, cited in Whitehead, xviii). David Stockton puts it this way: "Young boys must have early become accustomed to hearing about or watching their local deme meetings, and listening to their elders discussing deme business. The demesmen as a whole would find the idea of attending and voting on proposals at meetings of the 'national' ecclesia in Athens less formidable [than] would have been the case without this background of local experience, and would have been less daunted by having to serve as members of the central Council of Five Hundred." Stockton, *Classical Athenian Democracy*, 65–66. A study of members of the Vermont House of Representatives in Montpelier from 1945 to 1965 demonstrated clear parallels between what the experiences of the demesmen serving on the Council of Five Hundred must have been and what local Vermont legislators serving in the House of Representatives in Montpelier surely were. The House was about the size (246 members) of a typical town meeting and operated in much the same way. These 246 people represented a state of only 320,000 residents of all ages, and each member represented a median of only 783 citizens. The huge majority of House members served as town officers. The sound of the gavel in Montpelier fell on an assembly intimately familiar with doing the public's business face to face. Frank M. Bryan, *Yankee Politics in Rural Vermont* (Hanover, NH: University Press of New England, 1974).

It marks the place where lowlands along the southern end of the Gulf of Evvoiea begin to rise into the rougher (what used to be) grazing country just north of Mount Hymetto.[24] Athens, Vermont, is much more clearly akin to Pallenais than it is to Athens. First and most important, the two were about the same size. The Vermont Athens had 183 citizens eligible to participate in its democracy in 1992. Pallenais is estimated to have had 191 in 498 BC.[25] As core units of larger political entities to which sovereignty was owed, both were only partial democracies.[26] Yet Athens, Vermont, and Pallenais (and the systems of towns and demes of which they were but a tiny part) were undoubtedly cradles for the citizenship of the sovereignties that housed them. Athenian citizenship was administered by the deme as the jurisdiction of first resort.[27] In Vermont also, towns administer citizenship. Vermont citizens' right to vote in statewide elections is validated when their names appear on the town's "grand list." Athens, Vermont, in 1992 and Pallenais in 492 BC were represented at the next level by population, Athens in the state legislature in Montpelier (where it has shared a representative with several other towns in southern Vermont since 1965), Pallenais in the Council of Five Hundred in Athens.[28]

24. This entire area is now pretty much folded into the suburban extensions of the city of Athens.

25. In population, therefore, Pallenais was somewhat bigger than Athens, Vermont, since in Pallenais only men could vote. The population of Athens, Vermont, in 1990 was 313, making it one of the smallest towns in my study. The population of Pallenais is estimated at about 750. The basic source on the population of the demes is A. W. Gomme, *The Population of Athens in the Fifth and Fourth Centuries B.C.* (Oxford: Basil Blackwell, 1933). The authoritative summary and explanation of Gomme's work and other sources appearing since 1933 is John S. Traill, *The Political Organization of Attica: A Study of the Demes, Trittyes and Phylai, and Their Representation in the Athenian Council* (Princeton, NJ: American School of Classical Studies at Athens, 1975).

26. For most of their history both places were probably much more "full" democracies than partial ones. Taxes and military service were their principal obligations to the larger units they belonged to. Until the 1950s Athens, Vermont, and all the other Vermont towns cared for their poor, educated their children, maintained their own roads, and performed nearly every other important government function in the lives of their citizens. Thus, for three-quarters of their historical existence the towns, for all practical purposes, were pretty much full democracies. In a doctoral thesis written for the political science department at Syracuse University in 1957, Stanley T. Wilson concluded after studying the government functions of some of Vermont's smallest towns that they met the functional, structural, and democratic criteria of full polities. James Wilson, "An Inquiry into the Existence of the Ten Least-Populated Vermont Towns as Separate Legal and Administrative Entities" (Ph.D. diss., Syracuse University, 1957).

27. One of the most accessible and complete short takes on classical democracy in Athens is David Held's opening chapter in *Models of Democracy*, 2nd ed. (Stanford: Stanford University Press, 1996), 13–35. He does not discuss the demes' role in Athenian democracy but includes them in figure 1.1, with an arrow leading from the demes to the assembly, the ecclesia. This arrow intrigues me.

28. Traill's quota of representatives in the Council for Pallenais was set at six. Gomme gave the deme seven. *Traill, Political Organization of Attica*, 67; Gomme, *Population of Athens*, 65.

Some dramatic differences add spice to the comparison. For Athens, Montpelier is not the final repository of sovereignty. The United States of America is. In Pallenais a citizen did not have representation in Greece. Greece was not a sovereign nation, and the Greeks had no system of representation in any entity larger than the city-state. The 191 eligible citizens of Pallenais were *expected* to journey to Athens ten times a year and help in person to pass laws for the entire city-state. The citizens of Athens, Vermont, have no such opportunity. For the comparison to hold, the Vermont legislature would have to serve as a statewide "board of selectmen" (as did the Council of Five Hundred in Athens, Greece) that would submit proposals to mass meetings attended by Vermonters from all over the state.[29] But for all these differences, the comparison of Pallenais and Athens, Vermont, remains remarkable.[30] The demes anchored democracy in the most democratic Greek city-state (Athens), and the towns anchor democracy in the most democratic American state (Vermont).

In 1951 Alistair Cooke, a British journalist, radio and television commentator, and author of many books on America, including the popular *Letters from America*, commented on the Greek influence in the beautiful little town of Newfane, Vermont.

WITNESS

IN NEWFANE'S SMALL VALLEY (1951)

Walk into the center of this village of Newfane. It is a handsome common with a couple of shops, an inn and a quite magnificent courthouse. The town was settled in 1776, but the county courthouse didn't go up until fifty years later, and we can be thankful for that. For in the interval Americans conceived a passion for everything Greek, believing that they had just successfully established the first genuine democracy since the Greeks and the grandest Republic since Rome. In this small village in Vermont, the county courthouse is an exquisite symbol of what Americans did in wood with Greek forms.

Opposite the courthouse is the inn, which is also the jail. Newfane has kept up its habit of feeding its prisoners from the inn, and since the inn serves

---

29. Pallenais was also part of a tribe (a *phylai*) and, on the level below this, part of a *trittyes*. The *trittyes* was a cross-sectional link between the deme and the tribes. One cannot equate either *phylai* or *trittyes* with the New England "county," which is an unimportant structure. In the deme structure, citizenship remained locked to the deme of one's first male ancestor. In Vermont, of course, citizenship follows the individual. Nor do Vermont towns have an analogue to the *demarch*, which one scholar likens to a mayor (Stockton, *Classical Athenian Democracy*, 63).

30. For instance, for 150 years Vermonters in their towns created and elected officers such as "fence viewer" and "hog reeve." Although trivial offices today, for well over a century they were the towns' answer to problems of the "common." Athenians in their demes did the same. This office was called an *aixomp* (one who oversees pasture rights). Whitehead, *Demes of Attica*, 122.

the best food around here, it's sometimes hard to get the inmates out of jail. Theodore Roosevelt said he would like to retire here, commit some "mild crime" and eat his way through a cheerful old age.

If you went along the valley you would be walking without knowing it through another town called Brookline, for Brookline is simply the scattered houses of the valley. It has less than a hundred people, mostly farmers, and they are their own rulers. Its first town meeting was held in 1795 and the last one was held last week. The names at the first meeting are still there: Moore and Waters, and Ebenezer Wellman and Cyrus Whitcomb, and Christopher Osgood (there has always been a Christopher on the Osgood farm). Walking along the road you might run into the tractor of a Mr. Hoyt, to all intents a farmer. He is also the road commissioner of the valley. His wife, Minnie Hoyt, is the town clerk, a justice of the peace, and when she isn't doing the farming chores she's busy signing fishing licenses, or marrying a visiting couple, or telling the comfortable city-people who have made a summer home here that by decision made at the last town meeting their taxes will be twice as much next year. What is striking to an Englishman is that the few fairly well-to-do people are all what they call "summer folks," people who made a farm over as a summer retreat from New York or Boston. But the summer folks are strangers and underlings. The valley has heard many delicate sounds through the years. But it has never heard the advice of a squire or the accent of *noblesse oblige.* The farmers are ruled and rulers.

Alistair Cooke[31]

Why Not Town Meeting?

There is emotion in the study of Greek democracy. First comes wonderment at the panoply of laws and institutions created so long ago by a people committed to self-government. Accordingly, the effort expended to understand what happened there is equally wondrous. Over the centuries thousands of anthropologists, archaeologists, architects, historians, linguists, and students of drama and poetry have spent their professional lives unearthing the empirical evidence from which we now craft our own political science. Much remains to be done. Yet our poring over the existing record, our exploration of every nook and cranny of nuance, our attention to every scrap of evidence, every subtlety of argument, are profoundly impressive. We have probed our own interpretations of our own interpretations in an incessant stirring of the intellectual broth. We seem compelled to make sure we have

31. Alistair Cooke, *One Man's America* (New York: Alfred A. Knopf, 1952), 158, 160–161, reprinted in T. D. Seymour Bassett, ed., *Outsiders inside Vermont* (Canaan, NH: Phoenix, 1976), 121–122.

gotten right what we say about what we think we know. We care about real democracy. Deeply.

Then comes puzzlement. If this be so, why haven't we looked at real democracy where it exists, here in our own land?[32] For the fact is, we know much more about the Greek democracy of twenty-five hundred years ago than we do about real democracy in America today.[33] We have as accurate estimates (based on heroic efforts in the fields of archaeology, anthropology, and literature) of how many eligible citizens attended the assembly in the Athens of old as we have of how many eligible citizens attend a New England town meeting today. Until the publication of Joseph Zimmerman's book in 1999, the human race had *no* aggregate published data on attendance rates of the New England town meetings.[34]

Imagine the world twenty-five hundred years from now. And imagine that the archaeologists of that time could unearth intact the entire empirical record of town meeting democracy as it exists today—the newspapers, popular literature, scholarly works, private diaries, and even the town clerks' records. Practically nothing of what we would want to know about real democracy in America in the year 2000 would be knowable. It has never, literally, been recorded.[35] Imagine now that we could travel back in time to classical Greece, carrying with us the information technologies of the present. Would we let the practice of real democracy in the demes be lost to history? Would we condemn ourselves again to centuries of backbreaking discovery that, in spite of many ingenious undertakings, have produced only a frustrating tidbit of what we want to know?[36]

32. A rare exception is an example of survey research, which focuses primarily on face-to-face participation. See Jeffrey M. Berry, Kent E. Portney, and Ken Thomson, *The Rebirth of Urban Democracy* (Washington, DC: Brookings Institution, 1993).

33. Robert Brown's account of provincial and town meeting democracy in colonial Massachusetts exceeds in its care and precision any account of town meeting democracy since the Revolution. See Robert E. Brown, *Middle-Class Democracy and the Revolution in Massachusetts, 1691–1780* (Ithaca: Cornell University Press, 1955).

34. In bringing together descriptions of the legal and institutional structures of town meeting in the six New England states, Zimmerman's book is important and very useful. Problems with his attendance data should be considered in light of the difficulty of his task. See Joseph Zimmerman, *The New England Town Meeting* (Westport, CT: Praeger, 1999), and Frank Bryan, "*The New England Town Meeting in Action*" (Review), *American Political Science Review*, June 2001, 489–490.

35. The best sources might be scattered videotapes of very recent town meetings, most in bits and pieces but some in full. From these we might be able to extrapolate limited data on participation rates. But attendance levels would be mostly obscure.

36. Take the question of the secret ballot process in earlier town meetings. What we have is evidence like the picture of a ballot being cast in the Woodstock town meeting of 1940 on whether the town should license itself to allow liquor to be sold. The caption reads: "Harriet

Puzzlement provokes inquiry. Yet we need not long speculate over why serious scholarship on town meeting is rare. First, town meetings are found only in New England, and the greater portion of them in northern New England. Second, town meeting has hardly been ascendant in recent decades. In many places it seems near death. Third, town meetings do not affect most U.S. citizens. The participants do not start wars or write the federal budget. Fourth, political scientists are primarily liberals, not communitarians. Their interests turn their research away from real democracy. Fifth, political scientists tend to come from cities, not the countryside. I suspect most of my colleagues around the country would welcome three or four years in rural Vermont with the same enthusiasm I would feel for a similar stay in Pittsburgh, Milwaukee, or Los Angeles. Sixth, even those political scientists who are interested in face-to-face, communal participation (and there are more and more good ones these days) are unlikely to believe this form of participation can be attached to real legislative bodies making policy for real governments.

Indeed, the important work predating and that stimulated by Robert Putnam's celebrated enterprise to establish the civic underpinnings of democratic society rests on the assumption that governments are *manifestations* of the civic process.[37] The idea that a government could itself be an important, even primary component of civil society has been pretty much abandoned. Our eyes have understandably fastened instead on participation in groups that practice real democracy rather than governments that do. An exception was Jane Mansbridge, who as early as 1970 decided to include a government (the town of "Selby," Vermont) in her pathbreaking *Beyond Adversary Democracy*.[38]

Although all of these reasons explain, they do not suffice. Northern New England may be a bit of a trip for many scholars, but an entire subdiscipline of political science travels the globe to investigate governance in out-of-the-way places. Town meeting is in decline in some of the largest towns, but it is going strong in many more. So what if individual town meetings do little more than buy trucks, vote for local school budgets, rule on salt for the

---

Cummings and Blanche Goodsell check off Elmer Freeman. Mrs. Cummings reportedly said to him, 'if you vote "yes" for liquor, you'd better put your ballot in a box in another town.' Licensing won, 171–76." In the picture Mr. Freeman (his real name) is handing one of the women a slip of paper. It does not appear to be folded, and the woman he is handing it to appears to be looking at it too closely for it to be truly secret. Peter S. Jennison, *The History of Woodstock, Vermont, 1890–1983* (Woodstock, VT: Countryman Press for the Woodstock Foundation, 1985), 246–247.

37. Robert D. Putnam, *Making Democracy Work: Civic Tradition in Modern Italy* (Princeton: Princeton University Press, 1993). Putnam has been a godsend for communitarians like me, for he has challenged the discipline to reconsider the foundation of the Republic.

38. Mansbridge, *Beyond Adversary Democracy*.

highways, and determine when taxes come due? We are scientists. Physics can be learned and taught as well from the perspective of a spiderweb as from that of the Golden Gate Bridge. Surely the discipline has had enough enthusiastic communitarians over the past half century to produce more than the half-dozen studies that have been done. No article on town meeting has ever been published in a major political science journal. Never. Finally, are we sure that real democratic governance is impossible? And even if it is, are we convinced that knowing how real democracy works would tell us so little about other forms of democracy that we are willing to let it go completely unstudied?

A single point explains a great deal. Logistics. For the most part town meetings are held only once a year and most on the same day. Minutes are not required, and although most towns produce some kind of record, the thoroughness varies greatly. Even the very best minutes usually do not record complete attendance data. None produce an accurate record of verbal participation. In short, what happens at a town meeting can be known in only one way. Attend. A single meeting needs at least two, usually three, and sometimes even four persons to record data on such basic items as attendance, verbal participation, and voting results. Thus, to study more than two or three small town meetings a year requires a cadre of researchers. The expense would be enormous.[39] Consequently, no database on real democracy exists, and therefore there is no developed science. My intention in this book is to do something about that. I want to get the science of real democracy under way.

Going into the Outback

In the spring of 1969, while teaching at St. Michael's College in Colchester, Vermont, I tested the possibility that the logistics of an extensive town meeting study could be overcome. I developed a data-recording procedure, devoted two lectures to town meeting and instructions in its use, and sent sixty-two students (in two class sections) out to pretest the procedure on twenty-five town meetings. In brief, here is the kind of information they

---

39. Beginning in the late 1990s several Vermont towns began experimenting with Saturday meetings. Before that some towns instituted Monday night meetings. This means that if you plan correctly, are willing to drive fast, and know the right roads, it is possible to attend five meetings a year—Saturday, Monday night, Tuesday morning (for a town that finishes its meeting by noon), Tuesday afternoon (for a town that begins its meeting after lunch), and Tuesday evening (this would also be a very small town). In this way I personally have attended and recorded data for at least four town meetings a year since 1995.

recorded.[40] They counted how many people were present by gender. They counted four times: half an hour after the meeting began, half an hour before the lunch break, half an hour after the meeting began again after lunch, and at the time the next to last warning item was considered. The students also indicated on another form how each issue taken up was resolved: by voice vote, standing count, or ballot. Whenever votes were counted, they recorded the totals. They measured the time spent on each warning item by noting the time the discussion began on each article and the time it left the floor and discussion on the next item began.

Recording participation turned out to be easier than I had expected. A form allowed the students to do the following: When the first person speaks, she is identified by some unique marking ("red vest, blond hair") and by gender. Her act of participation is placed on a grid, represented by the number of the warning item on the floor at the time she participated. The next participator, say "big guy in green suspenders" is then recorded on the grid immediately under the line for the "red vest" participator. A number matching the warning item on the floor similarly marks this second participation. If these people participate again, that participation is recorded on their individual lines on the grid (next to their earlier participation), with the number of the article on which they participate the second time. And so on until the end of the meeting.

Since this is done *sequentially*, it shows the order of the participations of all the participators and the order of each one's entering the discussion for the first time, along with the issues on which they spoke and the number of times they participated on each warning item. The measure also produces the total number of people who participated and the total number of participations by all those participating. The *distribution* of the participations among those who spoke, the sequence of participation by gender (important for theories of feminine participation), and the kinds of issues that prompted the most or least discussion are also available.

In the Craftsbury meeting of 1999, for instance, we know that 152 people attended the meeting.[41] Of these, 55 participated a total of 185 times. In the three hours and forty-three minutes of the meeting, not counting the lunch break, the people of Craftsbury resolved seventeen articles on the town warning and seven on the school warning. They also considered six matters of "extra business" and eight items under the "new business" article. Five of

40. For a detailed explanation of the process see the methodological appendix, www.uvm.edu/~fbryan.

41. The participation grid for this meeting is available in www.uvm.edu/~fbryan.

the seventeen town articles required a ballot vote.[42] The closest was 106 yea, 43 nay on the question of producing a new town lot map.[43] None of the town officer elections were contested. During the school meeting only one of the seven warning articles, the budget, required a ballot, and it passed 109 to 19. In the closest vote of the day, for school director, Roy Darling defeated Melissa Phillips 70 to 55. On the highest attendance count, women outnumbered men at the meeting 89 to 63. The average of the four counts was 67 women and 58 men. Of the 55 participators, 25 were women. This is a very small sample of the kinds of things we now know about the Craftsbury town meeting, one of the 49 meetings studied in 1999, three decades after the pretest. None of these data are available anywhere else. Nor could they now be made available.

The following are directions to Craftsbury (seventy miles one way) that I found jotted down in Beth Tonneson's Craftsbury folder. Hers is representative of the kind of trip my students have taken for thirty-three years to make this book possible.

WITNESS

Take Interstate 89 to exit 10—Waterbury Stowe take left off ramp head through Waterbury and into Stowe at 3 way intersection go straight on that road into Morrisville in Morrisville come to 4-way intersection and go straight through it. At the end of that road is route 15—take a right—keep going on rt. 15—heading toward Hardwick well before that there will be a sign on the left for North Wolcott rd—take a left onto North Wolcott road—(you'll know it a little ways down on that road is Larische's farm it is split by the road) follow North Wolcott to the end, it will intersect with route 14 take a left onto 14 (be able to look up at the common)—then take your first *paved* [emphasis mine] right road leads directly to the common—Academy will be on the left across from the common.

Beth Tonneson

42. Most elections for town officers must (by law) be resolved by a ballot vote. If no contest develops, a motion is made that the clerk be instructed to "cast one ballot" for the lone nominee. When this motion has been approved (it almost always is) the election is official. Budgets do not require a ballot by law, but often a ballot is requested from the floor. If seven people at the meeting request a ballot, then one must be held on any issue before the meeting. Often you hear groans from the floor when a ballot is requested. The ease with which citizens may require secret ballots is perhaps the best example of the mix of adversary and communitarian forms of participation at a town meeting.

43. This relatively controversial item was on the floor for thirty-two minutes: 15 people participated, 8 men and 7 women, a total of 26 times. Men had 17 of the participations and women 9. Beth Tonneson, "As Craftsbury Goes...So Goes Vermont? An Analysis of Democracy in Craftsbury, Vermont," Burlington, University of Vermont, April 1999.

PRESTON RIDGE CAMPUS

This kind of comparative information about real democracy has never before been collected. We have not known what percentage of a town's registered voters go to town meeting. What percentage of these speak? What are the issues on which they speak the most? How long do the meetings last? Is participation dominated by a few? Do women share real democracy equally with men? Do women speak more often on some issues than on others? What is the nature of conflict within the meetings? How much conflict is there? Are the votes close? Are face-to-face elections more competitive than elections by ballot? On what kinds of issues does conflict occur? Do high-conflict issues take longer to resolve? Do they stimulate more or less participation? Do women participate on high-conflict issues at the same rate as they do on low-conflict issues? What is the distribution of time spent on the issues? Do officers dominate the discussion?

Beyond its descriptive value, this kind of data makes possible for the study of real democracy the kind of scientific inquiry that has been under way for so long in the study of representative systems—for instance, in the comparative analysis of the American states or samples of cities or even nations. Are variations in real democracy in a community related to that community's socioeconomic diversity, or socioeconomic status, or population dynamics, or sense of community "boundedness," or the size of the town? Simple stuff in the scheme of the discipline as it now stands for representative democracy—uncharted ground in the study of real democracy.

Here is what I mean. In 1969, with the pretest over and relatively successful, I decided to experiment with a simple predictive model just for fun and (perhaps) to convince myself that a long-range project was worth the time. With only twenty-three towns in my sample, I ranked each town by number of registered voters and by a number that combined (equally) the percentage of its registered voters at the town meeting and the percentage of those attending who spoke out in the meeting at least once. I called (rather awkwardly) this sum of attendance and speaking "democraticness." The results shown are in figure 1.1, plot 1.

The trend is clear enough. For every increase of one rank of its population size, a town's town meeting will lose about nine-tenths (0.88) of a rank in "democraticness." This remarkably rough, case-challenged scatterplot (clearly unpublishable) greatly advanced what we knew about real democracy. But its value came primarily from the underdeveloped state of the discipline. My purpose in this book is therefore quite modest. It is to take the guesswork out of fundamental things we ought to know about real democracy.

PRESTON RIDGE CAMPUS

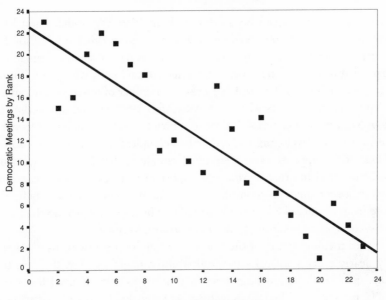

Town Size in Registered Voters by Ranks

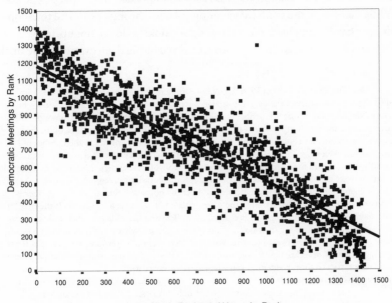

Town Size in Registered Voters by Ranks

Figure 1.1. Two samples of town meetings.

Telling the Story

Thirty-four years after I began this study in 1969, my students and I had obtained data on 1,669 meetings; 1,435 are used in this book.[44] Plot 2 of figure 1.1 demonstrates the explanatory potential of such a dramatically expanded database. The towns were selected randomly, with the following exception. Each year before 1980 I chose a number of towns at random and tried to match students with the towns. After 1980, in addition to the random list, I made a conscious effort to return to a select number of towns to be sure I was developing a more or less complete history on a few towns. These towns approximated a stratified sample in that I made certain they had characteristics that represented important features such as size, region, and socioeconomic composition. Throughout this process I was not afraid to vary from the model if logistics required it. The result has produced only one bias—overrepresentation of towns in northern Vermont.

In the description of the towns one condition overwhelms: their size. By nearly every standard a political scientist might employ, they are tiny. One-quarter of the meetings were held in towns that averaged fewer than 1,000 residents. Of the 1,435 meetings, 113 were held in towns that averaged fewer than 200. Only 2 percent of the meetings were held in towns of more than 5,000. Political scientists seldom make professional visits to places like these. Yet little towns allow us to gaze at the important inner space of politics. While many seek the truth by scanning galaxies through powerful telescopes, my eyes have been glued to a microscope—looking down, not up, inward, not outward. America has often seemed transfixed by big. I am captivated by small.

---

44. The database ends in 1998. The final editing of this book occurred in 2003. I am often asked about the accuracy of the data. Do students ever get it wrong? Sure. The question is how wrong. My judgment is that it is probably more *reliable* than survey research instruments. This is partly because the recording device is so simple and does not rely on assumptions of internal *validity*. On attendance counts my bet is the students are close to perfect. On the number of participators, even more so. On repeat participations I suspect they make a few more mistakes, but it is still very close. In the aggregate these errors are probably less egregious than the errors made by interviewers in someone's household, because it is much easier to record nonobtrusive data. If a student counts 200 people at a town meeting, I'd bet the house and the car the real number is between 195 and 205. If they say 40 of these participated, it is between 39 and 41. If they say "the man in the red hat" spoke 8 times, it is either 7, 8, or 9. Given the wide gaps that we know exist between what individuals say their political behavior is like and what it really is, I have no qualms about asserting that when I report in this book that 18 percent of a town's voters were at a town meeting, it is a more secure figure than a survey research schedule reporting a similar percentage based on a survey of town residents, even when allowances are made for sample size. For caveats to the science of survey research, see John Brehm, *The Phantom Respondents: Opinion Surveys and Political Representation* (Ann Arbor: University of Michigan Press, 1993), and the anthology Thomas E. Mann and Gary R. Orren, eds., *Media Polls in American Politics* (Washington, DC: Brookings Institution, 1992).

It is not a popular approach. For the policymakers of a continental republic this is understandable. For scientists investigating democracy I find it odd.

This, then, is a first cut at the study of real democracy. I want to show what real democracy looks like and how it works. To make this description more palatable, I garnish it with the herbs of science—simple hypotheses drawn from the larger scheme of the discipline. To do this requires numbers. Lots of numbers. But quantification must be conditioned by the other senses. And so we turn to Charles Kuralt and Marnie Owen.

WITNESS

CHARLES KURALT'S TOWN MEETING DAY IN STRAFFORD, VERMONT

This one day in Vermont, the town carpenter lays aside his tools, the town doctor sees no patients, the shopkeeper closes his shop, mothers tell their children they'll have to warm up their own dinner. This one day, people in Vermont look not to their own welfare but to that of their town. It doesn't matter that it's been snowing since four o'clock this morning. They'll be in the meeting house. This is town meeting day.

Every March for 175 years, the men and women of Strafford, Vermont, have trudged up this hill on the one day which is their holiday for democracy. They walk past a sign that says: THE OLD WHITE MEETING HOUSE—BUILT IN 1799 AND CONSECRATED AS A PLACE OF PUBLIC WORSHIP FOR ALL DENOMINATIONS WITH NO PREFERENCE FOR ONE ABOVE ANOTHER. Since 1801, it has also been in continuous use as a town hall.

Here, every citizen may have his say on every question. One question is: Will the town stop paying for outside health services? The speaker is a farmer and elected selectman, David K. Brown. And farmer Brown says yes.

DAVID K. BROWN: This individual was trying or thinking about committing suicide. So we called the Orange County Mental Health. This was, I believe, on a Friday night. They said they'd see him Tuesday afternoon [*mild laughter*], and if we had any problems, take him to Hanover and put him in the emergency room. Now I don't know as we should pay five hundred and eighty-two dollars and fifty cents for that kind of advice.

They talked about that for half an hour, asking themselves if this money would be well or poorly spent.

This is not representative democracy. This is pure democracy, in which every citizen's voice is heard.

JAMES CONDICT: We will vote on this before we go to Article four. All those in favor signify by saying "Aye."

PEOPLE: Aye.

CONDICT: All opposed.

PEOPLE: Nay.

CONDICT: I'm going to ask for a standing vote. All those in favor stand, please.

PRESTON RIDGE LIBRARY
COLLIN COLLEGE
FRISCO, TX 75035

It's an old Yankee expression which originated in the town meeting and has entered the language of free men: Stand up and be counted.

And when the judgment is made, and announced by James Condict, maker of rail fences and moderator of this meeting, the town will abide by the judgment.

CONDICT: There are a hundred votes cast—sixty-one in favor and thirty-nine against. And it then becomes deleted from the town budget.

This is the way the founders of this country imagined it would be—that citizens would meet in their own communities to decide directly most of the questions affecting their lives and fortunes. Vermont's small towns have kept it this way.

Will or will not Strafford, Vermont, turn off its streetlights to save money?

CONDICT: All those in favor—

MAN [shouting]:—Paper ballot!—

CONDICT:—signify by saying—

MAN [*shouting*]:—Paper ballot!

WOMAN: What?

MAN: That's my right, any member's right at a meeting—to call for a paper ballot.

CONDICT: Is that seconded?

WOMAN: I'll second it.

CONDICT: It's seconded.

MAN: It doesn't have to be seconded.

CONDICT: Prepare to cast your ballots on this amendment.

If any citizen demands a secret ballot, a secret ballot it must be. Everybody who votes in Vermont has taken an old oath—to always vote his conscience, without fear or favor of any person. This is something old, something essential. You tear off a little piece of paper and on it you write "yes" or "no." Strafford votes to keep the streetlights shining.

There is pie, baked by the ladies of the PTA. There are baked beans and brown bread, served at town meeting by Celia Lane as long as anybody can remember. Then a little more wood is added to the stove and a dozen more questions are debated and voted on in the long afternoon. What is really on the menu today is government of the people. . . . When finally they did adjourn and walk out into the snow, it was with the feeling of having preserved something important, something more important than their streetlights—their liberty.

Charles Kuralt[45]

That was Kuralt on Strafford. In March of the year 2000, one of my students, Marnie E. Owen, whose mother is a former town clerk of Strafford

45. Charles Kuralt, *On the Road with Charles Kuralt* (New York: G. P. Putnam, 1985), 288–291.

and whose father is a carpenter in town, did her paper on Strafford. Here (in part) is what she said about town meeting:

WITNESS

My observations of town meeting day this past March are much less romantic than Kuralt's. Strafford doesn't have a town carpenter; it has several, most of whom likely went to work on town meeting day. I didn't see many of them at the Town House. There is no town doctor either. Most Strafford residents go to Dartmouth-Hitchcock Medical Center in Lebanon, New Hampshire, when they need medical attention. As for snow, by March 7, 2000, most of the Strafford's snow had melted. Temperatures climbed to a least fifty degrees that day.

The media often portrays Vermont as a pure, primitive, simple place that modern technology has not yet pervaded and where (as Jefferson said) live "the chosen people of God." Accounts like Kuralt's reinforce these broad stereotypes.... This is precisely the sort of thinking that leads the many citizens in places like Strafford to participate in town government. Strafford's high turnout at town meeting likely stems in part from the misconception of the inherent virtue of rural people and newcomers' desires to make themselves part of something they see as highly moral.

When I went to town meeting in Strafford this year, I sat behind and frequently conversed with a relative newcomer, Donna Bliss. Donna and her husband Stephen retired to Strafford from Boston about five years ago. They've built a gorgeous mansion atop a hill that overlooks much of South Strafford. Donna is a graduate of Vassar and had a career as a journalist. Stephen was a high-powered corporate CEO. Stephen and Donna are not unlike many Strafford newcomers in that they were very excited to attend their first town meeting. Unfortunately, Stephen had the misfortune of being called back to Boston at the last minute and couldn't attend. Donna hadn't been in the Town House before and was looking forward to seeing the interior of a building that she'd recognized from magazines when she first moved to Strafford. Donna found the Town House to be a charming place with its old wood stove and natural light. She was amazed that the Town House remains without plumbing, running water or electricity, and though a bit annoyed by having to walk next door to a neighboring house to use the bathroom, she tried not to show it.

Marnie Owen[46]

46. Marnie E. Owen, "Strafford, Vermont: A Historical and Political Analysis," Burlington, University of Vermont, April 2000. Unlike nearly all other proper names used in this book, the Blisses' names are fictional. Over thirty years earlier when I began this study in 1969, Thomas Gallucci reported from the town of Calais: "The meeting place was an old church in need of repair.... The 'restroom' consisted of a small room in which was a long board with holes in it. (I waited until I got back to school!)" (Thomas Gallucci, "A Day in Calais," Colchester, Vermont, St. Michael's College, March 1969).

This is what comes of their wretched town meetings—these are the proceedings of a tumultuous and riotous rabble, who ought, if they had the least produce, to follow their mercantile employment and not trouble themselves with politics and government, which they do not understand.

Lord Germain (appointed by the king to be secretary of state to the colonies) when hearing of the Boston Tea Party

"Senator Quayle, you said it's not going to be the folks at town meeting who are going to resolve this thing, but isn't that what has happened? Isn't that the reason we're here tonight? Isn't that the reason the president's speaking on it tonight because people at town meetings . . . have raised the issue?"

"Our military experts say that we're in an inferior situation: the Soviet military experts believe that we are in an inferior situation. And they're not going to ask some grassroots caucus taking place in Vermont whether they're inferior or superior."

Senator Dan Quayle responding to a question (*The MacNeil-Lehrer Report,* Public Broadcasting System, March 31, 1982).

2

Town Meeting

An American Conversation

The heart of the American republic, it seems to me, beats to the rhythm of two philosophies: liberalism governs the center, democracy sustains the base. In the beginning, however, the voices of our history chronicle a passion for the life of the nation and the promise of liberalism. Democracy was distrusted, even feared.

From Fear to Celebration

The framers went to Philadelphia in 1787 dreading real democracy. Many say Americans adopted the Constitution *because* they dreaded real democracy. "Had every Athenian citizen been a Socrates," wrote Madison, "every Athenian Assembly would still have been a mob."[1] Mary Ritter Beard said of the founding period, "At no time, at no place, in solemn convention assembled, through no chosen agents, had the American people officially proclaimed the United States to be a Democracy.... [When] the Constitution was framed no respectable person called himself or herself a democrat."[2] The nation had discovered (as the British had tried to tell us only a few years earlier) that it takes a certain stability and unified purpose to run a continental enterprise. Troublemakers like Daniel Shay (reminiscent of those who threw

1. Alexander B. Hamilton, James Madison, and John Jay, *The Federalist Papers, Federalist* no. 55 (Middletown, CT: Wesleyan University Press, 1961), 374.
2. Charles A. Beard and Mary Ritter Beard, *America in Midpassage* (New York: Macmillan, 1939), chap. 17. Yet real democracy was happening on the ground all over the new nation and especially in the hills and valleys and along the shores of New England.

tea into Boston harbor) were raising hell in *America*, that is, just across the Connecticut River in western New England.

Yet it wasn't long before fear of democracy began to recede. Relief came with the opening of the frontier, where most of the moblike characters who might disrupt a town meeting or a fresh republic were wont to go. It came too from the acceptance of a new democracy-proof Constitution that would handle what at the time were considered (from the citizens' point of view) the rather incidental matters of the Republic itself. Our first important political upheaval replaced America's emphasis on urban, coastal mercantilism with small-town inland agrarianism. With Jefferson the town meeting democracy that once threatened the Republic ("shook it to its very foundations," he said) became "the wisest invention ever devised by the wit of man for the perfect exercise of self government."[3]

After Jefferson, our national perspective on real democracy was defined predominantly by the New England transcendentalist and romantic tradition and by Alexis de Tocqueville.[4] Henry David Thoreau and Ralph Waldo Emerson inscribed town meeting and the real democracy it implied into the annals of the American way. Town meeting became (for Thoreau) "the true Congress... the most respectable one ever assembled in the United States." In his famous speech before the people of Concord, Emerson seems almost driven in his praise. Town meeting reveals "the great secret of political science" and solves the "problem" it entails: how to "give each individual his fair weight in the government." In town meetings, he said, "the rich gave council, but the poor also; and, moreover, the just and the unjust... every opinion had its utterance, every fact, every acre of land, every bushel of rye, its

---

3. Ironically, Jefferson had little firsthand experience with real democracy, practiced as he was in the southern county tradition. After New England opposed the Embargo Act, Jefferson remarked, "How powerful did we feel the energy of this system in the case of the embargo....I felt the foundations of the government shaken under my feet by the New England township." And (in language that could have come straight out of Madison's *Federalist* no. *10*), "The organization of this little selfish minority enabled it to overrule the union." Letter to Joseph C. Cabell, Monticello, February 2, 1816, found in Joyce Appleby and Terence Ball, eds., *Political Writings/Thomas Jefferson* (New York: Cambridge University Press, 1999), 205. Jere Daniell argues that statements like these make Jefferson's recommendation that the town meeting be adopted throughout the United States even more remarkable. Jefferson concluded: "What could the unwieldy countries of the Middle, the South, and the West do? Call a county meeting?" Jere Daniell, "Town Meeting: Symbol for a Nation," Hanover, New Hampshire, unpublished working paper, n.d.

4. Lawrence Buell finds a connection between the writings of the Federalists and those of the New England romanticists. He says that reformers within the Whig Party who were attached to the Federalist tradition did the most to invigorate the town meeting tradition. Lawrence Buell, *New England Literary Culture: From Revolution through Renaissance* (Cambridge: Cambridge University Press, 1986), 94–95.

entire weight." About the same time, Tocqueville was writing, "Town Meetings are to liberty what primary schools are to science; they bring it within the people's reach, they teach men how to use and enjoy it." Later in the century John Stuart Mill seconded the motion. Town meeting was "a school of public spirit."[5] It seemed as though all had read and accepted the words of Yale's President Timothy Dwight, who wrote as early as 1821: "In these little schools men commence their apprenticeship to public life; and learn to do the public's business. Here the young speaker makes his first essays: and here his talents are displayed, marked, and acknowledged. The aged, the discreet, here see with pleasure the promise of usefulness in the young; and fail not to reward with honorable testimonials every valuable effort of the rising generation."[6] The litany could go on. But all in all it is hard to imagine how the central years of the nineteenth century could have provided town meeting with a more impressive pedigree.

By the century's end, the applause had found its way into the textbooks. James Bryce in his much read *American Commonwealth* says: "The town or the township with its primary assembly is best . . . it is the most educative of citizens who bear a part in it. The town meeting has been not only the source but the school of democracy."[7] Still more effusive was *Civil Government of the United States* by Harvard's John Fiske, published in 1890, which became a classic. The professor did not mince his words. The town meeting, he says, is "the most complete democracy in the world." While his praise is more broad-based than most, he too focuses on the schoolhouse metaphor: [8] "In the kind of discussion which it provokes, in the necessity of facing argument with

5. Henry David Thoreau, "Slavery in Massachusetts," in *Reform Papers* (Princeton: Princeton University Press, 1973), 99; Ralph Waldo Emerson, "Historical Discourse at Concord," in *Miscellanies*, vol. 2 of *Collected Works* (New York: AMS Press, 1968), 46–47; Alexis de Tocqueville, *Democracy in America* (Cambridge: Sever and Francis, 1862), 76. John Stuart Mill, *Consideration on Representative Government* (Chicago: Henry Regnery, 1963), 73.

6. Timothy Dwight, *Travels in New England and New York* (New Haven: T. Dwight, 1821), 32. Dwight also spends considerable time defending in glowing terms the lawmaking capacities of town meeting.

7. James Bryce, *The American Commonwealth* (New York: Macmillan, 1912), 601.

8. Civic education is by far the most pronounced strain in the praise for town meeting. In 1907 the Supreme Judicial Court of Massachusetts argued: "No small part of the capacity for honest and efficient local government manifested by the people of the commonwealth has been due to the training of citizens in the forum of the town meeting. . . . The practical instruction of the citizen in affairs of government through the instrumentality of public meetings and face-to-face discussions may be regarded quite as important as their amusement, edification, or assumed temporal advancement in ways heretofore expressly authorized by statute and held constitutional." *Wheelock v. Lowell*, 196 Mass. 220, 81 N.E. 977 (1907), cited in Lane W. Lancaster, *Government in Rural America*, 2nd ed. (New York: D. Van Nostrand, 1952), 37–38.

argument and of keeping one's temper under control, the town-meeting is the best training school in existence."[9] Summarizing the century's intellectual exuberance about town meeting, James K. Hosmer, a professor of English and German literature at Washington University in St. Louis, rhapsodized, "Is there anything more valuable among Anglo-Saxon institutions?"[10]

Nationalization and the Progressive Alternative

The timing was fortuitous. Town meeting made it into the textbooks just ahead of a band of progressives armed with shotguns and a rope. Historian Jere Daniell of Dartmouth College marks the time and place of the hinge in thinking as 1897, when the *Nation* published an article titled "The Decay of Town Government." Here the author, A. G. Sedgwick, begins by noting that to question the New England town meeting would be like questioning democracy itself. No matter. The truth is, says Sedgwick, the institution has fallen on hard times. New England towns have become corrupt to the core, their meetings dominated by "Village Tweeds," ignoring the will of the people. Elections are rigged. Pockets are lined. Town meeting is no longer a pretty picture (if indeed it ever was). In short, progressives like Sedgwick were not about to give town meeting a pass, hallowed ground or not.[11] In the next three decades the attack continued in both the local and the national press.

The Progressive Era dealt town meeting several blows. The first was perhaps the most devastating. Boredom. Looking for critiques of town meeting by the leading scholars of the period is like looking for Vermont dandelions in the snows of January. As Thoreau scholar Bob Pepperman Taylor says, "[Town meeting] wasn't where the action was."[12] The action was with referenda and reform, city machines and the national system. It was in the center, not the parts. At about the time the last state of the adjacent forty-eight joined the Union, the celebrated Progressive Herbert Croly expressed the exuberance and national perspective of the Progressive agenda. "[The] salutary aspect of the present situation is the awakening of American public opinion to the necessity of scrutinizing the *national* [emphasis mine] ideal and

9. John Fiske, *Civil Government in the United States* (Boston: Houghton, Mifflin, 1890), 30–32. Fiske's assessment is refreshingly clear-eyed.

10. James K. Hosmer, "Sam Adams, the Man of Town Meeting," in *Johns Hopkins University Studies in Historical and Political Science*, second series, pt. 4, ed. Herbert B. Adams (Baltimore: Johns Hopkins University, 1984).

11. A. G. Sedgwick, "The Decay of Town Government," *Nation* (1897), cited in Daniell, "Town Meeting."

12. Bob Pepperman Taylor, interview with the author, Burlington, Vermont, September 1999.

of working over the guiding principles of its associated life. The American democracy is becoming aroused to take a searching look at its own meaning and responsibilities."[13]

In his optimistic *Changing America*, published in 1912, University of Wisconsin professor of sociology Edward Alsworth Ross likewise shows no interest in local democracy. The closest he comes is an early, explicit, and prophetic affirmation of liberalism. The people are no longer "masses," he says. They have "broken up into individuals."[14] Even the quintessential Progressive John Dewey, a Vermonter himself and known for his admonition that democracy begins in the "neighborly community," finds no time to consider the role of town meeting as an institution of governance.[15] Those who did take the time to think about it at all gave it short shrift. Progressive man of letters Charles Russell went to high school in St. Johnsbury, Vermont, and he concluded of town meeting governance there that business ran things: "These men might be so good they were blue in the face; still the fact remained that without mandate from the people they were the government."[16]

13. Herbert Croly, *Progressive Democracy* (New York: Macmillan, 1914), 27. Croly's only attention to town meeting democracy is indirect and instrumental. He credits the towns of Massachusetts and New Hampshire with "stubborn insistence" (even before the end of the Revolution) that any proposed new scheme for post-British state governance be submitted to a statewide popular vote that was generated by a convention formed expressly to propose the new plan. He says: "The importance of this assertion by the people [the "towns" had become "the people" in one short paragraph] of New England of the reality of ultimate popular responsibility can scarcely be overestimated. Thereafter democracy obtained a new meaning and a new dignity." Ibid., 33.

14. Edward Alsworth Ross, *Changing America* (New York: Century, 1912), 6. In its denial of Greek (real) democracy, his defense of direct democracy is reminiscent of the founders: "There is no real likeness between a deliberate referendum vote in sparsely settled Oregon and the offhand, tumultuous decision of six thousand Athenians meeting in their *agora*." Ibid.

15. Many believe that Dewey's faith in face-to-face democracy was instilled in Vermont. Bob Pepperman Taylor, who knows as much about Dewey as anyone, resists the linkage between Vermont and Dewey's public philosophy. Dewey's thinking, says Taylor, is more apt to have come from his formal schooling and church experience *in* Vermont than from his experiences *with* Vermont. Dewey grew up in one of the few cities in Vermont, Burlington—a small city to be sure, but the biggest in the state. It had no town meeting. He left Vermont in his twenties and thereafter lived and worked almost exclusively in two of America's greatest cities, Chicago and New York. See Bob Pepperman Taylor, "John Dewey's Vermont Inheritance," in *The University of Vermont: The First Two Hundred Years*, ed. Robert V. Daniels (Burlington: University of Vermont; Hanover, NH: University Press of New England, 1991), 121–137.

16. Charles Edward Russell, *Bare Hands and Stone Walls: Some Reflections of a Sideline Reformer* (New York: Scribner, 1933). St. Johnsbury was home to the second most important business family of the century in Vermont, the Fairbanks of Fairbanks Scales. It would be hard to imagine a better setting for the "company town" thesis. Russell seems fair-minded in his recollections. He pays the people of the town about the highest compliment one can, saying he could think of no community "blessed" with citizens more "kindly, friendly, neighborly and good to know." He also is lavish in his praise of the company: "They gave money for good objects, they

With the war that settled the question of the Union still fresh in memory, the frontier closed, and the Industrial Revolution ascendant (and with it the threat of corruption and corporate greed), it was time to fashion a national democracy, a larger, more centralized expression of American nationhood. In local affairs the quest was for managerial politics engineered by politics-free professionals, a concept anathema to town meeting. The Progressives' democracy was defined in terms of direct voting rather than face-to-face deliberation.[17] In short, on the canvas of the Progressive dream, town meeting was nowhere to be found.[18]

The building of the American century—that unique blending of continental expansion and urban industrialism between 1830 and 1950—combined with the Progressive vision to spell more trouble for town meeting. With the American century came the decline of the New England town, a special conjunction of geographic cohesion and small population that had been the prime grassland of real democracy. New England was a major exporter of people to the West, and no state contributed more of its population to the movement than Vermont.[19]

---

financed the Academy [which Russell attended], built and presented to the town the really remarkable Athenaeum, stocked it with a marvelous library, added an excellent collection of paintings. Liberally they subscribed to foreign missions; they had built one of the most beautiful churches in all New England; they were flawless in the performance of every pious duty."

17. In 1912, while defending the gut-level institutional processes of the Progressive agenda, Delos F. Wilcox pretty much writes town meeting off. It is "a sort of national memory, a regret of days gone by and conditions that have passed." He continues in a passage prescient of the neighborhood government movement of the 1970s: "Even yet it occasionally happens that some ardent civic reformer, his soul burdened with the political failures of American city government, brings forward some complex and curious plan for reestablishing town-meeting methods in a metropolis. But these schemes are so manifestly visionary and impracticable that they hardly attract a passing notice. The town-meeting belongs essentially to the past." Delos F. Wilcox, *Government by All the People, or The Initiative, the Referendum, and the Recall as Instruments of Democracy* (New York: Macmillan, 1912), 5–6.

18. Some Progressives had been willing to link the spirit of town meeting to their favorite reforms. "Town meeting," one wrote, "gave great encouragement to the spread of the plebescital principle," because "the people in their town meetings had been made familiar with direct legislation representing their local concerns." Ellis Paxson Oberholtzer, *The Referendum in America* (New York: Da Capo Press, 1991), 108, 110. Indeed, it could be that the tradition of "instructing delegates" in Massachusetts did support the notions of referenda, initiatives, and recall. But these traditions could also be seen as simply a natural unfolding of the concept of representation in the colonies. John Phillip Reid, *The Concept of Representation in the Age of the American Revolution* (Chicago: University of Chicago Press, 1989), 90–93. I am inclined to agree with David Magleby that for referenda and initiatives "the town meeting has little relevance." David B. Magleby, *Direct Legislation: Voting on Ballot Propositions in the United States* (Baltimore: Johns Hopkins University Press, 1984).

19. Van Wyck Brooks calls this period New England's "Indian summer." Van Wyck Brooks, *New England: Indian Summer, 1865–1915* (New York: E. P. Dutton, 1940). See also Stewart H. Holbrook, *The Yankee Exodus: An Account of Migration from New England* (New York: Macmillan,

But to the dismay of people like Lewis Mumford, New Englanders failed to implant their democracy in the new lands they did so much to settle and fashion.[20] The New England democratic perspective may have had an influence, but the *institution* didn't take. The land settlement patterns (mostly agricultural) of the Midwest, and especially the middle border and the deep West, were not hospitable to communal, deliberative enterprise.[21] The township of the new America evolved on its own, influenced by the wider open spaces that New Englanders coveted. Besides, countervailing influences were at work, primarily the county, manor, and parish systems that were fresh in the memories of fellow settlers from New York to Louisiana.[22]

Within New England itself, urban industrialism played havoc with town meeting. In the south (Massachusetts, Rhode Island, and Connecticut), where town meeting had first taken hold, urbanization was chewing up the towns

---

1950). The depletion of small-town New England began in earnest with the Civil War. Vermont sent 10 percent of its *entire population* off to fight. The state had a casualty rate of 15 percent. Dead casualties. "For those who returned," writes Howard S. Russell, "ties to the old town had been loosened by absence and travel." See Howard S. Russell, *A Long Deep Furrow* (Hanover, NH: University Press of New England, 1976), 417–418. See also John O'Brien, "Vermont Fathers of Wisconsin," *Vermont History* 16 (July 1948): 74–82, and Lewis D. Stilwell, *Migration from Vermont* (Montpelier: Vermont Historical Society, 1937).

20. Said Mumford, "The political importance of this new form [the town and its town meeting] must not be under-rated, through the failure to grasp it and to continue it—indeed to incorporate it in both the Federal and the State Constitutions—was one of the tragic oversights of post-revolutionary political development." Lewis Mumford, *The City in History* (New York: Harcourt, Brace and World, 1961), 332–333.

21. Clyde Snider observed in 1957, "The geographical townships marked out by the rectangular land surveyors of the national government commonly provided the areas for new civil townships (except in eastern Ohio); and the artificial nature of these areas has been an important factor in preventing the township in these regions from attaining the social unity and political importance of the New England town." Clyde F. Snider, "Indiana Counties and Townships," *Indiana Magazine of History* 33 (June 1937): 119–152; Clyde F. Snider, *Local Government in Rural America* (Westport, CT: Greenwood Press, 1957), 20.

22. The best study of this process is Lois Kimball Mathews Rosenberry, *The Expansion of New England* (New York: Russell and Russell, 1962). To get out of New England by land one must go through New York. New York's county system of local governance developing next to New England's town system is an example of the subtle chemistry of tradition, geography, and governance. See Nicholas Varga, "The Development and Structure of Local Government in Colonial New York," in *Town and Country: Essays on the Structure of Local Government in the American Colonies*, ed. Bruce C. Daniels (Middletown, CT: Wesleyan University Press, 1978), 186–215. Townships in Indiana and Illinois bore clear similarities to the New England town, primarily in the central and northern regions where the New England influence was strong. The "Biblical Institute" that came to Evanston, Illinois, for instance, was modeled after the theological seminary in Newbury, Vermont. My first twelve years of education came in the seven-room Town Central School building on the site of the Newbury Seminary. It took only three teachers to get us through eight grades. Mrs. Merrill, Mrs. Whitehill, and Mrs. Butson did everything but the janitorial work—and now and then some of that. One of the best opportunities to study the transplantation of towns in this period is the "Vermontville Colony" in Michigan. See Douglas K. Meyer, "Union Colony, 1836–1870: Pattern and Process of Growth," *Vermont History* 41 (Summer 1973): 147–157.

and with them the potential for sustained real democracy. Connecticut started the process as early as 1784, incorporating the four cities of Hartford, New Haven, Middletown, and Norwich each *within* its respective town.[23] It was not yet a popular move. According to Harold A. Pinkham Jr., chronicler of early urbanism in New England, it was not until Boston broke out and "set the pace" that a rapid expansion of city charters began. In 1822, after a three-day town debate, Bostonians voted away their town meeting. Providence became a city in 1830, and Portland, Maine did so in 1832. In Connecticut, Waterbury, Bridgeport, and New Britain followed suit, all dismantling their town meetings. By the end of the century, aided by the arrival of the streetcar, suburbanization was added to the mix and further reduced the number of freestanding towns.[24]

The "north forty" of New England—Maine, New Hampshire, and Vermont—which by 1850 was the nation's best remaining natural range for real democracy, was hit especially hard by the movement down from the hills to the larger mill towns of southern New England or to the West. By the turn of the century a close observer of New England would write:

> The children left [the farm] drawn by dreams of gains the city or the sea or the far West offers: and the parents are gone, too, now. The shingles and clapboards loosen and the roof sags and within, damp, mossy decay has fastened itself to the walls, floor and ceiling of every room. Gaps have broken in the stone walls along the roadway, and the brambles are thick, springing on either side. In the front yard is a gnarled, untrimmed apple tree, with a great broken limb sagging to the ground, and about, a ragged growth of bushes. As time goes on, the house falls, piece by piece, and at last only the shattered frame stands, a grim memorial of the dead past.[25]

23. Thus the city dwellers had dual residency, city and town. This process was adopted in Vermont with the incorporation of "villages" within towns. Growing up on the "intervales" of the Connecticut River (just below the fall line) in Newbury, I had dual citizenship. I was a citizen both of Newbury village and the town of Newbury. Newbury has two incorporated villages—Newbury village and Wells River village. It was in another village (Orleans) in a two-village town (Barton) up in Vermont's Northeast Kingdom that I began my teaching career in the local high school.

24. For a treatment of the urbanization process through 1873 see Harold A. Pinkham Jr., "Plantation to City Charter: The Rise of Urban New England, 1630–1873," in *American Cities and Towns*, ed. Joseph F. Rishel (Pittsburgh: Duquesne University Press, 1992), 14–25.

25. Clifton Johnson, "The New England Country" (1893), quoted in Perry D. Westbrook, *The New England Town in Fact and Fiction* (Rutherford, NJ: Fairleigh Dickenson University Press, 1982), 161. When I was ten years old I spent a good part of the fall and winter on a hill farm on Wallace Hill in Newbury, Vermont. Rural electrification had not yet arrived. I remember Mr. McEachearn's face in the yellow light of a kerosene lantern as he milked. A fuzzy pride of barn cats (mostly kittens) surrounded a huge bowl of steaming fresh milk, the purring so

This picture is precisely on target.[26]

Although the demise of the hill farms left many valley villages intact,[27] the decline of rural, farm culture in so many places all at once in the very heartland of "town meeting country" had a debilitating effect on the public persona of town meeting. It fertilized the emerging antirural sentiment that accompanied Progressivism and the urban-industrial revolution and became a third element in the swing from good to bad of the national perspective on town meeting between 1895 and 1935. The more or less benign country bumpkin image evident throughout the nineteenth century turned sour in the twentieth. Critics began to doubt that country people were of the proper *quality* to sustain democracy, especially face-to-face deliberative democracy.[28]

In fairness, things did look bleak. Listen to Rudyard Kipling describe the outback of Vermont as he worked on *The Jungle Book* and *Captains Courageous* from his home in Brattleboro: "The land was denuding itself of its accustomed inhabitants, and their places had not yet been taken by the wreckage of Eastern Europe or the wealthy city-folk who later bought 'pleasure

---

loud it competed with the sound of four alternating teats filling the pail between my best friend Joe's knees. I milked my first cow there and shot my first gun. Now and then I got to drive the old jeep they used for a tractor. The family moved away when I was thirteen. Joe got killed on his motorcycle somewhere in California, I heard later. The last I saw of any of the McEachearn family was the night Joe's brother John beat the hell out of me at a dance at the town hall over a girl named Frances. (We danced, played basketball, watched plays, and marched in to graduate from high school on the same floor from which our parents practiced democracy.) The McEachearn house lasted longer than the barn; I watched it rot and lean and tumble over the years. Like dozens of other hill farms I knew as a boy, it died hard. I often take the shortcut over Wallace Hill on my way back to Burlington from visits home to Newbury (eighty-five miles). But the only trace of the old McEachearn place is in a faraway corner of my heart.

26. See John R. Stilgoe, "The Wildering of New England, 1850–1950," in *Settlement in New England: The Last 100 Years*, ed. Timothy J. Richard (Storrs: University of Connecticut, 1980), 1–6. The best overall source is Harold Fisher Wilson, *The Hill Country of Northern New England: Its Social and Economic History, 1790–1930* (New York: Columbia University Press, 1936).

27. See Joseph S. Wood, *The New England Village* (Baltimore: Johns Hopkins University Press, 1997). Many villages were commercial centers within a town, often near the depot. When incorporated they provided essential urban services like a fire department and streetlights. These villages were (and are) governed by their own village meetings. In Newbury village where I grew up in the 1940s and 1950s, the village plowed the three sidewalks (one of which ended at our house) and maintained lights on the three little streets that had them. It also provided water from a reservoir up on Moore Hill, which drained the "Adam's lot" where I spent my high school weekends and vacations in 1959 logging with Ira Chamberlain, Alex Greer, and an old white horse named Captain. Three dairy farms were within a few hundred yards of our house in the village. The village population was 723.

28. As late as 1973 the textbooks were reporting that "the popular urban expression of rural people is that they are ignorant, slow in thought and action, and very gullible." J. B. Chitambar, *Introductory Rural Sociology* (New York: Halstead Press, 1973), 130. Paul Carter, *The Twenties in America* (New York: Thomas Y. Crowell, 1968), 73.

farms.' What might have become characters, powers and attributes perverted themselves in that desolation as cankered trees grow out branches akimbo, and strange faiths and cruelties born of solitude to the edge of insanity, flourished like lichen on sick bark."[29] This kind of Kipling-like observation on the sorry condition of county folk can be found throughout the popular literature and serious scholarship of the period.[30]

Life was apparently so bad in Vermont in the 1930s that the federal government suggested saving the state by purchasing over 55 percent of it, abandoning most of the roads in the condemned areas, closing the schools, and moving all the farmers and townspeople—every living soul—down into the valley towns. Future governor and then future U.S. senator George Aiken (on Vietnam: "Why don't we declare victory and leave?") was lieutenant governor and chairperson of the committee to consider the proposal. His take on the situation: "They placed before members of the legislature the astonishing story that, not only were these people in certain areas of the state very unhappy because of their condition, but that the State itself was very unhappy because such people existed in such areas. Vermont was very, very sick.... What of the fact that the people of these areas concerned did not care to be moved from their homes? Well, possibly these people weren't of high enough mental capacity to understand that they were really unhappy."[31]

The blurring of exuberant Progressive reform and serious threats to liberalism emerged in a book authored by "Two Hundred Vermonters" in

29. Rudyard Kipling, *Something of Myself* (Garden City, NY: Doubleday, Doran, 1937). At the turn of the century Kipling was forced to take up residence in a cottage in Brattleboro belonging to his new bride's family. He had run out of money on his honeymoon, a trip around the world. See Derek Levin, "Rudyard Kipling's Vermont Years," *Window of Vermont* 3 (October 1986): 54–60.

30. Daniell remarked, "One can almost hear Emerson turning over in his grave." Daniell, "Town Meeting." Perhaps the best counterpoint to what is known as the degenerative or "dark age thesis" of rural life in northern New England in this period is Hal S. Barron's treatment of Chelsea, Vermont, *Those Who Stayed Behind: Rural Society in 19th Century New England* (New York: Cambridge University Press, 1984).

31. George D. Aiken, *Speaking from Vermont* (New York: Frederick A. Stokes, 1938), 8–10. The response in Vermont was not a conservative reaction against government as such. Aiken himself was an agrarian, Jeffersonian Republican. See Frank M. Bryan, *Yankee Politics in Rural Vermont* (Hanover, NH: University Press of New England, 1974), 85–93, and Duane Lockard, *New England State Politics* (Princeton: Princeton University Press, 1959), 8–45. *The Fifth Annual Report of the Eugenics Survey of Vermont* offered what historian Kevin Dann termed a "strange inversion of the frontier myth" as a solution to what eugenicists called the decay of rural Vermont. It argued that people living in "infertile" areas should move to more "progressive communities" so that "degeneration in the quality of the stock of future citizens" would not occur. See Kevin Dann, "From Degeneration to Regeneration: The Eugenics Survey of Vermont, 1925–1936," *Vermont History* 59 (Winter 1991): 5–29.

1931, which is mostly a compilation of plans for a better life through government. Written before Hitler's fall, it has no trouble comparing immigrants with native stock.[32] Early on, the movement had focused more purely on eugenics. Targets were rural families and ethnic groups, especially French Canadians and (to a lesser extent) the Irish. For example, Henry F. Perkins, professor of zoology at the University of Vermont and founder and leading light of the eugenics movement in Vermont, describes the French Canadians as congenial, not very bright ("many have a pretty low I.Q."), and liars ("You can't believe a thing they tell you"). Otherwise (especially compared with the Irish) they are a hell of a race.[33]

How could town meetings, which presumably draw on our best behavior and our best reasoning, prosper in such an environment? The following comments by H. L. Mencken illustrate the high-water mark of rural decline and the low-water mark of the public's perception of town meeting:

> Certainly no competent historian believes that the citizens assembled in a New England town meeting actually formulated *en masse* the transcendental and immortal measures that they adopted, nor even contributed anything of value to the discussion thereof.... [T]he New England town meeting was led and dominated by a few men of unusual initiative and determination, some of them genuinely superior, but most of them simply demagogues and fanatics. The citizens in general heard the discussion of several ideas and went through the motions of deciding between them, but there is no evidence that they ever had all the relevant facts before them or made any effort to unearth them, or that appeals to their reason always, or even usually, prevailed over appeals to their mere prejudice and superstition. Their appetite for logic, I venture, seldom got the better of their fear of hell, and the Beatitudes moved them far less powerfully than blood. Some of the most idiotic decisions ever come to mortal man were made by New England town meetings, and under the leadership of monomaniacs who are still looked upon as ineffable blossoms of the contemporary *kulture*.[34]

32. Two Hundred Vermonters, *Rural Vermont: A Program for the Future* (Burlington: Vermont Commission on Country Life, 1931), 21.

33. Dann, "From Degeneration to Regeneration," 16. Interested scholars everywhere are fortunate to have a thorough, careful, and sober analysis of the eugenics movement in Vermont. See Nancy L. Gallagher, *Breeding Better Vermonters* (Hanover, NH: University Press of New England, 1999).

34. H. L. Mencken, *Notes on Democracy* (New York: Alfred A. Knopf, 1926), 72–73.

Revival—Sort of

The American conversation on town meeting began to shift in the 1930s. The change featured resuscitation in the popular and literary press and in a new electronic medium, the radio. There would be no return, however, to the heady days of Jefferson, Emerson, and Tocqueville. The new tone seemed to be one of ambivalence.

A dramatic increase in national attention paid to town meeting began with the Depression and continued into the war years.[35] The *Atlantic Monthly*, the *New York Times Magazine*, *Scribner's*, *Life*, *Time*, and *Collier's* all painted a pleasant picture of town meeting between 1935 and 1945.[36] In 1938 Thornton Wilder's popular play *Our Town* idealized small-town life in a place he called Grovers Corners, New Hampshire. As Perry Westbrook reminds us, Wilder went out of his way (with accents and speech rhythms) to nail down its location in northern New England.[37] This renewed interest may have derived in part from a national backlash to the Depression.

A more likely stimulant was the influx of influential academics and intellectuals into the country that Frost called simply "north of Boston" (the title of his first book of poems). From E. B. White in Maine to Bernard DeVoto in Vermont, a cadre of writers, editors, scientists, and artists reestablished in the national mind the land that Arnold Toynbee had trivialized as "above the optimum climatic area" of the United States. These intellectuals were just the vanguard of a massive relocation into rural New England that began in earnest in the 1960s and was to peak in the early 1980s. Earlier settlers, like Sinclair Lewis and Dorothy Thompson, had come seeking peace and quiet to think and to write. Before the Depression a rampaging capitalism had brought huge vacation hotels to cool the rich in the summer

---

35. At the war's end the *New York Times Magazine* featured the century's most positive look at town meeting to appear in a journal of significant reputation. See L. H. Thomas, "Democracy Town Meeting Style," *New York Times Magazine*, March 23, 1947, 24. A book titled *Town Meeting Country* appeared in 1945 as part of an American Folkways series edited by Erskine Caldwell. Its importance does not lie in its content, because the author, Clarence M. Webster, is content to champion myths and folklore as reality. But "town meeting" could now be used as a title in a series that featured *Golden Gate Country*, *Blue Ridge Country*, and *Buckeye Country*—titles that commercial impulse had concluded would touch a positive chord among Americans. This would not have happened in 1910. See Clarence M. Webster, *Town Meeting Country* (New York: Duell, Sloan and Pearce, 1945). The other major book on town meeting featuring a town meeting in Maine was John Gould, *New England Town Meeting: Safeguard of Democracy* (Brattleboro, VT: Stephen Daye Press, 1940). Town meeting is romanticized in this book, and too much attention is paid to the "Yankee" character. Nevertheless, in its fundamental description of town meeting and how it works, the book reads and looks (with many telling black-and-white photographs) true to life.

36. Daniell, "Town Meeting."

37. Westbrook, *New England Town in Fact and Fiction*, 215.

mountains.[38] But the post-Depression newcomers were neither rich nor transient. They became "summer people." Heavily degreed, they bought abandoned farms and stayed from last frost to first. Their work, full of their accounts of country life, told a benign story.

There are times when there is no way to walk the hills of Peacham, Vermont, and not weep with the beauty of it.[39] Like most towns in Vermont, it has a published history that (in terms of words per capita) is one of the most extensive histories of a political entity ever written. In this paragraph chroniclers of modern Peacham, Shepard B. Clough and Laura Quimby, describe the arrival of the summer people in the 1930s:

> People of "back farms" also sold out and moved to better places.
> Sometimes the buyers were people from "away." Crane Brinton, a
> Harvard University historian, acquired the farm of Mark Abbott on
> Penny Street; Herbert W. Schneider, a member of the Philosophy
> Department at Columbia, bought two adjoining places on Cow
> Hill. . . . In the "in-migration" which took place, as in all migrations,
> pioneers blazed the trail and others, frequently their friends, followed.
> For example, Professor Schneider [of the Columbia group], who bought
> two places as early as 1929, had attracted fifteen of his friends to the area
> by 1939. Similarly, the first of the Harvard group had brought in a like
> number in the first ten years after the Depression began.[40]

38. Across the Connecticut River valley from my backyard in Newbury, fifty miles of peaks of New Hampshire's White Mountains marched uninterrupted north and south. But Mooselocke, which in its bulk is the largest single mountain east of the Mississippi, dominated. It was there that my brother David (a walker of mountaintops in his youth) and I had climbed on a summer's day in 1961 when I was twenty. Among the boulders in the rare air of the mountaintop we sat and schemed about ways to save our town from the ravages of centralism. President Kennedy was my hero when I started up Mooselocke that day. Like my mother, I was a Democrat. But by the time I came down David had convinced me my loyalties were misplaced. His ten-hour seminar (up and down the mountain) took. I ditched Kennedy and the Democratic Party and accepted communitarianism. The political journey from that day to now has been lonely.

39. I spent the summer of 1957 at age sixteen boarding at the Maple Corners Farm in Peacham while I worked for the State of Vermont mapping marl deposits under Eules Pond. I worked for Roger Wilder, the minister's son in Newbury, who managed to get me the job even though I was underage for state employees. This was my first real "paycheck" money. We came down every morning to a nice little dining room where usually sat a few tourists from here or there, and we were served breakfast with real juice, and bacon and eggs, and cereal. Days that summer were filled with blackflies, muck, bloodsuckers (huge ones, I still remember), and sweat. Still, I thought I had died and gone to heaven.

40. Shepard B. Clough and Lorna Quimby, "Peacham, Vermont: Fifty Years of Economic and Social Change, 1929–1979," *Vermont History* 51 (Winter 1983): 5–28. This article was an update of Ernest L. Bogart's first-class local history, *Peacham: The Story of a Vermont Hill Town* (Montpelier: Vermont Historical Society, 1948).

From the town of Arlington, Dorothy Canfield Fisher, an eclectic and best-selling author with a national reputation, worked hard to promote the image of rural America in the 1930s. More important, she worked directly to resettle the outback of Vermont with people like herself, a Ph.D. (again) from Columbia. Robert Frost, Sarah Cleghorn, Stephany Humphrey, and Norman Rockwell all lived close to Fisher's house in Arlington.[41] To Bethel, Vermont, in 1940 came Johns Hopkins's Marshall Dimock, a political scientist and a highly placed member of the Roosevelt administration, who became one of America's leading scholars in public administration. He and his wife, author Gladys Ogden Dimock, wrote dozens of books from their farm high in the hills of central Vermont.[42]

Hundreds of such examples could be listed. Yet no pair did more to na-tionalize the new image of the real "town meeting country" of northern New England than Bernard DeVoto and (to a lesser extent) Wallace Stegner. An ac-complished writer and essayist, Stegner lived on Caspian Lake in Greensboro, Vermont. DeVoto, a historian (*Across the Wide Missouri*), critic (*Mark Twain's America*), and columnist (*Harper's Magazine* for twenty years), lived on Lake Seymour in Morgan. Both lakes are deep, cold blue waters in Vermont's fabled "Northeast Kingdom." Both lie near rolling fields cast among the hard line ridges of a glacier's bygone passing. Both have villages and a little country store.

It was from Morgan that DeVoto wrote his famous description of the Green Mountain State: "There is no more Yankee than Polynesian in me. But whenever I go to Vermont I feel like I am traveling toward my own place."[43] It

---

41. Ida H. Washington, professor emeritus from the University of Massachusetts living in Weybridge, Vermont, a town that has provided several town meetings to the case base of this book, provides an excellent description of Fisher's contributions to the "summer people" movement. Ida H. Washington, "Dorothy Canfield Fisher's 'Tourists Accommodated' and Her Other Promotions of Vermont," *Vermont History* 65 (Summer-Fall 1997): 153–164. Fisher is clear-eyed about town meeting. It can be tedious, quarrelsome, and petty. But the empirical record tells her that "a bunch of quite ordinary men and women, if they are not permanently separated into rival competing classes or groups, are really able, in spite of human rancor, to get together on how to run things—for everybody's benefit, not for any one or any few." Dorothy Canfield Fisher, *Vermont Tradition: The Biography of an Outlook on Life* (Boston: Little, Brown, 1953), 409–410.

42. See Marshall Dimock's autobiography *The Center of My World* (Taftsville, VT: Countryman Press, 1980) and Gladys Dimock's *Home Ground* (Woodstock, VT: Countryman Press, 1985).

43. Bernard DeVoto, "The Easy Chair: Wayfarers Daybook," *Harper's Magazine* 203 (December 1951): 46. See also Bernard DeVoto, "New England, There She Stands," *Harper's Magazine* 164 (March 1932): 36.

was from Greensboro that Stegner wrote his joyful yet melancholy description of the social psychology of Vermont's weather:

> Though rains are frequent and often torrential in that country, which lies under the St. Lawrence storm track, the good days are like the good days in the western mountains. The light is intense, the deep sky is crossed by navies of fair-weather, strato-cumulus clouds, the horizons are cut with a diamond, the air has never been breathed. And those days come so infrequently between days of clouds and rain and violent thunderstorms, and are spaced through such a brief and fragile time, that a man believes he deserves them and has a right, because of what else he has to put up with, to enjoy them thoroughly.[44]

These men were not Vermonters. But whatever it was that touched their hearts, they found something in the hills of Vermont they understood, and they let it be known.[45] Americans everywhere seemed to want to listen.

During this period another kind of intellectual began to pay attention to the American outback. These residents were conservationists and practitioners of rural life to a degree that the summer people were not. From Wisconsin, Aldo Leopold gave us his classic *Sand County Almanac*. From Maine, Henry Beston wrote *Northern Farm*, a year's chronicle of human and natural events in a small town. Louise Dickinson Rich wrote *We Took to the Woods*. From Vermont (and then Maine), Helen and Scott Nearing came as close as anyone to fusing the lives of social commentator and naturalist advocate, writing back-to-back books on maple sugaring and economic theory. These and other

---

44. Wallace Stegner, *The Uneasy Chair: A Biography of Bernard DeVoto* (Garden City, NY: Doubleday, 1974).

45. In DeVoto's case it might have been the Quebec and Southeast Transportation Company, the name coined by members of the Harvard community for DeVoto's network for smuggling liquor across the Canadian border between Rock Island, Quebec, and Morgan, Vermont. DeVoto supplied not only visitors to his place in Vermont but also his colleagues at their homes in Cambridge, Massachusetts. It turns out he was an accomplished smuggler. Charles Morrissey relates the following account of one such shipment delivered in 1931: "Young Arthur Schlesinger, Jr., who would later be a student of DeVoto's and still later an ally and admirer and working colleague, was fourteen years old in the fall of 1931, and he first met DeVoto because the *Harper's* editor would often appear on the Schlesinger doorstep carrying packages for the senior Schlesinger, the eminent Harvard historian. For a long time young Schlesinger assumed that DeVoto was the family bootlegger." Charles Morrissey, "Wanted: An Oral History of Vermont during the Prohibition Era," *Vermont History* 43 (Fall 1975): 322. DeVoto was carrying on a long-standing Vermont tradition of free trade with Canada stretching back to the War of 1812.

voices from rural America cast a warmer, friendlier light on the possibilities of living "the good life" in town meeting country.[46]

Jere Daniell, however, offers a far bolder explanation for the rebirth of national interest in town meeting, one with a more populist resonance.[47] "What really put town meeting into the national limelight," he writes, "was the extraordinary success of the radio program, 'Town Meeting of the Air . . . .'" The first program began with the words 'Town Meetin' Tonight! Town Meetin' Tonight! Which Way America—Fascism, Communism, Socialism, or Democracy?'"[48] *Town Meeting of the Air* sponsored the formation of discussion groups around the country to discuss the program's weekly topics.[49] This was the golden age of radio, and the National Broadcasting Company made good use of it. Within three years of its first broadcast, the program expanded from one radio station and 500,000 listeners to seventy-eight stations and 2,500,000 listeners.[50] By the early 1950s its prestige was immense, with Peabody Awards in 1950 and 1954. Daniell is unequivocal in his assessment of the program's influence: "'Town Meeting of the Air' did for the legitimacy of twentieth century town meeting in America what de Tocqueville had for the nineteenth."[51]

Two fortuitous parallel factors emerged from the revolutionary 1960s to revitalize the more positive tone of the American conversation on town meeting. First, the energy crisis and other national ecoshocks led to a remarkable

46. Aldo Leopold, *Sand County Almanac* (New York: Oxford University Press, 1949); Henry Beston, *Northern Farm* (New York: Holt, Rinehart and Winston, 1948); Louise Dickinson Rich, *We Took to the Woods* (Philadelphia: J. B. Lippincott, 1942); Helen Nearing, *Maple Sugar Book* (New York: J. Day, 1950); Scott Nearing, *Economics for the Power Age: A Statement of First Principles* (New York: J. Day, 1952).

47. Daniell, "Town Meeting."

48. Recently *Town Meeting of the Air* has been put to sound academic uses. The most recent example is Barbara Dianne Savage, *Broadcasting Freedom: Radio, War, and the Politics of Race* (Chapel Hill: University of North Carolina Press, 1999), esp. 206–222. *Town Meeting of the Air* was far more populist in tone than its companion program, the *University of Chicago Round Table*. Although these two were the most popular, respected, and influential of the growing number of such programs, *Town Meeting of the Air* "had a much livelier and less pretentious tone than the staid atmosphere of *Round Table*." Savage, *Broadcasting Freedom*, 206.

49. An important text in rural sociology identified *Town Meeting of the Air* as a popular radio program in rural America that exemplified the impact of communications technology on small-town life. J. H. Kolb and Edmund de S. Brunner, *A Study of Rural Sociology: Its Organization and Changes* (Boston: Houghton Mifflin, 1940), 488.

50. Lawrence C. Zucker (executive director), the Town Hall (www.the-townhall-nyc.org/townmeetings.htm).

51. Daniell, "Town Meeting." Vermont scholar and writer Charles Edward Crane said of *Town Meeting of the Air* in 1942, "It is hard [for a Vermonter] to believe if most if not all the other states are getting on without town meeting. Of course there is The Town Meeting of the Air, but a mere open forum of broadcasting has slight similarity to town meeting as we know it in Vermont." Charles Edward Crane, *Vermont in Winter* (New York: Alfred A. Knopf, 1941), 292.

distrust of macrosystems and a growing willingness to pay attention to the small and decentralized—in energy sources and in governance. The politics of this awareness (it could not be called a movement) reinforced and reinvigorated the second factor—the ideology of the Left that had emerged from the antiwar, feminist, and civil rights revolutions of the 1960s.[52] Crossover academics began to pay more attention to small places and human-scale behavior, at least in metaphor. Charles Reich's *Greening of America* urged his readers to look for "flowers pushing up through the concrete pavement."[53]

This theme was sustained and developed by E. F. Schumacher[54] and his followers, who formed a small[55] but ideologically eclectic band of true believers around the rallying cry "small is beautiful." Scholars, activists, authors, and poets like Wendell Berry, Murray Bookchin, Leopold Kohr, John McClaughry, and Kirkpatrick Sale held that governments work better when they are small rather than big.[56] Later Rutgers University political scientist Benjamin Barber's *Strong Democracy* reinforced the drive for a more human-scale politics.[57] At the same time came a fresh look at community from the urban perspective.[58] The city could become in some limited but useful ways

52. An excellent anthology that appeared in 1971 provides an inclusive array of thinking about direct participatory democracy from the Left during the period. See C. George Benello and Dimitrios Roussopoulos, *The Case for Participatory Democracy: Some Prospects for a Radical Society* (New York: Grossman, 1971).

53. Charles Reich, *The Greening of America* (New York: Random House, 1970), 395. The new rural romanticism became so silly that in some places city people began trying to lug the country into downtown America. Even in usually level-headed Vermont, city planners in Burlington hauled huge boulders down out of the hills and scattered them along the city's new pedestrian mall. Here we've been working for two hundred years to get the damn things off our fields and out of sight, and the first time we go into town to soak in some urban atmosphere, there they are.

54. E. F. Schumacher, *Small Is Beautiful* (New York: Harper and Row, 1973).

55. What else could it be? A good summary of the "small is beautiful" movement is found in Richard Lingeman, *Small Town America: A Narrative History, 1620-Present* (Boston: Houghton Mifflin, 1980), 441–442.

56. Wendell Berry, *The Unsettling of America* (San Francisco: Sierra Club Books, 1977); Murray Bookchin, *The Ecology of Freedom* (Palo Alto, CA: Cheshire Books, 1982); Murray Bookchin, *The Limits of the City* (New York: Harper and Row, 1974); Murray Bookchin, *The Rise of Urbanization and the Decline of Citizenship* (San Francisco: Sierra Club Books, 1987); Leopold Kohr, "Critical Size," in *Time Running Out? Best of Resurgence*, ed. Michael North (Dorchester, UK: Prism Press, 1976); Leopold Kohr, *The Breakdown of Nations* (New York: E. P. Dutton, 1978); Frank Bryan and John McClaughry, *The Vermont Papers: Recreating Democracy on a Human Scale* (Chelsea, VT: Chelsea Green Press, 1989); Kirkpatrick Sale, *Dwellers in the Land: The Bioregional Union* (San Francisco: Sierra Club Books, 1985); Kirkpatrick Sale, *Human Scale* (New York: Coward, McCann and Geoghegan, 1980).

57. Benjamin R. Barber, *Strong Democracy* (Berkeley: University of California Press, 1984).

58. See Daniel Bell and Virginia Held, "The Community Revolution," *Public Interest* 16 (Summer 1969): 142–177; Harry C. Boyte, *The Backyard Revolution* (Philadelphia: Temple

a federation of little neighborhoods, each with avenues of direct participation for citizens. Not surprisingly, "town meeting" appeared more and more in the lexicon of the metropolis.[59]

Political scientists were beginning to take a scholarly interest, if not in town meeting directly, at least in more direct forms of face-to-face politics— in instruments of street-level bureaucracy, open hearings, and neighborhood decision making. "Maximum feasible participation" became a rallying cry for academics and reformers alike.[60] While political scientists of the inner city enhanced the intellectual credentials of town meeting from the inside out, elsewhere in America town meeting profited from the growing attraction of small, direct, local, and human-scale values—in a word, small-town and rural values.[61]

Serious scientific research on town meeting democracy got under way in the 1970s. Two doctoral dissertations appeared in 1974.[62] By the end of the decade a group of political scientists at Dartmouth College had skillfully integrated town meeting into the options for a citizenry grown restless with the national government. While they were not enthusiastic about town meeting's chances to reinvigorate the Republic, it was the first time a major textbook designed for undergraduates featured town meeting.[63] Most important,

---

University Press, 1980); Bill Berkowitz, *Community Dreams* (San Luis Obispo, CA: Impact, 1984); Mark O. Hatfield, "Bringing Political Power Back Home: The Case for Neighborhood Government," *Ripon Quarterly* 1 (1974): 9–15; Milton Kotler, *Neighborhood Government* (New York: Bobbs-Merrill, 1969); Robert A. Nisbet, *The Quest for Community* (New York: Oxford University Press, 1976); Douglas Yates, *Neighborhood Democracy* (Lexington, MA: D. C. Heath, 1973).

59. See "Town Meeting Gets Miami Tryout," *American City* 77 (August 1962): 93; Frank M. Bryan, "Does the Town Meeting Offer an Option for Urban America?" *National Civic Review* 67 December 1978, 523–527; Frank Bryan, "Town Meeting in Mass Society—What Role Remains?" paper delivered at the annual meeting of the New England Political Science Association, Durham, NH, April 6–7, 1979); and Aaron Levise, "Town Meeting Comes to Philadelphia," *American City* 69 (May 1954): 129.

60. Montana completely restructured its constitutional provisions for local government in its new constitution of 1972. One of the four forms of local government Montanans granted themselves the power to adopt was the town meeting. It didn't take. Frank Bryan, "Town Meeting: Pure Democracy in Action?" in *What This Community Needs* (Helena, MT: State Commission on Local Government, 1976), 31–37.

61. Even some progressives were beginning to rethink their position on town meeting. See J. Allen Smith, *The Spirit of American Government* (New York: Macmillan, 1967), 352.

62. Vivian Scott Hixson, "The New Town Meeting Democracy: A Study of Matched Towns" (Ph.D. diss., Michigan State University, 1974), and Neil G. Kotler, "Politics and Citizenship in New England Towns: A Study of Participation and Political Education" (Ph.D. diss., University of Chicago, 1974).

63. Denis G. Sullivan, Robert T. Nakamura, and Richard F. Winters, *How America Is Ruled* (New York: John Wiley, 1980), 26–38. Their thoughtful treatment of town meeting presents a strong challenge to those (like me) who hold that the merits of town meeting are sufficient to bequeath it a fundamental role in American democracy.

Jane Mansbridge left the comforts of Cambridge and headed into the hills of Vermont for intense on-the-ground research in "Selby." Her *Beyond Adversary Democracy* contained the first published account of town meeting to employ archival research, survey techniques, and in-depth interviewing. The book, I later learned, came very close to winning political science's most prestigious award, the Woodrow Wilson prize.[64]

While all this was happening, vociferous criticism of town meeting continued. It came primarily from community power theorists who undercut even the possibility of town meeting governance by questioning the legitimacy of democratic systems of *any form* in small communities. A goodly number of progressives also continued to suspect (correctly) that much of the new hoopla about rural life was no more than romantic nonsense.[65]

Serious scholarship generated by several community power studies published before 1970 called the efficacy of local government into question on a variety of fronts and set the tone for an entire generation of social scientists interested in the possibility for and the character of democracy in localities. On the model of the Lynds' early classic, *Middletown: A Study of Modern American Culture*,[66] Arthur Vidich and Joseph Bensman published their equally important *Small Town in Mass Society* in 1958.[67] In both "Middletown" and "Springdale" the authors question seriously whether the small town is capable of duplicating (even in a cursory way) the democratic models forwarded in the first half of the nineteenth century.

Neither of these studies involved New England towns with town meetings, but Robert C. Wood's well-received *Suburbia: Its People and Their Politics* did.[68] He was strongly critical of town meeting democracy in Lincoln,

64. Jane Mansbridge, *Beyond Adversary Democracy* (New York: Basic Books, 1980). In academia and the journals of opinion, Mansbridge's book is almost universally viewed as critical of town meeting. It was. But it was also balanced. I am perplexed by the degree to which political scientists seized on the negative and chose to ignore the positive in her chapters on "Selby."

65. Although Hofstadter doesn't fit the bill for a "die-hard progressive," see Richard Hofstadter, "The Agrarian Myth and Commercial Realities," in his *The Age of Reform: From Bryan to FDR* (New York: Alfred A. Knopf, 1955), 3–22.

66. Robert S. Lynd and Helen M. Lynd, *Middletown: A Study of Modern American Culture* (New York: Harcourt Brace, 1929), and Robert S. Lynd and Helen M. Lynd, *Middletown in Transition* (New York: Harcourt, Brace, 1937). About the same time as the appearance of *Middletown*, Thorstein Veblen laid waste what he called "the country town"; it was, he said, "an enclave of business elite where competition for sales precludes any hope of open, honest, democratic resolution of conflict." Thorstein Veblen, *Absentee Ownership and Business Enterprise in Recent Times* (New York: Viking Press, 1954), chap. 7.

67. Arthur J. Vidich and Joseph Bensman, *Small Town in Mass Society*, rev. ed. (Princeton: Princeton University Press, 1968).

68. Robert C. Wood, *Suburbia: Its People and Their Politics* (Boston: Houghton Mifflin, 1958). For a response see Joseph Zimmerman, "On the Other Hand," *National Civic Review* 55 (January 1966): 14–20, 28.

Massachusetts. These and other community power studies of small towns were not challenged by efforts of similar quality.[69] Even Aaron Wildavsky's critique of the Lynds' *Middletown* did little to suggest more than a liberal, pluralist alternative for small towns.[70] Beyond these strong empirical contributions, the negative implications of real democracy in small settings received theoretical support from scholars like Grant McConnell.[71] In effect an entire generation of political scientists was teaching that both big *and* small were bad for real democracy. In big settings, real democracy was impossible by definition.[72] The best one could hope for was pluralism.[73] In small settings, a clique would inevitably rule.[74] The best one could hope for was a benign village elite.[75] Either way, town meeting was out of the picture. Hannah Arendt's suggestion that town meetings were "public happiness" was perhaps the most notable town meeting gush of the 1960s.[76]

American government and politics textbooks beginning in the 1950s and 1960s and extending into the 1980s reflected this negativism.[77] Phrases

69. Granville Hicks, who was more sympathetic, still provided little to encourage anyone working to continue the town meeting in the modern world. Granville Hicks, *Small Town* (New York: Macmillan, 1946), 194. For one of the best counterpoints to the dominant negative strain in the small-town literature see French archaeologist Hervé Varenne's treatment of "Appleton," a small town in Illinois. Hervé Varenne, *Americans Together: Structured Diversity in a Midwestern Town* (New York: Teachers' College Press, 1978).

70. Aaron B. Wildavsky, *Leadership in a Small Town* (Totawa, NJ: Bedminster Press, 1964).

71. Grant McConnell, *Private Power and American Democracy* (New York: Alfred A. Knopf, 1966).

72. No one put it better than E. E. Schattschneider: "In other words an all American town meeting would be the largest, longest, and most boring and frustrating meeting imaginable. What would such a meeting produce? Total paralysis. What could it do? Nothing." E. E. Schattschneider, *Two Hundred Million Americans in Search of a Government* (New York: Holt Rinehart and Winston, 1969), 63.

73. Nelson W. Polsby, *Community Power and Political Party* (New Haven: Yale University Press, 1980).

74. In fact, the preponderance of these case studies claimed to show that *representative* democracy in small towns did not work. Little communities governed by town councils or village boards, the authors said, failed to parry the natural thrusts of oligarchy. That town meeting democracies would fail as well was (one can only suppose) assumed.

75. An engaging essay by a second-generation progressive that comes down hard on town meeting is Robert Cenedella, "A Lesson in Civics," *American Heritage* 12 (December 1960): 42–43, 100–102.

76. Hannah Arendt, *On Revolution* (New York: Viking, 1963), 165.

77. Authors of local government textbooks, who were more familiar with the terrain, treated town meeting more objectively. Their views of town meeting in the future, however, were still not optimistic. Clyde Snider's judgment is typical: "The New England town meeting has had an illustrious history, and it seems still to function effectively in many small communities, particularly those in strictly rural areas. In general, however, popular interest in town meeting seems to be on the wane." Snider, *Local Government in Rural America*, 198. In 1952 Lane W. Lancaster was supportive of town meeting, but in the past tense, accepting the standard hypothesis

like "attendance is often very poor" and "sparsely attended" typified the word choices of political scientists when they contributed a sentence or two to town meeting democracy.[78] They were not totally wrong. But equally correct and far more positive things could have been said as well. Limited by the availability of hard data, many textbooks resorted to pictures to augment their commentary. One shows an old man sleeping in the foreground of a town meeting in Vermont as the author emphasizes the point with his caption: "Direct Democracy: A Town Meeting in Vermont. You Will Note that Some of the Participants Appear to Be Sleeping."[79] Another textbook features a photograph of what appears to be a very lightly attended town meeting in Victory, Vermont. The student is not told that Victory is the smallest of Vermont's 246 incorporated towns and cities with, at the time, a *total* of twenty-nine registered voters. One can count nine people in a photograph that shows about one-third of the hall. If the other two-thirds of the hall held an equal number, that would amount to over 62 percent attendance.[80]

Outside the academic world, the ambivalence in the public mind on the question of town meeting emerged in two *Newsweek* articles. The first, appearing in 1962, slams the "Farce Down East." "Town meetings are poorly attended, manipulated by minorities, unrepresentative of the community, and cumbersome to the point of rendering town government unrespon-sive....Modern complexities in local government...have forced many a Maine community...to switch important decisions to either elected officials or appointed town managers. This evolution is inevitable."[81]

Only four years later the same magazine had changed its tune. "Farce Down East" was replaced with "New England: Basic Democracy," and the story told of town meeting working well in New London, New Hampshire:

> Thus did one of the oldest forms of democracy extant, the New England town meeting, resolve a major local issue—in a way that defied all the

---

that modernism and town meeting cannot cohabitate. Lane W. Lancaster, *Government in Rural America* (New York: D. Van Nostrand, 1952), 41.

78. Frank M. Bryan, "Direct Democracy in the New England Town Meeting: Establishing Empirical Parameters," paper delivered at the annual meeting of the American Political Science Association, Washington, DC, August 28–31, 1986.

79. Harry T. Burnham, *Government and Politics in America* (New York: Houghton Mifflin, 1983), 36. How many pictures of the Congress of the United States of America could be taken, one wonders, that would show the same thing?

80. Robert Weissberg, *Understanding American Government* (New York: Holt, Rinehart and Winston, 1980), 46.

81. "Farce Down East," *Newsweek* 59 (January 29, 1962): 74. Also see John Guy La Plante, "What Killed the Town Meeting?" *Nation* 180 (February 1958): 96–97.

defeatist discussion about modern man's alienation from his complex government. The town-meeting season wound up last week with hundreds of such gatherings having been held and decisions made in town halls, gymnasiums and school auditoriums from Maine to Massachusetts. And together they added up to solid testimony that this venerable and distinctly American institution, dating from 150 years before the Revolution, was still a spry and vital form of government.[82]

A decade after the *Newsweek* piece, *Time* Magazine spent town meeting day in Huntington, Vermont (just down the hollow from where I sit at this moment), and left impressed. "The budget was approved at 2:27. The meeting adjourned two minutes later, after one citizen's parting complaint that the dog-pound keeper was letting too many loose dogs run around town.[83] By and large Huntingtonians seemed to genuinely like and trust each other. Tocqueville would have been pleased."[84] About ten years later the *Washington Post* published an article on its editorial page titled "Town Meetings Don't Work," with the subtitle "In New England These Days, Small Isn't So Beautiful."[85] Less than six months earlier, New England's most important newspaper, the *Boston Globe*, had featured an article titled "Maybe It's Sloppy, but It's Good Government."[86]

In my review of the popular literature on town meeting since the 1940s (of which I have presented only a few examples), one thing stands out. Those who criticize town meeting or question its usefulness almost always seem repentant at the end. It's a strange thing, this craving to place in the record a final apology in the guise of a kind word or two or a nod to better times long past. No doubt some of this is disingenuous or patronizing. But most of it seems sincere. Here is an example from a retired reporter living in Pomfret.

82. "New England: Basic Democracy," *Newsweek* 67 (April 4, 1966): 32, 34.

83. I had a dog named Flip back in the old days. I often took him to work, and he'd wait patiently outside the classroom for me. He got shot running deer in Huntington. I never held it against the guy who shot him. I'd shoot a dog chasing deer in the deep snow too. I was a damn fool for letting him get loose.

84. "New England: Rites of March," *Time*, March 14, 1977, 18–19. Quite a compliment. Huntington has had more than its share of conflict over the past thirty years—over the school, taxes, plans for an upscale golf course-housing development, and moving the post office away from the village center. Earlier in 1970 *Time* devoted its "American Scene" report to the town meeting of Mount Vernon, Maine, the town from which Erskine Caldwell wrote *Tobacco Road*. It too was very positive. Gregory Wierznski, "American Scene: Participatory Democracy," *Time*, April 13, 1970, 24.

85. Robert Preer, "Town Meetings Don't Work," *Washington Post*, July 13, 1986), B5.

86. Raymond Clark, "Maybe It's Sloppy, but It's Good Government," *Boston Globe*, February 22, 1986, 14.

The town meeting had debated the matter of salt on the roads. Nearly all the people with blue-collar jobs (most of whom were "locals"), along with the road crew, were for it. Newcomers, the better-off, and the environmentalists were against it.

WITNESS

The mind tells us that Town Meeting is a government whose time, in this space age, has passed. Towns just aren't efficient enough to be worth saving. But let's not fool ourselves about what we're giving up. Nothing—and that goes for the new form of town/country government I've proposed—nothing can replace a town's and Town Meeting's rich sense of history, community, and close human association. These are the things that give life to social arrangements. These are the heart.

And this citizen's heart? Well, it is still up there in Pomfret, where the late afternoon sun is pouring through those old glass windows, turning our company to gold. Salt has just lost, but a moment later someone makes a motion to thank the road crew "for its fine work in keeping the roads open this winter."

Now, if seventeen years as a Washington reporter have taught me anything, they've taught me that the press never applauds anyone, not even the president. We'll stand for the president, but we'll clap for no one simply out of obligation. Point of professional chastity, I guess.

But when someone moved to thank the Pomfret road crew, and the motion was seconded and approved, friends and foes of salt applauded with a roar. As for me, I dropped my pen and notebook and banged my hands together as lustily as my neighbors.

You see, they *are* my neighbors.

John Pierson[87]

I know Pomfret well.[88] I do not know John Pierson well, but I suspect that his words are more than romantic nonsense. I think they are wise. If so, then they stand as an indictment of what is to follow. For the dominant

---

87. John Pierson, "The Decline and Fall of Town Meeting," *Blair and Ketcham's Country Journal*, March 1982, 98–101. For an excellent balanced account of the problems facing town meeting published about the same time, see David Shribman, "The Town Meeting: New England Staple Faces Tide of Change," *Wall Street Journal*, March 7, 1986, 24.

88. In the 1960s I spent time haying one of the little hill farms in Pomfret then owned by May Cole. One of my good friends, Bucky Cole (a first-class ox teamster and maker of fine yokes), was her grandson and the subject of a piece I published in a book of contemporary Vermont essays (Frank Bryan, "We Are All Farmers," in *Vermont Odysseys: Contemporary Tales from the Green Mountain State*, ed. C. L. Gilbert [New York: Penguin Books, 1991], 72–83). His father, Tom Cole, was the foreman of the road crew in Pomfret the day John Pierson rose to applaud.

national perspective on town meeting since the late 1970s is neither support nor attack. It is manipulation. In the national mind town meeting became a tool, used first by interest groups and then by politicians. By the year 2000, more ordinary citizens in America knew about town meeting than ever before. Yet fewer than ever before knew what it *is*.

Town Meeting: A Tool for Representative Nationalism

On Monday night, March 4, 1974, the little Connecticut River valley town of Thetford, Vermont, did something no duly constituted, legally incorporated, general-purpose municipal government of the United States had ever done before. In mid-February Jacqueline Lucy, a newcomer to Thetford and chair of the local Democratic committee, had gone to work gathering the necessary signatures to require the selectmen to put an especially controversial article on the warning for the March town meeting.[89]

Discussion had begun at 10:57 p.m. Voting on the article started about 11:30 and stopped (and the ballot box was closed) at 11:55 p.m. At ten minutes after midnight the vote was announced. The local and national press had been waiting since 7:30 p.m. On opening the town meeting and seeing how many press people had showed up, the town moderator, Matthew Wiencke, had issued an order. The press would "be kept to the bleachers and the back of the hall."[90] There were 420 citizens and thirty reporters in attendance at 7:30. By voting time, 31 percent of the citizens had left for home. The vote was 160 yea and 130 nay.[91]

Impeach him, said the town. Impeach Nixon.[92]

From that moment, the town meeting took on an entirely new meaning for Americans.[93]

89. Town of Thetford, *Town Report*, year ending December 31, 1973, 6–7.

90. Town of Thetford, "Minutes of the 1974 Annual Town and School District Meeting," *Town Report*, year ending December 1974, 64–66.

91. Do not think it odd that 31 percent of the citizens did not consider impeachment important enough to hang around for until midnight. Many were over fifty, out on a weekday when they had to be in the barn at 5:00 a.m. or warming up the dozer or starting the day shift at Mary Hitchcock Hospital at 7:00 a.m. These kinds of people are apt to conclude about 11 p.m. that either way, in or out, Nixon isn't worth it.

92. Lucy, who became a friend later in the 1970s, moved to Washington and took a job with conservative political scientist and future United States ambassador to the United Nations, Jeanne Kirkpatrick. If I ever see her again, I'm going to ask her how that went.

93. See also John Kifner, "Vermont Town Favors Impeachment of Nixon," *New York Times*, March 6, 1974, 23. Kifner reports the following exchange: After Jacqueline Lucy, the leader of the impeachment forces, said that "Democracy starts" in the town meeting, Robert White, a high school vocational education teacher, reminded Lucy that New England traditions were not

Between 1975 and 1985 interest groups descended on town meetings to solicit approval for their special agendas. Right-to-life organizations introduced ordinances to ban abortions in this town or that. The Vermont Public Interest Research Group introduced ordinances to prohibit trucks from carrying nuclear waste through town. Opposers of the leg-hold trap and nuclear power plants, champions and critics of guns, and limiters of legislative terms all organized to get ordinances or resolutions on the town warnings. Then they worked to get their supporters to town meeting, making sure the press got the results whenever they were positive. Although the Left was better at this game than the Right, players came from across the political spectrum.

What had often been cast as nests of Neanderthal Yankees holed up in their town meetings, fighting progress, skimping on public spending for good causes—and worst of all doing all this to protect a scheming little cadre of businessmen and their cronies—now became founts of wisdom and legitimacy. A band of scruffy college students hanging from the fences of a nuclear power plant could be dismissed, but a town meeting of farmers and loggers and teachers and owners of mom-and-pop stores voting to disallow a nuclear plant in their village was something else indeed. This was Tocqueville and Jefferson and apple pie and common sense all rolled into one.

Murray Bookchin understood the new American appreciation for town meeting and the power it held. He wrote in 1987: "Vermont's town meetings like those of its New England neighbors are often more effective nationally than they truly realize, precisely because they are hallowed by moral traditions that give America its national identity. It is the enormous weight of this moral voice, this invocation of an ethically charged past that haunts the present with its ambiance and freedom that gives them enormous political power for social change."[94]

In 1983 the nation's leading popular print news outlet, *USA Today*, devoted a cover story to town meeting in Vermont titled "Hands-on Democracy in Vermont." It was a quintessential portrayal of the new national "take" on town meeting. The front-page picture featured an old Vermonter in work clothes talking with an attractive younger woman across a woodstove in a country store in Ripton. The caption: "Town meeting day is as traditional as Howard Murray's chat at a country store with owner Sue Collitt." The article's

---

always to be emulated. For instance, "women believed to be possessed had the Devil burned out of them at the stake." To which Edward C. Kirkland, a "stooped, white-haired, retired professor of American economic history stood up and said in an indignant voice: 'If there is anything I dislike it's a joke that isn't true. No woman had the Devil burned out of her in New England—not ever.' He sat down amid applause and cheers. 'They hanged them,' the professor later confided."

94. Bookchin, *Rise of Urbanization*, 270.

message: town meeting is still lively, crusty, down-home democracy where quaint rural wisdom prevails. *USA Today* reporter Judith Horstman quoted Faire Edwards, a seventy-one-year-old woman from Waterbury: "Why you might as well say God is dead, or that all the maples have been struck by lightning as to say the town meeting is dead."[95]

National attention paid to town meetings reached its pinnacle in 1982 when over 160 Vermont towns passed resolutions demanding a freeze on the expansion of nuclear armaments. With great portions of the national media still stunned and smarting over the election of Ronald Reagan, the specter of the Vermont towns rising against Reagan's bombs much as they had risen against Jefferson's embargo or Richard Nixon's presidency was simply too sweet to resist. Favorable coverage abounded. But make no mistake. These were legitimate votes cast by citizens who came to town meeting (for the most part) to vote on local budgets, repair roads, and in general maintain the civil order.[96]

A few (including me) had opposed the use of town meetings as forums for special interest politics. The nuclear freeze vote took the wind out of our sails. It was hard to argue that the freeze organizers and what concerned them—nuclear holocaust—constituted just another special interest. The issue was of such importance that it seemed to me the very thing towns *ought* to speak up about every now and then. Yet my argument, expressed as a guest editorial in *Newsweek*, held in part: "What kind of logic suggests that communities that must be told how to bury their garbage or educate their kids are capable of advising presidents on foreign policy? Some of us hold they can *be trusted to do all three.* So we distrust those who would deny us the liberty to bury our garbage yet urge us to advise on matters of foreign policy."[97]

95. Judith Horstman, "Hands-on Democracy in Vermont," *USA Today*, March 1, 1983, 1.

96. One of my students was not impressed with NBC's coverage of the "freeze vote." "The main problem with NBC's coverage was that it stereotyped Vermonters and the Town Meeting itself. NBC included brief coverage of the nuclear proliferation vote, and of course showed an intelligent immigrant from Connecticut talking about it. Although a couple of Vermonters spoke about the issue, it seems to me that the editors at NBC did not feel that the rest of the nation would believe that a real Vermonter knew anything about nuclear proliferation." John Goodrow, "NBC Visits Lincoln Vermont," Burlington, University of Vermont, March 1982. Another student reported a humorous event early on in the meeting. "A young man of about thirty-five stood up and loudly asked that the *Tomorrow Show* should not be allowed to film the meeting. The request was 'cordially' denied by the moderator." Steve Fuchs, "Impressions of the Lincoln Town Meeting," Burlington, University of Vermont, March 1982.

97. Frank Bryan, "Trouble in the Vermont Hills," *Newsweek* 103 (March 5, 1984): 15. I made a similar point in the *New York Times*: "Town Meetings—a Relic," *New York Times*, April 3, 1982, 25. (Unfortunately one is not allowed to choose the title of an op ed. piece.) See also Jeffrey Goode's article on the town of Weston's debate on military aid to El Salvador. His view: "Local and

My fears were misplaced. Perhaps I underestimated the good sense of Vermonters, the sensitivity of the outside media people,[98] or the miserable March weather in Vermont. Perhaps the misuse of town meetings simply dissipated with the decline of activism that came with Reagan, the end of the cold war, the changing generation, and the hot economics of the 1990s. Whatever the reason, the incidence of using town meetings as democratically enshrouded public opinion polls began to slow in the mid-1980s. As the century closed, we saw the phenomenon only now and then.

But town meeting was not to escape unscathed. National news people began to leave us alone, but the politicians didn't. They knew that the town meeting reached deep into the American soul and stirred sacred longings. Thus came the final indignity: the use of "town meetings" as strategic devices in political campaigns. Here Bill Clinton was a master. A president of the United States standing before a crowd of ordinary people fielding questions in a seemingly ad hoc format is powerful imagery. Citizen-delivered questions are easier to handle than those offered up by seasoned reporters.

In their textbook on American government, one group of political scientists credited Clinton with inventing the staged town meeting as a campaign device, though some would argue that Ross Perot deserved the finder's fee. The authors include a picture of President Clinton under a huge sign that reads "Town Meeting" as he answers a question from a distant participant on a video screen before an audience in Providence, Rhode Island. The caption reads: "The town meeting of yesterday gave way to the electronic town meeting of today. Here Bill Clinton answers a question asked by a citizen in another location but whose image and voice were transmitted through video conferencing telecommunications equipment. As telecommunications that include video and voice become better and cheaper, politicians will be able to use Clinton's electronic town-meeting concept more and more."[99]

The most poignant example of the new town meeting consciousness appeared in the changing references in the introductory American government

---

outside activists and network executives must recognize the fragility of this most stubbornly Yankee of traditions and resist the urge to dilute it, to create still more illusion." Jeffrey Goode, "Vermont Spoilers," *New York Times*, March 26, 1983, 23.

98. They can be sensitive. In fact, on more than one occasion I've seen a heartwarming humility on their part when they walk through the doors of a town hall and are suddenly among, *really* among, common people doing real democracy. They somehow want to be careful.

99. George C. Edwards III, Martin P. Wattenberg, and Robert L Lineberry, *Government in America: People, Politics and Policy*, 3rd ed. (New York: Longman, 1995), 328. The same photograph with the same caption also appears in Steffen W. Schmidt, Mack C. Shelly, and Barbara A. Bardes, *American Politics and Government Today*, 1999–2000 (Belmont, CA: West/Wadsworth, 1999), 351.

textbooks that political scientists assign to their students. Before the mid-1960s references to town meeting were limited, brief, and structure-bound. References began to increase in the 1960s and to focus more on politics and participation (or lack of it). In the 1970s and 1980s notations became more positive. By the second half of the 1990s, although the textbooks still said little about town meeting (usually a sentence or two or a short paragraph), they remained positive or neutral.[100]

Throughout the postwar period and until about the 1990s, these references were nearly always found in the "What is democracy?" section of the first chapter of the textbook. Beginning about 1990 they began to be found as often in the electoral politics chapter and more and more in the media chapter.[101] As the century closed, some texts did not mention town meeting *except* as a campaign device or public relations tool.[102] The popular volume *We the People*, by Ginsberg, Lowi, and Weir, for instance, cites town meeting in three chapters. The *media* chapter explains town meeting as a media-driven campaign technique, the *campaigns and elections* chapter describes it the same way, and the *presidency* chapter shows how a "town meeting" organized by a president to help sell a policy can have positive effects.[103] Reference to town meeting as *democracy* is nowhere to be found.

It has come to this. The twentieth century's final, most powerful contribution to the American conversation on town meeting was titled "Ye Olde Town Meeting Gimmick." An essay by that name was published in *Time*

100. In textbooks published after 1995 I found the best treatments of town meeting (in the sense of integrating the town meeting into an account of face-to-face as opposed to referendum or representative democracy) to be James Eisenstein, Mark Kessler, Bruce A. Williams, and Jacqueline Vaughn Switzer, *The Play of Power* (New York: St. Martin's Press, 1996), 58–60; Edward S. Greenberg and Benjamin I. Page, *The Struggle for Democracy*, 4th ed. (New York: Addison Wesley Longman, 1999), 8–9; and Kenneth Janda, Jeffrey M. Berry, and Jerry Goldman, *The Challenge of Democracy*, 6th ed. (Boston: Houghton Mifflin, 1999). The worst was Morris P. Fiorina and Paul E. Peterson, *The New American Democracy* (Boston: Allyn and Bacon, 1998), 13–14. The text features a picture of nine or ten people scattered about in what looks like a beat-up old church; an old man wearing a hunting cap stands (he looks almost alone) by a woodstove with a stovepipe leading off into the foreground. The caption reads: "In towns like this one in rural New England, town meetings may be scheduled at unpredictable and rather unusual times, in order to obtain citizens' votes on pressing budget issues." The authors are totally wrong.

101. See, for example, Walter E. Volkomer, *American Government*, 8th ed. (Upper Saddle River, NJ: Prentice-Hall, 1988): 7, 87; Susan Welch, John Gruhl, John Comer, Susan M. Rigdon, and Jan Vermeer, *Understanding American Government*, 5th ed. (Belmont, CA: West/Wadsworth, 1999), 16, 88; and James Q. Wilson and John Dilulio Jr., *American Government: The Essentials* (Boston: Houghton Mifflin, 1998), 6, 8, 12, 273.

102. Milton C. Cummings Jr. and David Wise, *Democracy under Pressure* (Fort Worth, TX: Harcourt Brace, 1997), 224.

103. Benjamin Ginsberg, Theodore J. Lowi, and Margaret Weir, *We the People: An Introduction to American Politics*, 2nd ed. (New York: Norton, 1999), 301–303, 380, 494.

magazine in 1998 with the intention of further crippling the Clinton presidency.[104] Its target was Clinton's use of "town meetings," and in particular the one that backfired (with heckling and rudeness from the backbenchers) in Columbus, Ohio, when Clinton went forth to gain support for his foreign policy on Iraq. The event, carried by CNN, received broad coverage by the major television networks.

Columnist Andrew Ferguson's attack on fake town meetings was sound enough, but the article produced collateral damage. According to Ferguson, actual town meetings are "anachronisms today, surviving only in a few eccentric backwaters of Ye Olde New England." (There is some truth there—about 25 percent.) Real town meeting has "fallen from favor" because it was "disorderly and unpredictable." (The causal attribution is totally false—although sometimes I wish it were not.) In real town meetings "the balance tends to tip toward the fellow with the loudest voice [almost never the case]—the crank with the thickest sheaf of mimeograph papers under his arm." (This claim is about 10 percent true. But when it happens the perpetrators are not "cranks," they are bureaucrats.)

The piece is so well done that it is hard not to smile on reading it. It is also unlikely that Ferguson's easy, hackneyed, and dismissive inaccuracies have much influence on the American conversation about town meeting. But that is not the point. Now, when the term "town meeting" has for the first time in history achieved common day-to-day usage and taken a prominent position in the popular lexicon of politics, its meaning in the American conversation is counterfeit.

Oh, well. I look out my office window on this late November afternoon, and I see the ice blue of Lake Champlain tossing whitecaps into the teeth of a brisk Canadian north wind. New York's Adirondack range is ten miles west across the water, and it looks to be a mile, so clear the mountain air. My office is at the top of the tallest building (four stories) on the highest hill near the lake. The flat November sun casts long shadows *north*east this time of day, this time of year, sneaking under things from odd angles up and down the great valley through which Burgoyne sailed south to defeat at a place called Saratoga. It was from these waters that he wrote in his diary, "Vermont abounds with the most rebellious race on the continent and hangs like a gathering storm on my left."

It will become cold soon. Very cold. The leaves are gone from the trees, and the tourists have gone with them. The northland is quiet. It is time to hunker down for winter. There is no fighting it. But one month from now,

---

104. Andrew Ferguson, "Ye Olde Town Meeting Gimmick," *Time*, March 2, 1998, 88.

thirty short days, in the dark of a December afternoon the planet Earth will pause for a moment, and then ever so slowly this end of it will begin to tip back toward the sun. The journey away from the cold and back to the light and to the life that follows will begin. About three weeks after this moment passes, governments in over two hundred communities in Vermont will begin to plan the agendas for their springtime democracy, their town meetings. They have been doing this for more than two hundred years. It matters not what others say. Real democracy resides deep in America's dearest dreams. It is like the springtime. It is a longing.[105]

---

105. I have always wondered about the relish with which most scholars and many opinion elites in America feast on the evidence (when it appears) of town meeting's weaknesses—that it is not all it is cracked up to be. Jennifer Tolbert Roberts identified a tradition among students of Greek democracy "devoted to demonstrating the weaknesses of Athenian democracy with a passion that bordered on obsession." *Athens on Trial: The Anti-democratic Tradition in Western Thought* (Princeton: Princeton University Press, 1994), 311. Perhaps we are afraid that if real democracy offered so much more than the alternatives, we would be forced to deal with it. What then?

If liberty and equality, as is thought by some, are chiefly to be found in democracy, they will be best attained when all persons alike share in the government to the utmost.

Plato, *Politics,* book 4

"Walking the bounds" is the old Scottish tradition of walking a town's boundaries ("perambulating" the town) once a year to ensure its territorial integrity. Vermont still requires its secretary of state to perform such a task each year by visiting the four cornerposts of the state. The New England version, however, is more like Robert Frost's poem "Mending Wall," which celebrates two farmers walking the fence between their properties in springtime. The idea is to establish limits and parameters.

3

Democracy as Public Presence: Walking the Bounds

Plato would not be pleased with the modern world's most important example of real democracy. Town meeting may be a longing in the breast of Vermonters, but its pulse is not strong enough to turn out even a quarter of a town's voters. In my sample of 1,435 town meetings held between 1970 and 1998, an average of only 20.5 percent of the registered voters were in attendance.[1] One might argue, of course, that Plato would be even less happy with the American representative republic, which finds it difficult to persuade more than half its voters to spend the thirty minutes it takes once every four years to select the leader of the free world. Town meeting takes place every year, requires over four hours of time, and more often than not costs the citizens who attend a day's pay.[2]

Still, the single most important statistic I have discovered—20.5 percent turnout at town meeting—needs a lot of explaining. In doing the explaining I intend to set forth the empirical parameters of town meeting participation as one might want to see the details of participation in ancient Athens or the little towns that surrounded it—the demes. This is the easy part. The hard part is to discover why turnout at town meeting is as it is. Answers to the question most researched by political scientists in the second half

1. This percentage is remarkably similar to that reported by Berry, Portney, and Thomson, who found that 16.6 percent of city dwellers participated in face-to-face neighborhood association meetings. Jeffrey M. Berry, Kent E. Portney, and Ken Thomson, *The Rebirth of Urban Democracy* (Washington, DC: Brookings Institution, 1993), 293.
2. This argument is developed more fully in chapter 12.

of the twentieth century (why people participate in politics) do little to guide us in our search for the correlates of participation in real democracy. Participation in real democracy dances to a different tune. To begin to discover why, we need to visit town meetings held in two different towns, find out how many citizens attended, consider some of the things they did there, and get a feel for the meetings and the communities where they were held.

Democracy in the Kingdom and by the Great Lake

Newark, Vermont, is a town that (as those who know Vermont best would wager) leads the state in chain saws per capita. It is in the middle of the very coldest and loneliest region of Vermont, called the Northeast Kingdom. Here two thousand square miles of tough sledding pitch and snarl hard on the Canadian line, while off to the east across the long rolling Connecticut River[3] New Hampshire's high peaks stand guard. Here forty-eight little towns have reached accommodation with the land and with the moose and the bear and the beaver that share it with them. In Newark the town meeting is held in a schoolhouse on the only paved road in town—a three-mile stretch improved by the state when it decided to build a fish hatchery on Bean Brook. The other thirty-three miles of town highways in Newark are gravel and dirt.

The border town of Newport is thirty miles to the north, and St. Johnsbury, the gateway to the Kingdom, is twenty-five miles south. These are little places by American standards, but to Newark they seem big. Each has streetlights and sidewalks, restaurants, and even a movie theater. In 1992 Newark had only one store (it closed a few years later), no streetlights, and no sidewalks. The school (K-8), the town clerk's office, the old town hall (which had been converted into a recycling center), and the town garage (which doubles as a fire station) were the only public buildings. When the U.S. Census Bureau took its readings in 1990, it found the typical family in Newark made $27,000 while the average for the 210 towns in the sample was $33,000. Most of the residents are working people.[4] Only 19 percent were classified as managers or professionals (the average town had 25 percent), and only 17 percent of those over twenty-five years old had college degrees. The average town's percentage was 23.

---

3. The Connecticut River is to New England what the Mississippi is to America. It runs down the middle and marks a division that makes a difference.

4. By working people I mean generally blue-collar or service workers who draw low or low-medium wages or self-employed blue-collar workers like farmers, loggers, and individual contractors who own a bulldozer or an excavator. I do not mean to imply that people like college professors and other professionals do not work.

As has been the tradition in New England for more than three centuries, the citizens of Newark had "warned" themselves to be at their town meeting. It would begin at 10:00 a.m. with deliberation on eight issues concerning the schools. This took less than an hour.[5] Then the rest of the town meeting began. It too had been "warned" in the official town report in February. The warning read as follows: "The legal voters of Newark are hereby warned and notified to meet in the school in said Town on Tuesday, March 3, 1992, immediately following the Annual School Meeting to transact the following business."[6]

A list of thirty-two items followed, including: "(8) To see if the Town will vote to have Newark town roads open to snowmobiles which use these highways according to highway rules and do not exceed 25 miles per hour. The town will not be responsible for any accidents caused by snowmobiles" and "(22) To see if the town will appropriate the sum of $100 to Umbrella, Inc. to be used to provide services for adults and children in areas of domestic violence, sexual assault, child abuse prevention, child care and support groups."[7]

The snowmobile debate started just before lunch and lasted fourteen minutes. In that time 13 people spoke. Two of them spoke twice: Violet Carr, who had defeated incumbent Tom Girard for selectman at 11:30, and a man my students identified as "Bill with the plaid shirt and glasses." At 11:10 there were 87 people at the meeting, 46 men and 41 women, with 10 of them standing in the back and along the side walls of the school's "all purpose room." Eighteen chairs were empty. By the time the snowmobile question came to the floor at 11:51, there were 96 people in attendance—51 men and 45 women. This was the highest of the four counts taken during the meeting.

Two voice votes settled the snowmobile issue: yea to shut off debate on the question and nay to allowing snowmobiles on town roads. Money for victims of domestic violence and child abuse (article 22) was approved after a vote to include it with twelve other funding proposals for regional service providers and resolve them as one. The process began at 1:51 p.m., and the bundle passed by a voice vote at 1:59. At 2:40, there were 34 men and 30 women remaining at the meeting. At 2:45 they adjourned and left the little schoolhouse.[8] The sun, which had been struggling all day to get out from behind the clouds, was easing downward in the west, preparing to settle

5. In many towns the "town meeting" actually begins with the "school meeting" (or vice versa), even though in some towns like Newark the two are legally separate.

6. Town of Newark, *Town Report*, year ending December 1991, 28.

7. Ibid., 28–29.

8. Stephanie LaPoint, "The 1992 Comparative Town Meeting Study: Town of Newark," Burlington, University of Vermont, Real Democracy Data Base, March 1992.

behind Vermont's Green Mountains. It would freeze hard again that night, but tomorrow the sun would be as high as in early October.[9]

A bit to the south and across the state on Vermont's western border, it is usually warmer than it is in Newark. This is where Vermont and New York face each other across Lake Champlain (the sixth largest lake in America), which acts as a moderating thermostat in both winter and summer. The people of Shelburne, Vermont, one of that region's valley towns, had already been to their town meeting the night before. Shelburne is a fifteen-minute commute from Vermont's largest city, Burlington, which is in Chittenden County, the state's only Standard Metropolitan Statistical Area (SMSA). There one finds the state's major hospital, its only commercial airport, its university (and several other smaller colleges), its television station, and the region's major employer—the IBM Corporation.

The town of Shelburne is much flatter than Newark. In Shelburne the roads are easier to travel. Nearly all are paved. This is a place where the people have more formal education and higher incomes, are more apt to be classified as "professional or managerial workers," and are more likely to have been raised outside Vermont. In a word, they would be considered more cosmopolitan.[10] And they are younger. The median age in Shelburne is substantially lower than the statewide average. In Newark it is substantially higher.

Shelburne has lake frontage. It is the home of one of America's finest museums of nineteenth-century rural life (the Shelburne Museum), the sprawling "Webb Estate," and several upscale resorts. On clear, quiet mornings in the early fall, balloonists float their colorful craft over the countryside, while in Shelburne harbor dozens of sailboats begin a day on the ice blue lake, surrounded by mountains bathed in the brightness of New England's upland fall foliage.

Shelburne started its meeting at 7:34 Monday evening in the gymnasium of the middle school. Preliminary to placing the first article on the floor, town moderator Samuel Bloomberg called on Reverend Alfred Stefanik of Trinity Episcopal Church to give the invocation. Members of Junior Girl Scout Troop 98 and Brownie Troop 50 then led a flag salute, and a moment of silence was observed for two recently deceased local citizens. Only five articles were on the town's warning. Three of them, the election of town

---

9. For a further description of Newark and an update on the snowmobile issue that was still being discussed as late as the town meeting of 2002, see www.uvm.edu/~fbryan.

10. Vermonters like to joke that living in Chittenden County isn't too bad because it does, after all, border on the state of Vermont.

officers, approval of the budget, and a $15,000 request to support the acqui-
sition of land to "preserve open space and natural resources," could not be
decided at the meeting. Discussion was allowed under the "other business"
article, but the voting would take place the next day by what New Englanders
still call an "Australian" ballot.[11] Thus the first article was the only one that
required a decision: "To hear and act upon the report of the town officers and
the Auditor's Report for the budgetary period July 1, 1990, through June 30,
1991." It took less than a minute for the 131 people (69 men and 62 women)
present to approve article 1 by a voice vote.

The town meeting was then recessed, and the school meeting opened.
The school warning contained seven articles. The first five were to be dealt
with then and there, and the final two—election of the school directors and
a budget of $4,978,108—would be voted on the following day by Australian
ballot. Articles 1 through 4 were resolved in nine minutes with 11 acts of participation shared by 5 people. Pamela Pierce, a member of the school board,
led the discussion with 6 of the 11 participations. Presentations by the town's
two school principals and the chairman of the school board dominated the
new business article (article 5), which was on the floor for thirty-nine minutes.[12] Fourteen people participated, 3 who had already participated on an
earlier matter and 11 new participators. Each of the 11 new speakers participated just once, however, so the total number of participations was only 16.[13]

After the adjournment of the school meeting, the town meeting reconvened and discussed the town budget for sixty-eight minutes. It featured 20
new participators and 3 people who had already participated. When the town
budget debate began, 135 citizens were present. When it ended, fewer than
100 were left. At 10:00 p.m. the meeting recessed until 7:00 a.m. the next day
for voting by Australian ballot at the fire station. This did not mean that the
"meeting" would reconvene. It meant only that townspeople (whether or not
they had attended the town meeting) could vote by ballot the next day on all
those issues discussed (but not resolved) at Monday evening's meeting.

11. The Australian ballot is a paper ballot that allows people to vote for town officers (in
this case) and on other issues (in other cases) without attending town meeting.

12. The minutes of the school meeting put it this way: "School Board member Mike
Errecart presented the 1992–1993 school budget to the *audience*" (emphasis mine). I doubt whether
the people at the meeting in Newark would have considered themselves members of an audience.
Perhaps the attenders at Shelburne did not either. But somehow the term seems to fit Shelburne
better. Town of Shelburne, "Minutes 1992 School Meeting," *Town Report*, year ending December
1992.

13. Randy Huey, Christine Palmer, Jennifer Shanahan, and Tana Wolfson, "The 1992
Comparative Town Meeting Study: Town of Shelburne," Burlington, University of Vermont,
March 1992.

The examples of Newark and Shelburne make it clear that the structure of the meetings and the character of the communities where they are held vary considerably in Vermont's towns, much as they may have in Greek demes like Pallenais. To understand how this variation is related to turnout, let us begin with the number of citizens involved and then turn to the proportion. Indeed, assessments of democracy in the classical city of Athens itself always begin with the question, How many people were at the assembly? Such information may be forever lost to us for the demes. For the towns, it is not.

Walking the Bounds

The actual number of people at the Newark and Shelburne town meetings (an average of 81 in Newark and 122 in Shelburne) is representative of the norm for the entire sample of 1,435 meetings we studied between 1970 and 1998. When all the attendance counts for each of the meetings in the sample are averaged (four counts for day meetings and three counts for night meetings), the average number of people at the 1,435 town meetings was 114. The lowest average attendance throughout the day for a *single* meeting was 17, recorded in the southern Vermont town of Woodford in 1984. The average lowest attendance count for the day for *all* the meetings was 91. The highest average attendance throughout the day for a single meeting was 418 in 1992 at the meeting in Charlotte, a town adjacent to Shelburne. The average highest attendance count for the day for all the meetings was 137. The distribution of these averages is found in plot 1 of figure 3.1.

Averages hide things—things like ranges. Consider Maidstone, a town in the Northeast Kingdom (a couple of towns east of Newark) bordering New Hampshire on the Connecticut River. Maidstone has a population density of about four per square mile, 150 acres of land for every man, woman, and child who lives there.[14] At 9:53 p.m. on Monday, March 4, 1996, the issue was the fate of the town's old school bus. At that time 14 people were left in the town hall, which measures twenty feet by forty. We counted the number of people in attendance about 5,100 times in 1,435 meetings between 1970 and 1998, and Maidstone's 14 attenders in 1996 constituted the lowest count of all.

The highest attendance count recorded was taken at a town meeting in the town of Thetford. Thetford, like Maidstone, is on the Connecticut River. This is where the similarities end. Thetford is 100 miles south of Maidstone, where the river's wide meadows fashion a more pastoral landscape and way of life. Up north near Maidstone the water flows fast and narrow. Forested

14. Maidstone is best known for its beautiful lake, campground, and state forest.

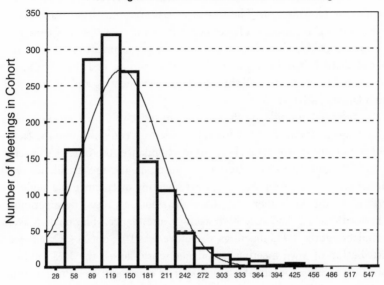

Plot 1: Highest Number in Attendance at Town Meeting

Cohorts of Highest Number in Attendance

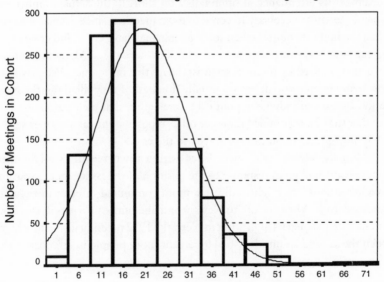

Plot 2: Percentage of Registered Voters Attending at Highest Count

Cohorts of Percentage of Registerered Voters Attending

Figure 3.1. Attendance at town meetings (1,435 meetings, 1970–1998).

mountains squeeze the river from both sides and create the culture of the woodsman. Downstream, Thetford is an easy commute from Hanover, New Hampshire, Dartmouth College, and a growing metropolitan center. It is the town introduced in chapter 2 as the first government in America to ask that Richard Nixon be impeached. On the evening of February 29, 1988, two of my students attended the Thetford town meeting and counted 547 in attendance at 8:10 p.m.[15]

Averages can hide another important piece of information—variance. An average attendance of 114 for 1,435 meetings could disguise the fact that half the meetings averaged about 30 in attendance, the other half averaged about 200, and none came close to the mean, an average attendance of 114. However, the only irregularity in town meeting attendance is a slightly extended tail on the higher end of the distribution caused by meetings like Thetford's, which had very high average attendance. The median average attendance at the 1,435 meetings, therefore, was 107, not 114. Otherwise the distribution of town meeting attendance scores across the 1,435 individual meetings nicely approximates a bell-shaped curve and contains no troublesome ups and downs.

For analytical purposes I prefer the highest attendance count and not the average attendance count. While highest count exceeds gavel-to-gavel town meeting attendance, it often falls a bit short of the actual number who expend the effort necessary to come to town meeting, since even at the point when the highest count is taken some people may have come and gone or will appear later and not be counted as additional attenders. Many measures of participation used by political scientists share this inaccuracy. We may know how many people voted, but we usually don't ask if they filled out the entire ballot. Indexes of individual political participation that code respondents on whether they have attended rallies or other types of political meetings seldom ask if they got there on time or stayed to the end.

Finally, variations of attendance within town meetings might mean people come and go in response to the position of the issues on the warning. Steadier attendance might indicate a more communal interest in the commonweal itself. A brief return to Newark and Shelburne provides illustrations. Attendance reached its high point in Newark's 1992 meeting just before lunch, when the second count identified 9 percent more people in attendance than

15. Kimberly Crossley and Katherine Glendenning, "The 1988 Comparative Town Meeting Study: Town of Thetford" Burlington, University of Vermont, Real Democracy Data Base, March 1988. This meeting is described in more detail in chapter 10.

did the first count. After the noon break a third attendance count turned out to be 22 percent lower than the second count. Five minutes before adjournment, a fourth count dipped to 15 percent of the third count. All in all, attendance in Newark at its low point was 67 percent of what it was at its high point. In Shelburne's night meeting, attendance was more stable. At its low point, 9:45, fourteen minutes before adjournment, attendance was 72 percent of what it was at its high point, reached at 9:00. Lowest attendance in the average town meeting was (as it was in Newark) 67 percent of the highest attendance.

Most of the variance in attendance at a town meeting occurs because people arrive late or (much more likely) leave early. When issues coincide with a legal break in the process (such as an adjournment of a town meeting to open a school meeting) or a break for lunch, attendance often goes down and (more rarely) may go up. If important issues appear near the end of the meeting, attendance throughout the meeting is often more stable than if they appear right before lunch or early in the afternoon. At night meetings especially, the resolution of a particularly controversial issue can signal a sharp decline in attendance. Otherwise variation in attendance seems to be governed more by human foibles of tardiness and fatigue than by strategic concerns.

The most important question asked of all democracies, however, is what *proportion* of citizens participate,[16] and we know that on average towns attract only 20.5 percent of their registered voters to town meeting. But the range of citizen participation at town meeting is wide. The very best meeting in the sample drew 72.3 percent of the registered voters, and the very worst drew 1 percent. Plot 2 in figure 3.1 summarizes the data for all 1,435 meetings by arranging them in a histogram according to percentages of registered voters who were present at the highest attendance count taken during the meeting. It groups the meetings into cohorts by increments of five percentage points. The cohort with the largest number of cases had 291 meetings averaging 16 percent of the town's registered voters in attendance at the highest count. Below this central cohort was a group of 273 meetings averaging 11 percent attendance, and above it was a group of 264 averaging 21 percent. The data

16. To determine these proportions I use the percentage of registered voters as the denominator. Figured as the percentage of eligible voters, attendance will be a bit lower than attendance measured as the percentage of registered voters, since not all those who are eligible are registered. Fortunately, such a strong relation exists between the two that it makes no difference from an analytical point of view which statistic is used. (The Pearson's r between eligible voters and registered voters is .98.) Vermont has no party registration, and the gap between eligible voters and registered voters is small.

in plot 2 of figure 3.1 show us for the first time (in the aggregate and in its most general dimensions) what real democracy looks like.[17]

The best meeting of all was held in Newark, whose meeting in 1992 was described at the outset of this chapter. Eighteen years earlier, on March 5, 1974, at 11:30 a.m., 72.3 percent (94) of the 130 citizens on the voter registration "checklist" were present. For twenty-eight years students made thousands of counts of citizens at town meetings. This is as good as it got.[18]

Vermont's smallest town, Victory, came in second on the list of highest attendance, with 70.1 percent of the registered voters present at town meeting in 1997. North Hero, a larger town on an island in Lake Champlain, turned out 65 percent of its registered voters for the 1994 town meeting.[19] Of the sample's 1,435 meetings held in 210 different towns, three towns accounted for seven of the top ten meetings on the highest attendance count.[20] Newark had two of these meetings; Athens (see chapter 2) had two, and Victory had three.

WITNESS

In 1996 the population of Victory was approximately seventy. These people were scattered over forty-three of the toughest square miles in New England. The following entry was on the inside of the back cover of the town report.

A LOOK BACK

The year started with a mild winter, followed by a not so muddy spring. Summer was in a hurry and rushed in the first part of June. It was a dry summer; lawns were turning brown and a little moisture was badly needed.

---

17. Thanks to the work of Menahem Rosner we know that, at least well into the 1980s, attendance at the assemblies of the Israeli kibbutzim was about 35 percent, and they met an average of three times a month. Menahem Rosner, *Participatory Political and Organizational Democracy and the Experience of the Israeli Kibbutz* (Haifa: University of Haifa, 1981); see also Joseph Blasi, *The Communal Experience of the Kibbutz* (New Brunswick, NJ: Transaction Books, 1986), 99, 109. See also Menahem Rosner, *Democracy, Equality and Change: The Kibbutz and Social Theory* (Darby, PA: Norwood Editions, 1982), and for more recent developments Avraham Pavin, "The Governmental System of the Kibbutz," in *Crisis in the Israeli Kibbutz*, ed. Uriel Leviatan, Hugh Oliver, and Jack Quarter (Westport, CT: Praeger, 1998), 97–109.

18. The average attendance that day for Newark was 60 percent. The lowest was 48 percent.

19. These meetings are described in more detail in chapter 10.

20. Victory's meeting in 1996 shows how the attendance counts may be conservative, especially in small towns where a handful of attenders affect the percentage turnout dramatically. Often potential voters are outside the hall smoking or talking. In 1996 the student who went into the very deepest part of the Northeast Kingdom to get the data for Victory tallied 39 in attendance at the highest count. But at 8:05 p.m. a three-way contest for lister developed, and on the third ballot 43 votes were cast.

We welcomed the rain on August 5th—at first. Before it was over, we experienced "the flood."

Two homes received damage, the folks on Victory Hill were stranded until John MacDonald could get out there and rebuild a path for them to get through. Judy and Keith went from house to house checking on folks and keeping us informed. Lots of people did lots of work. But on the whole, Victory did not fare too badly.

We were saddened by the loss of two gentlemen who affected our lives in one way or another. Conrad Gingue had done road work for the town and those who worked with him will miss him. Ross Baxter was our computer expert and those of us who were instructed by him and had the benefit of his sunny disposition feel the loss.

Neighbors, friends, and family moved on to another environment. We said good-bye to the Watsons, who went to another state; the Staats, who went up the road to Granby; and to Sandy Stocker, who went to St. Johnsbury to care for Betty Locke. Although he hasn't moved, Matthew Bush is off to college.

But we have new neighbors. Ilene Kanoff, a teacher in Whitefield, and Peggy Morris now live in the former Stocker homestead.

Janet Bouchard and "Uscar" Lynaugh have purchased the Alice Beaver place, Janet and Roland Copp are in their place on Victory Hill, and Jim and Helen Nichols are in the process of building their little hide-away on the hill as is Richard Prue. We also extend a welcome to Steve Bobrowsky, Jessica Hudson, and Fern Loomis.

Our year ended with a snowy December, which gives Victory its charm—to some of us anyway.

Have a healthy, happy 1996.

Victory Town Report[21]

The worst town meeting attendance occurred in the Burlington satellite town of Jericho, one of only five of Vermont's 246 cities and towns to be given biblical names (the others were Canaan, Corinth, Goshen, and Sharon). At the 1998 town meeting, attendance was counted at 9:30 and 11:00 a.m. and at 12:30 and 1:45 p.m.[22] The highest count numbered 36, exactly 1 percent

21. Town of Victory, *Town Report*, year ending December 1995. As we will see, Victory was not as happy as it seemed (chapter 10, page 236).

22. Kimberly Henry and Christopher Morris, "The 1998 Comparative Town Meeting Study: Town of Jericho," Burlington, University of Vermont, Real Democracy Data Base, March 1998. The low attendance in Jericho is probably the result of an experiment with Saturday meetings. Jericho went to Saturday meetings in 1995. In the previous four meetings in the sample (1987, 1989, 1990, and 1991), the average number of attenders was 190. In the next four it was 119, 116, 85, and 31. In 1998 Jericho had had enough, and after 9 people participated in a fifteen-minute debate, a voice vote moved the meeting back to Tuesday. Dee Dee Jameson

of the registered voters. This was as bad as it got. The second lowest turnout over the 29 years occurred in Swanton. Swanton was built on a great bend in the historic Missisquoi River, just before it enters Lake Champlain in the northwestern part of the state. In 1997, only 54 of the 3,622 registered voters (1.5 percent) were at the meeting in the Swanton Village Municipal Complex at 8:10 p.m. when the highest count of the evening was recorded.[23]

To summarize, the average meeting had 20.5 percent of its registered voters present when the highest attendance count was taken.[24] The towns this turnout is based on averaged a population of 1,442, with 894 names on the list of registered voters. Importantly, the variation within this average is far greater than it is for larger, representative systems. Elections held in high-turnout industrialized nations, for instance, seldom double the turnout of elections held in low-turnout industrialized nations. In America, high-turnout states almost never double the turnout of low-turnout states. In 1996, for instance, the state with the lowest turnout (Nevada) had 60 percent of the turnout produced by the highest-turnout state (Maine). In our sample of town meetings, however, the top 25 percent of the meetings on turnout doubled the turnout of the bottom 25 percent.

This range of variation improves our chances of discovering what it is about the towns where meetings are held that accounts for good and bad democratic performance—especially since the character of these towns varies widely as well. Consider again Shelburne and Newark. We have discussed how dramatically these towns differ from one another, and indeed these differences match a similar gap in their town meeting performances. But the connection between the character of these communities and their practice of democracy is opposite from what we would expect. The upscale,

---

seemed to sum up the argument for the move: the school winter break included the weekend before town meeting, and many families were away on vacation. (Jericho is an upscale town.) She also argued that a Tuesday meeting "would encourage that childcare be provided by a local group as a fundraiser" and recommended that the town meeting be combined with School Meeting on the same day. Ibid., and Town of Jericho, Cynthia Humphrey, Town Clerk, "Minutes of Annual Town Meeting February 28, 1998," *Town Report*, year ending December 1998. Turnout in Jericho since 1998 shows Jameson was right. Within a week of my manuscript's due date for final editorial changes, Jericho's 2003 town meeting turned out 219 at the highest count, an increase of about 500 percent. Tanya Osol, "The 2003 Comparative Town Meeting Study: Town of Jericho," Burlington, University of Vermont, Real Democracy Data Base, March 2003.

23. Jeremy Chevalier, Brad Messier, and Derek MacDonald, "The 1997 Comparative Town Meeting Study: Town of Swanton," Burlington, University of Vermont, Real Democracy Data Base, March 1997. The average attendance was 49. The meeting began at 7:00 p.m. and ended at 9:06.

24. When this highest count was averaged with all the counts taken at each meeting, producing an average attendance for each meeting, the mean of the average for the entire sample was 17.4.

highly educated, and more cosmopolitan town of Shelburne turned out 3.2 percent of its registered voters for town meeting, while the more working-class, rural town of Newark, whose citizens have far less formal education, turned out 39.5 percent of its registered voters.

A second comparison, the meetings in the towns of Calais in 1977 and Lunenburg in 1978, features equally different communities. Lunenburg is a conservative, blue-collar town in the Kingdom. Calais is a liberal, professional town within a manageable commute of the state capital, the city of Montpelier. In the late 1970s the median family income in Calais was 25 percent higher than that in Lunenburg. Calais had twice as great a percentage of college graduates as Lunenburg. In the 1980s the vote for Socialist Bernard Sanders in Calais was almost triple what it was in Lunenburg, and the vote for a constitutional amendment to Vermont's constitution to ensure equal rights for women was 64 percent yes in Calais and 65 percent no in Lunenburg.

Those most familiar with the literature on political participation in America would have little difficulty making the claim that Calais should have a more participatory citizenry than Lunenburg because the people in Calais share the characteristics of people most apt to participate in politics. But turnout at town meeting in Calais and Lunenburg (unlike Newark and Shelburne) was almost exactly the same—about the average attendance for the entire sample of 1,435 town meetings. Calais's meeting had 20.8 percent of the town's registered voters in attendance, and Lunenburg's had 20.7 percent.

These two examples do not bode well for our upcoming attempt to explain variations in attendance at town meeting, except for one thing. The populations of Lunenburg and Calais in 1980, towns with equal town meeting attendance, were nearly identical, whereas in 1990 the population of Newark (where attendance was 40 percent) was 354 and the population of Shelburne (where attendance was 3 percent) was 6,604.

Size and Democracy

I take it as a given: from participation to policy, size (the *scale* of things) is critical to any discussion of democracy. Yet the most often overlooked variable in political science is scale.[25] In 1973 Robert A. Dahl, later a president of the American Political Science Association and arguably the most distinguished scholar in the profession, and Edward R. Tufte, a professor at Yale, published

25. "Yet so far the size of social systems has scarcely become one of the central concerns of institution builders and social system designers." Alberto Guerreiro Ramos, *The New Science of Organizations* (Toronto: University of Toronto Press, 1981), 138–139.

a remarkable book, *Size and Democracy*.[26] In one incandescent paragraph in the epilogue, I found intellectual support for what was then becoming my life's work:

> It seems evident to us that among the units most needed in the world as it has been evolving lie several at the extremes: we need some very small units and some very large units.... Very large units that transcend the parochialism and inadequate system capacity of the nation-state are evolving, but too slowly—quite possibly too slowly for human survival. If the giant units are needed for handling transnational matters of extraordinary moment, *very small units seem to us necessary to provide a place where ordinary people can acquire the sense and the reality of moral responsibility and political effectiveness* [emphasis mine] in a universe where remote galaxies of leaders spin on in courses mysterious and unfathomable to the ordinary citizen.[27]

Unfortunately, political scientists did not take up the issue of size and democracy as Dahl and Tufte urged, nor did the profession explore the implications of such a discussion for issues of federalism, world government, and democracy.[28] Instead, we became entranced with the question of individual behavior in the very units that Dahl and Tufte downplayed (such as the national government of the United States), and scale was pretty much ignored.[29] This has had frustrating implications for my enterprise, because

26. Robert A. Dahl and Edward R. Tufte, *Size and Democracy* (Stanford: Stanford University Press, 1973).

27. Dahl and Tufte, *Size and Democracy*, 140.

28. Alas, there is little doubt that Dahl's vision of "very small units" did not match my own. Only three years earlier he said small towns "were filled with oppressive weight of repressive deviation and dissent, which, when they appear, erupt explosively and leave a lasting burden of antagonism and hatred." Robert A. Dahl, "Democracy and the Chinese Boxes," in *Frontiers of Democratic Theory*, ed. Henry Kariel (New York: Random House, 1970), 376.

29. Important exceptions are found in the work of scholars like Jane Mansbridge, *Beyond Adversary Democracy* (New York: Basic Books, 1980), and Benjamin R. Barber, *Strong Democracy* (Berkeley: University of California Press, 1984). Kirkpatrick Sale, *Human Scale* (New York: Coward, McCanon and Geoghegan, 1980), is a leading scholar on scale outside political science. An important popular literature grew from the efforts of such people as Wendell Berry, Murray Bookchin, Leopold Kohr, and E. F. Schumacher. See Wendell Berry, *The Unsettling of America* (San Francisco: Sierra Club Books, 1977); Murray Bookchin, *The Limits of the City* (New York: Harper and Row, 1974); Leopold Kohr, "Critical Size," in *Time Running Out? Best of Resurgence*, ed. Michael North (Dorchester, Dorset: Prism Press, 1976); Leopold Kohr, *The Breakdown of Nations* (New York: E. P. Dutton, 1978); and E. F. Schumacher, *Small Is Beautiful* (New York: Harper and Row, 1973). See also Jacques Thomassen, "Political Representation in Dutch Communities," paper presented at the annual meeting of the American Political Science Association, Washington, DC, August 28–31, 1986.

nearly all the literature available to direct the investigation deals with representative democracy, whereby individuals elect executives *of* and representatives *to* distant and remote governments.

The size variable receives theoretical support from models of rationality. In 1957 Anthony Downs's classic *Economic Theory of Democracy* established a baseline in the literature on rationality and voting in mass democracies.[30] The intellectual ecology of the field was then heavily influenced by two related propositions. One was that political participation in America was woefully low, and the other was that what remained of it was primarily limited to the act of voting. In the most important of the early studies of political participation, *The American Voter*, Angus Campbell and his associates put it bluntly: "For most Americans voting is the sole act of participation in politics."[31]

Downs's contribution was to begin the process of explaining voting (or rather the lack of it) in purely rational terms. In its simplest form his model reads: voting is unreasonable because the cost of voting far outweighs its benefits. As B. F. Skinner put it (speaking through his fictional Dr. Frazier), the probability of making a difference in an election is "less than the chance [of being] killed on the way to the polls."[32] Thus Downs left us with what has been called the "voters' paradox": the cost of voting always outweighs its benefits, yet the majority of the people vote anyway.[33] The dilemma is extended by a further paradox: one would expect that the more citizens know about the system (the more educated they are), the more rational they will be (about the possibility of enhancing their own self-interest at the polls) and, consequently, the less likely they will be to vote. Yet the empirical evidence is clear: people with more education vote more, not less.[34]

Where does this leave us? First, we are told that a stronger value can overcome self-interest.[35] People will vote more, even in the face of gigantic odds against its making a difference, because "making a difference" doesn't

30. Anthony Downs, *An Economic Theory of Democracy* (New York: Harper and Row, 1957).

31. Angus Campbell, Philip Converse, Warren E. Miller, and Donald E. Stokes, *The American Voter* (New York: John Wiley, 1964), 50.

32. B. F. Skinner, *Walden Two* (New York: Macmillan, 1948), 265, quoted in R. E. Goodin and K. W. S. Roberts, "The Ethical Voter," *American Political Science Review* 69 (September 1975): 926–938.

33. This strain in the literature of political participation is complex. For a review of many of these studies see www.uvm.edu/~fbryan.

34. Sidney Verba warns us not to get so intellectually involved with the voter's paradox that we forget the more interesting questions like why some people participate and others do not. Sidney Verba, "The 1993 James Madison Lecture: The Voice of the People," *P.S. Political Science and Politics* 26 (December 1993): 677–686.

35. Here I prefer "self-interest" to "reason," since self-interest is often ignored for reasonable ends—such as the good feeling you often get when acting for the common good.

matter as much as being a good citizen. Duty trumps reason. Or we are told that the size variable does matter because it makes participation on any number of smaller fronts meaningful enough to create an instinct for participation in much larger contexts. Habit trumps reason. Second, what may seem irrational really is not. A surrogate for small scale is created when mass elections are reduced in the minds of the voters by the perception that the outcome of the race is in serious doubt. Finally, it is argued that what may seem irrational (voting against all odds of its making a difference) becomes rational indeed when we factor in the regret associated with not voting when it would have made a difference.[36]

Why not back up and start over? The near dead end we find in the literature suggests it.[37] Our database of small-town democratic systems allows it. Our preliminary findings command it. We need to look at high-cost political participation in governments that are small enough to make salient the variations in the potential to make a difference and where the significance of the outcomes is high.[38] The ecological fallacy (and other cautions) notwithstanding,[39] our preliminary observation that socioeconomic status (SES) and town meeting attendance may not be related slaps us alongside the head. In matters of real democracy SES, the premier causal variable in the literature of political participation, may not suffice. The gap between this first peek at the data and a definitive conclusion is, of course, massive. But one thing is certain; community size must lead the attempt to build a working model of real democracy.[40]

36. For a review of the chronology of this research and the literature that supports these models, see www.uvm.edu/~fbryan.

37. For instance, Arend Lijphart, in his thorough review of the literature on political participation, makes this claim: "From the perspective of rational choice, it is to be expected that the careful reasoning voter will vote less in most second order than in first order elections." Why would this be so if the size of the electorate is much smaller in second-order elections? Is it that significance of the outcome trumps potential to make a difference? Or is it that in second-order constituencies the curvilinear pattern in the "making a difference" potential means the single voter still (even in a small city, for instance) cannot in any practical sense "make a difference"? Or could it be that American political socialization is biased in favor of national citizenship over local citizenship and it is this, not the significance of the issues, that draws people to the polls in first-order elections? See Arend Lijphart, "Unequal Participation: Democracy's Unresolved Dilemma," *American Political Science Review* 91 (March 1997): 1–14.

38. Most political scientists, I wager, would disagree with my "significance" claim. This question is in my view a key ingredient in the mystery soup of political participation and rational behavior. Which *is* (not "ought to be") more significant to a typical citizen: a school bus route, a zoning ordinance, or one's property taxes (on the one hand) or (on the other hand) who becomes president of the United States?

39. See the discussion in chapter 5.

40. For a review of the literature on the relation between size, urbanism, and political participation, see www.uvm.edu/~fbryan.

The Linear Relationship

The operating assumption is that voters will understand that participating in a meeting of, say, two hundred voters gives them a *real* chance to change the outcome (or to demonstrate one's commitment to the polity), and that this chance is far less likely in a meeting of one thousand voters. Further, a point exists at which the size advantage is so clear-cut that it ought to assume priority in any hypothesized chain of causal variables said to affect the decision to participate or not to participate.

First, a very simple hypothesis: the bigger the community, the lower the turnout at town meeting. Recall the meetings in Athens and Newark. They ranked first (51.4 percent) and third (39.5 percent) respectively on turnout at town meeting among the seventy town meetings studied in 1992. Now recall that Shelburne had a 3.2 percent turnout, the very lowest in 1992. Charlotte, another town on the lake just south of Shelburne, also ranked very high on upscale indicators and had 19.3 percent attendance. Now consider the size of these four towns. Athens had a total population of 313 in 1992. The town of Newark had 354. Shelburne and Charlotte, however, had populations of 6,604 and 3,148 respectively. If this pattern obtains for the entire range of data, the conclusion seems inescapable. Size matters, and it matters a lot.

To draw a more refined bead on the question, we need to compare the attendance at all 1,435 meetings with the size of the towns where they were held in the year when they were held. The result of such a comparison is best summarized by means of what for decades has been the hand shovel of analysis in the social sciences—the Pearson product moment correlation coefficient. The simplest utility of Pearson's *r*, as it is called, is its ability to roughly summarize both the strength and the direction of a relation between two variables. The correlation coefficient ranges between -1 and $+1$. In this case, the coefficient representing the relation between the percentage of the registered voters that attended town meeting and the size of the town where the meeting was held is $-.65$.[41]

The product moment coefficient has another useful property. When squared it tells us what percentage of the variance in the dependent variable is "explained" by the independent variable. An *r* of .65, therefore, indicates that about 42 percent of the variance in attendance at the 1,435 town meetings is associated with the size of the town where the meeting was held. The notation for this derivative is R^2. Although the R^2 fails to specify the direction of the

41. In comparing attendance at community and workplace assemblies in Israel, Rosner found it twice as high in the workplace, and he attributes this to size: "The community is much larger than the plants." Rosner, *Participatory Political and Organizational Democracy*, 12, 44.

relation, it is a more intuitively satisfying measure than the simple r because it provides a meaningful reference point: the best relation is one in which all (100 percent) of the variance in the "dependent" variable (in this case town meeting attendance) is explained by the "independent" variable (in this case town size) and the worst is one in which none of the variance in the dependent variable is explained by the independent variable. In this first look at the data 42 percent of the variance in town meeting attendance is explained by town size. We are still in the dark about 58 percent of whatever it is that makes attendance go up and down from meeting to meeting.

Still, the relation between size and democracy is very strong indeed. Most would call it impressive.[42] But is it reliable? The meetings, after all, are selected yearly and pooled over a twenty-nine-year period. It could be, for instance, that a relation that appears to be so strong overall is actually a product of its great strength in particular years. It adds significantly to the credibility of the size variable to be able to report that the association between size and attendance remains remarkably consistent over time.[43] A wide array of variables can affect attendance at town meeting; a snowstorm, a controversial issue, the structure of the town meeting itself, or the socioeconomic and political character of the community where the meeting is held. Yet if we drop randomly into the data set at any point over the period, we would come away with the same conclusion we drew from the pooled data: size matters, and it matters plenty.[44]

The Bend in the Data

As averages hide things, so do correlation coefficients. It is time to take a hard, squint-eyed look *within* the relation that produces this strong correlation. Let us begin on familiar ground by returning to the year 1992 and arranging the town meetings for that year in a scatterplot featuring town size

42. What is a "strong" relation between two variables (assuming the variables have statistical and paradigmatic legitimacy) is, of course, pretty much a judgment call. Hayward R. Alker Jr., writing from Yale University, quotes Karl Deutsch on this matter as follows: "Anyone who suggests a variable explaining an additional 10 percent of the variance has made a contribution to political theory." Hayward R. Alker Jr., *Mathematics and Politics* (New York: Macmillan, 1965), 89.

43. The R^2s for thirteen two-year clusters of town meetings studied between 1970 and 1998 (1970 and 1971 through 1997 and 1998) show that when the number of registered voters in each town is correlated with that town's average attendance at town meeting for all the towns in each group, the lowest R^2 is .27 and the highest is .59. The mean is .42 and the median is .41. All of these relationships are, of course, negative.

44. Size does not matter, however ($r = .08$), when voter turnout in statewide elections is substituted for turnout at town meeting.

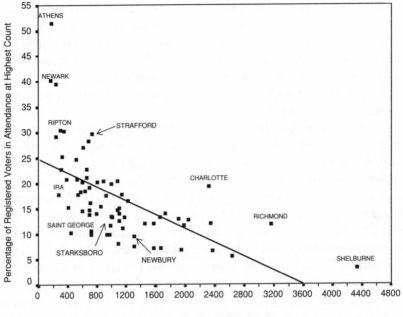

Figure 3.2. Town size and meeting attendance: the linear model (70 town meetings, 1992).

and town meeting turnout. Focusing on a single year reduces the number of cases (meetings) to a more manageable number. When too many cases are crammed into a scatterplot, individual towns like those we are becoming familiar with can disappear from view, and the scatterplot's descriptive utility can be compromised. Figure 3.2 arranges the meetings of 1992 by town size[45] (on the horizontal axis) and turnout, the percentage of the town's registered voters who came to the meeting (on the vertical axis).

Simple correlation coefficients can sometimes be misleading because the information they render is based on the *assumption* that the relation between the two variables involved is linear when in fact it is not. The association between town size and town meeting attendance is one of these instances. As the towns first increase in size (moving right across the horizontal axis), the

45. From this point on town size is defined as the number of registered voters in a town rather than a town's total population. The correlation between the two variables is .98. Given this, it seems more reasonable to express size in terms more directly operative to politics by eliminating, for instance, all underage citizens from the definition of size.

decline in attendance at town meeting is sharp. But this decline soon begins to level off. As the towns get bigger, increases in their numbers of registered voters do not reduce the percentage going to town meeting with anywhere near the same intensity as do increases in numbers at the lower end of the scale. A rough point of diminishing returns seems to appear, after which continuing enlargement of electorates does not produce as much decline in participation as it did earlier.

As the scatterplot demonstrates, a linear regression model like the one associated with Pearson's r predicts town meeting attendance well enough for individual parts of the distribution (of town size), but it is rather clumsy when applied to the entire array of meetings. It is more than clumsy. It is downright embarrassing. The straight line of "best fit" drawn through all the meetings in figure 3.2[46] predicts that towns with more than about 3,550 registered voters would have a *negative* number of citizens at town meeting. Moreover, the line underestimates the attendance for meetings in both the very smallest and the very largest towns. It tends to overestimate the attendance at meetings for those towns in the middle.

Based on their size, the linear regression line predicts that both Athens and Newark will have about 24 percent attendance. Athens exceeded its prediction by about twenty-eight percentage points, and Newark exceeded its by about sixteen. Strafford, the town where (you may remember from chapter 1) one of my students, Marnie Owen, and the popular CBS correspondent Charles Kuralt took different views on town meeting, was also a high achiever on town meeting attendance even when its small size is taken into account. The meetings in Shelburne and Charlotte, the much larger towns we discussed earlier in this chapter, also seem to be overachievers. They fall well above the line representing the linear relation between size and town meeting attendance. Middle-sized towns like Newbury, where I grew up and attended my first town meeting, and Starksboro, where I have lived since 1971 in a hollow where Appalachian-raised county music singer Loretta Lynn would feel at home, did not muster enough attendance in 1992 to meet the expectations of their size. Nor did the smaller towns of St. George and Ira.

Something is amiss. The coefficients do not take into account the bend in the data. This omission wreaks havoc with our ability to predict attendance levels at town meeting based on the size of the town where the meeting is held.

---

46. Statisticians call it the "line of best fit," since it would minimize to the greatest extent possible the total distance produced if the distances from each town to the line were added together.

A Size-Calibrated Measure of Real Democracy

Let's think about the dynamics involved here. In a group of one, the voter has 100 percent of the power because she controls 100 percent of the vote. As soon as someone else joins, her power is cut in half. A third person in the group means she has only one-third the power, and when a fourth comes this power is reduced to 25 percent. Note that the larger the group becomes, the smaller the loss if another person joins. Put it this way. If one's goal is influence over the group, a fifth person's joining a group of four is much more disheartening than a forty-first person's joining a group of forty.

The what's one more going to matter? hypothesis predicts that if (when considering their personal influence) people are willing to attend a meeting with three hundred potential attenders, an increase of ten more potential attenders at the meeting may make little difference to them. But if the total number of potential attenders may increase from thirty to forty (still an increase of only ten voters), this increase may mean a lot indeed. I call this familiar ratio of a single group member to the total group membership the voter power index.

A second way to look at the relation between group size and the power of an individual within the group is to determine the probability that the group will be evenly split on an issue so that one person could cast the decisive ballot. What is the probability that the other members of the group will produce a tie, which any one voter may then break? John Banzhaf, the first scholar to give this notion mathematical expression, explains: "The voter's ability to affect the election of his legislator decreases as the inverse of the *square root* of the population of the district rather than the simple inverse of the population."[47] I will call this probability that a single group member could break a tie among the other members of the group the voter decisiveness index. Voter decisiveness decreases less sharply than voter power as group size increases.[48]

Another popular technique for dealing with curvilinear patterns is to define the independent variable (in this case the number of registered voters in town) as its logarithm. Using the log of a variable has a successful history in the social sciences for precisely the kind of situation we find ourselves in.

47. John F. Banzhaf III, "Multi-member Electoral Districts—Do They Violate the "One Man One Vote Principle?" *Yale Law Journal* 75 (July 1966): 1323. See also Banzhaf, "One Man, 3312 Votes," *Villanova Law Review* 13 (Winter 1968): 304–332.

48. Banzhaf has been refined by Steven J. Brams, *Game Theory and Politics* (New York: Free Press, 1975), 260–261. See also G. Chamberlain and M. Rothschild, "A Note on the Probability of Casting a Deciding Vote," *Journal of Economic Theory* 25 (1981): 152–162, and H. Margolis, "Probability of a Tie Election," *Public Choice* 31 (1977): 135–138.

But the log index lacks theoretical grounding. It is at least conceivable that when citizens decide whether to attend town meeting, they might take into account the size of the group they expect to find there. Likewise, it is at least possible that they might imagine the size of the group in terms of a possible tie that they might break. It is highly unlikely, however, that they would muse over a logarithm as they eat breakfast and ponder whether to go snowmobiling or practice real democracy.

Yet of the three measures the best "predictor" of town meeting attendance turns out to be the log[49] of the registered voters in the town where the meeting is held. It explains 58 percent of the variance. Remember that the number of registered voters alone (the earlier linear model) explained 42 percent. Voter power explains only 43 percent and voter decisiveness 52 percent. Since the log transformation was theoretically the least satisfying, however, it seemed appropriate to further examine voter power and voter decisiveness to see if they could be improved either individually or in combination.

After exploring several alternative approaches, I joined two equations that in combination conformed both to the statistical mandates of regression analysis and to the theoretical assumptions of the curvilinear models. The first equation used voter decisiveness modified by voter power to predict attendance for towns with more than 345 registered voters. The second relied on voter decisiveness alone to predict attendance for towns with 345 or fewer registered voters. When these equations are combined, they account for 58 percent of the variance in attendance—as good a fit as the log term but, as I have suggested, more theoretically pleasing.[50]

The argument, put simply, is that smaller towns will have higher attendance at their meetings because the people who live in these places know they are more powerful decision makers than people in larger towns. It fits either the rational *self*-interest model ("I will use this power to promote my own interests") or the rational *community*-interest model ("I will use this power to try to accomplish what I think my community needs"). The curve produced by the combination of the voter power and voter decisiveness indexes demonstrates that town meeting attendance levels conform to this theory. See figure 3.3.

But the curve does more. It allows us to predict with remarkable accuracy the actual percentage of registered voters who *ought* to be in attendance at a town meeting *given* the size of the town where it is held. With this

---

49. A "base 10" logarithm will be used throughout the analysis.

50. For the statistical properties of this model, my reasoning for the particular combinations I used, and a suggestion for further research, see www.uvm.edu/~fbryan.

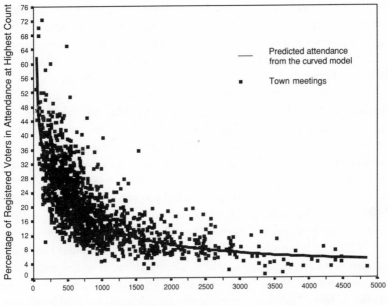

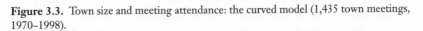

Figure 3.3. Town size and meeting attendance: the curved model (1,435 town meetings, 1970–1998).

information we may then score (or credit) a meeting for high or low attendance after taking into account town size. Accordingly, I created an attendance "effort" score for each of the 1,435 meetings in the sample. This score transforms the percentage of a town's registered voters at town meeting into a ratio of the actual percentage turnout at town meeting to the expected (according to the size-based curve established above) percentage turnout given the town's size. I call this the size-adjusted attendance measure (SAAM).

Thus, if the curved model of town meeting attendance predicted a 20 percent turnout for a town meeting based on the size of the town where it is held and the actual turnout was 20 percent, the SAAM would be 1.00. If the same town's actual turnout was 40 percent, the SAAM would be 2.00 because the town doubled its predicted attendance. On the other hand, if only 10 percent of the registered voters attended town meeting when 20 percent was predicted, the SAAM would be 0.50.

At the beginning of this chapter I briefly described the 1992 town meetings held in the Northeast Kingdom town of Newark and the Champlain valley town of Shelburne. This is a good time to reevaluate their attendance levels in light of the important refinement the SAAM contributes to assessments of town meeting attendance. Based simply on the percentage of their registered voters attending town meeting, Newark's attendance, which was 39.5 percent of its registered voters, was about twelve times Shelburne's, which was only 3.2 percent of its registered voters. In other words, Newark did hugely better than Shelburne on town meeting attendance.

This picture changes dramatically, however, when we compare the meetings in Newark and Shelburne on the size-adjusted attendance measure for 1992. When we consider the size handicap these towns labor under, Newark was predicted to have 30.9 percent attendance and Shelburne was predicted to have 6.3 percent. This means that Newark's 39.5 percent attendance *exceeded* expectations by a ratio of 1.28 to 1.00 (39.5/30.9), while Shelburne's 3.2 percent attendance *fell short* by a ratio of 0.51 to 1.00 (3.2/6.3). Newark's SAAM is only about 2.5 times better than Shelburne's, while its nonadjusted attendance was twelve times Shelburne's.

This makes sense. Since we know that size is a profound handicap to attendance, it seems only fair to take this into account as we judge the democratic performance of Shelburne's citizens. The value of the SAAM goes well beyond "fairness," however. As we begin to explore other variables that may account for the ups and downs of town meeting attendance across the 1,435 meetings in our sample, it is critical that we first control for size. The SAAM does this by substituting a measure of attendance that has already taken size into account. It is also helpful to ask questions such as, How are the education levels of the citizens of a town associated with town meeting attendance? without continually having to add the disclaimer "with the size of the town controlled."[51]

To summarize, we now know the answer to a question that generations of political scientists must (at some level) have wondered about: If we held a real democracy, how many would come? The answer is, on average 20.5 percent of the registered voters. But the answer does not tell the whole story. In small towns this percentage is much larger. In larger towns it is much

---

51. I am always on the lookout for data on which I can levy my formula for predicting attendance. I spotted one such case in the *New York Times* in 1987. In an excellent article on town meeting in Litchfield, New Hampshire, in 1987, the author reports that 148 registered voters from a list of 2,300 turned out on March 27. This is only 6.4 percent. Our size-based model predicts that a town with 2,300 voters should have 8.4 percent of them in attendance. Thus Litchfield's attendance was 2 percentage points below prediction, and its SAAM was therefore 0.76 (6.4/8.4). Matthew L. Wald, "Poignancy Presides at Town Meeting," *New York Times*, March 29, 1987, 20; another sample was reported in 1998 in *USA Today*, where the town of Peterborough was reported to have 196 in attendance. Since it had 4,200 registered voters, my model predicted 5.6 percent attendance, and Peterborough had 4.7 percent for a SAAM of 0.84. Fred Bayles, "Venerable Town Meeting Is Slowly Losing Its Voice," *USA Today*, April 14, 1998, 3A.

smaller. When we take into account its curvilinear properties, the size variable is extremely powerful, explaining 58 percent of the variance in attendance at town meeting. As far as citizen presence is concerned, real democracy works best in small towns. Of this there is no doubt.

Now comes a more difficult task—to uncover the 42 percent of the variance in town meeting attendance left unexplained. This unexplained variance will not be easy to flush out, for its components are subtler and more difficult to measure, and they share complex connections that are theoretically and empirically skittish.

Do night meetings have higher attendance than day meetings? Do towns with upscale populations do better than working-class towns? Do towns that have higher turnout at the polls have higher attendance at town meeting? Do towns that consistently vote Democratic have higher attendance than towns that consistently vote Republican? Does the political culture of the town matter? What about something as simple as weather conditions? In short, why did Newark have so many more citizens at its 1992 meeting than its size predicted? The good news is that we have hundreds of published studies on representative democracy that deal with similar questions to help direct the inquiry. The bad news is that for real democracy there are none.

...the task is not to construct ever-larger structures but to decompose the organizations that overwhelm us, and to seek less abstract and remote dependencies.

Sheldon S. Wolin

This epigraph is quoted in L.S. Stavrianos, *The Promise of the Coming Dark Age* (San Francisco: W. H. Freeman 1976), 83

4

Attendance

The Architecture of Governance

Real democracy works better in small places—dramatically better. Moreover, as we are about to discover, smallness fights off every variable I mobilized to intercede with this relationship. Many of these competitors have impressive empirical credentials of proven influence on other forms of democracy. Others seem logically connected to changes in town meeting attendance. Yet in addition to failing to topple town size from its lofty position, none of these variables demonstrate more than limited connections with real democracy on their own. In short, with the size-connected variance we discovered in the previous chapter secured, a long list of potentially important supplementary indicators accounted for less than ten percentage points of the explained variance remaining.

I treat these competing variables in two categories. The first (the subject of this chapter) contains elements associated with the structure or architecture of town meeting, such as the kind of voting system in use or when the town meeting is held. The second category of variables (the subject of the following chapter) comprises community life indicators such as the level of formal education of the town's citizens or the strength of the Democratic vote in the community. The relative weakness of the variables found in these two categories (town meeting architecture and community life) is best understood in the context of another variable, the presence of controversial issues before the town. Because this variable defies precise quantification, I will deal with it later in the book. But for now it is helpful to understand that the presence or absence of controversy soaks up a great deal of the remaining variance in town meeting attendance after size is controlled.

Issues before the town change from year to year. Variables associated with the architecture of town meeting and the socioeconomic and political life of the town, on the other hand, hold steady. By understanding how much of the variation in attendance at town meeting is associated with the coming and going of contentious issues from year to year within individual towns (and is thus separated from the influence of structural and community life variables), we can better appreciate why these more stable variables account for an amount of variance that, while important, is nevertheless limited.

Consider my hometown of Newbury, Vermont, the only town in the sample with a complete, year-to-year set of town meetings (see fig. 4.1, plot 1). Little of the dramatic drop in attendance at Newbury's town meeting between 1970 and 1971 could have been caused by population increase. Nor could the slow growth in the number of the town's registered voters cause the drop in attendance between 1982 and 1983 or the jump between 1987 and 1988. Other things that might matter to town meeting attendance, such as how the voting takes place (an architectural variable) or the percentage of college graduates in the citizenry (a community life variable), are even less likely to change radically from year to year within a single town.

This principle can be generalized into a rough surrogate for the impact of issues on town meeting democracy or (at a minimum) an explanation of why architectural and community life variables do not perform well. My sample of towns and their meetings between 1970 and 1998 has twenty-four back-to-back yearly comparisons: 1970 with 1971, 1971 with 1972, and so forth through 1997 with 1998. Fourteen of these year-to-year comparisons had at least twenty towns with meetings in the sample for both years of the comparison. For each of these fourteen back-to-back comparisons, the towns' attendance at town meeting in the first year of the comparison (for instance, 1979) was correlated with their attendance in the next year of the comparison (1980). This process was repeated for each of the fourteen "trials." In short, I used a town's attendance in one year to predict its attendance in the following year, and I did this fourteen times. The median percentage of variance explained (R^2) in the towns' attendance from one year to the next in these fourteen sets of comparisons was 0.68.[1] Plot 2 of figure 4.1

1. More efficient statistical methods are available to measure this variance, but efficiency with numbers (like efficiency in love) sometimes smothers what really matters. In our case it is seeing what happens in real towns with names we may come to know as they go about the year-in, year-out business of conducting their town meetings.

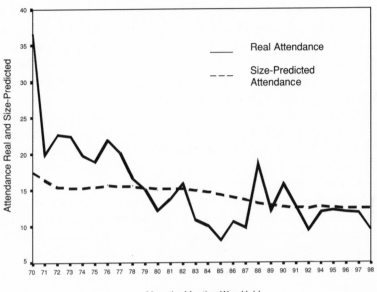

Plot 1: Real and Size-Predicted Attendance in Newbury, 1970-1998

Year the Meeting Was Held

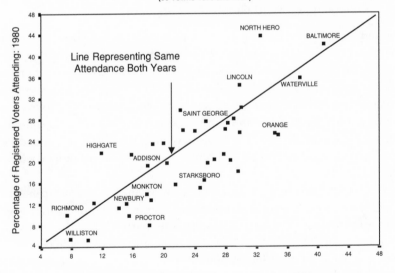

Plot 2: Attendance at Town Meeting: Subsequent Years Same Towns
(36 Towns 1979 and 1980)

Percentage of Registered Voters Attending: 1979

Figure 4.1. Year-to-year variance in town meeting attendance.

demonstrates this with the year-to-year comparison whose strength most closely approximates the median. The solid line represents the prediction if each town had exactly the same percentage of registered voters at town meeting in 1980 as it did in 1979. Thus Starksboro had significantly higher attendance in 1979 than in 1980, while North Hero had more in 1980 than in 1979. But most of the towns are like Newbury, St. George, and Waterville. Their attendances were about the same both years.

Since a year-to-year comparison of meetings within the same town shows (roughly) that all contextual variables (town meeting structure, community life, *and* town size) explain about 68 percent of the variance in town meeting attendance, and since we know that the relation of town size to attendance (size explains 58 percent of the variance in attendance) is real, no more than about ten percentage points of variance in attendance (68 percent minus 58 percent) is left to be explained by both structural and community life variables. Thus, with size out of the equation, architectural and community life variables have the potential to capture at most about 24 percent of the remaining 42 percentage points of the total variance in town meeting attendance.

Before I begin to explain how structural variables make use of this potential, it is important to put first things first.

Tough Sledding on Hard Ground

In Vermont, the first thing is the weather. It won't budge. True, many Vermonters (especially recent arrivals to the state) have tried wrapping their lives up in technological cocoons designed to keep planetary prerogatives from interrupting human activity. They don't work. The North Country sees to it. Many an upscale "sports utility vehicle" carefully equipped with four-wheel drive, positive traction, and antilock breaks ends up pastured in the snow in a curveside meadow. To know why some town meetings have higher attendance than others, it is best to begin with this most independent of independent variables.

As winter slips back across the border into Canada around town meeting day, several things happen in northern New England. None of them are good. As the weather turns warmer, the temperature constantly oscillates across the freezing point. The cold but sunny days of February give way to clouds and precipitation. The frost inches upward to the surface of the earth, taking with it everything in its path and signaling the beginning of Vermont's fifth season—mud season. On the gravel and dirt of Vermont's "back" roads (which make up most of the roads in the state), the mud is pervasive. It waylays school buses. It mocks the four-wheel drive. It sasses newcomers. Paved roads escape the mud, but not the frost. "Frost heaves," nature's own speed bumps, become asphalt catapults at speeds over thirty miles an hour.

But you can't count on the frost. The state can be hard as a rock in early March when spring is "late." Or the twisting of the planet toward the sun may bring the worst snowstorm of the winter, called by meteorologist David Ludlum the "crown of winter storm." To reach several town meetings that fell in the 1971 sample, for example, my students had to cross a gap in the eastern range of the Green Mountains named "Orange Heights." There a little town named Orange is nestled in a granite wrinkle just below the place where the highway reaches the height of the land. Eighty-eight inches of snow were on the ground in the town of Orange that day—more than seven feet. Down in the Winooski valley to the west, Montpelier had about five feet of what Vermonters call "level deep" snow.[2]

All in all, if one were to try to imagine the most difficult conditions for highway travel anywhere in America any time of the year, it would be hard to beat Vermont in early March. Moreover, attending town meeting means driving somewhere, parking the car, going into a building for three or four hours, and then coming out of that building to God knows what. Thus the weather has far more potential to inhibit real democracy than to interfere with the voting act.[3]

Judging what the conditions were on town meeting day in any particular town, however, is tricky business. The state is split north to south by a chain of mountains. Elsewhere are swirls of lesser peaks, and here and there a stately monadnock.[4] In the west the weather is affected by the great basin of Lake Champlain, which lies flat on the sunrise side of New York's high Adirondacks. In the east the Connecticut River valley rolls southward between the Green Mountains of Vermont and the still loftier White Mountains of New Hampshire. In between the lake and the river and the mountains are

2. At 1:30 in the afternoon the students recorded the highest attendance of the day at 88. This was 29 percent of the towns 305 registered voters. Of these, 30 (19 men and 11 women) participated at least once. J. Guy Isabelle and Larry Spargo, "The 1972 Comparative Town Meeting Study: Town of Orange," Burlington, University of Vermont, Real Democracy Data Base, March 1972.

3. Now and then the start of a town meeting is delayed by bad weather. This from the minutes of a meeting in Charlotte in 1985: "The Annual Town Meeting of Charlotte was called to order by Moderator Gordon Sprigg at 10:00 a.m., March 5th, 1985, at the Town Hall in Charlotte, Vermont. A short recess was immediately called because of bad weather. The meeting resumed at 10:15 a.m." Town of Charlotte, Hazel Prindle, Town Clerk, "Abstract of the Town and School District Meetings, March 5, 1985," *Town Report*, year ending December 1985.

4. This commonly understood name in Vermont is the Abenaki word for "mountain that stands alone."

Perhaps that is why the framework variables of our political system (at any level) are rarely paroled from the dungeons they were placed in during the behavioral revolution. Still, framework is fundamental—especially as we look at a political process like real democracy for the first time.

The question for us is theoretically fresh: What are the *design* factors that may limit or expand the number of people who practice real democracy by attending town meeting? I shall investigate four. The first is when the town meeting is held, during the day or at night. The second is whether electoral processes are in place that allow for voting without being present for discussion at the meeting. Third is the way school district meetings fit into the process on town meeting day. Finally comes the size of the town's meeting place itself.

Night Meeting/Day Meeting

Many Vermont towns have decided to hold their meetings at night instead of during the day. Although some very small places like Walden and Victory hold their meeting on the night of town meeting day, the great majority of night meetings are held the previous evening. Night meetings presumably give many more people a chance to attend, especially working people. Unfortunately, town meeting day is not a holiday in Vermont. Thus hourly wage earners are more disadvantaged than professional people, who have greater latitude to adjust their workday. Night meetings, on the other hand, may be more difficult for senior citizens. Night meetings also compete with what most Americans believe to be leisure time or, as the television networks call it, "prime time." Whatever the merits of the argument for changing the time of the town meeting from the traditional meeting on "the first Tuesday after the first Monday in March" to the Monday evening of the first Monday in March, such a move has long been touted by reformers as a good thing.

But how good? On the face of it, Monday night meetings seem to have precisely the opposite effect from what was intended. The average attendance for the 1,085 meetings in the sample that were held during the day was 21.6 percent of the registered voters. The 346 towns that held their meetings on Monday night averaged 17.3 percent. This seems to mean that the average town would lose 4.3 percentage points of its attendance if it shifted from Tuesday during the workday to a night meeting. This is 20 percent of its total attendance, a substantial loss.

But we know something very important about towns that hold their meetings at night. They tend to be larger towns like Shelburne rather than smaller towns like Newark and Athens. The average number of registered voters in towns we studied that held their meetings Monday night was 1,153. The average number of voters in the towns that held their meetings during the day on Tuesday was only 812. Could the relations between night meetings and lower attendance be spurious—that is, caused by the fact that larger towns, which are more apt to hold their meetings at night, have lower attendance because of their size, not because of their night meetings?

I divided the towns of the sample into seven categories that seem to make sense based on their size and then measured the average attendance at the town meetings of the towns in each category depending on whether the meetings were held during the day or at night. Irrespective of the time the meeting is held, as the size of the town increased the attendance at town meeting dropped like a rock. But the negative association between night meetings and attendance reappeared in somewhat reduced form within each category of town size.[8]

Statistical associations, however, do not prove causation. When one looks at those towns that switched their meeting times from day to night or vice versa, troubling inconsistencies emerge. Although 210 of the 237 towns in Vermont made it into the database, only 19 of these switched their meeting times between 1970 and 1998, and only 6 of the 19 had enough meetings clustering around the year of the switch to make comparisons reasonable. Only in Brighton, the old railroad town in the Kingdom, did a drop in attendance seem clearly related to a change to night meetings. Even there one wonders if the relatively high attendance in the 1970s (which may have been associated with an influx of counterculture groups from "away")[9] produced the "drop" in the latter half of the 1980s and the 1990s after night meetings had been adopted. In Lincoln, on the other hand, switching to night meetings seemed associated (given a few years for the change to take hold) with a solid *increase* in size-controlled attendance.

The town of Alburg borders Canada on an island in Lake Champlain. It is a Catholic, French working-class town an hour or so from Montreal. Norwich is a traditional upscale New England Protestant valley town on the Connecticut River five minutes from Dartmouth College and two hours from Boston. In the spring the people in Alburg give up ice fishing and go to

8. The correlation between attendance and night meetings (−.18) is reduced only to −.16 under controls for town size. The correlation between attendance and town size, remember, is −.76. Under controls for when the meeting is held, it remained at −.76.

9. Brighton was just down the road from the progressive "Earth People's Park" and the home of the traditional Northeast Kingdom Community Church. These two organizations raised some hell in the Kingdom, but on balance they were a healthy expression of Vermont's rural, human-scale, liberal tradition.

spearing eels. The people of Norwich rake their lawns. Both towns changed to night meetings and may have increased attendance—at least for a while. Yet even here the data are ambiguous. Alburg's increase was small and didn't last long. Norwich's improvement could have been an extension of rising attendance already under way.

Finally, in two instances towns reversed the process and went from night to day meetings. The ski resort town of Stowe, which had tried night meetings beginning in the late 1970s with mixed results, went back to day meetings in 1984. At first attendance failed to improve. Later on (in the 1990s) Stowe's attendance did increase dramatically. But I suspect this happened because the town became a battleground in the war between development and environmentalism that has gripped Vermont since the late 1960s. Grand Isle, another town on the Lake Champlain islands, returned to day meetings in 1994. Early results show no effect on the downward slide in size-controlled attendance Grand Isle has been experiencing since the 1970s.[10]

The Australian Ballot

Some of the inconsistency in the relation between when the meeting is held and town meeting attendance is explained by a second structural factor, the voting system, in particular the "Australian ballot." The Australian ballot is simply a written ballot, prepared ahead of time to allow people to vote on questions before the town or for election of town officers without going to a town meeting and waiting for issues to reach the floor.

The Australian ballot has been the object of the progressives' passion over the past half century. As a hedge on the bet that real democracy is good democracy, it reads: presence isn't enough; voting in private outside the context of the meeting is also necessary. Over the years, I have sat through many a debate on the issue.[11] They nearly always boil down to quantity versus

10. In 1988 the town of Grand Isle experienced a poignant (perhaps pungent is a better word) example of the frustrations town meeting democracies face in Vermont because of regulation by the state. The *Burlington Free Press* reported: "The Grand Isle Elementary School doesn't measure up very well to state standards, according to the Public School Approval Report. Along with a laundry list of requirements . . . state committee members apparently didn't much care for the fact the school is located in a rural area. They found 'the smells from the adjoining farms distracting to the educational process.'" This from a state government that has been touting its farms and lamenting their decline for fifty years. "Barnyard Smell," *Burlington Free Press*, September 4, 1988, 5E.

11. One of the best days of the year for me has been returning in early March to collect the data for my hometown of Newbury. I missed a series of years after I realized that my citizenship in Starksboro precluded such indulgences. In recent years, however, Starksboro has gone to a Saturday meeting, and now I can attend both. I was in Newbury for the 1977 meeting. The town

quality—more people will participate in a less meaningful way if the Australian ballot is adopted. These discussions sometimes become classic contests between liberal and communitarian ideals.[12] Of the meetings in the database, 55 percent used the Australian ballot in one way or another. Most towns that use it, however, limit it to the election of town officers.

Reason suggests that the Australian ballot will lower attendance at town meeting. If you are interested in the race for town selectman, for instance, but little else, you can stop at the polls, cast your vote for town officers, and be gone. The more items that appear on the ballot, the more decision making can be done without actually attending town meeting.[13] The attendance at the highest count for the 787 meetings in the database that used the Australian ballot was 15.6 percent of the registered voters. For the 647 meetings that did not use the Australian ballot the average attendance was 26.6 percent. This 70 percent increase is dramatic and in the expected direction.

But again there are complications. These complications help explain why night meetings do not draw attendance any better than they do. Once

---

debated the Australian ballot issue (for officers only) for only ten minutes, from 2:36 to 2:46 p.m., and approved it with a voice vote. That was the year Barbara Welch defeated Annie Murphy for town clerk 111 to 49. This vote took place by a secret ballot held during the meeting after nominations had been made from the floor. This race became the last contested vote for a town officer nominated from the floor during a town meeting in Newbury. The town also voted "to exclude the operation and construction of commercial nuclear reactors or any other nuclear facilities, and the transportation, storage, and disposal of radioactive waste from such reactors in and on the land, air, and water in the town." Nuclear materials used for medical purposes were exempted. The vote was 92 to 39. Melissa Bryan and Frank Bryan, "The 1977 Comparative Town Meeting Study: Town of Newbury," Burlington, University of Vermont, Real Democracy Data Base, March 1977.

12. Debates on the question of "going to" the Australian ballot are often long and heated. Although they are carried on by everyday people in the most humble of settings, they are usually well reasoned. If the oratory is not refined, it contains an eloquence of its own—a mixture of Yankee brevity and rural pragmatism.

13. In my youth when Newbury voted each year whether to go "wet" or "dry" by means of the Australian ballot at town meeting, the local grocery store owner (the town had only one store) could always be seen entering the town hall about 11 a.m., soon after his part-time helper (my neighbor, who was married to the road commissioner) arrived to spell him at the counter for a few minutes. He was "from away" (New York City), and his arrival in Newbury doubled the Irish Catholic population. The storekeeper was a good citizen of the town, liked and respected by all. But he never stayed at town meeting. He came. He voted by Australian ballot. He left. In fact, he had seldom even gone to town meeting before the year when forces for good in the community had staged a "still hunt" and gunned down his right to have a second-class liquor license. Newbury had voted "dry"! The Beer, Ale and Wine sign disappeared from the store window. And down went his earnings. Way down. Not because people bought a lot of booze in Newbury, but because when you went shopping only once a week (as most families did then) it didn't make much sense to shop where you couldn't buy *any*. The dry vote damned near did him in. But he managed to survive the year, and he never missed another Australian ballot on the wet or dry question. We don't vote on the liquor question anymore.

again, town size is directly involved. The degree to which the Australian ballot is employed is closely associated with both town size and whether town meetings are held in the evening. All but a handful of towns that meet in the evening do so on Monday evening[14] and use the Australian ballot during the day on Tuesday at least for the election of town officers. A small number of towns meeting Monday evening use the Australian ballot on Tuesday for other matters as well, especially money items. A very few have all the discussion Monday night and all the voting on Tuesday.

Many towns, however, use the Australian ballot throughout the day on Tuesday (while the town meeting is in session), but only for the election of officers. Since the polling place is also the meeting place, people who choose to vote only and not take part in the meeting itself come and go throughout the day. State law also prohibits any discussion of Australian ballot items "from the floor" while voting is taking place. This means that a zoning ordinance, for instance, that is on the warning to be voted on by Australian ballot cannot be discussed at a town meeting that is held while the polls are open on Tuesday. The following is an example of a warning in a town having nearly all issues on Australian ballot:

> The legal voters of the Town of Randolph, the Randolph Police District, the Randolph Water District and the Randolph Sewer District are hereby warned to meet at the Chandler Music Hall, Main Street in Randolph, Tuesday, March 7, 2000 at 10:00 A.M. to vote on the Articles herein set forth. **Articles 1 through 32 are to be voted by Australian ballot.** The polls open at 10:00 A.M. and close at 7:00 P.M. Polls will be located at the Gallery, Chandler Music Hall, Main Street in Randolph. **Articles 33 through 38 are to be called for consideration from the floor** at the business meeting of said legal voters which is hereby warned to convene at 10:00 A.M. Tuesday, March 7, 2000 at the Chandler Music Hall, Main Street, Randolph, Vermont. A Public Hearing and Information Meeting on the Town Budget and warned items will be held on Tuesday, February 29, 2000 at 7:00 P.M. in the Studio, Room SR3 of the Randolph Area Vocational Center.[15]

Sometimes issues that by law should not be discussed because voting is going on at the same time are discussed anyway in more or less indirect ways. If the matter gets too direct, the moderator will most usually cut off

---

14. In the entire sample of 1,435 town meetings, only 13 were held Tuesday evening. None of the towns with Tuesday evening meetings used the Australian ballot.

15. Town of Randolph, *Town Report*, year ending December 1999, 2 (boldface in original).

discussion. If the moderator is new to the job and forgets, a voter may yell out, "We're not supposed to talk about that, are we?" (The "are we?" is a kindness to the moderator.) When this kind of challenge arises, the oldtimers usually mutter to themselves about the stupidity of "the state" or "Montpelier," while newcomers may click their tongues at this most insidious denial of the democratic impulse. One of my students once reported that a person she identified as a "flatlander like me" rose on such an occasion to make a pious speech about the value of open discussion and the evils of "censorship," to the silent amusement (followed by patience and then boredom) of the voters assembled. Often, wrote this student, "even the best intentioned speakers have trouble finding an opening in their own rhetoric in which to shut themselves up."

WITNESS

BALLOT DEBATE IN RANDOLPH

The minutes for the town of Randolph held on Tuesday, March 2, 1999, contain the following under article 37, the "New Business" article. (Articles 2–32 were Australian ballot items, and articles 33–36 had been quickly resolved.)

Article 37. To do any other business proper to come before this meeting. The due date for payment of property taxes has not been set. Carolyn Tonelli made a motion to set the due date as November 9, 1999. The motion was seconded and passed by unanimous voice vote.

Dick Drysdale [a local newspaper publisher] asked if there could be any discussion about the articles, whether they were properly warned.

Lew Whitaker expressed disappointment when the Town voted to go to Australian ballot. He felt a lot of discussion was lost in the process. The pro's and con's of discussion in addition to the written materials distributed would help people make better decisions when voting. He would like to go back to the old Town Meeting.

Warren Preston commented that he had worked on getting the Australian ballot and has seen an increase in the number of people voting by ballot. He also noted that there also has been a decrease in discussion. His suggestion was for everyone to contact their legislators to make a law so there can be discussion of issues on Australian ballot.

Carolyn Tonelli, Selectboard Chair, told the audience that discussion was allowed on these issues at the informational meeting which was held last week. No one came to that meeting. She urged people to attend the informational meeting.

Horace Puglisi wanted to know if there could be discussion on any part of Articles 2–32. The response was that there could not be discussion on these articles.

Douglas Shane felt there should be more advance warning of meetings. Meetings are warned as far in advance as is possible and the warning is posted in 3 public places (Town Offices, Floyd's Store, East Randolph Country Store) as required by State Statute. . . .

Terri Burgee did not understand why discussion could not be done at both the informational meeting and town meeting.

Mr. Whitaker would like to see discussion, not merely voting by Australian ballot.

Charles Russell commented that the intent of the Australian ballot was not to cut off discussion.

Dick Drysdale felt that the Town of Randolph, as a sovereign body, should overrule the statutes and discuss the Australian ballot articles. He made a motion to overrule the Moderator, to ignore the state statutes and to permit discussion. The motion was seconded.

Chris Recchia asked if by discussing the articles this would invalidate the vote.

Peter Nowlan [the town moderator] read the statute to the audience which states that Annual Meeting can be held on any of the 3 days preceding Town Meeting Day and you would be allowed to have discussion, but not if the meeting and the balloting are on the same day.

Mr. Drysdale asked the audience to not be timid and vote to overrule the moderator.

Mr. Russell commented that this is a democracy and the majority rules.

Mr. Adams voiced concern that taking this action might invalidate the vote. He also commented that you can't violate the statutes—it is up to the legislature to change the statutes.

Mr. Wright asked if the meeting had been held the night before if there could be discussion.

Mr. Preston suggested we close the meeting and then stay to have a discussion.

Mr. Nowlan ruled that the motion to overrule the moderator was out of order.

Mr. Whitaker was confused about whether or not there could be discussion on the same day. Mr. Nowlan responded and clarified by citing the statute.

Wendy Wells asked what was the date of the statute.

Mr. Drysdale asked for clarification for why Mr. Nowlan overruled the motion. Mr. Nowlan answered stating the decision was based on his interpretation of the statute.

Randolph Town Report[16]

A typical warning for a Tuesday town meeting using the Australian ballot for the election of officers reads only as follows: "The legal voters of

16. Ibid., 10–11.

the Town of Newfane, Vermont, are hereby warned and notified to meet at Williamsville Hall, in Williamsville, VT on Tuesday, March 3, 1992 at 9:00 a.m. to transact the following business of the Town. (Voting for Town Officers will be by Australian ballot. The polls will be open from 9:00 a.m. to 7:00 p.m.)"[17]

Many towns do not use the Australian ballot at all. These are called "traditional" town meetings, and all voting (for officers and all other issues) takes place as each warning item reaches the floor. Traditional town warnings often consist of one sentence: "The legal voters of the Town and School District of Roxbury are hereby notified and warned to meet in the Town Hall in Roxbury on Tuesday, March 6, 1984 at (ten) 10 o'clock in the forenoon, E.S.T., to act on the following articles."[18]

In the battle for supremacy in predicting town meeting attendance among multiple kinds of Australian ballot procedures, varying town sizes, and differing times the town meeting is held, town size again wins hands down.[19] But the Australian ballot does reduce attendance on its own as well. The percentage differentials in town meeting attendance *within* levels of town size indicate that ballot use has an important negative influence on attendance independent of town size, especially in the four groups of towns with fewer than a thousand registered voters (see fig. 4.2).

When the Australian ballot is used and size is not controlled, the median-sized town with its 684 registered voters is predicted to have 107 in attendance. Without the ballot the data indicate it should have 181 in attendance, a gain of 73 registered voters, or nearly 70 percent over what it would have if it used the ballot. But when the size-adjusted attendance measure (SAAM) is applied to the data, this gap is reduced sharply. A town with 684 registered voters is predicted to have 148 in attendance without the Australian ballot and 128 in attendance with it. Abandoning the ballot would

17. Town of Newfane, *Town Report*, year ending December 1991. Williamsville, Vermont, is a little village in the town of Newfane. It gets its name from William H. Williams, who was born in Chester, Massachusetts, in 1776. An orphan, he "bound out" to a farmer and then a cloth-dressing manufacturer. He arrived in Newfane in 1797, and by his death in 1866 he had become an important citizen operating several cloth mills and carding mills and a gristmill at what is now called Williamsville. Esther Monroe Swift, *Vermont Place-Names* (Brattleboro, VT: Stephen Greene Press, 1977), 496–497.

18. Town of Roxbury, *Town Report*, year ending December 1983.

19. The partial correlation coefficient (which gauges the relation between two variables controlling for one or more other variables) between size and attendance when the dummy variable for the presence of the Australian ballot is controlled is −.68, only a mild reduction from the −.76 first-order correlation coefficient. The partial correlation coefficient between the Australian ballot and attendance when size is controlled is −.29, down from a first-order coefficient of −.54.

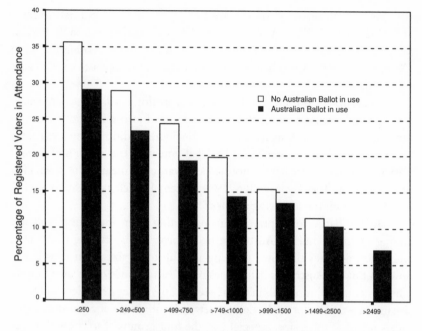

Town Size in Cohorts of Registered Voters

Figure 4.2. Attendance by Australian ballot use and town size (1,434 meetings, 1970–1998).

therefore produce an increase of 20 registered voters at the meeting, not 73 as was estimated when size was not controlled. This is an attendance gain of 16 percent, not 70 percent.

Nevertheless, even with size controlled the Australian ballot remains a powerful inhibitor of attendance. The loss of 20 voters a year when a town switches to the Australian ballot is a hefty chunk of the 148 voters the meeting might otherwise have. Moreover, the Australian ballot deals the day/night variable a serious blow. A good portion of the drop-off in attendance at night meetings remaining after town size is controlled seems to be caused by the use of the Australian ballot in so many night meetings.

To summarize, the worst case for town meeting attendance is a Monday night meeting called for discussion only with all (or nearly all) voting by Australian ballot on Tuesday.[20] The SAAM for these kinds of meetings is

20. In a few cases the town tries to hold a "discussion" meeting early in the morning on Tuesday and then open the polls for Australian ballot voting on all the issues throughout the day. This was the case in Randolph in the "Witness" above. One of my students, Justin Smith, attended the Burke town meeting in 1997, which opened at 9:00 a.m. and then closed at 10:00 a.m. for

Table 4.1. Town Meeting Structure and Size-Controlled Attendance

Type of Meeting Structure	N	SAAM
Traditional day meetings; no Australian ballot	610	1.13
Night meetings; no Australian ballot	37	1.09
Day meetings; Australian ballot	474	1.01
Night meetings; Australian ballot next day (officers only)	256	0.94
Night meetings; Australian ballot next day (all articles)*	57	0.85

* Includes four Saturday meetings with all articles by Australian ballot the following Tuesday.

only 0.85. (These meetings have about 85 in attendance for every 100 their size would predict.) The SAAM improves to 0.94 when the budget and other substantive matters are resolved by vote during the Monday night meeting and only the election of town officers occurs on Tuesday. Size-controlled attendance improves still more, to 1.01, when town meeting is held on Tuesday and the Australian ballot is used for the election of town officers throughout the day. If all matters including the election of officers are voted from the floor at a town meeting held Tuesday night, the SAAM improves to 1.09. Finally, town meeting attendance is best when the meeting is held during the day on Tuesday with no Australian ballot in use at all. In this situation the SAAM rises to 1.13, indicating that the meeting had 113 percent of its size-predicted attendance at the town meeting—113 attenders for every 100 predicted. (See table 4.1.)

School Meeting/Town Meeting

The third structural consideration brings the content of discussion directly into play. Unlike most other states, Vermont allows its citizens to govern their school systems as they do their towns, directly in open meetings. As in other states, however, Vermont's school districts are separate legal entities. Traditionally the "town meeting" and the "school meeting" were one—warned

---

Australian ballot voting on all warning items throughout the day. He says in his report: "The meeting had a really bad turnout because people could show up any time between 10 a.m. and 7 p.m. to vote, and did not have to be present at the meeting in order to vote. This was disappointing to watch because those who did make the effort to attend the meeting engaged in some meaningful discussion and were much more informed about each warning item than those who just showed up and voted. Burke, by changing to the Australian ballot format, got rid of everything that was good about town meeting." Justin, who lived in Burke, was aided in his work at the meeting by his father, Donald Smith, and Dan Jackson. Justin Smith, Dan Jackson, and Donald Smith, "The 1997 Comparative Town Meeting Study: Town of Burke," Burlington, University of Vermont, Real Democracy Data Base, March 1997. These kinds of meetings have the poorest attendance of all.

together and held at the same time. Over the past half century, but especially in the past three decades, many towns in Vermont have moved the school district's annual meeting to another day entirely so that almost no issues involving this most local of local concerns come up for discussion at town meeting.

The reasons for this are partly technical, partly political. At town meeting time in early March, towns seldom know the amount of supplemental money they will receive from the state; they do not find out until later in the spring. It makes sense to wait for this information before voting on local school budgets. My data and the minutes of the town meetings themselves also indicate that after a particularly long and tiresome meeting (where school and town are combined), citizens will suggest moving the school meeting to another day.

Yet sometimes mischief is afoot. Many educational leaders view the town meeting as a thorn in the side of sound education policy. Town meetings, they reason, are more likely to be attended by generalists (citizens) or, worse yet, angry taxpayers with no children in the school. It would be better for education, they believe, to keep the school gathering small and focused. This could be done, for instance, by meeting on an evening in the good weather of early May. The farmers (who often are sensitive to property taxes) would be busy with spring work, usually until dark. A society thawing out after a long winter's cold would be less apt to give up such an evening to go inside and debate school issues.[21]

Whatever the intent, one might imagine that a town meeting with school issues embedded in the warning along with roads and social services would have higher attendance than a town meeting where school issues were completely absent, especially given that the great preponderance of locally raised taxes in Vermont goes to education. The towns' solutions to the school meeting/town meeting problem take several forms. In our sample of 1,435 town meetings, 583 had school meetings conducted on the same day, either directly before or after the town meeting. Another cluster of school meetings (343) occurred by interrupting the town meeting, conducting the school meeting, and then returning to finish the town meeting. My data in

21. In fact, however, this strategy may have proved counterproductive to education interests. Smaller, single-issue meetings are as vulnerable in hard times as they are secure in good times. Although in general the movement to separate town meetings from school meetings continues, several towns have moved back to the traditional practice of having town and school meetings on the same day. It may be that Vermonters who came into Vermont from "away" in the 1960s and 1970s with left-leaning political views now (with twenty Vermont winters under their belts) are leading their communities back toward democracy in education.

combination with the minutes from a town meeting in the Champlain valley
town of Charlotte indicate, for instance, that in 1985:

> [At 12:08 p.m. by my data the meeting was in the middle of article 6.]
> Will the Town adopt the Selectmen's Budget of $488,046.00 for the fiscal
> year July 1, 1985, to June 30, 1986, less anticipated revenues? [They had
> just voted down an additional $20,000 for an ambulance by a "show of
> hands" 53 to 59 when] the Moderator called a recess until 1:00 p.m. and
> discussion of Article 6 to continue after the Town School District meeting.
> [At 1:02 p.m. by my data the school meeting officially opened as
> warned in the Town Report:] The legal voters of the Charlotte Town
> School District are hereby notified and warned to meet at the Charlotte
> Town Hall..., at one o'clock in the afternoon on Tuesday, 5 March
> 1985.... [After the resolution of article 7 (the last article) of the school
> meeting's warning ("To transact any other business thought proper when
> met"), the minutes report:] The Town School Meeting was adjourned at
> approximately 2:30 p.m. [actually it was 2:50 p.m.] and the Town Meeting
> was resumed.[22]

Other town meetings (295 in the sample) make no formal distinction
between the town and school district in the way they conduct their local
governance. School items simply appear in the warning of the town meeting
and are considered in order as they appear. Year after year in my town of
Starksboro the warning tells us that school business is part of the town meeting
with typical formality: "The legal voters of the Town of Starksboro and the
Town *School District* [emphasis mine] in the County of Addison and State of
Vermont are hereby notified and warned to meet at the Robinson School
multi-purpose room within said Starksboro on Tuesday the second day of
March A.D.[23] 1993 to transact the following business viz." Only two of the
fourteen articles that follow are directly related to school business, but one
of them is the budget. ("Article 8: Will the voters adopt for the support of
the Starksboro School District the proposed budget for the ensuing year
[FY 1993–1994], being *$1,118,915* less receipts, with the remainder being

22. Hazel Prindle, Town Clerk, Town of Charlotte, "Abstract of the Town and School
District Meetings 1985," *Town Report*, year ending December 1984; John K. Butler, Ann K.
Byington, Kristin Camp, and Craig Garland, "The 1985 Comparative Town Meeting Study, Town
of Charlotte," Burlington, University of Vermont, Real Democracy Data Base, March 1985.

23. As long as the people of the town consider what we do of sufficient historical
importance to justify a notation to future historians that the meeting took place *after* the death of
Christ, I am confident that our democracy is alive and well.

raised by taxes on a tax rate set by the Selectmen according to State Statute?")
With the school budget as subject matter, almost anything related to the
schools can be discussed.

Finally, some towns (217) have separated the two meetings completely.
A handful of these schedule their school meetings within a week or two of the
town meeting, but most hold the school meeting in May or early June when
it is reasonably certain the legislature will have allotted the all-important
financial assistance to the school districts.

The predicted effects of the presence of school issues on town meeting
attendance are straightforward. Meetings mixing school and town business in
a single meeting should have the highest attendance, followed by those that
hold a separate school meeting embedded *within* the town meeting, followed
by separate but sequential meetings held the same day, followed finally by
town meetings with no school meeting at all scheduled for town meeting day.

In general the data behaved as expected. When controls for size are
introduced by the SAAM, a town meeting in a town whose size predicts that
100 registered voters will attend will have 107 in attendance if school issues
are placed directly on the town meeting warning, 105 if they are considered separately at a meeting conducted during an adjournment of the town
meeting, 97 if two separate meetings are held in sequence, and 90 when the
school meeting is scheduled for another day completely, leaving the townspeople no educational matters to resolve on town meeting day. All in all, the
difference between a meeting that integrates school business into the town
meeting warning and one that has no school business at all considered on
town meeting day is substantial—a loss of about 17 voters in attendance for
every 100 predicted from its size.

When the type of school meeting and use of the Australian ballot are
compared, each affects attendance at town meeting independent of the other,
although the Australian ballot has the stronger effect. Switching to the Australian ballot will cost a meeting 13 attenders if it has school business to do
on town meeting day and 20 attenders if it does not. Switching the school
meeting to another day, however, will cost the town meeting only 8 attenders
if it is using the Australian ballot and 15 attenders if it is not. Overall, the
combination of the two variables makes quite a difference. If a town changes
its school meeting to another day and begins to use the Australian ballot
for its town meeting, it will lose about a quarter of the attendance generally
achieved by towns that did not make similar changes.

Overall, however, the dominance of the Australian ballot is demonstrated by a stepwise regression equation that adds night meetings to the
school meeting and Australian ballot mix. The ballot and school variables

explain all the difference that is seemingly caused from a shift from a day to a night meeting, and the school variable itself adds only a single percentage point of variance explained after the town size and Australian ballot variables enter the regression equation. The end result is that size explains 58 percent of the variance, the Australian ballot an additional 4 percent, and school meetings an additional 1 percent.

Town Halls and Church Basements

The places where the people gather on town meeting day vary almost as much as the scratch and claw geography that surrounds them. In Brandon in 1987 the people met in the modern auditorium of Otter Valley Union High School. In Braintree they met in the West Braintree town hall, described by my students as "small and very *old*" (emphasis in the original).[24] They met in the elementary school gym in Cambridge in 1992. In Calais they met in a "quaint little church that had been converted to a town hall some time ago,"[25] in Ira in the cellar of the Ira Baptist Church, in Washington at "the small elementary school, that looked like a converted chicken barn,"[26] in Tinmouth at the Grange hall, and in Bolton in the fire station. Up on the Canadian border in the town of Troy, one of the students described the meeting place as a "tiny bingo building."[27]

No matter where they were situated or in what kind of building the citizens met, all these meeting places shared one feature. They were too small— far too small—to hold all the registered voters of the town had these voters decided to attend. Most were too small to hold even a majority of the town's registered voters. In fact, the meeting place of the average town meeting in our sample of 1,435 would have to increase its capacity by 50 percent to do so. The situation is often even worse. In a typical town meeting in my old hometown of Newbury (1996), for instance, 158 townspeople were in attendance at its highest point in 1996. At that time 47 seats were empty and 13 people were standing. If those standing had sat down, 34 empty seats would have remained. Thus, 192 seats were available. But Newbury had 1,302 registered

24. Nicole Bourassa, John Cain, Adelaide Haskell, and C. Tasha Sprague, "The 1987 Comparative Town Meeting Study: Town of Braintree," Burlington, University of Vermont, Real Democracy Data Base, March 1987.

25. Sara Eastman, "Town Meeting Essay, Calais 1992," Burlington, University of Vermont, March 1992.

26. Eileen Riley, "Washington 1992," Burlington, University of Vermont, March 1992.

27. It was actually held at the Sacred Heart parish hall. Tom Butler, "Town Meeting: A Democracy? Troy 1992," Burlington, University of Vermont, March 1992.

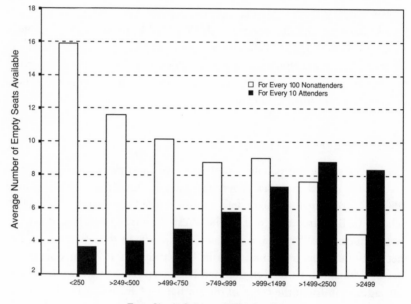

Town Size in Cohorts of Registered Voters

Figure 4.3. Empty seats available for attenders and nonattenders (1,369 town meetings, 1970–1998).

voters in 1996. To accommodate even half of these, Newbury would have had to more than triple its seating capacity.

Bigger towns lack the most space. In the smallest towns of our sample (those with fewer than 250 voters), an average of 16 seats were available for every 100 registered voters *not* in attendance. Meeting places in the largest towns (those with over 2,500 voters) had only 4 seats available for every 100 registered voters not in attendance. But while town meetings in the bigger towns were potentially more crowded, the meetings in the smaller towns were actually more crowded.

The data (see fig. 4.3) also show that in the 132 meetings held in the towns of fewer than 250 registered voters, an average of fewer than 4 empty seats were available for every 10 attenders. In the meetings with more than 2,500 voters in town, 8.4 empty seats existed for each person in attendance. Crowding *increases* as the number of voters potentially available to make the hall crowded *decreases*. One might argue, therefore, that if the lack of adequate meeting space inhibits attendance anywhere, it is in the smallest towns. On the other hand, it may be that the perception of potential crowding in the bigger towns lowers attendance and thus crowding. In any event, people go to town meeting when their presence counts more, even if there is typically less space for them to sit and conditions will be more crowded.

To this point we know that the most important thing Vermonters could do to improve attendance at their town meetings is to dramatically reduce the size of the towns where they are held. The analysis in this chapter makes it clear that the great amount of variance in attendance accounted for by town size leaves little room for other variables to come into play. Still, because on average town meeting attendance is low (20.5 percent), small improvements have stronger relative effects. The most important improvement would be to eliminate the Australian ballot. Night meetings should be abandoned, because bad weather reduces attendance much more at night meetings than at meetings held during the day. The data also show that attendance could be increased somewhat if school meetings were reunited with town meetings. At this time, expanding the size of the meeting places would probably produce no improvement.

It is now time to turn from the relation between attendance and the way meetings are held and explore the relation between attendance and the kinds of communities (the life of the community) where the meetings are held. Can we match particular kinds of communities with particular levels of attendance? If so, does this relation hold when other variables like town size and the Australian ballot are controlled? Do particular kinds of communities tend to adopt the Australian ballot, which then generates its own impact on attendance independent of the nature of community? Thus the investigation becomes more complicated. It also becomes more interesting.

One cannot help wondering how much the geography of Greece helped to stimulate this vision [of the small polis] for that land of mountains, valleys, islands and the sea provided magnificent natural boundaries for each community. . . . it is only the barest poetic license to say that nature herself suggested the small, autonomous city-state.

Robert Dahl

The epigraph is from Robert A. Dahl, "The City in the Future of Democracy," *American Political Science Review* 61 (December 1967): 953–970. For insights on community and Athenian democracy see also L. B. Carter, *The Quiet Athenian* (Oxford: Clarendon Press, 1986). Dahl suggests further that it was this "hint from nature" that helps explain why "a people to whom Prometheus himself had given the first elements of civilization were bound to elaborate among themselves the ideal form of the harsher and very often uglier reality they knew so intimately."

5

Attendance

The Context of Community

One day in the summer of 1760 Jacob Bailey, a soldier in the service of the Crown, was walking overland from Canada to a town in Massachusetts called Newbury. His journey home led him down the Connecticut River valley. Just below the fall line where the waters turn deep and canoes no longer scrape bottom in August, he came upon a huge bend in the river. It turned out to be a half loop that snaked off east toward New Hampshire, veered south for about a half mile, and then headed back toward the Green Mountains of Vermont before once again bending south on its journey to the sea.

This is now called the "great oxbow." Immediately below it the river repeated itself on a smaller scale and created the "little oxbow." For ten thousand springtimes the water had rolled across the meadows within these huge bends as the river grew impatient and took the direct route south. Consequently there is no better soil in New England. Bailey knew it. In 1763 he returned to the region the Abenaki called *coos* (where the great pines grow), built a town, and named it Newbury after the place he had called home. It was in this same little village on the banks of this same deep-flowing river of dreams that I grew up.

In 1969 I returned home with Kenneth Bruno, one of my students at St. Michael's College, to test the methodology for this book. Except for the year 1993, I have returned (or one of my students has) every spring thereafter from 1970 to 1998.[1] The

---

1. In 1993 I was studying rural politics in Mississippi and could not get home for the meeting. I continue to record Newbury's town meeting data. See www.uvm.edu/~fbryan.

account of how the nature of community life explains (or does not explain)
the practice of real democracy therefore appropriately begins in the land of
the coos.

WITNESS

There was the river that led away to God knows where. Give a kid a raft and
a little pluck and an eleven year old had adventure enough to last a
childhood. We never considered "running" away from home. Hell, we'd float
for it. There was a railroad too and a railroad station where passenger trains
stopped twice a day. It was a perfect place for hanging out and watching the
strangers watch you—many with pity in their eyes at the sight of ragged kids
without the brains to know how unhappy they were. I have met many of
these people later in life.

They still don't get it.

Memory. We had a cemetery, a long pretty one just above the river north
of town. The hornpouting was always good down behind the cemetery. But
you fish for hornpout (some call them bullheads) at night by lantern. Then you
have to walk home through the cemetery—carefully and with your heart in
your throat. My mother rests there now and I have reserved a little slice of the
coos next to her for myself. The village had a post office, a general store
named Jim's, and Harley Slack's Garage where it was always dark and cool
in summer and the men there moved slowly about in their cavern of oily tools
and off-limit wall calendars.

A paved road (that soon changed to dirt) went into the hills beyond the
village to "out back." A little pond called the "fishpond" lay hidden about a
half-mile through the woods on an old logging road northwest of town.
Mayflowers grew in abundance on checkerberry mound, and lady slippers
and hepaticas too. It was there I shot my first partridge.

Here and there little trout-filled brooks flowed into the Connecticut. We
had neat old buildings, a few abandoned barns, and even a rich person's
beautiful house surrounded by a white picket fence. It was an exact square
acre located next to the green in the middle of town. A rock out front
displayed the inscription "Dream Acre." The owner's name was Mrs. Charles
Bailey.

As in: "Let's go down to Pop Green's barn, fill these bags with manure,
and tonight we'll dump it all over Mrs. 'Chaaaarles' Bailey's lawn!" Could it
have been more perfect?

The village had a Sunday school, a grade school and a high school where
in 1959 I and six others graduated in a small lilac-filled town hall. We had little
league baseball, and even a barbershop until I was ten. Then it moved down
to Bradford. In the late '50s we watched out for Russian planes armed with
nuclear bombs from the Ground Observer Corps building that Frank Cass
and others built down by the creamery.

> We had junior proms and basketball games and senior plays and March of Dimes drives. "Summer people" could be shamed (very subtly, mind you) into a variety of gratuities for seemingly deprived country kids who had to live "up here" all year long. A little library up the street, named the Tenney Memorial Library, operated by Mary Hale and then Katharine King, was open Tuesday and Thursday from 3 to 9 p.m. and Saturday morning. In early spring (if you kept your mouth shut and behaved) you could hang around in the back of the town hall between snowball fights on the common and watch "pure democracy in action." Once in awhile you got to see grownups sass each other in public.
>
> Frank Bryan[2]

If, as Robert Dahl suggests, a bounded geography is part of the story of real democracy, then Vermont, which is filled with places like Newbury, seems to fit the bill. One finds no grandeur in Vermont, no temptation to pretension. Valleys and hills, twisting ridges, dark gulches, and bright slopes create a mosaic of opportunity for little clusters of settlement. They also preclude big ones. Vermont topography offers no wide-open spaces where people can spread out. Nor does it feature vast watersheds that funnel commerce into great cities. Lacking too are mountain-grassland junctures where large batches of people are wont to gather. No seaports congregate the crowds of enterprise. Vermont's largest municipality has only 39,391 people, and the state capital has only 8,247. It is the smallest in America. No state has a larger percentage of its population living in places of under 2,500. This complication of settlement can be traced back to the cold. Vermont was fashioned in ice, by ice. About 12,000 years ago, when the Laurentide glacier retreated back into Canada,[3] its tremendous weight gouged and scattered and piled and spewed, cutting and carving the face of Vermont into a thousand wrinkles, dips, and swirls and leaving a geographical underpinning perfectly suited to the small community.[4]

---

2. Frank Bryan, "Townscape Newbury," *Vermont Magazine* 1 (November–December 1989): 74–76.

3. For treatments of this phenomenon see Christopher McGrory Klyza and Stephen C. Trombulak, *The Story of Vermont: A Natural and Cultural History* (Hanover, NH: University Press of New England, 1999), and Harold A. Meeks, *Vermont's Land and Resources* (Shelburne, VT: New England Press, 1986).

4. Vermont hill farmers, me included now and then (mostly, thank goodness, then), have spent lifetimes picking up after Laurentide. Russell Thompson introduced me to the glacier in back of his chicken farm in the spring of 1958. The lesson involved a stone boat, a crowbar, physics, and parenting. I had walked the eight miles out to his place, drawn by the smiles of his

Unfortunately, the remarkable democratic potential of Vermont's geography was compromised from the beginning when the Crown-appointed governor of New Hampshire formed Vermont's 251 towns in a checkerboard of 251 similar-sized squares. No attention was paid to bioregional integrity.[5] Although minor adjustments have been made to accommodate the more egregious disconnections between governance and geography, the grid map of the towns in the year 2000 looked almost exactly as it did in the year 1800. In the aggregate, Vermont's geography is conducive to the small town and thus fundamentally supportive of real democracy. But the bioregional insults "granted" to Vermont by New Hampshire have made town-based democracy more difficult.

First, bioregional enclaves and settlements create competition for civic attachment within the towns. My hometown of Newbury, for instance, has two legally incorporated villages, each with its own annual "village meeting": Newbury village, which in 1990 had a population of 412, and Wells River village, a little commercial settlement upriver about five miles, with a drugstore, a restaurant, a convenience store or two, its own little library, and so forth. In 1990 Wells River's population was 424. The other 1,149 citizens of the town of Newbury are scattered over hill and dale, clustering here and there in several unincorporated "places" such as "West Newbury," "South Newbury," "Newbury Center" (which has one of the town's three polling places), and a bunch of other places like "Boltenville," "Leighton Hill," and "Hebs Corner"—all this social structure for fewer than 2,000 people.

The second negative effect of imposing squared, geometric town boundaries on Vermont's naturally diverse topography is that bioregional cohesions often transgress town lines, snatching the day-to-day concerns of the citizens in a corner of one town and placing them in another. Starksboro, where I have lived since 1972, has a little settlement called Jerusalem in the southeastern part of town. It is on a nice paved road that leads down out of the mountains. But because of the rugged hills between Jerusalem and the rest of the town, the road slopes south toward the larger commercial center of Bristol rather than north toward Starksboro village. This kind of push-pull geographical dynamic on the communities of Vermont is found throughout the state.

---

youngest daughter, Susan, only to be recruited at the door to pick stone from their corn piece up on the hill behind the house. By dinnertime (noon) my amorous anticipations had been replaced by fatigue. But Russell did throw a compliment in my direction I've never forgotten. When his wife Adeline, a schoolteacher, mother of three daughters and two sons, and the soul of the family, asked brightly over her potatoes and gravy: "How'd it go up on the hill this morning?" he said matter-of-factly: "Well Frank doesn't know much yet but he tries hard." Susan smiled.

5. For an extended discussion of this process see www.uvm.edu/~fbryan.

The cohesion of community life in Vermont is threatened in another way. At almost the precise moment this study began, Vermont was at last fully emerging from what historians call its great dark age, a period lasting over a century when Vermont led the American states in out-migration.[6] For most of its history Vermont was a place for "getting out" of.[7] But after 1960 a tremendous influx of new people to Vermont produced a dramatic turnaround—a population increase not equaled since the late eighteenth century.[8] Note this profound dynamic in three typical small towns in figure 5.1.

Most of these newcomers to Vermont settled not in the large towns or even in the bigger places like villages in the smaller towns. They went to the "outback"—the dirt roads between the "places"—buying up abandoned family farms with a view. In Newbury there were over a hundred farms in 1950. In the year 2000 there were fewer than ten. In Newbury village the train station is gone, the creamery went out of business, the barbershop went down to Bradford, and the high school soon followed. That finished the junior prom, the senior play, and all the dances and sporting events and other activities sponsored by the school. This while Newbury town's population almost doubled. The post office left South Newbury, and the little store in West Newbury closed.

The greatest change came with the interstate highway. An interchange in Bradford (to the south) and one on the northern edge of town west of Wells River means buses no longer go through the village. It also means you can live in the village, drive a few miles south to Bradford or north to Wells River, get on the interstate, and then drive north upriver to work in St. Johnsbury

6. Horace Greeley, a Vermonter who grew up and came of age in East Poultney, is credited with the famous quotation "Go west, young man, go west." Actually, John L. B. Soule said it in an editorial in the *Terre Haute (IN) Express*. Greeley said, "Go west, young man, and grow up with the country." Greeley's Vermont youth taught him well. He prefaced his "go west" dictum with the following prophetic passage from his essay "To Aspiring Young Men": "The best business you can get into you will find on your father's farm or in his workshop." If you can't do that, he advised, "turn your face to the great West." When Greeley was growing up in Vermont young men (and women too) couldn't and did. In one of those fascinating turns of history that seem to happen to people from small places, George Jones, Greeley's fellow apprentice in a tiny print shop in East Poultney, turned out to be Greeley's chief competitor later in life in the nation's largest city. Greeley was founder and editor of the *New York Tribune*, and Jones was cofounder (with Henry Raymond, another Vermonter) and editor of the *New York Times*.

7. Harold F. Wilson, *The Hill Country of Northern New England: Its Social and Economic History, 1790–1930* (New York: Columbia University Press, 1936).

8. The town Jane Mansbridge calls "Selby" in *Beyond Adversary Democracy* (New York: Basic Books, 1980) turns out to be a model of the dark age thesis: remarkable growth until 1830, steady decline until 1950 (when the population was almost 20 percent lower than in 1790!), and then a rocketlike takeoff after 1970. Other towns peaked later. Newbury had nearly 3,000 people in 1850 and declined to about 1,450 in 1970. Newark, the town discussed at some length in chapter 3, dropped from its 1800 high of almost 700 to 150 in 1970.

PRESTON RIDGE LIBRARY
COLLIN COLLEGE
FRISCO, TX 75035

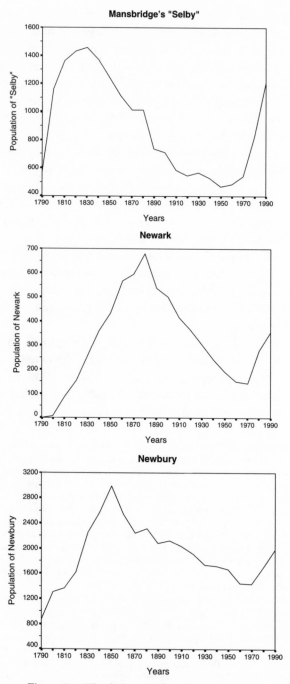

Figure 5.1. The dark age in three Vermont towns.

or south downriver to White River, both about thirty miles. Culture leak. It's not all bad, of course. Fewer cars go through town. But even that traffic, while sometimes a nuisance in the summer, brought the village a presence that is now lacking.

The changes that began in Newbury with the closing of the 1950s are not unlike those that came to the rest of Vermont's towns in the second half of the twentieth century. It is a principal finding of this book that these beautiful little New England communities, so rich in history and tradition, yet so widely varying in their social and political composition, tell us almost nothing about why they practice real democracy so differently. Almost no match exists between the socioeconomic and political lives of these towns (in their stability and in their changes) and their rates of attendance at town meeting.

The scholarship on the linkages between community life variables and political participation is wide and deep. But it has limitations. One is the predominance of representative democracy as the fundamental construct and the emphasis (understandably) on the voting act. Nearly all studies on political participation in general (as opposed to strict voting studies) treat variables that are kin to real democracy—variables like going to rallies, participating in public forums, and such—primarily as components of general participatory constructs.[9] Seldom does attendance at (or public participation in) public meetings take center stage.[10] Moreover, most of these studies use national samples. It is nearly impossible to find survey research studies of even one small town, to say nothing of a *series* of small towns. Consequently the context of participation in the studies of representational systems seldom reflects the context in which town meeting democracy is practiced.[11]

9. For more recent examples, see, for instance, Norman H. Nie, Jane Junn, and Kenneth Stehlik-Barry, *Education and Democratic Citizenship in America* (Chicago: University of Chicago Press, 1996); Steven J. Rosenstone and John Mark Hansen, *Mobilization, Participation and Democracy in America* (New York: Macmillan, 1993); and Sidney Verba, Kay Lehman Schlozman, and Henry E. Brady, *Voice and Equality: Civic Voluntarism in American Politics* (Cambridge: Harvard University Press, 1995).

10. A recent interest in political deliberation, however, has added a new and hopeful component to the participatory literature. See especially James Bohman, *Public Deliberation: Pluralism, Complexity, and Democracy* (Cambridge: MIT Press, 1996); James Bohman and William Rehg, *Deliberative Democracy: Essays on Reason and Politics* (Cambridge: MIT Press, 1997); James S. Fishkin, "Bringing Deliberation to Democracy," *Public Perspective* 7 (December 1995–January 1996): 1; and Benjamin I. Page, *Who Deliberates? Mass Media in Modern Democracy* (Chicago: University of Chicago Press, 1996).

11. An important exception, which contains microlevel research from local, *face-to-face* decision-making government institutions in American cities, is Jeffrey M. Berry, Kent E. Portney, and Ken Thomson, *The Rebirth of Urban Democracy* (Washington, DC: Brookings Institution, 1993). Unfortunately (but understandably), the authors report no hard counts of how many citizens

A second difficulty is that nearly all the research on political participation uses individual-level data and does not concern itself directly with the context of community. An exception is the work of Robert R. Huckfeldt and John Sprague and a small cadre of political scientists who labor at the difficult task of stitching community context variables into the complex quilt of political behavior. This work, like that dealing primarily with individual-level associations, has been a source both of insight and caution.[12] For comparing individual-level data with community-level data is risky business. If we discover, for instance, that upscale communities have higher levels of attendance at town meeting, we have not proved that upscale *citizens* are more apt to attend town meeting.[13] Still, this literature provides the only map of the territory we are entering, and I have followed its principal trail markers. The first and the most important of these is the familiar upscale-downscale continuum.[14]

Upscale, Downscale? So What?

If political science produced a "law" of political behavior in the second half of the twentieth century, it is that socioeconomic status (SES) is strongly and positively associated with political participation. Yet town meeting democracies seem to violate this law with impunity. Sidney Verba and Norman Nie put the matter succinctly in their watershed volume *Participation in America*,

---

are present at the meetings, how long the meetings last, how many people speak out at the meetings, and so on.

12. For a review of this research, see Robert Huckfeldt and John Sprague, "Citizen, Contexts, and Politics," in *Political Science: The State of the Discipline*, vol. 2, ed. Ada W. Finifter (Washington, DC: American Political Science Association, 1993). See also Robert R. Huckfeldt, "Political Participation and the Neighborhood Social Context," *American Journal of Political Science* 23 (August 1979): 579–592; Robert Huckfeldt, *Politics in Context: Assimilation and Conflict in Urban Neighborhoods* (New York: Agathon, 1986); Robert Huckfeldt and John Sprague, "Networks in Context: The Social Flow of Political Information," *American Political Science Review* 81 (December 1987): 1197–1216; Robert Huckfeldt, Paul Allen Peck, Russell J. Dalton, and Jeffrey Levine, "Political Environments, Cohesive Social Groups and the Communication of Public Opinion," *American Journal of Political Science* 39 (November 1995): 1025–1054; and Robert Huckfeldt and John Sprague, *Citizens, Politics, and Social Communication: Information and Influence in an Election Campaign* (New York: Cambridge University Press, 1995).

13. Several solutions for the ecological fallacy have appeared since the 1950s. The most recent is Gary King, *A Solution to the Ecological Inference Problem* (Princeton: Princeton University Press, 1997).

14. See Amy Liu Qiaoming, Vernon Ryan, Herbert Aurbach, and Terry Besser, "The Influence of Local Church Participation on Rural Community Attachment," *Rural Sociology* 63 (Fall 1998): 432–450, and John J. Beggs, Valerie A. Haines, and Jeanne S. Hurlbert, "Revisiting the Rural-Urban Contrast: Personal Networks in Nonmetropolitan and Metropolitan Settings," *Rural Sociology* 61 (Summer 1996): 306–325.

published in 1972: "Citizens of higher social and economic status participate more in politics."[15] Try as I might, however, I was unable to establish a
meaningful connection between the income, education, or occupation levels
of a town's citizens and its town meeting attendance. Education alone survived the multiple regression equation provided at the end of this chapter
(table 5.1), and it explained only 1 percent of the variance in attendance.

Consider Goshen and Granville, mountain towns deep in central
Vermont's most rugged terrain. Our sample turned up two meetings each for
these towns between 1987 and 1992. Situated about halfway up the state be-
tween Massachusetts and Canada, Goshen begins at the crest line of the Green
Mountains and slopes west. Most of the town lies in the Green Mountain
National Forest, but the people of Goshen live in two little hamlets, Goshen
and Goshen Four Corners, one near and one exactly on Route 73, a major (by
Vermont standards) road that extends over the Green Mountains (through
Brandon Gap) to the east. Route 73 also runs west down into Brandon, which
has fifteen times the population of Goshen. There it connects with Vermont's
major north-south highway in the western half of the state, providing a manageable commute south to Rutland (Vermont's second largest "city") and
north to the college town of Middlebury.

Over on the eastern slope of the mountains and a bit to the north is the
town of Granville. Granville drops quickly into a deep valley between parallel
ranges of the Green Mountains. There it marks the headwaters of the White
River system that finally empties into the Connecticut far to the southeast.
The Northfield Mountains' steep ridges run along the eastern third of the
town, cutting off the morning sun. It's difficult to go east from Granville. The
best way is to drive down Route 100 to Rochester, over Rochester Gap to
Bethel, and then to the interstate, but it's a long haul even in good weather.
Going north up through Granville Gulch leads to the towns of Warren,
Waitsfield, and Fayston. In these towns nearly everyone houses or feeds or in
some way services skiers in the winter and upscale rural loungers the rest of the
year. Everywhere in Granville the mountains edge up to the highway. There,
on a ribbon of topsoil created by a million beaver damming the little brooks
that spawn the White River over a period of 10,000 years, live the people.[16]

15. Sidney Verba and Norman H. Nie, *Participation in America* (New York: Harper and
Row, 1972), 125. The analogue to Verba and Nie for Great Britain is Geraint Parry, George
Moyser, and Neil Day, *Political Participation and Democracy in Britain* (Cambridge: Cambridge
University Press, 1992). An important recent refinement of the SES model is Verba, Schlozman,
and Brady, *Voice and Equality*.

16. One of the student team members who went to the Granville meeting of 1987 wrote
the following: "Granville is a nice little town. I stress the word little because we drove right through

Both Goshen and Granville are very small towns. About the time the meetings we are comparing occurred, 220 people lived in Goshen and 313 lived in Granville. In Goshen 36 percent of the population over twenty-five years old held college degrees—well above the 23 percent average for the 210 towns in the sample. In Granville only 11 percent were college graduates. In Goshen, the median family income was $38,750. In Granville it was $26,875. Forty-two percent of the workforce were labeled "managers and professionals" in Goshen. In Granville only 18 percent were. With town size pretty much controlled, we might expect the upscale Goshen to outperform working-class Granville on town meeting attendance. But precisely the opposite occurred.

The two town meetings in the more "upscale" town of Goshen averaged about 30 percent of the registered voters in attendance, while the two meetings in the more working-class town of Granville, averaged about 40 percent. A similar analysis conducted for the entire sample of meetings obtained a similar result. The higher the education level of a town's citizens, the more the income, and the greater the percentage of managers and professionals in the workforce, the smaller the percentage of registered voters at town meeting. When town size was controlled (a necessary precaution, since larger towns in Vermont score higher on SES variables), however, this reversal of the SES "law" disappeared. But the conundrum remained. Attendance at town meeting was not associated with the socioeconomic level of the towns' citizens. Neither education, income, nor occupation explained more than 1 percent of the variation in SAAM (the size-adjusted attendance measure).

The importance of this finding called for a final check. I combined income, education, occupation, and several other SES variables into a single summary measure called "upscale" (a factor score) and matched it with

---

it before we even knew we were in it." But he liked his day in Granville, was amazed at how the one-room (K-5) school (next door to the church where the meeting was held) could be so modern ("a microwave oven, typewriters, computers with printers, a VCR, a TV and a copying machine"), and was impressed with the discussion. "I found the meeting really interesting and I probably would have enjoyed it more if it wasn't seven and a half hours long." David Vale, "Granville Town Meeting 1987," Burlington, University of Vermont, March 1987. Another student, Lee Hannauer, who studied the Granville town meeting in 1994, described the town as follows: "Granville is a small and beautiful Vermont town seemingly isolated from the rest of the state. The first part of Granville one encounters is the Granville Gulf Reservation, a spectacular valley road running through six miles of wilderness." But the description of the town meeting was less than spectacular. Hannauer concludes: "Though it pains me to say so, I think town meeting is a dying tradition in Granville." This after recording data for a meeting attended by 38 percent of the town's registered voters, in which 75 percent of the attenders spoke. Lee Hannauer, "1994 Granville Town Meeting," Burlington, University of Vermont, March 1994.

town meeting attendance after controlling for town size. Plot 1 of figure 5.2 displays the flat association between size-adjusted town meeting attendance for 1,244 meetings and the summary SES score for the towns that housed these meetings. Plot 2 of figure 5.2 then acts as a microscope by limiting the number of meetings and allowing a visual return to Granville and Goshen to see how they fit in the context of the 91 meetings studied in 1987 alone.[17]

Meetings in other towns we are becoming familiar with also appear in the scatterplot. The 1987 meeting for upscale, Dartmouth-influenced Norwich is a perfect fit for the SES model, as is Barton—a more isolated town up in the Northeast Kingdom. But meetings with countervailing positions on the scatterplot similar to the one in Athens (low SES/high attendance) and the one in Shelburne (high SES/low attendance) balance meetings like those in Norwich and Barton. Other meetings, like those held in Newbury, Charlotte, Underhill, and Ripton,[18] combine with these examples to produce a pattern that dooms the SES hypothesis.

If this disconnect between SES and real democracy, which we have established at the community level, holds at the individual level, it will confound expectations, since the positive association between SES and political participation, so prevalent in the literature of political science, is said to be especially strong when more demanding forms of participation are involved. Town meeting attendance is surely more demanding physically, economically, and psychologically than nearly any form of participation in representative systems.[19]

17. For the statistical parameters of this and other factor scores used later on, see www.uvm.edu/~fbryan. The number of meetings used in this particular statistical routine (and some of the others used throughout the book) are reduced because of missing data. In this case faulty SES data from the 1970 Census for small towns means towns that had meetings in the sample for 1970–76 cannot be used. I applied 1980 Census data to the towns with meetings in the sample for 1977, 1978 and 1979.

18. Goshen and Ripton abut one another high in the Green Mountains. An incredibly beautiful little road, especially in early October (Route 32, the "Goshen-Ripton" Road), joins them and will bring you out a stone's throw west of the Robert Frost Interpretive Trail in Ripton if you're headed north from Goshen. That Ripton and Goshen score about the same on size-controlled attendance will surprise no one who lives in these hills.

19. One study compares the act of registering to vote with voting (or not voting) after registration and finds that the effect of education is "overwhelmingly focused on the registration stage." Given that registering to vote traditionally required a much larger investment of time and effort than voting itself, one might argue that town meeting attendance (which requires a much greater investment than registering) ought to be more closely associated with education levels. See Richard J. Timpone, "Structure, Behavior, and Voter Turnout in the United States," *American Political Science Review* 92 (March 1998): 145–158.

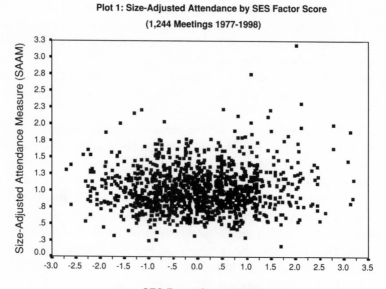

Plot 1: Size-Adjusted Attendance by SES Factor Score

(1,244 Meetings 1977-1998)

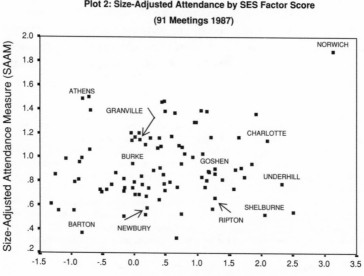

Plot 2: Size-Adjusted Attendance by SES Factor Score

(91 Meetings 1987)

Figure 5.2. Socioeconomic status doesn't matter.

Exploring the SES Conundrum

Does this finding hold at the individual level? I would bet the house and car that it does. But I have no hard data to prove it, and important findings suggest I am wrong. The most important of these is Jane Mansbridge's research on "Selby." Mansbridge shows that town meetings there were associated with disadvantages for the very poor.[20] Findings from Switzerland (another place that has known real democracy) report that forms of direct, plebiscite democracy cause "the choir of Swiss direct democracy" to "ring in upper or middle-class tones."[21] Jeffrey M. Berry and his colleagues showed that "lower SES people are significantly underrepresented and higher SES people are significantly overrepresented among community participants."[22]

On the other hand, the only group Berry and his colleagues found to be advantaged by the presence of opportunities for *face-to-face neighborhood democracy* was not the wealthy but the middle class. Also, Jack M. McLeod and his colleagues discovered that demographic variables were not associated with increased participation (attendance and speaking) in public forums,[23] and Menahem Rosner found no relation between education (or demographic variables in general) and attendance at the governing assemblies of the Israeli kibbutz.[24] More direct evidence comes from Joseph Zimmerman, a longtime observer of the New England town meeting, who claims that town meeting attendance is a "virtual" microcosm of a town's population,[25] and Vivian Scott Hixson, who found that for citizens of a town meeting town in Vermont, SES was less apt to predict rates of political involvement than it was for citizens of a "matched" town council town in Michigan.[26]

Moreover, theoretical explanations for the disconnection between SES and town meeting attendance are available. Brady, Verba, and Schlozman discovered that a cluster of civic skills intervenes between SES and participation, and certain of these civic skills are not strongly related to SES. They are tied instead to affiliations with institutions that are more or less independent of

20. Mansbridge's findings demonstrate that some class distinctions bear a newcomer/old-timer imprint as well. Mansbridge, *Beyond Adversary Democracy*, 77–88.

21. Wolf Linder, *Swiss Democracy*, 2nd ed. (New York: St. Martin's Press, 1998), 95.

22. Berry, Portney, and Thomason, *Rebirth of Urban Democracy*, 82–83.

23. Jack M. McLeod et al., "Understanding Deliberation," *Communication Research* 26 (December 1999): 743–774.

24. Menahem Rosner, *Participatory Political and Organizational Democracy and the Experience of the Israeli Kibbutz* (Haifa: University of Haifa, 1981), 13.

25. Joseph Zimmerman, *The New England Town Meeting* (Westport, CT: Praeger, 1999), 242.

26. Vivian Scott Hixson, "The New Town Meeting Democracy: A Study of Matched Towns" (Ph.D. diss., Michigan State University, 1978), 107.

SES. The town itself and more importantly the town *meeting* may provide the civic instruction that neutralizes the standard effect of social and economic status.[27] Samuel Popkin and Michael Dimock argue that nonvoting is caused by lack of political knowledge—what is going on in government. My experience in Vermont tells me that working-class and middle-class people are better informed about local matters than upper-class people. If so, SES may not be the requirement for participation in town meeting that it is for participation in larger representative systems.[28]

Finally, strong personality, which has been found to translate into social capital independent of SES, may be more closely associated with small social systems than with large ones.[29] My observation over the years has been that Vermont's towns have many "local characters" with strong personalities who are apt to come to town meeting and participate. I have hundreds of student essays in my files that refer to or even focus on (not always in complimentary terms) local personalities of this sort. Often the students seem surprised by the mere *presence* of "the lady in the front row in a Robin Hood cap with a red feather in it" or "the man who thinks he's Gandhi sitting just behind us." The commonality in these essays is the judgment that such people have "odd" social capital, not that they have none at all. Most important, these essays leave little doubt that the presence of such people at town meeting is *not* the result of their higher socioeconomic status.

Still, the evidence that best supports my claim is the "thick evidence" I referred to at the beginning of this book. Sit with the people of town meetings in many different towns for nearly forty years. Read the accounts of town meetings by thousands of students over three decades. Collect and inspect an extensive, ongoing file of hundreds of photographs by authors, journalists, and ordinary citizens. Do this and you see the face of Vermont. The emotion returns again and again, year after year. You find yourself saying almost in amazement, "These are the people."

I have but one caveat. On the margin, town meeting does advantage the middle class, because the clearly down and out sometimes find town meeting uncomfortable. Mansbridge was the first to provide evidence of this. In my

27. See Henry E. Brady, Sidney Verba, and Kay Lehman Schlozman, "Beyond SES: A Resource Model of Political Participation," *American Political Science Review* 89 (June 1995): 271–294.

28. Samuel L. Popkin and Michael A. Dimock, "Political Knowledge and Citizen Competence," in *Citizen Competence and Democratic Institutions*, ed. Stephen L. Elkin and Karol Edward Soltan (University Park: Pennsylvania State University Press, 1999), 117–146.

29. Dietram A. Scheufele and Dhavan V. Shah, "Personality Strength and Social Capital: The Role of Dispositional and Informational Variables in the Production of Civic Participation," *Communication Research* 27 (April 2000): 107–131.

view, however, working-class people have no such problem. Moreover, the very well-off are as apt to be absent at town meeting as the very disadvantaged. Civic "skills" associated with high-class status often backfire at a New England town meeting.[30] My guess is that if the American electorate over the past thirty years had had the class bias of the town meeting, an entire generation of political scientists would have been much happier.[31]

Socioeconomic Diversity

A second consideration with less uniform theoretical underpinning—socioeconomic heterogeneity—likewise refuses to obey expectations. On the one hand, scholars say that the degree to which the community is divided into a number of distinct groups ought to increase participation in politics, since studies tie political participation to membership in groups. Also, heterogeneity often causes political conflict, which may increase participation.[32] On the other hand, many social scientists argue that open conflict can smother participation.[33] People shy away from public disagreement. In open forums like

30. Who would ask Luciano Pavarotti to sing "Blue Eyes Crying in the Rain" if Willie Nelson was in the house?

31. SES has a strong relationship ($r = .51$) with turnout in Vermont's general elections.

32. From his study of neighborhood politics in Baltimore, Matthew Crenson argues that citizen involvement is increased by the existence of social differences. Matthew A. Crenson, *Neighborhood Politics* (Cambridge: Harvard University Press, 1983). Curt Ventriss puts it this way in his essay on political participation from the public manager's perspective: "Neighborhood action is invigorated not only when neighbors know one another, but also when a little distrust exists among them." Curtis Ventriss, "Emerging Perspectives on Citizen Participation," *Public Administration Review* 45 (May–June 1985): 433–440. In 1968 Alford and Lee's study of turnout in American cities found higher participation in cities with more "explicit class or ethnic differences." Robert R. Alford and Eugene C. Lee, "Voting Turnout in American Cities," *American Political Science Review* 62 (September 1968): 796–813. See also Peter M. Blau, *Inequality and Heterogeneity: A Primitive Theory of Social Structure* (New York: Free Press, 1977), 22, and McLeod et al., "Understanding Deliberation," 743–774. Other studies that link heterogeneity with increased incidence of discussion spiced with conflict are M. A. Krassa, "Political Information, Social Environment, and Deviants," *Political Behavior* 12 (1990): 315–330; Michael MacKuen, "Speaking of Politics: Individual Conversational Choice, Public Opinion, and the Prospects for Deliberative Democracy," in *Information and Democratic Processes*, ed. John A. Ferejohn and James H. Kuklinski (Urbana: University of Illinois Press, 1990), 59–99; and Jack M. McLeod, Mira Sotirovic, and R. Lance Holbert, "Values as Sociotropic Judgments Influencing Communication Patterns," *Communication Research* 25 (October 1998): 453–485.

33. In his definitive account of early New England towns, Michael Zuckerman puts heavy emphasis on the link between social homogeneity and early town meeting "democracy." In a recent interview he claims that these early town meetings (controlled by the church hierarchy) were "a device to mobilize consensus, to maximize homogeneity." Heather Stephenson, "New England's Early Town Meetings Were Anything but Democratic," *Rutland Herald*, March 5, 2000, B1, B8. See also Michael Zuckerman, *Peaceable Kingdoms* (New York: Random House, 1970.)

town meeting, many breathe easier in the consensual atmosphere found in homogeneous communities.[34]

To test these two hypotheses, I classified the towns by how evenly the people of a community were distributed in cohorts of data within five demographic categories:[35] native Vermonters, education level, homeownership, income level, and occupation. The score for the town with the least diversity was set at zero, and the score for the most diversity was set at one hundred.

This index of heterogeneity was intuitively satisfying. It separated, for instance, a diversely populated mountain town like Ripton where high-income and low-income people, loggers and professors, and newcomers and native Vermonters must balance interests from the very homogeneous town of Whiting (nearby but down in the Lake Champlain lowlands), where a low-income, native Vermonter, agricultural culture dominates. Yet the heterogeneity index was not associated with either high or low levels of town meeting attendance. When town size is controlled, the correlation coefficient is just about as small as it can be and still register at all: $-.01$.[36] The complexity of town populations tells us nothing about turnout at town meeting.

Community Structure

I was not surprised when variants of class status failed to predict town meeting attendance. I was surprised when community structure variables related to time and place—like population growth and community "boundedness"— followed suit.

---

34. The homogeneity model has a long pedigree beginning with Aristotle. A leading text specifically devoted to rural government taught that for a town meeting government to "get along quite well" (which would presumably mean attendance was high) it would need a "stable and homogeneous population." Lane W. Lancaster, *Government in Rural America* (New York: D. Van Nostrand, 1952), 42–43. Now and then I have heard Vermonters, for instance, say things like: "I'm not going down there [to town meeting] anymore. All they do is argue and fight." Mansbridge recorded many similar reactions in "Selby." Mansbridge, *Beyond Adversary Democracy*, 59–76.

35. John L. Sullivan, "Political Correlates of Social, Economic, and Religious Diversity in the American States," *Journal of Politics* 35 (February 1973): 70–84.

36. The heterogeneity index and town population correlated at only .06 (Pearson's *r*). Beginning with Wirth's classic essay in 1938, studies have long shown that size is associated with SES heterogeneity. See Louis Wirth, "Urbanism as a Way of Life," *American Journal of Sociology* 44 (July 1938): 1–24. For a review of this literature and a probe of the connections between size, heterogeneity, and attitude constructs, see Thomas C. Wilson, "Community Population Size and Social Heterogeneity: An Empirical Test," *American Journal of Sociology* 91 (March 1986): 1154–1169.

Population Growth

The relation between high population mobility and low political participation is well established.[37] Moreover, I can think of no measure that better captures the sense of what happened to Newbury between 1970 and 2000 than the rate of population growth. In short, I felt population growth would be a fair surrogate for a more nebulous concept—culture shock—that I tried (and failed) to quantify. In any event, I was certain the correlation between town meeting turnout (with town size controlled) and population increase would be negative and significant. I was wrong.

On March 3, 1971, three of my students traveled 150 miles up across Vermont and then along over through down into[38] the historic Nulhigan River passageway to attend town meeting in the Kingdom town of Bloomfield. Except for the loggers, a few farms along the river, and a bit of outdoor summer trade (the country is too wild for most tourists), Bloomfield has little economic activity. The summer when I made the final editorial changes to this book, a little store in Bloomfield (Debanville's) finally closed. It had been selling stuff like clothing, food, ammo, Eagle Claw hooks, bug repellant, and beer for as long as I can remember. Of the 1,435 meetings we studied between 1970 and 1998, none was held in a town that had lost population faster in the two decades preceding its meeting. Attendance at town meeting was far below what the SAAM predicted for Bloomfield.

---

37. See Lancaster, *Government in Rural America*, 42–43. In 1972 Verba and Nie, through their integration of the concept with community boundedness and suburban growth, developed a more explicit argument. Sidney Verba and Norman H. Nie, *Participation in America* (New York: Harper and Row, 1972), 232–247. Axelrod's formulation that "cooperation requires that individuals have a sufficiently large chance to meet again so that they have a stake in their future interaction" might also mean that swiftly growing communities will have lower percentages of citizens attending town meeting. Robert M. Axelrod, *The Evolution of Cooperation* (New York: Basic Books, 1984), 20. If longevity in a community leads to more neighboring behavior, then population mobility may have an indirectly negative effect on participation. See David M. Chavis and Abraham Wandersman, "Sense of Community in the Urban Environment: A Catalyst for Participation and Community Development," *American Journal of Community Psychology* 18 (February 1990): 55–81. See also Paul Florin and Abraham Wandersman, "Cognitive Social Learning and Participation in Community Development," *American Journal of Community Psychology* 12 (December 1984): 689–708, and Abraham Wandersman and Paul Florin, "A Cognitive Social Learning Approach to the Crossroads of Cognition, Social Behavior, and the Environment," in *Cognition, Social Behavior and the Environment*, ed. J. H. Harvey (Hillsdale, NJ: Erlbaum, 1981), 393–408. Another study that treats population mobility is Paul Florin and Abraham Wandersman, "An Introduction to Citizen Participation, Voluntary Organizations, and Community Development: Insights for Empowerment through Research," *American Journal of Community Psychology* 18 (February 1990): 41–54.

38. Real Vermonters like prepositions.

Far to the southwest of Bloomfield in Chittenden County is the town of St. George. In 1791, the year the Republic of Vermont joined the United States, 57 people lived in St. George. By 1960, even though St. George is in Vermont's most populous county and only a stone's throw from its largest city, its population had grown to only 108. Over the next two decades, however, St. George's population leaped upward. When my students went there in 1980, it had increased over 500 percent, to 677. No town meeting in the sample was preceded by such rapid population growth in the town where it was held. However, attendance at St. George's 1980 meeting, like Bloomfield's 1971 meeting, was below what would be expected for a town its size. Thus meetings in the fastest-growing town (St. George) and the town losing population the fastest (Bloomfield) had poorer attendance than their size would predict.

Our sample of 1,435 town meetings reflected the ambiguity of the connection displayed by the meetings in Bloomfield and St. George. The relation for the full sample was in the predicted direction; the faster the towns grew, the lower the turnout at town meeting. But population increase explained less than 1 percent of the variance in SAAM.[39] Accordingly, I tested three shorter-term indicators of population mobility: the ten-year population change in the town, the percentage of a town's population living in the same house they were living in five years before the Census count was taken, and the percentage of a town's population that had moved into town in the five years before the Census count. None of these measures produced more than trivial associations with attendance at town meeting.

Another way to look at population growth is through the lens of the most dominant cultural cleavage in Vermont's public mind, the one that everyone knows and talks about. Newcomer to native Vermonter: "Lived here all your life old-timer?" Reply: "Not yet." The differences between newcomers (flatlanders) and native Vermonters (woodchucks or simply "chucks")[40] are real and to some extent class-based. The suspicion has always been that native Vermonters care more about their town meetings than do the newly arrived "from away." That suspicion is probably wrong. Data for 1,435 meetings held

39. An important study of voter turnout and mobility estimated in 1987 that turnout would increase by nine percentage points if the influence of moving from one place to another could be neutralized. Peverill Squire, Raymond E. Wolfinger, and David P. Glass, "Residential Mobility and Voter Turnout," *American Political Science Review* 81 (March 1987): 45–65. See also Ruy A. Teixeira, *The Disappearing American Voter* (Washington, DC: Brookings Institution, 1992).

40. In the 1980s a friend and I had some fun with this cultural divide in a book that went through seven printings, sold 70,000 copies (in a state with about 600,000 residents), and appeared on the *New York Times* best-seller list for regional humor. Frank Bryan and Bill Mares, *Real Vermonters Don't Milk Goats* (Shelburne, VT: New England Press, 1983).

in 210 towns do not suggest that town meeting is more popular in towns with more "Vermonters" than newcomers. The correlation coefficient between native Vermont population and higher attendance at town meeting and the SAAM was −.03.

WITNESS

THE "JERICHO RECYCLERS" GO TO TOWN MEETING

About halfway through the meeting was interrupted by the opening of the stage curtain right behind the selectmen's table, revealing an elaborate game-show set, around which pranced "The Jericho Recyclers," an acting troupe unequaled in their gall, who insisted on playing out a game show which would involve anyone in attendance at the meeting who wanted to answer questions about recycling. If answered correctly, contestants would win an environmentally safe prize (which a good percentage of the crowd would probably throw away as soon as they went home anyway, creating more waste).

Unfortunately, and yet quite predictably, the show met with little cooperation and went over about as well as an added agenda item. People wanted out. Scanning the room I saw a couple of men I knew to be farmers who were visibly less than pleased with this unforeseen waste of time. The climax of the show was when the players ran around the gym distributing recycle-wheels, with which one can compute exactly what to do with certain recyclable materials as well as determine how to dispose of certain toxic wastes. These discs, I noticed, nearly covered the floor as the meeting adjourned.

These folks had the right idea, but they just plain went about it wrong. Most of the townspeople were starting to think about lunch, getting home to their soap operas, and even getting back to the farm to finish the day's chores. Few wanted to be preached to by a bunch of recent college graduates who were acting very goofy and yet, in a way, a little bit condescending.

Kevin P. McGonegal[41]

Community Boundedness

Down in the southeast corner of the state where Vermont, New Hampshire, and Massachusetts meet, is the little town of Guilford. A couple of hundred years ago Ethan Allen rode into town with a crowd of his "Green Mountain

41. Kevin P. McGonegal, "Jericho 1991 Town Meeting and the Crisis of the Yuppie," Burlington, University of Vermont, March 1991.

Boys" and threatened to "lay it as desolate as Sodom and Gomorrah" if it did not subject itself to his will. It must, he thundered, abandon its plan to secede from the Republic of Vermont and join New York. Allen's will prevailed (as it often did), and Guilford remains in Vermont—a town of 1,941 people rich in its history and (one hopes) satisfied with the outcome of the infamous "Guilford Raid" of long ago.

Guilford, like many other places in Vermont, is a small town adjacent to a much larger town, in this case the town of Brattleboro, with a population of 12,241. Brattleboro could sap the community strength from Guilford— economic, social, and cultural—and jeopardize interest in the community's political life. The same could happen to Cornwall and Weybridge (populations 1,101 and 667 respectively), immediately west of the town of Middlebury up in the Champlain valley. Middlebury has 8,034 people, a McDonald's, several shopping centers, the union high school, a movie theater, and—most important—Middlebury College and the many cultural amenities associated with it. What chance do Weybridge and Cornwall have of maintaining their community identity, caught as they are in the socioeconomic and cultural magnetic field emitted by Middlebury?

Many of the towns we studied are like Guilford, Weybridge, and Cornwall. But an equal number lie far from the influence of larger towns, where it is very clear to the traveler "coming into town" just where the boundaries of the community are etched, not only in topography but also in social and economic institutions—a mom-and-pop store, a couple of gas stations, a clustered village center. Such is Canaan, which borders both Canada and New Hampshire and is thus the most northern and eastern town in Vermont's wild Northeast Kingdom. Such is the island town of Isle La Motte in Lake Champlain, which saw European settlement as early as 1642. Such is the valley town of Granville discussed above.

Scholarship is in near agreement that "community boundedness"[42] should improve political participation. Early on Verba and Nie were explicit on the matter: "As a community loses its clear border and identity, it should become more difficult or less meaningful for the individuals to participate.... Isolation and small size seem to work together to increase participation." This finding was especially strong for the "communal" activity component of their participation index.[43] Nearly three decades later Robert Putnam agreed, attaching a "civic penalty" to commuting and the "spatial

42. The term originated with Verba and Nie, *Participation in America*, 229–247.
43. Verba and Nie, *Participation in America*, 240, 241, 245.

fragmentation between home and workplace that is bad for community."[44] Many other studies confirm the boundedness hypothesis in other forms and situations.[45]

Vermont towns and their town meetings, however, continue to be obstinate. Summary indexes of "rural isolation" and "community boundedness" and other individual measures much like those employed by Putnam and others refused to predict important fluctuations in attendance rates at town meeting.[46] Only the percentage of the workforce working out of town operated in the correct direction. With town size controlled, town meeting attendance declined as this percentage increased. The correlation coefficient, however, although statistically significant, was weak: $r = -.12$.[47] When entered into the final all-variable regression equation displayed at the end of this chapter (table 5.1), it disappeared altogether, further evidence that attendance at town meeting seems to ignore the causal connections others find linked to civic involvement.

Population Density

It stands to reason that the more citizens are scattered around town, the harder it will be for them to attend town meeting. This would be especially true for

44. Putnam's research shows that "each additional ten minutes in daily commuting time cuts involvement in community affairs by 10 percent—fewer public meetings attended . . . and so on." Robert Putnam, *Bowling Alone: The Collapse and Revival of American Community* (New York: Simon and Schuster 2000), 213–214.

45. Using individual-level data, Berry and his associates found a strong relation between "sense of community" and participation in urban neighborhood assemblies. Berry, Portney, and Thomason, *Rebirth of Urban Democracy*, 236–243. Gerald M. Pomper and Loretta A. Semekos find what they call "bake sale" variables to be key components in their model for participation decline. In distinctly communitarian language, they call for a rebuilding of American communities with references to town meeting. Gerald M. Pomper and Loretta A. Semekos, "Bake Sales and Voting," *Society* 28 (July–August 1991): 10–16. For the relation between community boundedness, SES, and political information, see Kasisomayajula Viswanath, Gerald M. Kosicki, Eric S. Fredin, and Eunkyung Park, "Local Community Ties, Community-Boundedness and Local Public Affairs Knowledge Gaps," *Communication Research* 27 (February 2000): 27–50, and L. L. Pearson, "Desert Storm and Tundra Telegraph: Information Diffusion in a Media Poor Environment," in *Desert Storm and the Mass Media*, ed. Bradley S. Greenberg and Walter Gantz (Cresskill, NJ: Hampton Press, 1993), 182–196. For the link between local media, community boundedness, and participation, see Jack M. McLeod, K. Daily, Z. Goo, W. P. Eveland, J. Bayer, S. Yang, and H. Yang, "Community Integration, Local Media Use and the Democratic Processes," *Communication Research* 23 (April 1996): 179–209.

46. The correlation coefficients (Pearson's r) with attendance were as follows: rural isolation .03; community boundedness .06.

47. For further discussion of these indexes and displays of the data see www.uvm.edu/~fbryan.

the aged or infirm. Moreover, the back roads of early March in Vermont might hinder attendance at town meeting for all kinds of people. Indeed, Mansbridge found villagers were more apt to attend town meeting in "Selby" than people who lived out in the hills. This is an important finding, since compared with many Vermont towns, it is relatively easy to get to the village from the surrounding hills of Selby.[48] Other studies tout the civic-enhancing attributes of increased population density rather than its spatial convenience.

Most social scientists measure population density as a jurisdiction's population per square mile. While this measure has the advantage of simplicity, I believe its conceptual limitations render it pretty much useless. In Vermont many towns have their citizens clustered in one location, whereas others with the same number of people per square mile have them scattered all over the place. I therefore totaled the miles of maintained roadway per town as a more precise quantifier of *living* territory than square miles.[49] An inspection of the findings convinced me that if the "scatteredness" of a town's population has any bearing on its town meeting attendance, that fact has a better chance of appearing if we use population per road mile rather than people per square mile.

This measure of population density outdid any of the community life measures employed in this chapter. It correlated with the SAAM at $r = -.23$, survived a series of controls, and emerged to influence town meeting attendance in the final equation. Maddeningly, however, it points in the wrong direction. Towns where the people are spread out over a more extensive road

48. Mansbridge, *Beyond Adversary Democracy*, 102–104. Years ago I hunted in the hills of "Selby" now and then. In Selby, no other villages scattered the town's population away from the town center. Esther Munroe Swift, *Vermont Place-Names* (Brattleboro, VT: Stephen Green Press, 1977). I have omitted page references to honor Mansbridge's wish to preserve the anonymity of the real town of "Selby." Kirkpatrick Sale argues that density along with small size helps improve participation. Many urban scholars such as Jane Jacobs agree, arguing that density and the "hustle-bustle" of the crowd are key components of public safety, helping behavior and a sense of civic space that fosters participation. Kirkpatrick Sale, *Human Scale* (New York: Coward, McCann and Geoghegan, 1980); Jane Jacobs, *The Economy of Cities* (New York: Random House, 1969). Some literature on helping behavior, which indicates that "crowding" is negatively associated with social participation, includes Dale O. Jorgenson and Fred O. Dukes, "Deindividuation as a Function of Density and Group Membership," *Journal of Personality and Social Psychology* 34 (July 1976): 24–29, and Charles Korte, "Helpfulness in the Urban Environment," in *Advances in Environmental Psychology: The Urban Environment*, ed. Andrew Barum, Jerome E. Singer, and Stuart Valins (Hillsdale, NJ: Lawrence Erlbaum, 1978). Individual-level studies of the link between community population density and political participation are scarce as hen's teeth, although the linkage between small towns and rural places and civic engagement is well documented. See Putnam, *Bowling Alone*, 204.

49. For further discussion of this measure and the dimensions of its statistics, see www.uvm.edu/~fbryan.

system have higher attendance. If distance and isolation are an impediment to attendance at town meeting, this fact slithered through the analysis undetected. My guess is that population per road mile is a variable that reflects an issue as well as a condition of life. As the miles of roads per person increase, the people are more scattered over "back roads." The condition of these roads is thus more important to them. Since, after education, roads are the single most important issue to come before a town meeting, this variable should increase attendance if issues matter more than the accessibility of the meeting place.

Enough. We have prowled at length through the underbrush of socioeconomic structure. Thickets of variables that in other times and places have produced either theoretical or empirical ties to political participation have been flushed with almost no success. Connections do exist, but they are frail. The literature overflows with findings that connect the social and economic characteristics of the people in a society with how their living places are linked to their political behavior. Community-level data suggest, however, that in the town halls where real democracy is practiced, attendance floats relatively free of these standard currents.

Elements of Political Culture

If real democracy does not dance to the melodies of social life, I thought, perhaps it moves to the cadence of political life. The backbeat of representative democracy that permeates the townspeople's public consciousness would surely better foretell how much they practice real democracy. But it did not. Once again real democracy stands apart from the context of community. Here I treat four indicators—the participant culture of representative democracy, the ideological posture of the community, the partisan division of the electorate, and the progressive politics of Vermont's Socialist-independent congressman, Bernard Sanders.

Ballot-Box Participation

The act of voting is remarkably different from the act of attending town meeting. In the one, citizens act in private to choose someone else to legislate on their behalf. In the other, they act in public, legislating for themselves. Yet a fertile literature suggests that the urge to vote for a United States senator and the urge to go to town meeting are probably related—that political "cultures" exist promoting (or discouraging) political participation of many kinds and at many levels.[50] One possibility is that people who turn out at the polls year after year to vote in state and national elections develop a participatory mentality urging them to attend town meeting. Another possibility is the reverse—that attending town meeting reinforces turnout at the polls. Or these activities could be mutually supportive.

The gap between voting and face-to-face political participation in Vermont's towns is substantial. The average proportion of the registered voters who voted in the two elections closest to each of the 1,435 meetings in the towns that held the meetings we studied was about 68 percent. The average attendance at town meeting was about 20 percent. Voting participation is over three times as great as town meeting participation. The highest turnout at the polls for a town with a town meeting in the database was 91 percent. The highest turnout we recorded at town meeting was 72 percent. The lowest voter turnout for a single town in a single election year was 30 percent. The lowest turnout at town meeting was 1 percent. If it's quantity you want, representative democracy is the way to go.

Do these different kinds of participation respond to similar impulses? This is a most important question for political science. It speaks to what is perhaps the best hope we have generated in my lifetime for salvaging the American republic. By resuscitating *civil* society in our localities, we can rescue *political* society in our nation. Critical to this endeavor is a positive "spillover effect" from face-to-face democracy at the periphery to representative democracy at the center. Is real democracy simply a higher stage of participation, a more "costly" act than stopping by the polling place on your way home from work? If so, we might expect a correlation between a town's degree of electoral participation and its town meeting attendance.[51]

50. Vermont is one of the better examples of what Daniel Elazar calls the "moralistic" culture, which holds that participation is an inherent good that should be practiced by all citizens to advance the commonweal, as opposed to the "individualistic" culture (more apt to be found in New Hampshire), which holds that political participation is utilitarian in nature, to be practiced by professional politicians to advance individual interests. Daniel Elazar, *American Federalism: A View from the States* (New York: Crowell, 1966).

51. The evidence of a spillover effect is mixed. See for instance Robert A. Dahl, *A Preface to Economic Democracy* (Berkeley: University of California Press, 1985); J. Maxwell Elden, "Political Efficacy at Work: The Connection between More Autonomous Forms of Workplace Organization and a More Participatory Politics," *American Political Science Review* 75 (March 1981): 43–58; Edward Greenberg, *Workplace Democracy* (Ithaca: Cornell University Press, 1986); and Robert E. Lane, "From Political to Industrial Democracy," *Polity* 17 (Summer 1985): 623–648. C. D. H. Cole pointed out in 1918 that participation in a large, centralized state wouldn't work unless citizens had an opportunity to learn "the rudiments of self-government with a smaller unit." C. D. H. Cole, *Self Government in Industry* (London: G. Bell, 1918), 234. A good summary of the scholarship on this critical paradigm is Steven L. Schweizer, "Participation, Workplace Democracy, and the Problem of Representative Government," *Polity* 27 (Spring 1995): 359–377.

It bothers me no end that I could not find such an association. The Pearson r correlation coefficient for the relation between the SAAM and turnout at the polls is $-.06$.[52] All in all, we would be about as successful predicting town meeting attendance by the color of the town moderator's eyes as by the town's turnout percentages in general elections.

Political Ideology

In 1986 Vermont placed an equal rights amendment to the state constitution on the ballot. Like much of the everyday conversation in Vermont, it was brief and to the point: "Equality of rights under the law shall not be denied or abridged by the State of Vermont or any of its political subdivisions on account of the sex of the individual." In Strafford, a Vermont hill town of 850 people in the rugged uplands of Orange County, 67 percent of the voters agreed. Two years later on town meeting day Strafford cast 49 percent of its votes in the five-way Democratic presidential preference primary for the underdog, helping the whitest American state lead the nation in its delegate percentage for Jesse Jackson. Only seven of Vermont's 246 cities and towns would be stronger for Jackson. Finally, in a three-election average of votes cast for Socialist candidate Bernie Sanders, who finally won a seat in the U.S. Congress in 1990, Strafford's vote for Sanders was 45 percent when the state itself averaged 35 percent.[53]

Up north in the town of Concord the situation is quite different. Concord is a valley town situated above the fall line of the Connecticut River. Here the water flows fast enough to gurgle and draw trout, and the great peaks of New Hampshire's Presidential range of the White Mountains edge

52. In their groundbreaking study of neighborhood democracy in five American cities, Berry, Portney, and Thomason find no significant relation between overall levels of political participation in the five cities they studied with strong face-to-face community involvement and that in the control cities where face-to-face involvement was not available. Berry, Portney, and Thomason, *Rebirth of Urban Democracy*, 81. Verba and Nie also reported countervailing aggregate and individual-level findings but suggested that a spillover effect was possible. Verba and Nie, *Participation in America*, 243. Schweizer found the connection missing as well. Schweizer, "Participation, Workplace Democracy, and the Problem of Representative Government," 359–377.

53. Driving down out of the hills from Strafford to Norwich early on an autumn morning is a quintessential example of an upland New England experience that occurs wherever there are hills and stream-fashioned valleys (which is just about everywhere). The bright sun and glorious colors of the highlands are lost as you drift downward into a cool white damp of a fog so thick that you know your neighbor's farm is there only by her rooster's crowing. I spent the autumn mornings of my youth fogbound (until 9:30 or 10:00 a.m.) in a little valley town upriver twenty-five miles north of Norwich. Most of my friends came down from the hills. Today we still argue about the merits of the deep mists that mark the boundaries of our most tender memories.

close from the east. The 534 registered voters of Concord were not impressed with the campaign for the ERA. Only 79 of them (28 percent of those who voted that year) voted yes. In the presidential primary of 1988, Jesse Jackson could squeeze only three votes out of the entire town. Gary Hart did better with four. Bernie Sanders's vote in Concord over the years has been dismal. It is fair to say that in the accepted parlance of American politics Strafford, Vermont, would be considered a very liberal community and Concord a very conservative one. To summarize this concept I factor-analyzed a cluster of town-level electoral results that included the Jackson and ERA votes to form a measure that places each Vermont town on a liberal-conservative numerical continuum. The results were generally consistent with my naked-eye estimates. I then used this measure to predict levels of town meeting attendance.

"Blind empiricism" is the best way to characterize this exercise, for political science has failed to establish a clear reason to suppose ideology might forecast the nature of political participation. The literature is full of bits and pieces. A recent study, for instance, concluded that "self identified liberals and self identified conservatives are slightly more active than the population as a whole, with ideological moderates somewhat below average in activity."[54] But this was a prediction based on intensity of belief rather than content of belief. Yet in the end I could not bring myself to believe that towns so remarkably different in their politics as Strafford and Concord would have similar levels of town meeting attendance. Liberals, after all like the *idea* of governance.

In fact, however, the town meetings in liberal towns are no more heavily attended than town meetings in conservative towns. The correlation coefficient produced by comparing the factor score for liberalism with town meeting attendance controlled for town size is only $-.03$. Another clear and important differentiating characteristic of Vermont's towns failed to penetrate the size-adjusted attendance measure.

Party Identification, Party Competition, and Bernie Sanders

The same is true for the other variables I used to identify variations in the political cultures of the towns in the sample: party identification, party competition, and the Bernard Sanders movement. In fact, these variables seemed doomed from the start. Evidence suggesting that Democrats tend to vote

54. Sidney Verba, Kay Lehman Schlozman, Henry Brady, and Norman H. Nie, "Citizen Activity: Who Participates? What Do They Say?" *American Political Science Review* 87 (June 1993): 303–318. I checked to see if the most intensely liberal towns or intensely conservative towns would have higher turnout at town meeting, and they did not.

more than Republicans or vice versa is scarce and often contradictory. Even less evidence suggests that party identity affects participation in local politics. The most promising aspect of party identity—the competitiveness of the two-party split—is simply another example of the "conflictual community" hypothesis that has already failed for socioeconomic heterogeneity and the liberal-conservative continuum. Finally, although the grassroots nature of his progressive movement in Vermont politics would lead one to believe that towns demonstrating strong support for Sanders would be towns with more active town meetings, with few exceptions little evidence indicates that Sanders's voter mobilization efforts extended importantly beyond Burlington.[55]

As I feared, these three variables (like the turnout score and the political ideology factor) did almost nothing to explain why some town meetings had higher attendance than others. Since the effect of one variable is often hidden by another variable, I experimented with combinations of all five political culture variables to determine if more light could be shed on the link between representational and real democracy in the context of community. None was. In short, neither the electoral turnout score, nor the liberal factor, nor a Sanders-Democratic factor score (nor any of the single variables used to construct these aggregates) survived the final regression equation to help determine why town meeting attendance varies as it does.[56]

The Passage of Time

Many of the variables treated here covary with the passage of time over the twenty-eight years of this study. The best example is the population growth of the towns involved. While the towns have been growing, attendance at town meeting has been dropping. In the early years of the study, 1970–1975, the 185 meetings we studied averaged 26.7 percent attendance (at the highest count), and the towns where they were held averaged 600 registered voters. In the last five years of the study, 1994–1998, the 273 meetings we studied averaged only 16 percent attendance, and the towns where they were held averaged 1,101 registered voters. The question is obvious. How much of the decline in attendance at town meeting is associated with this increase in town size?

55. In his sympathetic yet balanced description of Sanders as mayor of Burlington, Vermont, Steven Soifer praises Sanders for his "role in increasing voter participation." Steven Soifer, *The Socialist Mayor* (New York: Bergin and Garvey, 1991), 93.
    56. For an extended discussion of these variables, scatterplots of the relations involved, and the statistical parameters of the measures, see www.uvm.edu/~fbryan.

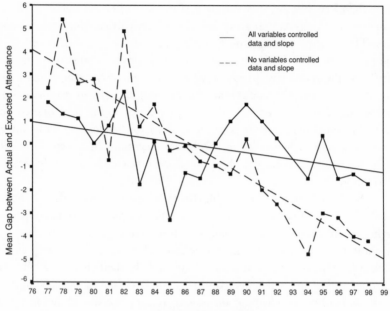

Year the Meetings Were Held

Figure 5.3. Decline in town meeting attendance, 1977–1998.

Figure 5.3 demonstrates the effect of the passage of time on attendance at 1,244 meetings held after 1976[57] by showing the percentage point gap between the average attendance at the meetings held in each year and (1) the average actual attendance each year and (2) the predicted attendance each year controlling for town size and other variables found to have additional impact on attendance. Thus in 1977 the average town meeting had about 2.5 percentage points *higher* attendance than the average town meeting in the entire database of 1,250 meetings studied after 1976. In 1998 the average meeting had about 4.2 percentage points *lower* attendance than the average town for the period 1977–1998.

When town size and other factors that affect attendance (see table 5.1) are controlled, however, the effect of time levels out considerably. Figure 5.3 shows that attendance at the average meeting in 1977 was only about 1.7 points above the average for the entire period, while attendance at the average meeting in 1998 was only about 1.7 percentage points below the average. The

57. I used the 1980 Census data for the towns with meetings in the sample for 1977–1979. Before that time reliable Census data were unavailable for Vermont's small towns. All meetings in the sample held before 1976 are omitted from the analysis anytime a Census variable is used.

trend lines summarize the slope in the data, account for the idiosyncrasies in individual years, and demonstrate that while actual attendance dropped about eight percentage points over the twenty-year period, from a positive 3.8 in 1977 to a negative 4.5 in 1998, controlled attendance dropped only about two percentage points, from a positive 0.8 in 1977 to a negative 1.2 in 1998. In other words, 75 percent of the drop in attendance is explained by the variables discussed in this chapter and in chapters 3 and 4. The most important of these variables by far was the size of the town.

Still, a fair amount of the variance in attendance for the pooled sample of meetings seems to be associated with the year the meetings were held. Meetings held in the later years of the study have lower attendance than meetings held in the early years irrespective of the size of the town, the presence of the Australian ballot, and so on. Town meeting may be suffering from the general participation malaise that has gripped the nation since the early 1960s. I will suggest in a concluding chapter that a continuing erosion of the number of issues of significance the towns are permitted to resolve at their meetings may explain much of the decline. For now, however, the year the meeting was held must be included in any summary of variables that explain why attendance is higher at some meetings and lower in others.

All Things Considered

The year the meeting was held becomes the third most important variable behind town size and the Australian ballot when entered into a regression equation along with all the other variables that account for at least an additional half a percentage point of explained variance in attendance at town

Table 5.1. Predicting Town Meeting Attendance (1,244 meetings, 1977–1997)

Variable	r	R^2	Improvement in R^2	Beta
Town size (adjusted)*	.777	.604	—	−.623
Australian ballot use	.796	.634	.030	−.195
Passage of time	.811	.657	.023	−.216
Population per road mile	.819	.670	.013	−.108
Education index	.824	.679	.009	.159
Time to work	.827	.684	.005	.096

Note: Dependent variable = percentage of registered voters at town meeting; all coefficients are significant at the >.01 level.
* See the voter power and decisiveness terms on page ●●●.

meeting. These three variables explain about 66 percent of the variance in attendance. Population per road mile enters the equation fourth, explaining a bit more than an additional 1 percent of the variance, while the education index comes in fifth, contributing a bit less than 1 percent of additional variance. The town's distance from its major source of out-of-town employment, defined by the time it takes commuters to get to work, squeezes into the calculation by adding a final half a percent. In total these six variables account for 68 percent of the variance in town meeting attendance.

When all is said and done, size remains dominant. Not only did none of the covarying relations that might have diminished size's stature pan out, but the process of controlling these variables actually strengthened the size variable. Size entered chapter 4 explaining 58 percent of the variance in town meeting attendance. It leaves chapter 5 explaining 60 percent. Only five of the many variables considered in this and the previous chapter were statistically significant, and they (in combination) reduced the variance in town meeting attendance by only an additional eight percentage points. For real democracy small not only is beautiful, it is essential.[58]

58. This table and the other tables in the book are based on a stepwise regression routine. From a group of independent variables the most important variable (the one that explains the most variance in the dependant variable) is selected first. Then the next most important variable of all those remaining is selected and its influence is reported, and so on until all the variables have been considered. For many, however, the "beta coefficient" is the measure of choice for gauging the effect of independent variables on a dependent variable. Beta simply standardizes the variables and then tells us what the effect of an increase (or decrease) of one standardized unit of an independent variable has on one standardized unit of the dependent variable. In table 5.1 readers will note, for instance, that for every increase of one unit of education, town meeting attendance will go up about 0.16 of a unit, while an increase of one unit of "population per road mile" produces a decrease of only 0.11 of a unit of town meeting attendance. I am including both measures throughout the book, even though by and large both render similar judgments. Beta, however, has the handy utility of specifying the direction of the relationship.

I turn pale at the outset of a speech and quake in every limb and in all my soul.
Cicero

The epigraph is from Cicero, *De oratore*, vol. 1 (Cambridge: Harvard University Press, 1942), quoted in Michael J. Beatty, "Situational and Predispositional Correlates of Public Speaking Anxiety," *Communication Education* 37 (January 1988): 28–39.

6

Democracy as Public Talk

Walking the Bounds

Norman Rockwell was America's most popular illustrator of the twentieth century. His renderings of Franklin Roosevelt's "Four Freedoms" (freedom *of* speech and worship and freedom *from* fear and want) touched chords deep in the heartland of a democracy caught in the passions of war. Rockwell's image of Carl Hess standing to speak at town meeting in Arlington, Vermont (*Freedom of Speech*), may be the most familiar to us. Rockwell lived in Arlington,[1] and (cutting him a little slack for romanticism) it must be said he nailed the distinguishing characteristic of town meeting right on the nose. Above all else, town meeting is public talk—common people *standing* for something.[2]

Town meeting is more than free speech, of course. It offers a fifth freedom, freedom to *govern*. After Hess and his neighbors finished talking, they often voted. They made a decision. Voting after

1. A New Yorker who made a summer trip to Arlington and fell in love with its peace and tranquillity, Rockwell was typical of the writers and artists who came to Vermont in the 1930s. In his introduction to Rockwell's *Rockwell on Rockwell: How I Make a Picture* (New York: Watson-Guptill, 1979), Alden Hatch says: "One summer showed Rockwell that Vermont was his spiritual home" (14).

2. Rockwell's illustration does not capture aspects of town meeting such as the participation of women and the nervousness and fear that some people have when speaking in public. It does capture, however, the sense that what happens in town meeting is almost never "social conversation." It is not done for pleasure, although nearly every town has one or two citizens who seem to enjoy the participatory act far too much. See M. Schudson, "Why Conversation Is Not the Soul of Democracy," *Critical Studies in Mass Communication* 14 (1997): 297–309, and Joshua Cohen, "Deliberation and Democratic Legitimacy," in *Deliberative Democracy: Essays on Reason and Politics*, ed. James Bohman and William Rehg (Cambridge: MIT Press, 1997), 67–92.

speaking is to governance what keeping the score is to sports. It changes everything.[3] But it is in the speaking, the direct face-to-face link between talk and power, that real democracy transcends nearly every other definition of democracy issued since the Greeks. This is what enfolds our imagination, sparks our sense of democratic adventure, and conjures up ancient and hopeful possibilities. It is time to explore the boundaries of these images—almost sacred in the Athenian tradition, but unexplored—and to prepare a match with reality.[4]

In his essay on Rockwell's famous painting of speech in town meeting, John Frohnmayer describes Rockwell's citizen as "relaxed and confident."[5] True in the image. But in reality many people standing to speak at town meeting may be scared to death. The literature on speech anxiety is extensive.

3. Political philosophers seem analytically and normatively averse to the joining of participation and decision making. Gerard Delanty interprets this tendency in the work of Jürgen Habermas: "Participation does not have to amount to decision-making." Civil society will produce "streams of communications" that will then "coalesce into bundles of topically specified *public opinion*." Then the political institutions take over to make the decision. In this way, he argues, Habermas is able to "avoid the problems that accompany the simple model of direct or strong democracy." Gerard Delanty, *Social Theory in a Changing World: Conceptions of Modernity* (Cambridge, UK: Polity Press, 1999), 86–91. For a more complete examination of Habermas and the separation of public opinion and decision making, see James Bohman, *Public Deliberation: Pluralism, Complexity, and Democracy* (Cambridge: MIT Press, 1996). In his insightful critique of the argument that social complexity at a national level precludes deliberative popular sovereignty, Bohman comes down hard on town meeting: "It is certainly clear that . . . town meetings are no longer the best way to maximize opportunities for citizenship." I assume he is talking about national citizenship, but I can't be sure. I run up against this maddening circumstance again and again. I always want to ask: Do you claim town meetings fail to "maximize citizenship" in the only context that any reasonable person would assume they might be able to—the small town? James Farr asks us, for example, to look at deliberation, where it occurs "over a wide range of issues" where "actual decisions" are made: "One might think of the sort of discussions that are still held in New England town meetings." Farr also emphasizes Harold Lasswell's admonition that "the methods of talk need to aid in the discovery of sound public policy. If the practice of discussion does not create a sense of achievement, there is contempt for talk." Harold Lasswell, *Democracy through Public Opinion*, cited in Farr, *Public Deliberation*. See also James Farr, "Framing Democratic Discussion," in *Reconsidering the Democratic Public*, ed. George E. Marcus and Russell L. Hanson (University Park: Pennsylvania State University Press, 1993), 379–392.

4. The coming of television, and with it the importance of televised imagery to the *representative* republic, has stimulated innovative work on the importance of visual communication in politics and suggests frameworks for similar analysis in *communal* democracies like town meeting. See, for instance, Denis G. Sullivan and Roger D. Masters, "Nonverbal Behavior, Emotions, and Democratic Leadership," in *Reconsidering the Democratic Public*, ed. George E. Marcus and Russell L. Hanson (University Park: Pennsylvania State University Press, 1993). See also Peter Laslett, "The Face to Face Society," in *Philosophy, Politics and Society*, ed. Peter Laslett (Oxford: Blackwell, 1956).

5. John Frohnmayer, "Freedom of Speech," in *Norman Rockwell's Four Freedoms: Images That Inspire a Nation*, ed. Stuart Murray and James McCabe (Stockbridge, MA: Berkshire House, 1993), 101.

Textbooks on oral communication typically identify symptoms such as "butterflies in the stomach, a rapid pulse rate, inability to sleep, rapid breathing, a dry mouth, clammy palms, perspiration, trembling, shortness of breath," and so on.[6] In 1978 the *Book of Lists* reported that Americans were more frightened of public speaking than of anything else: heights, sickness, insects, death, flying—you name it.[7] An extensive review of the scholarship on shyness reported by the *New York Times* in 1984 listed public speech second from the top on the list of "social anxieties": 74 percent of respondents said it caused them the most anxiety, just below being at a party with strangers.[8] All this needs to be kept in mind as we explore the degree to which people speak at town meeting.[9]

When Frohnmayer, a former chairperson of the National Endowment for the Arts, looks at Rockwell's painting, he also discovers that the argument being made by Carl Hess, a gas station owner (which in a small Vermont town means he pumped gas and had grease under his fingernails), is "compelling." Perhaps. But I have seen many a working person (and college professor as well) make arguments that are far from compelling. Indeed, as many of my students have pointed out over the years, some of the arguments made at town meeting are downright silly. Further on in his essay Frohnmayer says that freedom of speech depends on liberal interpretions of what it means. That freedom "will erode," he says, "when we scream at our congressional representatives to ban difficult or confrontational art." What would he say if Carl Hess was speaking for just such brands of censorship, which one can be certain many people (even majorities) at town meeting sometimes do?

---

6. Jimmy G. Cheek and Larry R. Arrington, *Effective Oral Communication* (Danville, IL: Interstate, 2000), 101. See also Mary Hinchcliff Pelias, "Communication Apprehension in Basic Public Speaking Texts: An Examination of Contemporary Textbooks," *Communication Education* 38 (January 1989): 41–53. Rush W. Dozier calls public speaking "the most common of the social phobias," telling us that the first time Mohandas Gandhi was called on (in a courtroom in India) he was so overcome he could not utter a word. Dozier's claim is that like all fears, fear of speaking before others is tied to the experiences of early humans, when the mere presence of others meant trouble. Rush W. Dozier Jr., *Fear Itself: The Origin and Nature of the Powerful Emotion That Shapes Our Lives and Our World* (New York: St. Martin's Press, 1998), 234–235, 244. Social psychologist Robert B. Zajonc's seminal article reviews the findings before 1960. Robert B. Zajonc, "Social Facilitation," *Science* 149 (July 16, 1965): 269–274.

7. David Wallechinsky and Irving Wallace, *The Book of Lists* (New York: Bantam, 1978).

8. Daniel Goleman, "Social Anxiety: New Focus Leads to Insights and Therapy," *New York Times*, December 18, 1984, C1.

9. When people were asked why they didn't speak out at meetings of the governing assembly in the Israeli kibbutz, the predominant reason among a sample of respondents was a general fear of speaking before large groups. Menahem Rosner, *Democracy, Equality and Change: The Kibbutz and Social Theory* (Darby, PA: Norwood Editions, 1982), 53.

Yet, given these caveats, Rockwell was right to use town meeting to portray freedom of speech.[10] In this chapter, however, I will not deal with questions of speech as governance or with the quality of the speech itself.[11] Here the task is far more basic; to analyze the quantity, the distribution, and the equality of that speech.[12]

WITNESS

The night we met in a special town meeting to reconsider the school budget, it was warm and the school's multipurpose room was filled to capacity. A group opposing new taxes to support the school had petitioned to have two issues decided. The first was to place future school budgets on an Australian ballot. One could then vote on the school budget without attending town meeting. This would be fairer, it was argued, since it hurt working people more to take a day off without pay and spend it at town meeting than it did professional people. Everyone would have a better chance to vote. There would be, of course, no more institutional, public, *democratic* deliberation— that is, public discussion on a real issue spiced by an impending decision that those doing the deliberating would have to live with. Also, defenders of school budgets could no longer blackmail opponents with a public question like "We're only doing this for the kids. Do you have something against kids?"

10. One (and perhaps the most qualified) interpreter of *Freedom of Speech* reads into the picture the idea that Carl Hess represented "a lone dissenter at a New England town meeting." Maureen Hart Hennessey, "The Four Freedoms," in *Norman Rockwell: Pictures for the American People*, by Maureen Hart Hennessey and Anne Knutson (Stockbridge, MA: Norman Rockwell Museum, 1999). Maybe. Maybe not.

11. Town meeting participation offers opportunities to study many of the characteristics of democratic participation. The quality of deliberation is only one. For recent definitional discussions of deliberative democracy, see Amy Gutmann, "The Disharmony of Democracy," in *Democratic Community*, ed. John W. Chapman and Ian Shapiro (New York: New York University Press, 1993), 126–160, and Jack Knight and James Johnson, "Aggregation and Deliberation: On the Possibility of Democratic Legitimacy," *Political Theory* 22 (May 1994): 277–296. The field of deliberative democracy was advanced dramatically by the essays published in James Bohman and William Rehg, eds., *Deliberative Democracy: Essays on Reason and Politics* (Cambridge: MIT Press, 1997).

12. David Sally argues, "No other variable has as strong and consistent an effect on results as face-to-face communication." David Sally, "Conversation and Cooperation in Social Dilemmas: A Meta-analysis of Experiments from 1958–1992," *Rationality and Society* 7 (January 1995): 58–92. In her 1997 presidential address to the American Political Science Association, Elinor Ostrom provides an excellent and thorough review of the literature on face-to-face communication. Her conclusions: "Consistent, strong and replicable findings are that substantial increases in the level of cooperation are achieved when individuals are allowed to communicate face to face. . . . the efficacy of communication is related to the capacity to talk face to face." Elinor Ostrom, "A Behavioral Approach to the Rational Choice Theory of Collective Action," *American Political Science Review* 92 (March 1998): 1–22. See also Elinor Ostrom, Roy Gardner, and James Walker, *Rules, Games and Common-Pool Resources* (Ann Arbor: University of Michigan Press, 1994), and the review of this literature in Jane Mansbridge, *Beyond Adversary Democracy* (New York: Basic Books, 1980), 270–277.

The second issue on the special warning was the current budget, passed earlier at the March town meeting. If this article was approved, deliberation on that year's school budget, along with the possibility of reductions, would be entertained.

Considerable discussion ensued on the first item (the Australian ballot). Most of the talk came from people who opposed it. These people (including me) tended to be professionals. Many were on salary, which made attendance at a Tuesday town meeting relatively painless from an economic point of view. We also were more apt to have kids in the school or to simply be passionate defenders of education. But the arguments we made were for democratic deliberation, not education. This was only right, since the issue was the Australian ballot. Eliminating the deliberative component would kill town meeting, we said. It is better to maintain the capacity to compromise and even trim an expenditure than to force the voters into a simple uninformed yes or no, up or down vote, we argued. Public discussion is vital to the democratic process, we contended. Thank God we lived in a place where open, public, deliberative democracy was possible! Except for a few "let every one have a chance to vote" declarations, the pro-Australian-ballot people were silent. They didn't want to talk about it. They asked for a secret ballot. They figured they had the votes. They didn't.

With the deliberative character of real democracy duly rescued, the moderator then called the second issue to the floor. Would the town meeting call the current school budget to the floor for deliberation? Would those who only moments before had extolled the virtues of open, public, democratic debate open any part the school budget to such a thing? No. We didn't want to talk about it.

We asked for a secret ballot.

We figured we had the votes.

We did.

Frank Bryan

I have no doubt that the attendance levels at town meeting we discussed in the preceding chapters appear (at first glance) to be discouragingly low. I have no doubt that the verbal participation at town meeting we are about to discuss will appear to be surprisingly high and well distributed among those in attendance. In this chapter I will treat the descriptive parameters of this participation, and in the next I will treat the correlates of their variation. To begin, let us return to the land of the coos in Newbury as it was in 1970 and meet some of the people who participated over the years in the town meetings that met in the town hall on the village green.

Signa Carbee, one of the very few female town moderators in Vermont in 1970, opened the Newbury town meeting at 10:39 a.m. She was a daughter of the retiring road commissioner, Theron "Buster" Carbee, and my next-door neighbor as I grew up. Scott Mahoney was the ninth person to speak. Scott was my social studies teacher in high school. He also ran a little inn and sold antiques. His hobbies were cooking, the theater, and raising local hell as a populist and a Democrat. (Not a particularly happy mix in those days.) By the time the meeting adjourned at 4:34 p.m., Scott would contribute sixteen more participations to a meeting that had 197 discrete acts of participation by a total of 57 of the 293 persons who made an appearance at town meeting that year.

Only one person would speak more than Scott Mahoney—a selectman, Milo Leighton. In almost all town meetings one of the selectmen unofficially answers questions for the Board of Selectmen and thereby piles up a lot of participations. Richard "Son" Darling, who taught me how to handle a canoe in between beers with my mom at our kitchen table when he was home on leave from the army, spoke the next most often, fifteen times. Year after year following the discussion of the town reports, Son, then a retired career sergeant, would rise and make the motion (it was usually article 3) that the town appropriate a sum of money (in 1970 it was $150) to observe Memorial Day.

In the same town meeting Lloyd Rogers, the man who won the most contentious race for selectman in years, spoke nine times, one fewer than the fourth-place participator, town clerk Barbara Welch. In 1970 it took four ballots to elect Rogers, a farmer who lived out back on Rogers's Hill. His place had the most beautiful view in New England of the White Mountains of New Hampshire. But you got the idea Rogers didn't spend a lot of time looking at the view. He had three sisters named Faith, Hope, and Charity. Hope was the principal of the high school for my last three years there.

A year later, in the 1971 meeting, Lloyd Rogers, now a selectman, led all participators with 23 discrete acts of participation; Scott Mahoney had 12; and Son Darling had 2. In the meeting of 1971 only 117 attended (116 fewer than the year before), but they talked a lot more often, 354 times as opposed to 197 in 1970. In 1970 only 57 participated. In 1971, 74 did. They also talked longer in 1971. Despite the several time-consuming paper (secret) ballots taken in 1970, the 1971 meeting took more than an hour longer than the 1970 meeting—382 minutes in 1971 as opposed to 302 minutes in 1970.[13]

The most important event in the town meeting of 1971 was the defeat of Signa Carbee as moderator. Voting down a moderator is unpleasant

---

13. A paper ballot for meetings of this size usually takes from ten to twenty minutes. During this time formal discussion is suspended.

(and therefore rare). The procedure goes as follows: The moderator from the past year calls the meeting to order and immediately asks a selectman (or the town clerk) to preside over the election of a moderator for the current year. Then she or he steps aside (literally) while the selectman asks for nominations from the floor. Opposition rarely exists, and the incumbent is duly nominated and reelected by acclamation. When opposition does develop, the moderator usually prevails. Since the office is the town's most prestigious, being thrown out of it is especially embarrassing. In Newbury that day opposition came from Gerry Brooks. The town voted. (A secret ballot.) The town counted. (Neighbors talked. People visited.) Signa Carbee waited. All this took fourteen minutes. Then the town announced the vote: Signa 70, Gerry 93. She walked alone down off the stage where she had received her high school diploma fourteen years earlier. She sat in a chair among her neighbors who had defeated her. In better times she had been the star of the girls' basketball team on that very floor, a floor so small that the center jump circle intersected the top of the "key," the painted half circle five feet from the foul line. There is nowhere to hide in the Newbury town hall.

Signa Carbee was not interested in hiding, however. The next year (1972) she participated from the floor 10 times. Only 6 of the 220 attenders participated more. Son Darling participated 10, times and Lloyd Rogers 23 (again). Scott Mahoney is not recorded as speaking.[14] All in all, 56 participators produced 234 individual acts of participation. In 1973, 219 attended, and 71 of them spoke a total of 239 times. Scott Mahoney was the first to speak and finished with 13 participations. Lloyd Rogers had 26, Son Darling had 1, and Signa Carbee had 3. The next year (1974) the meeting lasted 300 minutes, within which time 70 people participated 277 times. Lloyd Rogers, still a selectman, had 30 participations, Son Darling 3, and Signa Carbee 6, Scott Mahoney was aparently not in attendance.

As the 1970s progressed these kinds of participation profiles continued. In 1978 Son participated 13 times, Scott 16, Signa 9 (she had been elected to the budget committee a year earlier), and Lloyd 20, even though he was no longer a selectman. In 1982, the year Vermont town meetings attracted global attention by their overwhelming support for a nuclear weapons freeze referendum, Son—as usual—asked for and got money to observe Memorial Day. Scott was most interested in where the revenue-sharing money went. All in all, he participated 11 times. Signa spoke 8 times, and Lloyd, now a town agent and a justice of the peace, spoke 11 times.

---

14. Unfortunately, I cannot tell if he was present and not speaking or if he was simply absent. Knowing Mr. Mahoney the way I did, I'd bet he was absent. He wasn't one not to talk.

This 1982 meeting was not well attended (156 present at the highest count) and didn't last long (133 minutes). In that time 55 people participated. They took up the nuclear freeze resolution (article 15) at 11:37 a.m., voting to move it up a couple of notches on the agenda to make sure the debate took place before lunch, after which it was assumed (correctly) that attendance would drop off. Seven minutes after it began, discussion on the nuclear freeze article ended. Only 6 people participated. Of the 245 participations made that day at the Newbury town meeting, only 7 were on the nuclear freeze resolution. Son Darling participated once. Scott, Signa, and Lloyd did not participate on it at all. Just before the vote began I counted the attendance, finding 136 people in the hall. Only 117 of them voted on the resolution. It took eleven minutes to do the secret ballot. When the counting was over, the town had approved by a vote of 75 to 42 a resolution calling on Vermont's legislature to pass a resolution calling on the Congress to pass a resolution that would "request the President of the United States to propose to the Soviet Union a mutual freeze on the testing, production and deployment of nuclear weapons and of missiles and new aircraft designed primarily to deliver nuclear weapons, with the verification safeguards satisfactory to both countries."

Although Lloyd Rogers did not speak on the nuclear freeze resolution, he did speak a total of 11 times on six other articles. He had not missed a town meeting since I began this study thirteen years earlier in 1969. Sometime in the thirty-two minutes between 2:26 p.m. and 2:58 p.m. on March 2, 1982, Lloyd spoke on article 14, the town budget. It was to be his last participation in town meeting. He got sick in the spring of 1983 and died up on his farm on May 26. He was seventy-nine. That year 229 names were on the delinquent tax list (out of about 1,000 taxpayers) published in the town report. Lloyd's was not among them.[15]

It snowed heavily the night of March 5, 1985. Twelve inches had come down by the time the Newbury town meeting was to begin at 9:00 the next morning. Gerry Brooks (still moderator after defeating Signa Carbee fourteen years earlier) postponed the opening of the meeting for twenty minutes. In all, only 87 voters showed up that year. One was Son Darling. At 10:52 he rose at town meeting for the last time. He asked the people to appropriate $300 for the observance of Memorial Day. They did. It took two minutes. He was sick even then. He missed the meeting of 1986 and died later that year. His single participation in 1985 was one of only 177 in Newbury's worst-attended meeting between 1970 and the end of the century.

15. IBM, however, was. They owed the town $1.78 in property taxes.

Scott Mahoney also made it to town meeting that day in 1985. At 10:59 he was one of 12 attenders to speak on article 6, "To fix compensation of all town officers." He also entered a property tax debate (one of 12 participations among 9 people—6 men and 3 women), spoke three times on the revenue-sharing article, and spoke once on snow removal. Then sometime between 2:17 and 2:33 p.m., near the end of the meeting under the "new business" article, Scott, (then seventy-one) participated one last time. Along with four others (Signa Carbee being one of them), he spoke on the sixth item of new business, whether the town meeting should continue to be held during the day or be held at night. His remarks were covered in the *Journal Opinion*, a little weekly paper printed in the neighboring town of Bradford: "Scott Mahoney suggested the idea be put to a vote and survey sheets be available at various places, so voters can pick them up and make their feelings known. He said the Town Meeting could be a pot luck supper, allowing working families time to get home from their jobs and come to the town meeting for a meal and business."[16]

He died a year later. It was appropriate that this democrat's final participation be a vision of working families eating their supper and governing themselves. The last time I saw Scott he was flat out and in pain at the veterans' hospital in White River Junction, Vermont. But he still managed a grin as my mother and I walked into his room. My mother (protecting me even in my forties) would not tell me exactly what ailed him. It was, she said, some strange variety of cancer. He died on July second.

I don't know exactly what disease killed Scott Mahoney at age seventy-two. I do know that almost two years earlier his picture had made the front page in the state-and-local section of the *Burlington Free Press*, Vermont's largest newspaper, under the headline: "Gays Hold Celebration in Burlington." The accompanying story read in part: "He fought in a tank in George Patton's army in World War II. Born in Barre, this lifetime Vermonter married, had a child, taught in a local university and participated in local school boards, parents associations and local clubs. Three years ago, shortly after his wife died, he took a male lover. Saturday, Scott Mahoney, white haired and 70, marched along Bank Street past the Church Street Marketplace as part of Burlington's second annual Lesbian Gay Pride March."[17]

Signa Carbee, Son Darling, Lloyd Rogers, and Scott Mahoney are typical of the thousands of people participating in town meeting every year all

16. "Newbury," *Journal Opinion*, March 6, 1985, 1, 5.

17. Scott taught me world history (as it was called in the 1950s), U.S. history, and civics in high school. He never told any of us he was a tanker for Patton. Michael Powell, "Gays Hold Celebration in Burlington," *Burlington Free Press*, June 17, 1984, B1.

over Vermont throughout the three decades I studied these meetings.[18] Nor
is the Newbury town meeting unusual. My students and I counted 196,055
people like Scott Mahoney, Signa Carbee, Lloyd Rogers, and Son Darling
at town meetings. Of these, 61,474 participated verbally at least once. The
data allow an analysis of the town meeting talk of these kinds of people from
meeting to meeting and from town to town in the 1,389 meetings[19] in the
210 towns we studied.

The Parameters of Participation

I defined participation as including any verbal act that "commanded the attention" of the meeting itself. Thus one did not have to be recognized by the
moderator to have participated. But grumblings and asides that were more or
less localized in the meeting hall were not counted. Also not counted were
"seconds" of motions. Although seconds are formal participations, in many
cases when the moderator asks, "Do I hear a second?" the response is so subtle
that it would take a skilled auctioneer to identify who made it. Participations
by the moderator were not counted either, since they are fundamentally a
constant and their function for the most part is to guide the progress of the
meeting.[20] Also, if all the moderators' participations were counted, this would
deceptively inflate the participatory landscape of town meeting.

To simplify the lexicon, I will refer to anyone at a town meeting who
participates verbally as a "speaker" rather than a "participator," since all those
in attendance are "participators" in several respects whether or not they speak.
The amount of verbal participation will be called "speech," as in "speech was
strong at the Newbury town meeting" rather than "participation was strong at
the Newbury town meeting." Similarly, I will refer to individual acts of speech

---

18. Signa Carbee is still going strong. At the 2002 town meeting in Newbury she
participated 38 times, more than any of the other 51 participants in a town meeting with 152 in
attendance. She was elected selectman several years earlier and now is the most powerful officer in
town.

19. Of the 1,435 town meetings studied, 1,389 were used to analyze the talk at each
individual meeting. Forty-six cases tripped one of the many cords laid out to ensure that the
database was clean. They were discarded. Setting rigorous requirements for accuracy was an
affordable luxury because of the large sample size.

20. When moderators left the podium to speak on an issue they were counted as
participators. No doubt some moderators influence the decisions made at town meeting through
subtle forms of participation and through their capacity to guide the debate. My sense, however, is
that the moderator who "makes things happen his way" is pretty much a fictional character. This
may be because the role of moderator has been the subject of continuing attention by the Vermont
League of Cities and Towns, an organization that has sought to professionalize it through
workshops and seminars.

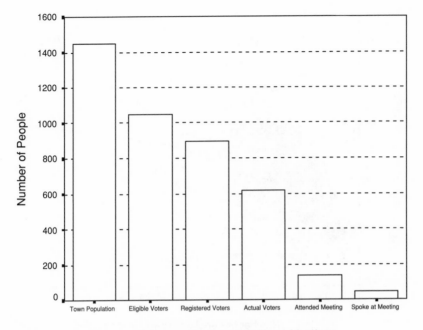

Averages for the 1,389 Town Meetings

Figure 6.1. Summary of participatory data for town meeting.

(verbal participation) as "talk." Thus a meeting where a large number of persons participated verbally at least once but very few participated verbally more than once will be called a meeting where "speech was strong but talk was not."

The average population of the towns where the town meetings of this study were held is about 1,450. The average number of eligible voters in these towns is about 1,050. About 900 of these registered to vote, and about 600 actually did so in the general elections held closest to the year when each meeting was held. But the average number of people who attended their town meetings in these towns in these years was only 137, and on average only 44 of those in attendance spoke out during the meeting. The dramatic drop in numbers of town residents who participate when the democracy becomes real rather than representative is displayed in figure 6.1.

In all, 238,603 discrete acts of participation were recorded over 4,816 hours of actual deliberative time.[21] The baseline number of most importance is the one telling us that on average 44 people will speak out at a typical

21. It took minute-by-minute recording of participation for an aggregate time span of 100 weeks of five eight-hour days to establish the database. These hours do not include time the meeting spent in recess or was adjourned for lunch.

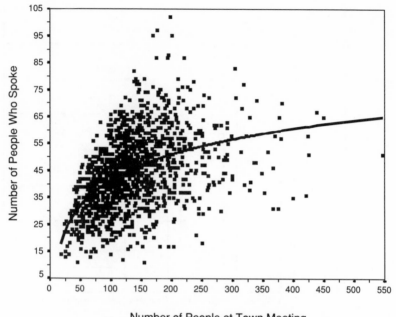

Number of People at Town Meeting

Figure 6.2. Speakers (at highest count) by attendance at town meeting.

town meeting. Great variation in this statistic exists, however, and within this variation are footprints that lead to the nature of face-to-face democracy. At the lower end of the distribution were two meetings with only 11 speakers and 8 others that had fewer than 15. At the upper end were fourteen meetings in which more than 75 persons spoke. One, the Newfane meeting of 1980, had 102. Between the extremes, the data follow a normal curve.

The number of speakers is obviously connected to the number present at the meeting, and the relation is curvilinear. The steep positive slope between attendance and speech flattens out dramatically as attendance begins to exceed 150 people. When attendance is 50, about 30 speak. When it is 100, about 40 do. When attendance doubles again to 200, the average number of speakers is only 50; at 400 it is 52. The number of speakers levels out when attendances reaches about 150. This makes theoretical sense. Wide variation also exists around the predicted slope in the data. The log of the number of people in attendance explains only 23 percent of the variance in the number who actually speak (see fig. 6.2).

Meetings where "everyone has a say" are precious few. Only 6 of the 1,389 meetings had over 90 percent participation. Two of these were in

Victory,[22] the tiny town in the Northeast Kingdom that was pictured in a political science textbook to demonstrate poor attendance at town meeting. Conversely, town meetings where only a small fraction of those in attendance speak out are also hard to find. Only 4 of the 1,389 meetings in the sample had fewer than 10 percent of the attenders participating.[23] One of these occurred in 1979 in Shelburne, a larger upscale town introduced in chapter 3.

The amount of speech in the average town meeting is 44 speakers for every 100 in attendance when attendance is measured as the average of several counts.[24] Compared with other rates of group participation (from classrooms to public hearings), this rate is high. Still, a majority of the attenders at town meeting speak in only 23 of 100 cases. In no meeting did a majority of a town's registered voters speak. Victory came closest in 1990, with 46 percent of the town's registered voters speaking. But in the Shelburne town meeting of 1985 the 24 citizens present who spoke out (18 percent of the average number in attendance) represented only 0.06 percent of the town's 3,753 registered voters.

How Much Talk Is There?

The majority of people who *speak* at all at town meeting will *talk* more than once.[25] Thus, while the number of speakers at the average town meeting is 44, the amount of talk (the average number of individual acts of participation) in the average town meeting is 173. An average of 3.9 individual acts of verbal participation (talk) are therefore issued for each person speaking at least once (speech). Talk ranges from the 21 recorded for the 12 speakers in the 1977

22. See the Witness in chapter 3.

23. The reduction in cases from the full sample occurs because participation is more difficult to record than attendance and nearly fifty meetings lacked reliable data on participation.

24. Coincidently, Rosner reported that 56 percent of those present at the assembly in a kibbutz usually spoke at least once. Menahem Rosner, *Participatory Political and Organizational Democracy and the Experience of the Israeli Kibbutz* (Haifa: University of Haifa, 1981), 12. For analytical purposes it makes no difference which measure is used (speakers as a percentage of highest attendance or average attendance), since they are so strongly related ($r = .98$). I use the average attendance because, while the highest attendance produces a better indicator of the percentage of a town's registered voters who take the time to "go" to a town meeting, it probably overestimates a meeting's potential talkers.

25. At the 1999 town meeting in Plymouth, Vermont, John Wheeler stood to receive a plaque from the town for twenty-eight years of service as town moderator. His advice to the 61 people in attendance (34 men and 27 women): "Stand up to be seen. Speak up to be heard. Sit down to be appreciated." Evidently the ghost of Calvin Coolidge still haunts Plymouth. David Grover, Betsy Kreimer, and Prasoeur Prum, "The 1999 Comparative Town Meeting Study: Town of Plymouth," Burlington, University of Vermont, Real Democracy Data Base, March 1999.

meeting in the ski town of Warren to the 539 participations made by the 95 speakers at the meeting in the very same town eleven years later in 1988.

It comes as no surprise that as speech (the total number of individuals who speak at all) increases, the total talk increases as well. What may be surprising is that the ratio of talk to speech (which averages 3.9 to 1) does not vary with the size of the group that speaks at least once. I expected, for instance, that a town meeting of 80 speakers would have a different ratio of talk to speech than a town meeting of 20 speakers. But the correlation between the size of the speaker group and the amount of talk that group produces is nearly nonexistent ($r = -.01$). Town meetings with 20 speakers have a talk/speech ratio of 4 participations per speaker, while town meetings with 60 speakers have a talk/speech ratio of 3.9.

The situation changes when the talk/speech ratio is compared with the total number of attenders rather than the total number of speakers. A clear but curved decline in the talk/speech ratio accompanies increasing attendance at town meeting. The 71 meetings with, on average, more than 200 persons in attendance at any point during the meeting averaged 2.9 acts of talk per speaker. The 590 meetings with fewer than 100 people in attendance averaged a talk/speech ratio of 4.6. Yet the *variation* in this talk/speech ratio from meeting to meeting increases as the meetings get smaller. Small meetings do not guarantee more talk per speaker, but they allow it.

How Long Do Speech and Talk Last?

The average town meeting takes the better part of four hours (three hours and forty-eight minutes) of actual deliberative time. It lasts long enough to give each of its attenders about two minutes to speak. Since many fewer speak than attend, each speaker averages about five minutes of talk.[26] In the average town meeting the average "talk" lasts about one minute and twenty-one seconds.

The average town meeting begins with a baseline of about twenty speakers, adding about six speakers for every additional hour the meeting lasts. About 40 percent of the variance in the speech at a meeting is explained by the number of minutes it lasts. Meeting length explains slightly less (35 percent) of the variance in the total amount of talk that occurs in the meeting. Each additional hour the meeting lasts produces about eighteen more acts of talk.

26. This statistic is exaggerated to the extent that some towns do not have discussion while voting by ballot is taking place. Others have visits from state legislators who give a short speech that takes up additional time.

Increases in the number of speakers begin to level off at about the three-hour mark. Meetings that last less than three hours add about five new speakers with every thirty-minute increment of meeting time. Those that last more than three hours add about two new speakers with every half an hour of additional time. A similar effect holds for the total amount of talk.[27]

"Presentations" or "Conversations"

That the average act of talk lasts about 1.3 minutes tells us little about the rhythm of deliberation at town meeting. On this matter two contradictory myths prevail. One holds that town meetings are staid political institutions where wise citizens rise carefully to address their fellow townspeople in measured tones reminiscent of Puritan town fathers or Roman senators. The other myth is that town meeting democracy is a give-and-take of many citizens speaking often and quickly. One vision is of ordered individual "presentations" by a relative few. The other is of a "conversation" by the many. To separate presentational meetings from conversational meetings and determine what was normal and what was not, I grafted a standardized length of meeting variable onto standardized speech and talk scores. This statistic weights the amount of speech, talk, and time equally. More speech and talk in fewer minutes ranks a meeting as more "conversational."

Of the 1,389 meetings studied between 1970 and 1998, the most conversational was held (again) in Warren, this time in 1987. Seventy-eight people spoke 430 times in three and a half hours. My hometown of Newbury earned a very high conversational score in its meeting of 1982 when 55 people spoke 245 times in a bit over two hours. This was the year Newbury debated the nuclear freeze issue (see above).[28] The town meeting that scored lowest on conversation (or, conversely, the highest on presentation) occurred in 1983 in Berlin, a town of about 1,200 registered voters situated near the state capital in Montpelier. The meeting lasted six hours and seven minutes, and in that time these 26 people combined to speak only 93 times.

But meetings like those in Warren and Berlin were exceptional. The typical town meeting on the presentation/conversation measure is like the

27. The ecological fallacy warns that these statistics ignore dynamics *within* the meetings themselves. Logic predicts, however, and inspection of the *sequence* of the talk in individual meetings shows, a predictable, curvilinear decline in new speakers (speech) as time passes.

28. The nuclear freeze debates, although receiving more national and international attention than any town meeting issue since Jefferson's embargo, were clearly more presentational than conversational in Vermont.

one held in the hill town of Roxbury in 1992, where 50 people made 286
verbal participations in 284 minutes, or the meeting in Alburg (a town bordering Canada on the Lake Champlain islands) in 1971 (52 participations by
22 people in 90 minutes). These findings match my own expectations and
the observations of my students. Verbal participation in town meetings is
seldom purely conversational or presentational. While it varies from town
to town, from meeting to meeting, and from issue to issue, the talk of town
meeting is probably best summarized as a mix of presentations (short ones)
and conversation with less presentation than conversation.[29] This mix is also
generally well ordered and mostly polite. Outbursts occur, but they are rare.
At the extremes (although neither suffices), "tedious" is a more apt adjective
for most of the talk of real democracy than "exciting." Similarly, "work" is a
better descriptive noun than "fun."

The Equality of Participation

Central to any definition of democracy is the equality of participation among
citizens. The statistics used so far begin our understanding of this question,
but they may camouflage inequality in the distribution of verbal participation. Even in the most conversational meetings (featuring more speakers and
more talk), a few individuals could dominate. A meaningful picture of the
equality of participation at town meeting requires an index sensitive to both
the percentage of those in attendance who speak at all and the degree to
which certain individuals dominate the discussion within the participating
group.

I have chosen a measure of equality that statisticians call the Gini coefficient because I find it intuitively pleasing. The logic behind the Gini
coefficient appears in such a familiar statement as "The wealthiest 10 percent
of the population earned 50 percent of the income last year." For our purposes a similar statement might read, "The most talkative 10 percent of the
citizens at town meeting were responsible for 50 percent of the talk," or "The
least talkative 30 percent of the citizens at town meeting were responsible for
only 5 percent of the talk." The Gini index itself is a summation of this logic
for ten cohorts, each representing 10 percent of the total attenders at a town

29. Over the years I have been tempted to ask my students to time each act of participation.
I have not because I am afraid it would be too difficult to do it accurately. But I do intend to see if
tape recordings might be permitted. If done unobtrusively, they might be of sufficient quality to
obtain "length of talk" data for individuals. To my knowledge the literature on public, verbal
participation provides no help in defining the quantitative parameters of public "conversation."

meeting.[30] It ranges from 100 (each cohort of attenders had 10 percent of the participations) to 10 (the top cohort had 100 percent) of the participations. The average Gini index for the 1,376[31] meetings in the sample was 24, the highest 58, and the lowest 10. The remainder was pretty much normally distributed within these parameters.

A meeting in my own town of Starksboro, a medium-sized (population 1,660 in 1990) foothill town that lies at the juncture of the Green Mountains and the Lake Champlain basin, represents the norm. In 1997 Starksboro's meeting had a Gini index of 24.3. In that year 53 of the 122 people present produced a total of 188 individual participations. The 10 percent of the attenders who spoke most often accounted for 60 percent of the total acts of speech. The 10 percent who spoke next most often had 23 percent of the total participation, the next 10 percent had 9 percent, the next 10 percent had 7 percent, and the last 10 percent of the attenders who had any speech or talk at all had 2 percent of it. This left half of those present with none.

Starksboro's average distribution is demonstrated in plot 1 of figure 6.3. The shaded area under the diagonal represents the degree to which its meeting met the expectations of a perfectly egalitarian system. The most equal distribution of the talk among the attenders at a town meeting in our sample occurred in the town of Panton in 1982, not surprisingly a small meeting with an average attendance of only 47 (plot 2 of fig. 6.3). The number of participators was also 47.[32] One woman (an officer of the town) spoke twelve times; two others spoke nine times each; four spoke seven times; four, six times; four, five times; two, four times; four, three times; and seven, twice. Each of the remaining nineteen people spoke only once. The total of 155 participations thus spread out over the 47 citizens in attendance produced a Gini index of 58. In no other town meeting did it get any better than that.

On the other extreme came Shelburne in 1979, with a meeting in which fewer than 10 percent of those in attendance spoke up. Shelburne is a relatively large town and had 348 present at its 1979 meeting (plot 3 of fig. 6.3).[33]

30. The Gini index is strongly related to other measures we have been using, namely the percentage of the total attenders who participate and the number of participations per attender. The former explains 83 percent of the variance in the Gini and the latter explains 49 percent.

31. Here another 13 meetings were discarded because the data, while accurate in the aggregate, contained uncertainties at the individual level.

32. I used the average attendance in calculating the Gini index because it is a better indicator of the number of people at town meeting at any given time during the meeting.

33. Since I built the Gini coefficients by breaking down participations into cohorts of ten percentage points, the index can go no lower than 10. This happens because in cases like Shelburne where fewer than 10 percent of the attenders speak at least once, all the participators are in the last cohort, so that at least ten percent of the area under the diagonal must be covered.

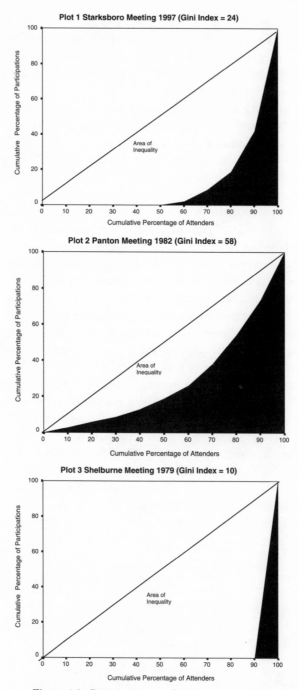

Figure 6.3. Participation equality in town meeting.

Seven of the remaining 1,375 town meetings in the sample scored the same as Shelburne. They also produced the lowest Gini coefficients possible (10) because 100 percent of the acts of speech at these meetings were made by 10 percent or fewer of those in attendance. Only ten meetings had Ginis over 50. If it is the goal of real democracy to equalize the number of times citizens in attendance at a public assembly speak out on issues, town meeting gets only a quarter of the way there.

Size Matters (Again)

Once again scale is at the heart of the matter. In general town meetings with the smallest number of people in attendance have the largest percentage of participators and the best distribution of participation among those present.[34] The relation between the size of town meeting and the spread of the participation over the meeting appears constant over the years and across the sample of towns. This may happen for the same reason a student is more likely to speak in a small seminar than in a large class.[35] It might also happen, however, because aversion to public speaking increases with the size of the group you must speak to.[36] Thus a town meeting with only 50 people in attendance

34. Rosner found meeting size to be negatively related to rates of verbal participation in the Israeli kibbutz. Rosner, *Participatory Political and Organizational Democracy*, 12.

35. The literature on class size and student behavior is often related to student performance, not verbal participation as an independent construct. Glen E. Robinson and James H. Wittebols, *Class Size Research: A Related Cluster Analysis for Decision-Making* (Arlington, VA: Educational Research Service, 1986). One study, for instance, found no relation between class size and participation in "class-run tasks." Stan M. Shapson, Edgar N. White, Gary Eason, and John Fitzgerald, "An Experimental Study of the Effects of Class Size," *American Education Research Journal* 17 (Spring 1980): 141–152. But beginning as early as 1934 (Helen C. Dawe, "The Influence of the Size of Kindergarten Groups upon Performance," *Child Development* 5 [1934]: 295–303), evidence continues to demonstrate that bigger classes mean less verbal participation, less equally distributed over the class population. An exception is James L. Scott, "The Effects of Class Size on Student Verbal Interaction in Five English Classes" (Ph.D. diss., Rutgers University, 1972). For a summary of this scholarship, see Leonard S. Cahen, *Class Size and Instruction* (New York: Longman, 1983).

36. Michael Beatty, chairman of the Department of Speech Communications at the University of Missouri and a central figure in the literature of the field, argues that although there are positive correlations between audience size and fear of speaking, the causal chains are complicated and the relationship may be curvilinear. Speaking before a very large group may allow a certain disassociation between the speaker and the audience (reducing anxiety), and speaking before a very small group may trigger anxiety based on familiarity and thereby constitute a threat to one's status. Nevertheless, in the four fundamental settings for communication (dyads, groups, meetings, and public audiences—smallest to largest), fear is most acute in the last. Michael Beatty, telephone interview, August 31, 2000. According to Karen Dwyer, associate professor of communication at the University of Nebraska, Lincoln, misunderstanding the ordering of different constructs (such as shyness, reticence, and apprehension) in the causal sequence also complicates the research on fear of public speaking. Karen Dwyer, telephone interview, September 12, 2000.

ought to have a larger percentage of those participating than a meeting with 200 present.[37]

Since the number of people who speak at town meeting does not keep up with the increase in the number of people who attend, the statistical relation between the number of people at town meeting (its size) and the percentage participating is negative—strongly so.[38] A similar, yet bumpier, relation exists between meeting size and the equality of verbal participation. Like the bond between town size and attendance, the connection between attendance and speaking is curvilinear. While the logged number of registered voters in town explains 58 percent of the variance in the percentage of registered voters in attendance at town meeting, the logged number in attendance at town meeting explains 57 percent of the percentage of those in attendance who will speak at town meeting and 43 percent of the variance in the Gini index of participation equality (see fig. 6.4).[39]

37. One "improvement" made to town meetings in recent decades is more use of microphones. But they don't seem to help. Since 1996 I have been including microphone use in the database. In the 216 meetings where data were available, 109 used a microphone and 107 did not. The percentage of attenders who spoke was 38 when microphones were used and 53 when they were not. A good deal of this difference is attributable to meeting size. Bigger meetings have relatively fewer speakers *and* tend to use microphones. Still, microphones may add their own influence to nonparticipation. Degree of "conspicuousness" has been shown to be associated with fear of public speaking, as has degree of "formality" in the speaking situation. Using a microphone (even from one's seat) in a town meeting hall certainly adds to both. Beatty, "Situational and Predispositional Correlates of Public Speaking Anxiety," 28–39, and A. H. Buss, *Self-Consciousness and Social Anxiety* (San Francisco: W. H. Freeman, 1980).

38. Finding comparative data in the literature on group size and participation in other settings is difficult because seldom do the groups vary in size as much as the town meetings I am studying. One study I found useful indicated that in twelve college classes of from six to twenty students, 41 percent of the students participated. In twelve classes of twenty-one to fifty students, 19 percent participated; and in twenty-seven classes of more than fifty students, 7 percent did. In our town meetings participation levels for similar-sized groups were much higher. This ought to be the case given that they lasted longer and that town meetings are *designed* to be more participatory than college classes. See Franklin D. Becker, Robert Sommer, Joan Bee, and Bart Oxley, "College Classroom Ecology," *Sociometry* 36 (December 1973): 514–525. For supportive findings see Roger G. Barker and Paul V. Gump, *Big School, Small School: High School Size and Student Behavior* (Stanford: Stanford University Press, 1964).

39. Sociologists estimate the number of possible interactions between members of a group (Bossard): interactions $= [N^2 - N]/2$) and subgroups (Kephart: interactions $= [3N - 2^{(N+1)} + 1]/2$). The more moderate curve established by Bossard produces a close approximation of a reasonable model of town meeting participation. See J. J. S. Bossard, "The Law of Family Interaction," *American Journal of Sociology* 50 (January 1945): 292–294, and W. M. Kephart, "A Quantitative Analysis of Intergroup Relationships," *American Journal of Sociology* 55 (May 1950): 544–549. As I have noted, the difficulty in using the findings from small-group analysis is that nearly all its research is conducted on groups that by definition are too small (under thirty members) to approximate town meetings. George Simmel, "The Number of Members as Determining the Sociological Form of the Group," *American Journal of Sociology* 8 (1902): 1–46, quoted in J. S. B. Lindsay, "On the Number in a Group," *Human Relations* 25 (February 1972): 47–64.

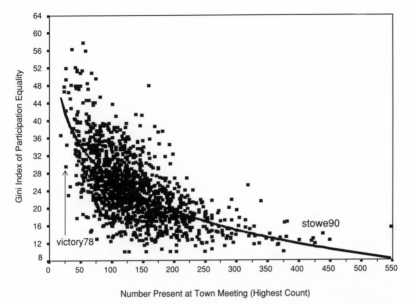

Figure 6.4. Participation equality by meeting size (1,373 town meetings, 1970–1998).

Earlier the concern was the size of the town. Now the concern is the size of the meeting.[40] The measure I will use to compare meetings on the amount and distribution of their verbal participation is (as it was for attendance) the ratio of what was expected, given size, to what was attained. The size control reminds us, for instance, that although the meeting held in Stowe in 1990 (see fig. 6.4) had a much lower level of participation than smaller meetings like the one held in Victory in 1978, Stowe's participation equality *effort* was much better than Victory's. In other words, citizens of Stowe overcame the burden of size associated with their meeting, whereas the citizens of Victory did not. With the effect of size thus statistically controlled, we can look to see if other variables beyond size make the equality of verbal participation at town meeting vary as it does.

40. An interesting explanation for this (beyond the obvious time constraints and the inclination to fear public speaking more as audiences get larger) is that larger gatherings are more apt to *draw* persons with speaking anxiety because they feel less threatened in a larger group. While this has negative implications for attendance in small towns (keeping shy people away), it also means that after the meeting size has been controlled larger meetings may have relatively more people in attendance who have higher speaking apprehension. K. David Roach, "Teaching Assistant Communication Apprehension, Willingness to Communicate, and State Communication Anxiety in the Classroom," *Communication Research Reports* 15 (Spring 1998): 130–140.

WITNESS

STANDING TALL FOR TOOTH DECAY

Things were going smoothly at the Starksboro Town Meeting.

Too smoothly.

One after another the usual list of "Warning" items requesting small amounts of money to fund human services in the region were being approved. Five hundred dollars for a Home Health Agency. One hundred fifty dollars for the Retired Senior Volunteer Program (RSVP) of Addison County. Six hundred dollars for the Champlain Valley Mental Health Agency. And so on.

I was voting "aye" along with everyone else when it struck me. If this keeps up, we'll be out of here by noon. Where was the debate, the skepticism Vermonters are known for?

What was needed was a little strategic cussedness. "NAY," I gruffed loudly on the next item, a call for $350 to help support a much needed rural dental clinic. Several others must too have sensed the danger of creeping benevolence and they also voted no. The "yea" forces, lulled by success, had managed only a perfunctory murmur and the moderator called for a standing count.

Oh m'god.

Dilemma: should I retreat into cowardly silence and stare at the floor—or rise grandly for tooth decay?

OH M'GOD!

"All those in favor please stand," intoned the moderator. Melissa's eyes grinned their most cruel, "Now, what are you going to do?" as she rose (along with nearly everyone else in the hall—about 175 people) to vote in the affirmative.

As the count began, my mind searched for salvation like the condemned at death's hour. There is safety in numbers! The moderator would see that the ayes clearly had it. Why waste time counting the nays? I wanted to yell triumphantly, "Stop the count! Stop the count! The ayes have it."

"All those opposed?" said the moderator. Standing proudly before my fellow townspeople in the cause of plaque, cavities and tooth aches I looked around me and gained a new appreciation for two words: "minority" and "chagrined." I had also confirmed in one fell swoop the very worst suspicions of my friends and neighbors: "Good Lord, he *is* to the right of Genghis Khan."

Frank Bryan[41]

---

41. Frank Bryan, "Town Meeting Debate," *Vermont Life* (Spring 1986): 36–39.

Democracy needs a new way to talk.
Harold Lasswell, 1941

The epigraph is from Harold Lasswell, *Democracy through Public Opinion* (New York: George Banta, 1941).

7

Democracy as Public Talk

Exploring the Contexts

As I have worked through the data on the tens of thousands of individual acts of public participation at town meetings over the past three decades, read my students' papers, and kept myself busy reading press accounts, talking to local town officers, and attending as many town meetings as possible, one constant has emerged. Variation. Some town meetings bubble with talk, while others seem much quieter. What is it that makes a meeting talkative? Is it something about the meeting, about the town where it is held? What?

The answer is complicated in ways that should whet the appetites of social scientists. While town size stands first in the causal ordering of all variables that might add to our understanding of town meeting attendance, meeting size does not stand first for verbal participation at town meeting. Meeting size is dependent in part on town size. Increasing town size thus hurts real democracy in two ways. First, as we know, it dramatically reduces the percentage of citizens who attend town meeting. Second, town size increases the number of citizens who attend, which dramatically decreases the percentage of these attenders who participate.

The situation is further confused by the presence or absence of hot issues before the town. As these issues draw more people to town meeting, this increased attendance reduces the percentage of those in attendance who speak out. At the same time, the presence of hot issues ought to have its own independent and positive effect on participation, causing citizens to speak out more than they might otherwise have done. Conversely, the lack of hot issues, while reducing attendance, increases the probability that verbal participation will be more equitably spread throughout the town meeting.

When all is said and done, unambiguous answers to the conundrums that arise from these and other complications are hard to come by. But we can clear away much of the underbrush. We will find, for instance, that meeting size retains its status as the dominant influence on participation (as town size did for attendance). We will see why and how other respectable explanations for variations in verbal participation in town meeting do not pan out. Surprises will be provided by two variables: town size (independent of meeting size) and the socioeconomic diversity of a town's population. Something as simple as the length of the meeting will emerge as a fundamental qualifier of democratic participation. Finally, we will discover again that reforms often backfire.

The Architecture of the Meeting

To begin, let us reconsider the "best-laid plan" that went astray—the move to night meetings. Earlier we discovered that night meetings hurt attendance, mostly because they nearly always use the Australian ballot. We also know they exacerbate the negative effects of bad weather. Now we discover that because they reduce the time available for deliberation, they hurt verbal participation as well. Badly.

Day Meetings versus Night Meetings

When the gavel fell for the last time in Middletown Springs, Vermont, on March 6, 1980, it was 10:05 at night. The meeting had begun at 7:30 p.m. In the meantime, 31 people had spoken 123 times, and the distribution of this participation over the body of 88 citizens assembled had produced a Gini index of participation equality of 22.7, 4.6 points below the score predicted by its size. That same year in the town of Monkton a meeting of similar size (90 attenders) was held during the following day, ending at 4:35 p.m. But Monkton's participation was much more egalitarian. Fifty-two people spoke 169 times, and the meeting exceeded its size-adjusted Gini index (of 26.6) by 7.4 points.

These cases reflect a pattern in the data as a whole. In the 1,091 meetings held during the day, 46 percent of the attenders participated, whereas in the 347 town meetings held at night 39 percent did so. Day meetings averaged Gini indexes of 25, while night meetings averaged Ginis of 22. When meeting size was controlled, the percentage of attenders who spoke at day meetings averaged three percentage points above what was expected given attendance, and the percentage of attenders who spoke at night meetings averaged ten percentage points below size expectations. The average Gini was five points above expectations for day meetings (given attendance), and at night it was seven points below expectations.

Consider, however, that Middletown Springs' night meeting lasted only two hours and thirty-five minutes, while Monkton's day meeting lasted five hours and thirty-five minutes. Monkton's citizens had more time to talk. In general, day meetings last an average of three hours and forty-eight minutes; night meetings generally end after two hours and thirty minutes. When the length of town meetings is controlled, the difference in participation between day and night meetings vanishes. The correlation coefficient between size-controlled night meetings and percentage speaking is reduced from $-.21$ to $-.01$, and the coefficient for the Gini index effort drops from $-.23$ to $-.06$.[1]

The random sample of 200 meetings in figure 7.1 demonstrates the interplay of these variables. Equality in the distribution of talk in a town meeting slopes upward as time for talk increases, whether the meeting is held during the day or at night. In both cases it takes a 185-minute meeting (a little more than three hours) to produce a one-to-one ratio in participation equality effort. Wide variation in participation equality surrounds these slopes, but this variation occurs both at night and during the day. The difference in the participatory averages between the two sets of meetings results from the fact that night meetings cluster on the bottom end of the axis for length of the meeting.[2]

Australian Ballot Meetings

As I explained in chapter 4, many Vermont towns have decided to resolve some (or in a few cases all) of the issues before the town by an election held throughout town meeting day rather than by voting on these issues as they

---

1. Franklin D. Becker and his colleagues reported that while almost exactly the same number (seven) participated in class irrespective of class size, the average total time used for student participation doubled between classes of under and over twenty students. This means that although no more students may participate in a big class than in a small one, in a smaller class those who do participate talk longer. Franklin D. Becker, Robert Sommer, Joan Bee, and Bart Oxley, "College Classroom Ecology," *Sociometry* 36 (December 1973): 514–525. For an excellent analysis of group size as it interrelates with time the meeting lasts and the dual impact of these variables on human interaction, see Bruce H. Mayhew and Roger L. Levinger, "Size and the Density of Interaction in Human Aggregates," *American Journal of Sociology* 82 (July 1976): 86–110.

2. Summary data for these relations are provided at www.uvm.edu/~fbryan.

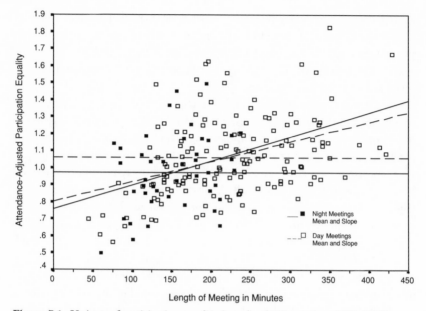

Figure 7.1. Variants of participation equality (sample of 200 meetings, 1970–1998).

come up and are discussed during the town meeting itself. To do this towns prepare a paper ballot, called the Australian ballot, on which to place the votes to be taken. Since use of a paper ballot transfers conflict from the openness of the meeting hall to the privacy of the polling both, its use or nonuse bears directly on a principal criticism of real democracy: that open participation is too psychologically costly, especially for citizens without the requisite status or personality resources to overcome it, and too socially costly, especially in small towns, where intimacy and overlapping political and social roles are more apt to prevail. Yet it is the small towns that have resisted adopting the Australian ballot. Our task is to discover whether citizens will be more apt to talk when the Australian ballot is in use.

Several reasons suggest they will. First, since we know from chapter 4 that Australian ballots reduce attendance at town meeting, and we know from chapter 5 that lower attendance is associated with better participation, ballot meetings possess a built-in statistical bias for more participation. Second, the Australian ballot option may remove from town meeting those citizens who attend traditional town meetings with no intention of speaking anyway and plan only to vote on the issues when they come up. These smaller "discussion only" meetings would be apt to have greater percentages of potential speakers. Third, I have often sensed in a meeting that if people did not have to do something about the issue then and there, they would have been more likely to discuss it.[3]

Finally, stopping proceedings to elect town officers during the meeting takes time. When the office is contested, secret ballots are often either required by law or requested from the floor. The people must leave their seats and line up to deposit a "ballot" (often just a strip of paper taken from the town report or provided by the ballot clerk). The time used in voting this way is time that cannot be spent in formal participation, and time is the one variable we know has a strong positive and independent effect on participation.

On the other hand the Australian ballot could hurt participation, since so many towns use it to elect town officers while the meeting is in session. In these meetings participation may be weaker, since by law candidates cannot be nominated from the floor or discussed in any formal way during the meeting. At the very least towns electing their officers at town meeting must nominate candidates from the floor. Even when opposition to a particular candidate fails to appear, participation often ensues as motions to "close the nominations" or "instruct the clerk to cast one ballot" for the uncontested nominee.[4]

As it turns out, the amount of participation associated with this most personal (and therefore difficult) kind of face-to-face activity—electing town officers from the floor—varies considerably from meeting to meeting. Consider the 1984 meeting in the town of Cambridge. Warning item 8 read as follows: "To elect all Town Officers required by law for the year ensuing: [There followed a list of twelve offices to be filled]." My data show that article 8 was brought to the floor at 10:16 a.m. and left the floor at 10:27. It took the town of Cambridge eleven minutes to elect its twelve officers.

During those eleven minutes 7 different people participated a total of 17 times; 10 of these times were by one man alone. Over the course of the meeting 39 attenders combined to conduct 174 discrete acts of participation. Since only one of these 39 participators participated only on article 8, the absence of the article would have reduced the total number of participators by only one and the percentage of the attenders who participated would have been reduced by less than 1 percent. Electing officers by Australian ballot would have reduced the total number of participations by 17. But since a

3. I believe this is an important impulse in certain situations. I have witnessed many instances when the people at a meeting where a difficult issue is on the floor seem to want to get it over with. Sometimes the public nervousness is palpable.

4. This is a time-saving process for officers who by law must be elected by ballot and not simply a voice vote; for example, "All those in favor of Ken Welch for cemetery commissioner respond by saying 'Aye.'"

majority of these were by one person, the absence of article 8 would have very little impact on the Gini index of participation equality.

A far different outcome occurred at the Ryegate town meting of 1977. The process of electing fourteen officers began at 1:13 p.m. and ended at 2:52, taking well over half the length of the meeting. Some of this time was spent actually voting, and some was spent counting the ballots.[5] We also know that 19 of the 82 people present (the town had only 818 registered voters at the time) participated on the article to elect town officers either by nominating a candidate or in some other way. This was over half of the total (33) participators. Moreover, 13 of the 19 participated only on these articles. They might have participated on other articles had they not participated in electing officers, but their participation in the election of town officers clearly boosted Ryegate's participation profile.

In the sample of 1,434 meetings for which we have similar data, 787 of the meetings used the Australian ballot at least for the election of town officers, and 647 did not. In the ballot towns an average of 40 percent of the attenders spoke at least once, compared with 49 percent in the nonballot towns. The Gini index, which gauges the egalitarian distribution of the talk of the meeting, averaged 23 points in the ballot meetings and 26 in the nonballot meetings. These are significant differences. But this positive relation between nonballot meetings and face-to-face participation disappears when meeting size and length are controlled. Moreover, the use of the Australian ballot fails to appear in the final multiple regression equation presented at the end of the chapter (table 7.1).

In short, while strong theoretical reasons suggest that using the Australian ballot might improve verbal participation at town meeting, it does not. Citizens do not speak more when town meetings are reserved for speaking only, and they are not discouraged from speech in the face of impending, often public, "stand and be counted" decisions made by the group they are a part of.

WITNESS

WINKING AT MARK

Mark came to town from away, articulate, poised, and confident. For several town meetings he behaved appropriately. He kept his mouth shut. But then came an especially severe mud season and Mark participated for the first

---

5. It is during the ballot counting that towns often let the district representative(s) to the legislature speak. As one moderator once told me with a wink after a meeting, "It saves time, don'tchaknow."

time. He was new to town he said but hoped that was okay. He and his family had found Vermont "just as beautiful as everyone said it would be." (Hmmmm.) He tried to be a good citizen and always paid his taxes on time. And "I pay a lot of taxes," he said. (Ah . . . so he was a rich flatlander.)

Last spring, Mark spoke quietly to what he apparently thought was the rapt attention of the meeting. He missed work in Burlington on three different days because the mud "precluded" (oh, oh) him from getting down off his hill. And as you may know (few did), he said, I have a job in Burlington that requires I be there. (His half-apologetic smile bespoke a man of great import on whom worldly matters bear heavily.) Mark concluded: . . . so I would just like to suggest that the Selectmen name a committee to meet to determine what we can do to help the road crew with the mud from now on. (Nice touch, he must have thought. No real criticism. Just an offer of help.)

It was quiet for a long moment before Nowi Gotcha rose from the back. She is not a down-and-outer, but she is close to it. Blue-collar working person all the way. She had just come in from the parking lot and a cigarette.

"I vote we thank the road crew for all their hard work," she half shouted.

Thunderous applause. Everyone stood except Mark and his wife.

While I was clapping, I tried to relieve his mortification with a wink across the several rows of chairs that (thank God) separated us. I couldn't catch his eye. He and his wife were staring hard at the floor.

Frank Bryan[6]

Town Meeting/School Meeting

Few issues elevate citizens' blood pressure more than education. From taxes to school choice, one is hard put to imagine an issue in modern American politics that has mattered more at the grass roots, to localities. It is to the schools that two-thirds of a Vermont citizen's property taxes go. Certainly there is reason to suspect that school issues increase verbal participation at town meeting. Yet education can be difficult to discuss in the open forum.[7] Teachers and school administrators (often living in town but working out of town at another school) may dominate discussion or intimidate with their expertise. Supporters of the schools often up the ante on public criticism

6. Frank Bryan, "Direct Democracy and Civic Competence: The Case of Town Meeting," in *Citizen Competence and Democratic Institutions*, ed. Stephen L. Elkin and Karol Edward Soltan (University Park: Pennsylvania State University Press, 1999), 220.

7. One of my students reporting on Charlotte's meeting in 1985 (with references to East Montpelier, with which he was also familiar) commented: "The school budget is presented with such an aura that to question any item makes the questioner feel like a subversive who risks unpopularity with the teachers and his neighbors." John K. Butler, "The 1985 Charlotte Town Meeting," Burlington, the University of Vermont, March 1985.

with not so subtle suggestions that those who raise questions have something against children. To speak or not to speak—which impulse prevails?

Let's see what happened in Montgomery in 1986. The seventy-four-word description of the town of Montgomery's town meeting that found its way into the *Burlington Free Press* stressed the school budget debate with these words: "Voters grudgingly approved a school budget they thought was too high."[8] Montgomery is a little mountain town in northwestern Vermont. When two of my students, Sarah Monneux and Leslie Sacco, went there to code events at town meeting March 4, 1986, the sky was slightly overcast and the thermometer read twenty-eight degrees. Not a bad day for a town meeting.

The meeting was held in the town hall in Montgomery Center, just below Hazen's Notch on the Trout River. This is the place through which (more than two hundred years earlier) the colonists decided to build one of the first military roads in North America. It was to stretch across the Green Mountains from Vermont to Montreal. This gigantic task began in Newbury, a hundred miles through uncharted forest to the east on the Connecticut River.[9] But the road never made it through the mountains of Montgomery. Up Route 242 a few miles from Montgomery Center is the Jay Peak ski area. This explains the six restaurants in a town of 681 people with 445 registered voters.

When the gavel fell to open the 1986 Montgomery town meeting, turnout was poor. Only 81 of the town's 445 registered voters attended, or 74 percent of the 110 its size predicted. However, 46 of these people would participate verbally that day, 71 percent of the average number present throughout the meeting (65). The experiences of all the 1,435 meetings in the database predict that a meeting with an average attendance of 65 will have only 58 percent participation. Thus Montgomery's participation effort for the meeting was 13 percentage points higher than expected, giving the meeting a strong positive ratio of 1.22. The Gini index of participation equality was high as well—120 percent of expectations. In short, even after controlling for the low turnout, Montgomery's meeting was more vocal than most.

How the towns handle their school business, remember, varies from town to town. There were 638 meetings in the sample that included school

---

8. "Montgomery Passes School Budget," *Burlington Free Press*, March 5, 1986, 4B.
9. As a boy I hunted partridge on what remained of the beginnings of the Bailey-Hazen Road. It was called the "old county road" in those days and was no more than a path whispering its way through the timber. But an abundance of thorn apple trees grew along it, and on a crimson blue October afternoon a twelve-year-old could sneak through the trees in the quiet bliss of preadolescence hoping to surprise a plump partridge or two.

matters as separate warning items in the town meeting or, like Montgomery, stopped the town meeting, convened the school meeting, and when it was over went back and completed the town meeting. In this group, the citizens interested only in school issues or only in town issues would likely be present for both. In another group of meetings (583 of them) the towns finished one of the meetings (either school or town) and then went on to the other one. This pattern made it more likely that someone interested in only one of the meetings would not stay (or come early) for the other. Finally, some towns decide town and school matters on separate days altogether. In these meetings (217 of them) it is even more likely that those interested only in school politics would not be at town meeting.

Montgomery's moderator, Joseph Sherman,[10] opened the meeting at 10:05 a.m. After preliminary remarks, the first article (to elect a moderator for 1986) was taken up at 10:14. Fifteen minutes later the town had reelected Sherman moderator, approved the town reports, authorized the selectmen to appoint a road commissioner, and elected fifteen town officers. Thirteen people had participated twenty-three times in sixteen minutes.[11]

At this point a member of the school board (whom the students identified as a man with "tinted glasses and a large gold ring") moved that the Town of Montgomery's meeting be formally adjourned and the meeting of the Town School District of Montgomery be formally convened. By 10:34

---

10. Joseph Sherman is the author of a popular modern history of Vermont, *Fast Lane on a Dirt Road* (White River Junction, VT: Chelsea Green, 1991). Sherman grew up in a small Vermont mill town and knows the state well. Yet he mentions town meeting only twice, once as an adjective in reference to my own work and once on page 49, where he makes this remark: "Many of these people [Sherman is referring to those who in the 1960s still believed in "local control"] simply refused to accept that local control had slipped away, leaving them little but the annual Town Meeting, where they could exercise an old-fashioned ritual of democracy, New England style, spew some rhetoric, and, in some instances, applaud jingoism wrapped up in often blurry history epitomized by the mythic individualism of Ethan Allen and the Green Mountain Boys."

11. It doesn't take long to elect a town officer if no opposition exists: Moderator, "To elect a town agent. What is your pleasure?" Man with white hair and half glasses: "Nominate Doug DeVries." Moderator: "Do I hear a second?" Unidentified Citizen: "Second." (We don't attempt to identify those who second a motion.) Moderator: "All those in favor of electing Doug DeVries your town agent for one year signify by saying aye." Citizens: "Aye." Fifteen seconds or so does the trick. Sarah Monneux and Leslie Sacco, "The 1986 Comparative Town Meeting Study: Town of Montgomery," Burlington, University of Vermont, Real Democracy Data Base, March 1986, and Town of Montgomery, Theresa Lamore, Town Clerk, "Minutes of the Annual Town Meeting March 4, 1986," mimeograph, 1986. This kind of participation, while brief and seemingly perfunctory, is important. It signifies satisfaction with the town's governors. These crisp, matter-of-fact (often no more that grunts) participations have two hundred years of history behind them. They are listened for. As when you listen to the sounds of the forest while sitting on a deer stand in late November, nuances become critical. The people of Montgomery were simply saying: "Our town officers did OK this year. Let's get on with our work."

this had been done, and the town moderator, Joseph Sherman, was elected moderator of the school meeting. For the next hour and forty-eight minutes the town debated school matters. It had taken less than a minute to elect the moderator, three minutes to approve the school directors' reports, and one minute to elect a member to the school board. Discussion of the school budget lasted fifty-eight minutes. The vote on the budget (a secret ballot) was close, 44 yeas to 30 nays. An additional minute was needed to authorize the school directors to borrow money in anticipation of taxes, and thirty-one minutes were used to discuss new business. The school meeting ended at 12:21. Then a hungry town meeting listened to the local state representative speak for twenty minutes and finally adjourned for lunch at 12:41.

In the 108 minutes of school debate, 27 people participated a total of 101 times. One-third of these were women, two-thirds men. This was almost the same ratio of men to women participators as at the entire meeting. Of the 27 school meeting participators, 11 participated only on school issues. They contributed only 32 of the 101 participations on school matters. It is possible that those 11 would have attended town meeting anyway even if school matters were not on the warning. If so (because no school matters were on the warning), they may not have participated verbally in the meeting. The total number of participators would then have been reduced to 35, the attendance would have remained the same, and Montgomery's verbal participation would have dropped below average. Moreover, if the 16 who participated on both town and school matters had not (in the face of having no school items to discuss) compensated for their loss of school-related participations by speaking more on town-related matters, the general participatory flavor of the meeting would have dropped still more.

Overall, the data from our 1,435 meetings show a slight decrease in percentage speaking as town and school meetings separate. On average 38 percent of the attenders speak when the school meeting is embedded in the town meeting (as it was in Montgomery), 37 percent when the school meeting comes on the same day either before or after the town meeting, and 36 percent when the school meeting is held on another day. But the Gini index hardly budges when these patterns are considered. It is 25 when school meetings are embedded or inserted and 24 when they are held another day. When the size and length of the town meeting are controlled, even this weak association melts away.[12]

12. These findings were confirmed through time-series analysis of individual towns that switched from holding their school meetings on the same day and in the same place as their town meetings to holding them on a different day.

In other words, separating the town meeting from the school meeting hurts participation a bit because it leaves the people less to talk about. But education issues as such show no special inclination to enhance democratic discussion and debate. Perhaps local educational professionals actually deter debate through the intimidation of their expertise. I have seen this happen many times. Or perhaps these numbers reflect on the inability of town meeting, with its face-to-face deliberation, to translate local conflict into democratic opportunity when the passion of the debate and the outcomes at stake increase.

The Size of the Meeting Place

Compare talk among a group of fifty in a crowded town hall where a lack of space creates forced intimacy with talk in a place where the same number of people have room to spread out and produce gaps in the human tapestry. Town meetings in Berlin and West Haven, for instance, had equal attendance (sixty-three in Berlin and sixty-four in West Haven) at their 1983 meetings. For every ten chairs filled by a citizen in Berlin, however, thirty were left empty. For every ten chairs filled by a citizen in West Haven fewer than two were left empty. At the same time, the percentage of attenders participating at least once in West Haven was six points higher than meeting size would predict, and in Berlin it was ten points below the meeting-size prediction. Similarly, the Gini index of equality of participation was 8.8 points above the expected in West Haven and 5.1 points below the expected in Berlin.

Some scholars do not find this situation surprising. They find that an aversion to standing out—being conspicuous—may be an important variable intervening between crowdedness and participation, because being conspicuous is an important reason respondents give for their reticence in public forums. A town hall where large gaps separate the people in attendance may trigger a greater fear of conspicuousness than a meeting place where nearly all the seats are filled.[13] On the other hand, others argue that increases in crowding (social density) lead to withdrawal.[14]

---

13. Michael J. Beatty, "Situational and Predispositional Correlates of Public Speaking Anxiety," *Communication Education* 37 (January 1988): 28–39; Arnold H. Buss, *Self-Consciousness and Social Anxiety* (San Francisco: W. H. Freeman, 1980). From time to time my students provide evidence that supports this theory. "Before any person spoke he had to walk to one of the two microphones in the center aisle and introduce himself to the assembly. This inhibited many people from participating." Kit O'Leary, "Elite Government in Norwich," Colchester, St. Michael's College, March, 1974.

14. For an early summary of this literature see Andrew Baum and Stuart Valens, *Architecture and Social Behavior: Psychological Studies of Social Density* (Hillsdale, NJ: Lawrence Erlbaum, 1977).

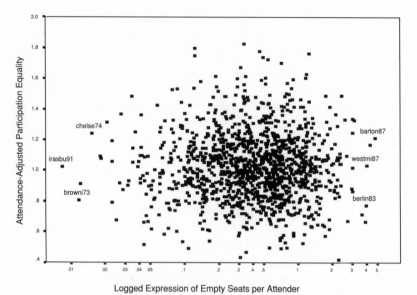

Figure 7.2. Crowdedness doesn't matter (1,271 town meetings, 1970–1998; meetings with zero empty seats per attender excluded).

Figure 7.2 provides a descriptive feel for these spatial arrangements of citizens at town meetings and shows that no connection exists between crowdedness and public speaking. The median town meeting had about forty empty seats for every one hundred persons in attendance. On the very crowded end of the distribution, meetings in towns like Irasburg, Brownington, and Chelsea had fewer than two empty seats for every one hundred attenders. These were standing room only meetings. On the other end of the distribution, meetings like those in Barton, Westminster, and Berlin had four hundred or so empty seats for every one hundred attenders—four empty seats for every filled one. When the number of people in attendance was controlled, the Gini index of participation equality was completely unrelated to this crowded-to-spacious continuum.

Some towns, however, set up the chairs in anticipation of turnout, providing just enough chairs to handle the number they expect to attend. Thus an average crowd may contain no empty chairs (maximum crowdedness) because chairs were provided on the expectation of an average crowd—but the town hall is less crowded than when a lot more people came than were expected and additional chairs were set up to accommodate them.[15] Because the space

15. Another possibility is that to the extent townspeople perceive that a given year's attendance might be high, they might act differently because of their anticipation of crowding.

inside the town hall seldom changes, I compared year-to-year variations in participation with year-to-year variations in attendance within the same hall. Thus measured, degrees of crowdedness for meetings in the twenty towns for which we had data on fifteen or more meetings in the same building (so that meeting place size was a constant) were unassociated with levels of public talk predicted by attendance size.[16]

The Weather

I have no theory regarding weather's direct effect on talk democracy. Nor does anyone else. If atmospheric pressure affects inclination to engage in open political discussion, the evidence has yet to be published. On the other hand, wind rattling the windows of the town hall or people's memory of sensing an impending storm on their way to town meeting might urge matters to a quicker resolution, which would shorten the time available for talk.[17] Bad weather at night could affect participation in the same way it reduces attendance. Night storms are more fearsome, and those who do attend will be more anxious to leave early.

I examined these relationships in great detail, and the findings were reduced to a single weak correlation: with size of the meeting controlled (which neutralizes the marginal tendency for bad weather to reduce attendance in the first place), participation is better in mixed weather than it is in either bad or good weather, and it is not much better in good weather than it is in

---

That behavior might actually limit attendance at town meeting. Andrew Baum and Carl I. Greenberg, "Waiting for a Crowd: The Behavioral and Perceptual Effects of Anticipated Crowding," *Journal of Personality and Social Psychology* 32 (October 1975): 671–679, and Andrew Baum and Stuart Koman, "Differential Response to Anticipated Crowding: Psychological Effects of Social and Spatial Density," *Journal of Personality and Social Psychology* 34 (September 1976): 526–536.

16. Visions of a crowded meeting hall often give way to notions of democracy by mob. The psychology of crowds has sometimes been grafted indiscriminately onto town meetings. "The realities of human behavior under the influence of agglomeration" (as Schumpeter put it in 1950) cause "the sudden disappearance, in a state of excitement, of moral restraint and civilized modes of thinking and feeling, the sudden eruption of primative impulses, infantilisms and criminal propensities." These are "gruesome facts that everybody knew but nobody wished to see and . . . thereby dealt a serious blow to the picture of man's nature which underlies the classical doctrine of democracy." Although Schumpeter oddly excuses English and Anglo-American crowds from such behavior and focuses instead on the example of "a Latin town," others also sometimes use the paradigm of the mob to describe a crowded town meeting. Joseph A. Schumpeter, *Capitalism, Socialism and Democracy*, 3rd ed. (New York: Harper and Brothers, 1950): 256–257.

17. I myself have never left a town meeting early, but there are times I should have, including one night when I eased out of the Kingdom town of Irasburg at 10:35 p.m. in a snowstorm that stretched a two-hour drive home into a four-and-a-half-hour white-knuckle slide. But I have seen people leave because of it, and the student essays refer to it on occasion.

bad weather. The length of the meeting explains this. In both day and night meetings the meetings were shorter during bad weather and good weather than during mixed weather, and shorter meetings inhibit participation.[18]

In summary, once an adjustment is made for the number of people at the meeting, the length of the meeting is by far the most significant structural variable. In combination these two variables explain 69 percent of the variance in the percentage of the attenders participating in town meeting and 57 percent of the variation in participation equality. Beyond this, no evidence suggests that crowdedness or the weather has much independent effect on participation. Night meetings are bad for talk democracy primarily because they decrease the time available for talk. If (and how) school issues are treated on town meeting day matters only a little and primarily only when school matters are decided another day altogether. The absence of school issues lowers participation not because they are school issues per se but because they extend the agenda of decisions to be made.

The Character of Community Life

Reporters often ask, "What kind of town should I go to in order to see a really exciting town meeting?" My students often ask, "Is this the kind of town where a lot of discussion takes place?" How does one respond? Given meeting size, would we expect a more lively discussion in the mountain towns or the valley towns, in small towns or large towns, in farming towns or bedroom towns, in rich towns or poor towns, in growing towns, or liberal towns, or the towns where more people turn out to vote for national and state candidates? At a minimum the answer (in upland Yankee) would be, "Hard to say."[19]

Big Town, Small Town

A book of Vermont humor titled *"Yup"... "Nope": And Other Vermont Dialogues* relishes the sparse talk of small-town people.[20] Many believe rural

---

18. This makes sense (see above, page 89). If the weather is good, people may want to do other things, especially in early March. There comes a certain longing to be gone from town meeting when a warm sun streams through the town hall window about noon on a clear March day. If nothing else, one might spot the first robin of the year. Democracy is one thing, first robins are another. I have been at town meetings under these conditions (and as you may have guessed, I love town meetings) when I have prayed for the words "motion to adjourn."

19. Often heard in response to questions like "Do you think you can get it out of the ditch?" or "Why doesn't she milk better?" or "What's he talking about?"

20. Keith Warren Jennison, *"Yup...Nope": And Other Vermont Dialogues* (Taftsville, Vermont: Countryman Press, 1976). Brevity in matters of the tongue has elevated prepositions to a

people guard their tongues and favor monosyllables. Question: "Where'd you find that horse everyone's been looking for, Sonny?" Answer: "I thought if I were a horse where would I go and I did and he had." Seventeen words, seventeen syllables. Perfect.[21] Fill a meeting hall with this kind of people, and silence would dominate. Yet others argue that small-town people are more "open" and friendly than city folk and will "talk your head off" if given a chance.

The most popular hypothesis in the serious scholarship on the issue goes like this: As communities get smaller, societal roles of individuals tend to overlap. As this occurs, public talk about politics may be stifled by the unwillingness to jeopardize other relationships. Thus the barber will keep his views on a zoning ordinance obscure lest he antagonize his customers. A member of the bridge club protects her relationships there. A father hesitates to alienate the mother of his daughter's best friend. An employee is careful not to annoy an employer sitting six rows over and three rows back. It all boils down to the old saying: "In small towns you have to be careful what you say!"[22]

---

position of high esteem in Vermont. They serve as indigenous road maps. For instance, a simple trip from Greensboro to Lyndonville (over Stannard Mountain Road) might be described as follows: "I'm going along up over through down around into Lyndonville." Ten words. Seven prepositions. Anyone who knows that trip will tell you this sentence is equivalent to pages of detailed topographical insight.

21. Keith Warren Jennison, *Vermont Is Where You Find It* (New York: Harcourt, Brace and World, 1941). My brother David, who turned a Ph.D. in ancient Semitic languages from Johns Hopkins University into a rural ministry (Catholic) in northern Vermont, once related to me the most succinct (and accurate) analysis he ever heard of the hard life in Vermont: "Dad drank. Mom ran." Mark Twain, having given one of his humorous lectures in the town of Bennington, Vermont, was perplexed at the tepid reception his witticisms provoked. On his way to his carriage afterward the reason became clear to him as he heard a Vermonter say to his spouse, "Gosh that man was funny.' Twas all I could do t'keep from laughing."

22. This is part of the argument that real democracy can work only in small places that feature homogeneity. If contentious issues do emerge, small-town people will work hard to hide or defer them to avoid the inevitable pain of conflict in the raw. But a counterposition is available. Sociologist George Homans's classic work on group behavior set the theoretical underpinnings of a model suggesting that the high number of interpersonal interactions possible in a small group creates favorable conditions for group solidarity. Mancur Olson argued in 1965 that in small groups each member can participate in a more contributory fashion. This higher status in the group leads to group solidarity. Mancur Olson, *The Logic of Collective Action: Public Goods and the Theory of Groups* (Cambridge: Harvard University Press, 1965), 65. For a summary of Homans's work see George C. Homans, *Social Behavior: Its Elementary Forms* (New York: Harcourt, Brace, Jovanovich, 1974). The question is, Does this "solidarity" lead to a diminishing of conflict that is then associated with less participation or at least less important participation? Hard evidence that it does is sketchy, and countervailing findings exist. My own observations suggest that town meetings in small towns are not less contentious (see chapter 11). Robin Donovan, a community activist in the New Hampshire town of Chichester in the 1980s, put it this way: "When you lose on an issue, you get over it because the person who voted against it'll be working with you on Old Home Day."

A return to the seventy meetings in the 1992 sample, for instance, shows that in Ripton, the little town that lies high along a gap in the mountains east of Middlebury, 90 of the 297 registered voters were present at town meeting. About fifty miles to the south in Proctor about the same number were in attendance (99), even though Proctor has about four and a half times more registered voters than Ripton. Given the size of their respective meetings, Ripton should have had 43 percent of its attenders speaking out at least once, and Proctor should have had 42 percent. But the people of Ripton had 44 percent participation in their town meeting (a percentage point above expectations), while Proctor had only 19 percent of its attenders speaking out, 23 percentage points lower than expected.[23]

This unexpected negative relation between town size and verbal participation reappears, but faintly, in the entire 1970–1998 database of 1,435 meetings. When both the size of the meeting and its length are controlled, the correlation between town size and percentage participating is −.19, statistically significant but not very strong. No relation exists between the Gini index of participation equality and town size. That the Gini index does not improve in small towns the way the percentage participating does may mean that small-town people are more likely to "get in their say" at town meeting than people in large towns, but that is all.

Also, longer meetings are not as apt to generate an increase in the number speaking in a small town as in a big town. What is going on? It may be that small-town people are briefer in what they say, freeing up time for others to speak. It may be that meetings in small towns are more "conversational" than "presentational," allowing a greater percentage of those present to get their say in. It may be that electing town officers in the meeting itself rather than by Australian ballot outside the meeting process (which is more apt to happen in small towns) brings in more participators making brief presentations ("I nominate Bill Brown for lister"), increasing the likelihood that

---

Gardner Hayes, "Town Meeting," *New Hampshire Profiler,* March 1987, 32–35. Students of fear of public speaking note, moreover, that our anxiety about strangers leads to fear of speaking in public. "We tend not to be afraid to speak around our closest friends and family, even a large group of them." Rush W. Dozier Jr., *Fear Itself: The Origin and Nature of the Powerful Emotion That Shapes Our lives and Our World* (New York: St. Martin's Press, 1998), 104. Others show that small-town people are more willing to interact with newcomers to town, a tendency that should boost participation in the meetings of small towns over larger towns. Joseph Newman and Clark McCauley, "Eye Contact with Strangers in City, Suburb and Small Town," *Environment and Behavior* 9 (December 1977): 547–558.

23. Proctor's size-adjusted percentage participating measure, which is a ratio of meeting-size-predicted participators to actual participators, was 0.45. (For every 100 participators predicted to speak, they had only 45.) Ripton's was 1.02. (For every 100 participators predicted, Ripton had 102.)

more people will get to say something in a small town. It also may mean that small-town people who don't intend to speak don't.

In any event, we may reject the hypothesis that small towns stifle democratic talk. If anything is happening, it is probably a mild tendency for more small-town people to speak at least once, especially in shorter town meetings. Although the evidence is too weak to propose that small towns promote participation, it is certainly fair to conclude that they do not inhibit it. Open, often adversarial, political talk in the context of impending decisions that make a difference is not closed off because neighbors are more familiar with one another.

WITNESS

Political Talk: A Town Meeting in Vermont's Smallest Town

Twenty-six of the town's 38 registered voters came through the snow to South Victory's school on Town Meeting Day to transact [Victory's] business.

The flag in the schoolroom [unused for years] has 48 stars; a faded portrait of George Washington stares down from the wall; and, on an old globe hanging from the ceiling, most of Africa still belongs to Britain and France. . . .

Shirley Lund [who currently held the offices of road foreman, tax collector, and constable] wanted to be selectman, since Gerard Beauchesne had decided not to run again.

Another selectman, Richard Kerr, a bearded young man in his 20s, was determined Lund wasn't going to get the job.

Kerr has been on the Board of Selectmen for two years. For the last year, he said, the other two selectmen haven't bothered to tell him when they have a meeting. His name was not signed to the official town meeting warning, he said, because the other two didn't consult him about it.

"We couldn't ever get hold of Richard. He lives way up there on Victory Hill and he's never home when you call," Beauchesne said.

Then Beauchesne had a few words of his own to say. "I'm not running again because I'm tired of working with those two," he said. He declined to elaborate, and left the meeting.

When the vote finally was taken, Lund lost the selectman race to George Stanley, an engineer who is the son of a town lister and the nephew of the town clerk. The vote was 15–11. While Beauchesne said Lund lost because he wanted to run the town—"there shouldn't be one man run the town," other Victory residents explained Stanley's victory in other ways.

Some said Lund's defeat was due to hard feelings in the town over his management of road repair funds; some said it was partially the result of a long-standing feud between folks in two areas of the town, Gallup Mills and Victory Hill; others mentioned another feud over a road abandoned by the town in 1913.

Lund said the present selectmen have done a "bad job." "They've spent all the road money from the state for this year already and the year isn't over. They don't know what they're doing." . . . And, finally, there was the matter of the town Planning Commission. Somebody asked what had happened to it.

"I'll tell you what happened to it," said Maltby, jumping up. "I'm the moderator and I'm supposed to sit here and not say boo, but I'm going to, whether it's illegal or not.

"We don't have a town Planning Commission anymore because whenever we came up with something, people didn't like it, but when you asked them for ideas, they shut up like clams."

Maltby was chairman of the now defunct Victory Planning Commission.

"I'm looking straight at you," he said, pointing at one of Victory's 26 voters. "You fouled up the only information meeting on planning we managed to have."

The audience smiled and one woman said to another about the unfortunate voter Maltby was pointing at, "Came in drunk and broke up the meeting. With planners there from Montpelier and all."

"We can have a Planning Commission, but I don't want any dumps outside my house," an elderly woman said, speaking into the dead silence that had followed.

At Kerr's suggestion, Victory elected a new Planning Commission.

Then, with an air of relief, Maltby declared the meeting adjourned.

As the voters filed out, Gerard Masten, whose family has lived in Victory for five generations, said, "mildest town meeting we've had in years."

Candace Page[24]

The Socioeconomic Context

As we found that the socioeconomic status (SES) context of the community had little to do with attendance at town meeting, so too do we find that the SES context of the community has little to do with verbal participation at town meeting. Moreover, I claim (as I did for attendance) that there is very little SES bias attached to verbal participation at the individual level within town meetings.

No one has been more poignant in describing the effects of class on face-to-face democracy than Jane Mansbridge. Her conclusions: "The face-to-face assembly lets those who have no trouble speaking in public defend

24. Candace Page, perhaps Vermont's most respected journalist in the last three decades of the twentieth century, wrote this for the *Burlington Free Press*. In its entirety it received the New England Associated Press's yearly award for reporting. Candace Page, "Victory's Townsfolk Speak Their Minds," *Burlington Free Press*, March 5, 1975, 1.

their interests; it does not give the average citizen comparable protection." I fundamentally agree. My caveat is simply that what she calls the "emotional tension" of face-to-face assemblies that leads to "trouble speaking in public" has traditionally not been uniformly associated with SES. (Mansbridge never made an explicit claim that it was.)[25] Even here, however, I will grant Mansbridge this point. If she is talking about what William Julius Wilson calls the "underclass" of "truly disadvantaged" citizens (and I think she is), then she is clearly right. The Vermont town, I should judge, has been no more successful in integrating the deeply suffering rural poor into the democratic process than has the inner city. But in nearly every Vermont town there are many citizens with very modest education levels and below-modest incomes. These working-class people often participate in ways that most Americans of all classes can only dream about.

In 1995 Sidney Verba was elected president of the American Political Science Association. His presidential address concerned the status gap in public participation. Work with Kay Lehman Schlozman and Henry E. Brady had demonstrated that skills learned on the job positively affect political participation. "Among people with advanced education and a professional level job," Verba pointed out, "about 90 percent say they plan meetings and give public presentations. The comparable figure for workers with high school education in lower status jobs is around 5 percent."[26] If, as I claim, town meeting participation is not dependent on SES, it may be because town meeting communities develop civic skills among "lower-status" citizens just as on-the-job

25. I think Mansbridge (especially in her well-known discussion of what happened to "Clayton Bedell," the uneducated farmer who was ridiculed by a lawyer in "Selby"), is on to something more subtle than simple class. As town meeting decision making becomes more ancillary and tertiary in nature, its complexity has changed and deciphering it often depends on formal education—not, mind you, brains. Trucks are complex items. They are often more complex (if less dangerous) than zoning ordinances. I suspect Clayton Bedell would have stood up pretty well against his lawyer antagonists on the matter of differentials and rear ends. But as procedural complexity increases and substantive complexity decreases, I fear Mansbridge's model may indeed become more and more securely attached to variables like formal education. Jane J. Mansbridge, *Beyond Adversary Democracy* (New York: Basic Books, 1980), 274; Jane J. Mansbrige, "The Limits of Friendship," in *Participation in Politics*, ed. J. Roland Pennock and John W. Chapman (New York: Lieber-Atherton, 1975), 261. For further empirical evidence that variations in the nature of participation vary with SES in a way that supports Mansbridge, see Jack H. Nagel, *Participation* (Englewood Cliffs, NJ: Prentice-Hall, 1987), 58.

26. Sidney Verba, "The Citizen as Respondent: Sample Surveys and American Democracy," *American Political Science Review* 90 (March 1996): 1–7. My observation and the observations of my students over the years clearly suggest that a hefty proportion of the people at town meeting lack college degrees, have lower-status jobs, and participate verbally at town meeting. Nor would I wager that upscale people at town meeting who are adept at giving public presentations elsewhere participate more at town meeting than their numbers at the meeting warrant.

experiences do for professionals.[27] Town meeting itself, I believe, is the principal (but not only) institution of small-town life where this kind of on-the-job training takes place.

Let us begin in the late 1980s in Williston, Vermont, an upscale community in Chittenden County where jets drop out of the sky to land next door in Burlington at Vermont's only airport with gates. Just down the road (the main artery into the Burlington metropolitan area, if we may call it that) is the state's only university, its dominant medical center, and its only commercial television stations. Situated in Vermont's most urban county, Williston has for over twenty years been a battleground where the forces for growth square off against the forces for protecting what they believe is the way Vermont used to be.[28]

Williston scores very high on upscale indicators and is a large town by Vermont standards, with 2,934 registered voters in 1987. Its median family income in 1990 was $47,731 compared with only $24,736 for the average town in the sample. Its education index was in the top 5 percent of all the towns.[29] In Williston 41 percent of the workforce were classified as "managers and professionals," compared with 24 percent in the average town.

Up north on the Canadian border, things are apt to be different. In the town of Swanton in 1987 the number of registered voters was almost exactly the same as in Williston (2,951), but the median family income was only $29,613. The education index in Swanton was below average, and only 17 percent of the workers were managers or professionals. In Swanton a good portion of the community is bilingual (French-English), and a sizable portion of the rest are Native Americans (Abenakis). Dairy farms still dot the landscape, critters own the woods at night, and the fear of strip development

27. In Athens, while attendance was not class-based, verbal participation was. During the fourth century B.C., noble birth waned as a predictor of participation, but wealth continued to matter. Josiah Ober, *Mass and Elite in Democratic Athens: Rhetoric, Ideology, and the Power of the People* (Princeton: Princeton University Press, 1989), 112–118. See also Harvey Yunis, *Taming Democracy: Models of Political Rhetoric in Classical Athens* (Ithaca: Cornell University Press, 1996), 11, 12.

28. Actually the protectionists want to protect the way Vermont used to look (and who wouldn't?), not the way Vermont used to be. I doubt that more than a few know the way Vermont used to be. Those of us who want to protect both the small-town way of life and its physical structure are called conservatives. The visual protectionists are called liberals. Neither are.

29. Findings at the individual level show that academically talented students feel less apprehension about speaking in groups than do "at risk" students: James W. Chesebro et al., "Communication Apprehension and Self-Perceived Comunication Competence of at Risk Students," *Communication Education* 41 (October 1992): 345–360; Lawrence B. Rosenfeld, Charles H. Grant III, and James C. McCroskey, "Communication Apprehension and Self-Perceived Communication Competence of Academically Gifted Students," *Communication Education* 44 (January 1995): 79–86.

does not register in the hearts of people with too many troubles in the here and now to search the horizon for more.

These two towns so remarkably different in socioeconomic makeup have nearly identical participation in their town meetings when meeting size and length are taken into account. The sample of 1,215 town meetings studied between 1977 (when accurate Census data became available) and 1998, in over 200 towns, confirms the ambiguity of the data from Williston and Swanton. When all is said and done, only one of the sixteen community life variables introduced in chapter 5 (from education level to community boundedness) is importantly associated with speaking out at town meeting.

The lone survivor is the SES diversity index. It measures how evenly the population of a town is spread within the cohorts of important socioeconomic characteristics. Thus a socially diverse town would have closer to 50 percent of the population owning their homes than either 20 percent or 80 percent. Or if the Census divides occupation into five cohorts, a "diverse" town would have 20 percent of its workers in each cohort. In the final stepwise regression equation, where variables are entered into the mix according to how much influence they have on the dependent variable, SES diversity ranks third most influential for both dependent variables—the percentage participating and participation equality. Still, the association is weak. Once meeting size (attendance at the meeting) and meeting length (time the meeting lasts) are accounted for, SES diversity contributes only 1.5 percentage points of additional explained variance in the percentage of attenders participating and 2.3 percent in the Gini index of participation equality.

While not a muscular variable like meeting size or meeting length, the persistence of SES diversity may be important, for it suggests (if those in attendance at a town meeting approximate in the aggregate the diversity of the community at large—something I believe to be generally true, although I have no data to prove it) that a complex socioeconomic setting may enhance participation rather than retard it.[30]

It should be comforting to supporters of democracy to note that the importance of status to face-to-face democracy could be in its mix, not its level. Perhaps we ought not be surprised that levels of class status in the community do not correlate with variants of public talk at town meeting. From personal experiences at town meeting in his own town in Connecticut,

30. SES diversity and the "upscale" factor score exhibited some multicolinearity ($R^2 =$ .41). Under controls the modest link between SES diversity and the Gini index of participation equality was strengthened a bit from $r = .14$ to $r = .23$, and the weaker coefficient between upscale and Gini was wiped out ($r = -.01$).

Robert Dahl, one of this century's leading democratic theorists, recalls: "As in Vermont, discussions at town meeting are not dominated by the educated and the affluent. Strong beliefs and a determination to have one's say are not by any means monopolized by a single socio-economic group."[31] Nor (as I explained above) do I see any automatic contradiction between Dahl's observations and the more developed findings of Jane Mansbridge. I suspect that the differences between the two could easily be ironed out by fine-tuning the operational definition of class with the addition of very small cohorts at either end of the class continuum for the very rich and the very poor.

WITNESS

We got through the first eleven articles in less than an hour. Then we spent the rest of the morning arguing—"debating" is too elevated a term for town meeting style—Article 12 [to replace a covered bridge with a new concrete bridge]. It came near time to vote. Then one of the proponents of the new concrete bridge got up, holding a formidable list in his hand. He is a leader in town. He told us he liked the old wooden bridge as well as anyone—but he wasn't sure we realized how much it would cost to repair it. And he began reading specifications and prices from his list: the number of new $12'' \times 12''$ bridge timbers required, and what each would cost; numbers and prices for joists, and so on. The total kept mounting; we taxpayers began having second thoughts.

Then a young fellow in back stood up, a workingman with a lumberjack's shirt on and a three-day growth of beard. "I don't know where he got them prices from," he said, "but I know this. I work up to the mill in Ely, and we can sell you all that stuff a hell of a lot cheaper than what he said." Every head turned to stare. Undeterred, he went from memory through each item the other man had mentioned, repeating the figures and then quoting the lowest price his mill could offer.

After that we voted. Usually we have voice votes to save time, but this was an important decision, and the selectmen passed out slips of paper. We wrote "Yes" if we wanted a new bridge, "no" if we didn't. We filed by the ballot box and dropped the slips in, and when we finished the selectmen counted them. It took fifteen minutes. The first Selectman then walked to the microphone. "Guess we're keepin' it," he said.

Noel Perrin[32]

31. Robert A. Dahl, *On Democracy* (New Haven: Yale University Press, 1998), 111.

32. Sonja Bullaty and Angelo Lomeo, photographers, with text by Noel Perrin, *Vermont in All Weathers* (New York: Viking Press, 1973), 18–19, as reprinted in Charles T. Morrissey, *Vermont: A Bicentennial History* (New York: W. W. Norton, 1981), 176–177.

The Political Context

I had considered it at least possible, if not probable, that towns with a more active citizenry at the polls in general elections would reflect a civic culture more supportive of verbal participation at town meeting. The theory that conflict spawns action might be held responsible for the idea of a link between more partisanship in town and more discussion of issues at town meeting.[33] On the other hand, it is doubtful that Democrats are more loquacious than Republicans. Nor are there strong reasons to believe that towns demonstrating strong support for independent-Socialist congressman Bernie Sanders or towns enthusiastically supporting Vermont's ERA would have more participatory town meetings. In fact, all these political culture variables, which offer intriguing possibilities in other contexts, rested on some very thin conceptual ice when asked to account for variations in verbal participation at town meeting.

Accordingly, they fell through. No single political culture variable associated with Vermont's towns (all were introduced in chapter 5) had an effect on either the percentage of those present participating at least once at town meeting or the egalitarian distribution of the participations throughout the total body of the meeting. Nor did the summary measure I called the "liberal" factor score. The only measure to survive was the Bernie Sanders vote, an aggregation of his support in elections close to the year town meeting was held. But even this strongest of the political culture variables disappeared under the ice in the final regression equation.

Summary

Beyond the number of people at the meeting (fewer is better) and the length of the meeting itself (longer is better), explanations for the variance in verbal participation from meeting to meeting and from town to town are hard to come by. SES diversity (diverse is better) and town size (small is better) combined to increase the variance explained in the percentage of those in attendance making at least one act of speech (participators—what was summarized as "speech" in chapter 6) by only two percentage points over the 70.5 percent explained by meeting size and length. SES diversity was by far the

33. Early on in the voting behavior literature Angus Campbell and his colleagues argued that intensity of partisan attachments was associated with a psychological disposition to participate in politics. It is at least arguable that this would stimulate town meeting participation in those towns where partisanship was keenly felt if (and it is a big *if*) a close balance between the parties in the town triggered a sharper sense of partisan loyalty. Angus Campbell, Philip E. Converse, Warren Miller, and Donald E. Stokes, *The American Voter* (New York: John Wiley, 1964).

Table 7.1. Correlates of Talk Democracy: The Final Equation

Variable	r	R^2	Improvement in R^2	Beta
Dependent variable = Percentage of attenders speaking				
Log of attendance	.752	.565	—	−.859
Length of meeting	.840	.705	.140	.362
SES diversity	.849	.720	.015	.122
Town size	.851	.724	.004	−.067
Sanders factor score	.852	.725	.001	.039
Dependent variable = Gini Index of Participation Equality				
Log of attendance	.662	.438		−.799
Length of meeting	.762	.580	.142	.355
SES diversity	.776	.603	.023	.101
Stable community	.779	.607	.004	.074
Night meetings	.782	.611	.004	−.060
Upscale factor score	.784	.614	.003	.083

Note: All coefficients are significant at the .01 level.

stronger of the two. SES diversity, "stable community" (stable is better), and day/night (day is better) increased the variance explained in the distribution of talk (the Gini index) by only three percentage points over the 58 percent explained by meeting size and length alone. Diversity was by far the strongest of the three. (See table 7.1.)

The appearance of the diversity variable may be important because it moves in the opposite direction from what is predicted by its very prestigious scholarly heritage, beginning with Aristotle, which holds that egalitarian, face-to-face, out in the open, community politics (in a word, real democracy) works best in homogeneous social structures. That diversity is especially good for real democracy is not established by these data. That it is not harmful may be. Similarly, the failure of higher SES to predict higher participation allows us to say with a little more confidence that lower SES is not associated with depressed levels of verbal participation at town meeting.

If I were asked . . . to what the singular prosperity and growing strength of that people [the Americans] ought mainly to be attributed, I should reply: to the superiority of their women!

Alexis de Tocqueville, *Democracy in America*

8

The Question of Equality

Women's Presence

For women the core promise of liberal democracy has been kept. Women may vote, and they do vote. Still, in the arenas of representative democracy where the expressions of this fundamental guarantee are worked out, women remain a minority. This fact is hugely embarrassing for liberalism. Women are the only majority "group" in society that has minority status—glaring minority status—in the halls of governance.

If attendance at town meeting is seen as analogous to the voting act, real democracy has failed to keep pace with liberal, representative democracy. Between 1970 and 1998, women averaged only 46 percent of the attendance at town meeting. If seen for what it is, however (the legislative body of the town), town meeting is remarkably successful.

From city councils to the halls of Congress, no representative institution can match the town meeting on women's presence. Moreover, with a pair of minor adjustments, Vermont's local democracies could be the first to provide full representation for women. These adjustments stand out because of a most heartening surprise in the data: it is otherwise impossible to predict variations from town to town in women's attendance at town meeting. In the context of the following analysis, lack of predictability is perhaps the most important indicator of equality.

Town meeting has come a long way. In the beginning, women were even apologetic about their "intrusion" into the places where men had for so long controlled the decisions of the town.

WITNESS

The Town Meeting was some fun, however, though I imagine, not nearly as much as it used to be. I am afraid that is one institution the zest and flavor of which have been spoiled by Woman Suffrage. In the old days, the floor of the hall used to be prepared with a significant coating of sawdust;[1] now it is left uninvitingly bare; sufficiently sad indication of emasculating change. And the flow of language is, I am sure, not anything as full and racy as it was. Too bad! The men, flocking to what was once their social high tide of the year, must hate us women intruding our decorum into the rude freedom of their intercourse.

However the tradition still holds that Town Meeting is an occasion for the interchange of wit and wisdom, and that tradition is lived up to as well as possible. Trying to shut our petticoats from the tails of their eyes, the men do still rally and vilify one another; and I am chokingly able to say that they still smoke. The town buffoon, whose great day this is, still opposes every motion and cracks resounding jokes. The moderator still has real need of the gavel.

Just to look at, however, they are a source of satisfaction, this assembly of real country people, met on their own merits, according to their own standards, with no contamination of the "city people" influence that, in the summer, tarnishes them.

Zephine Humphrey[2]

By 1978 things had changed. At 10:05 a.m. on the morning of March 7, 1978, Ruth French was the second person to participate in the Monkton town meeting. She wore a green outfit.[3] The weather was excellent, the roads were clear, and the moderator, William Bird, had opened the meeting promptly at 10:00 a.m. (It was to be his last year as moderator.) French seconded a motion made by Clark Thomas to hold the town meeting before the school meeting. Thomas was a school director for the town in the Mount Abraham union school district (where my youngest two kids went to high school), next door in the town of Bristol. French was a library trustee for Monkton. The town immediately approved the motion by a voice vote. It was 10:06 a.m. French

---

1. The sawdust was spread on the floor to absorb the spit that inevitably accompanied chewing tobacco.

2. Zephine Humphrey, *Winterwise*, quoted in Charles Edward Crane, *Let Me Show You Vermont* (New York: Alfred A. Knopf, 1942), 160–161.

3. This was how the students identified her. By matching up comments in the minutes of the meeting with these kinds of identifications, which are coded by the issue on which the person participated and the sequence in which the participation took place, I am able to identify participators by name at least half the time when the minutes are as good as they were for Monkton.

also made the motion to accept article 2, "To receive and act on reports as submitted."[4] She was seconded by Edgar Baker. The town approved by a voice vote. It was 10:07 a.m.

Just after the lunch recess ("ham, mashed potatoes, coleslaw, and home-made pie—good!"),[5] Ruth French participated for the third and last time on article 18, an appropriations article for a series of eight town expenditures such as cemeteries ($500), dump ($2,688) and library ($825). French made the motion to fund the library. Louella Murton seconded her. It was so voted.[6]

Throughout that day in Monkton Ruth French was one of (an average of) 98 citizens in attendance at the town meeting. On average, 53 of these were women. At 10:32, there were 55 women and 42 men present. At 11:28 the count was 63 women and 51 men. At 1:46 it was 47 women and 46 men, and at 2:31 there were 62 women and 49 men.[7] Then at 2:40 p.m. the town meeting adjourned and the school meeting opened. At 3:15 p.m. the students counted attendance again. Only 79 citizens were still at the meeting, and for the first time men outnumbered women. The count was 42 to 37. Most would find it odd that men were more apt to stay for the school meeting than

---

4. Town officers are required to report to the town annually, and these reports are printed in the *Town Report*. Some towns take time to consider each report individually. Most (like Monkton) lump them all under one question.

5. Michael Gilbert and Geoffrey Liggett, "The 1978 Comparative Town Meeting Study: Town of Monkton," Burlington, University of Vermont, Real Democracy Data Base, March 1978. The meal was prepared and served by the Women's Auxiliary of the Fire Department.

6. Town of Monkton, Carmelita C. Burritt, Town Clerk, "Minutes of the Annual Town and School Meeting, Held on March 7, 1978," mimeograph 1978. Monkton's minutes were better than most for the late 1970s.

7. I have noticed (especially in the 1970s) that now and then women's attendance declined a bit around lunchtime. In the most explicit verification of the thesis, one of my students reported in her essay on the town meeting in Granville in 1987: "I almost felt as if I had been out in a time warp that day. Their treatment of the women was typical of days long past. All morning the women were busy preparing a feast for the menfolk, so very few of them were able to participate in the town meeting. I could see from the attitudes of the townspeople that they viewed the women as subservient." But the team's data didn't confirm her impressions. Of the meeting's 60 people in attendance, 26 (40 percent of the town's registered voters, 32 men and 28 women) had participated by noon, and 13 were women. Elizabeth Bell, "The Granville Town Meeting, 1987," Burlington, University of Vermont, March 1987. Granville elected twenty-eight officers in 1987. Half (fourteen) were women, but most of these were "traditional" female officers—all five library trustees, two out of three school directors, two out of three auditors, and the town clerk and treasurer (one person). Still, even here percentages were high for women and did include one lister (typically a male position) and a second constable (almost always a male position). Of the twenty-three appointed officers listed, nine were women. Town of Granville, *Annual Report*, year ending December 1986, 3.

women.[8] Twenty-nine minutes later the school meeting adjourned after the fourth item of new business: applause and thanks were given to William Bird for his years of service as moderator.

The most contentious of the articles resolved at town meeting was article 6 on the school meeting warning: "To see if the voters will authorize the School Board to hire a nurse for one day per week during the school year." The motion was made by Ellen Thompson, seconded by Sallie Havey, and voted down on a voice vote eleven minutes later. In that time nine people spoke up, five women and four men. The women initiated nine acts of speech and the men six. Jeannette Deale, a member of the school board, spoke the most, five times.

Between 1970 and 1998, nineteen teams of students counted women at the Monkton town meeting. The 54 percent female attendance in Monkton's 1978 meeting (the meeting described above) placed it eleventh out of the eighty meetings studied that year. Only 47 percent of the attenders at the average town meeting studied in 1978 were women. Of the remaining eighteen meetings studied in Monkton between 1970 and 1978, only two produced a higher percentage of female attenders—the meeting of 1985 (58 percent) and the meeting of 1991 (57 percent).[9]

Women's Attendance: Walking the Bounds

Monkton's record for women's attendance, although a bit better than the average town's, was illustrative of the entire sample in its levels and its variety. The average town meeting of the 1,418 town meetings for which reliable data were available posted a low count of 41 women in attendance, an average count of 53, and a high count of 64. The average maximum attendance level for women was 64 percent higher than their average minimum attendance, exactly the same as it was for men.

---

8. Perhaps. But it is also true that this is about the time children would be returning from school and women might have to return home. I have no systematic evidence of this, however, because too few cases match Monkton's situation; that is, a school meeting held after a town meeting and beginning about 3:00 in the afternoon. For an excellent essay on feminist theory and the heuristic framework of political science (one that underscores the limits of my project), see Diana Owen and Linda M. G. Zerilli, "Gender and Citizenship," *Society* 28 (July–August 1991): 27–34.

9. The literature on women's participation in public life, which has grown in tandem with political science itself, is extensive. More and more scholars are broadening definitions and widening constructs. See, for instance, Vicky Randall's call for expanded research agendas. Vicky Randall, *Women and Politics: An International Perspective* (Chicago: University of Chicago Press, 1987). In taking a first cut at women's participation in town meeting democracy, I hope to set the framework for one such agenda.

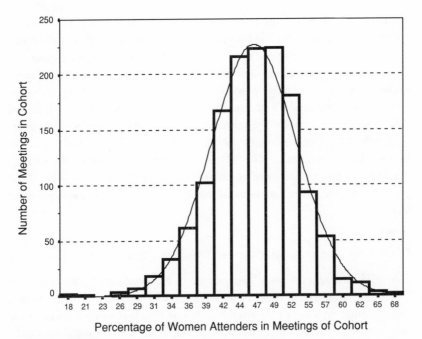

Figure 8.1. Percentage of persons in attendance that were women (1,418 town meetings, 1970–1998).

These raw numbers are critical to a proper understanding of the scale of women's role in real democracy, town meeting style. More important is the equality between women and men at town meeting. As noted above, the ratios of women to men at town meeting are closer than in any other general-purpose legislative body in America. At the average meeting in the sample, 46 percent of those in attendance (on average throughout the day) were women.[10] These data, arranged in a histogram (fig. 8.1), vary from 17 percent women's attendance at a meeting in the tiny farming town of Waltham in 1981 and in the larger quarrying town of Williamstown (population 2,284) in 1984 to 67 percent at a meeting in Burlington's bedroom suburb of St. George (population 677) in 1984 and 65 percent in the Northeast Kingdom town of Lunenburg (population 1,138) in 1980.

As the years passed between 1970 and 1998, the role of women in American political life became more and more legitimate, even expected. Although

10. In the Israeli kibbutz Rosner found attendance about equally divided between men and women. Menahem Rosner, *Participatory Political and Organizational Democracy and the Experience of the Israeli Kibbutz* (Haifa: University of Haifa, 1981), 13.

Vermont was ahead of the curve on this issue,[11] the national movement influenced us also. We would thus expect to find, and do find, that the mean of 46 percent attendance for women in our entire sample hides an increase in the percentage attending over time. Most of the increase, however, came in the 1970s. In the first five years of the study women's attendance averaged 45 percent of the total. By the middle of the 1980s (the five-year cluster of meetings studied between 1983 through 1987), it had climbed to 47 percent. A decade later (1994 through 1998), women's attendance had increased by only half a percent to 47.4. If the 1970s pace had continued, women would have achieved parity of attendance with men by the year 1990. If the post-1970s slope in the data remains the same, women will not achieve equal status until 2029.

Predicting Women's Attendance: The Size Variable

Size might influence women's attendance in two ways. First, meetings with larger raw numbers of citizens of both sexes in attendance might have a higher proportion of female attenders. If it is true that women do not have the same political legitimacy as men and therefore feel estranged by a politics as open and as visible as town meeting, it is possible that a large crowd might draw relatively more women than a small crowd, where anonymity is more difficult. Second, and more plausible, the kinds of women who live in the more complex environment of larger towns might be more at ease as participants in the political process, especially such a physically open process as town meeting. Or small towns may harbor old taboos and cultures unassociated with expanded political roles for women. Larger towns may contain the diversity that generates cosmopolitan norms encouraging non-traditional patterns of behavior while small towns remain homogeneous and

11. By 2001, Vermont was one of the few states to have elected a woman governor. It was the first state to elect a woman lieutenant governor (in 1952), the first to establish a college for women, and the second to elect a woman speaker of the state house of representatives. The presence of women in the state legislature has always been higher in Vermont than in nearly all other states. Edmond Constantini and Kenneth H. Clark, "Women as Politicians: The Social Background, Personality, and Political Careers of Female Party Leaders," *Journal of Social Issues* 28 (1972): 217–236. In Vermont percentages ranged from 10 percent to 15 percent before 1970. Frank M. Bryan, *Yankee Politics in Rural Vermont* (Hanover, NH: University Press of New England, 1974), 48. In their study of women in state legislatures between 1981 and 1993, Darcy, Welch, and Clark found that Vermont ranked fourth nationally on women in the lower house of the state legislature. No state east of the Mississippi was higher than Vermont save New Hampshire. R. Darcy, Susan Welch, and Janet Clark, *Women, Elections, and Representation*, 2nd ed. (Lincoln: University of Nebraska Press, 1994), 53–54.

conservative.[12] Indeed, survey research is deep with findings that small-town inhabitants have been less likely than city dwellers to approve public roles for women.[13]

On the other hand, substantial empirical evidence suggests that little places encourage women's participation in politics. Vermont, for instance, one of the smallest states, elected the first woman lieutenant governor at the very time it led the nation in the percentage of its population living in places of less than 2,500. In my own review of 3,690 elections to the Vermont House of Representatives between 1934 and 1964, I found that the larger towns lagged substantially behind the smaller towns in electing women to the statehouse in Montpelier.[14] In a study of local officeholders in Vermont town government between 1921 and 1941, Ann Hallowell discovered a moderately strong negative association between town size and the percentage of local offices held by women.[15] Hallowell's explanation is that rural life creates circumstances where women are needed more, and so small-town pragmatism prevails. If someone was needed to fill the office of town auditor in a town so small that willing men were scarce, women were asked. Necessity may have been the mother of invention.

When all is said and done, larger towns do have lower percentages of women at town meeting, although the variance in women's attendance explained by town size is not great. The correlation coefficient is only −.08. Nevertheless, the impact of this relationship is important. Women's attendance in the very smallest towns averages nearly 50 percent at day meetings and 46 percent at night meetings. Attendance in the very largest towns averages about 47 percent during the day and about 41 percent at night (see fig. 8.2).[16]

12. Reviews of this literature usually begin with Louis Wirth's seminal piece, "Urbanism as a Way of Life," in *Cities and Society*, ed. Paul K. Hatt and Albert J. Reiss (Glencoe, IL: Free Press, 1957).

13. Frank M. Bryan, *Politics in the Rural States* (Boulder, CO: Westview Press, 1981), 24–25.

14. Bryan, *Yankee Politics in Rural Vermont*, 46–50. See also Sharyne Merritt, "Winners and Losers: Sex Differences in Municipal Elections," *American Journal of Political Science* 21 (November 1977): 731–743. In Montana, Jobes found that size was unrelated to gender differences in the selection of administrative positions but that small agricultural communities elected more women than small "recreational" towns did. Patrick C. Jobes, "Gender Competition and the Preservation of Community in the Allocation of Administrative Positions in Small Rural Towns in Montana: A Research Note," *Rural Sociology* 62 (Fall 1997): 315–334.

15. Ann Hallowell, "Women on the Threshold: An Analysis of Rural Women in Local Politics (1921–1941)," *Rural Sociology* 52 (Winter 1987): 510–521.

16. Thus we see a case where variance explained (represented by R^2) is weak but impact (represented by beta) is strong. See table 8.1.

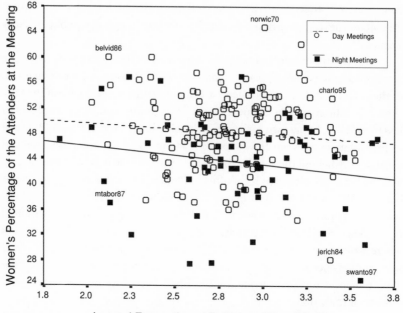

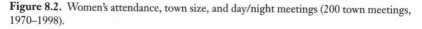

Logged Expression of Registered Voters in Town

Figure 8.2. Women's attendance, town size, and day/night meetings (200 town meetings, 1970–1998).

Predicting Women's Attendance: Structural Variables

With the size question resolved for the moment, we can continue the search for the correlates of feminine attendance in other places. The inquiry follows a pathway that should by now be familiar. The markers are town meeting structure and community life, including politics. But first we need to consider one of the clearest theoretical bridges to women's involvement on a wide range of fronts.

Peer Influence

Town meeting is a highly interactive affair where visual factors have considerable influence. Very early on in this study I became convinced that towns that had larger percentages of their town offices held by women would have higher feminine attendance at town meeting and more verbal participation. Town officers play an important role at town meeting. Several sit at the front of the hall and participate in a more or less formal way. Others are called on during the meetings to provide information and to comment on various matters of interest to the town. The presence of female town officers as role models ought to improve women's attendance.

In 1975 I coded the officers for the towns holding the eighty-two meetings in the 1970 and 1971 sample by sex and kind of office held for the years 1968–1971. The percentage of a town's major elective officers who were women became the independent variable and was matched with women's share of the town meeting attendance. A series of potentially contaminating measures were placed under control. But the percentage of town offices held by women was not associated in the slightest with women's share of town meeting attendance.[17] I duplicated this study for the years 1996 and 1997 with the same results.[18] A strong correlation between town size and women officeholders, however, confirmed Hallowell's earlier findings (see above, page 195).

Daytime versus Nighttime

The reformers who advocated holding town meeting at night in order to increase attendance may have biased the practice of real democracy against women.[19] Assume the traditional family situation. The man works outside the home and the woman works in the home. They have school-age children. Traditionally, the meeting is held during the day on a Tuesday beginning between 9:00 and 10:00 in the morning and ending between 2:00 and 4:00 in the afternoon. The man goes off to work. It may well cost the family a day's pay if he does not. The kids get on a school bus at 7:30. They will return home between 3:00 and 4:00. Women with school-age children have

---

17. Frank M. Bryan, "Comparative Town meetings: A Search for Causative Models of Feminine Involvement in Face-to-Face Politics," paper presented at the annual meeting of the Rural Sociological Society, San Francisco, August 21–24, 1975.

18. Frank M. Bryan, "How Does Town Meeting Treat Women?" paper presented at a Research in Progress seminar sponsored by the Center for Research on Vermont, University of Vermont, February 1999.

19. An important recent study questions the assumption that women have less free time to devote to politics than men do. Affiliation in voluntary associations has extended to women a special opportunity to enter political life. Kay Lehman Schlozman, Nancy Burns, and Sidney Verba, "Gender and the Pathways to Participation: The Role of Resources," *Journal of Politics* 56 (November 1994): 963–987. These observations make sense to me in the context of traditional town meeting democracy. Women's organizations in Vermont towns always have been equal to or exceeded men's organizations in *quantity*. (The "Ladies' Aid," "Women's Club," Daughters of the American Revolution, and even to some extent the Parent-Teacher Association, are examples.) Historically these segregated organizations gave women as much opportunity as men to learn civic skills, and they became very good at conducting public meetings. Moreover, women made time for them. Without these groups, the transition from home to politics would have been nearly unthinkable. Merritt, "Winners and Losers," 731–743.

an opportunity to attend town meeting. Change the meeting time to 7:30 p.m. Supper is finished. The woman does her evening chores in the home while the husband, with babysitting provided by his wife, is able to go to town meeting.[20]

Will a woman in a traditional family feel free to go off to town meeting alone even during the day? In farming families, which used to abound in Vermont, the man can structure his work to make attendance possible. In fact, town meeting was modeled on this very premise. But if small children are in the home, the woman is a convenient babysitter. In fact the data show that there is no relation between the ratio of women to men in a town's workforce and women's attendance at town meeting. These and other factors notwithstanding, however, it is hard to see how night meetings would have advantaged women in the days when traditional family arrangements dominated. This said, we consider two expectations. The first is that night meetings will depress women's attendance. The second is that this relation will decline over time as the availability of "free time" is equalized for men and women, and gender norms are modernized.[21]

An important negative connection does exist between night meetings and lower attendance for women. The 1,081 meetings we monitored that were held during the day averaged 47.3 percent female attendance. But attendance at the 337 night meetings averaged only 43.6 percent women.[22] To put it in perspective, we noted earlier that over the past twenty-eight years women

20. Anne Phillips's discussion of these issues in the context of feminist theory is both insightful and disquieting for communitarians. She argues, "Considering the intense pressures on women's time, it is remarkable that feminists have been so wedded to a politics of meetings. We might more readily expect male politicos to warm to a politics of continuous meetings and discussion and debate, all of them held conveniently outside the home and away from the noise of the children." Anne Phillips, *Democracy and Difference* (University Park: Pennsylvania State University Press, 1993), 111. Given this most pessimistic assessment, women's attendance at town meeting seems rather high. My sense is that the reason for this is the difference between face-to-face meetings and face-to-face governance. "Meetings" are more valued in large-scale, liberal democracy. In the small polities involved in face-to-face governance, citizens learn to keep "meetings" to a minimum.

21. The equalization of "free time" finding noted above (Schlozman, Burns, and Verba, "Gender and the Pathways to Participation," 970) has been reinforced and amplified. See Linda Thompson and Alexis J. Walker, "Gender in Families: Women and Men in Marriage, Work, and Parenthood," *Journal of Marriage and the Family* 51 (November 1989): 845–871, and Cathleen D. Zick and Jane L. McCullough, "Trends in Married Couples' Time Use: Evidence from 1977–78 and 1987–88," *Sex Roles* 24 (April 1991): 459–87. Both of these are cited in Nancy Burns, Kay Lehman Schlozman, and Sidney Verba, "The Public Consequences of Private Inequality: Family Life and Citizen Participation," *American Political Science Review* 91 (June 1997): 373–389.

22. The correlation coefficient is .25 and is significant at the .0001 level.

enhanced their position relative to men by about two and one-half percentage points, from an average of 44.8 percent of the attendance before 1976 to an average of 47.4 percent after 1993. During that time night meetings have not ceased to be a depressor of women's attendance. Thus, towns that switched from day to night meetings may have cost women all the gains they made since 1976.

How the night meeting reform hurt women's attendance is demonstrated in figure 8.2, which arrays a sample of two hundred meetings according to the size of the town where they are held and plots the slopes for night and day meetings separately. The lines of best fit can be seen as the average women's attendance at any given level of town size. The differential favoring day meetings is apparent and seems to grow slightly as towns get bigger. While wide variation exists, the overall pattern is clear. Meetings in the rim of positive outliers from Belvidere in 1986 to Norwich in 1970 to Charlotte in 1995 were all held during the day. The opposite relation from Mount Tabor in 1987 to Swanton in 1997 (with the exception of Jericho's 1984 meeting) appears for the negative outliers. Women's attendance is most apt to be equal to men's at the traditional day meetings in the small and often-isolated hill towns.[23]

When School Issues Are Present

A substantial literature suggests that traditionally women are more apt to be involved in local politics when "women's matters" like education are on the agenda.[24] Educational issues are usually the most family-centered items on the warning, and women are more apt to serve on the school board than in any other town office except town clerk. Indeed, in Vermont women were elected to school boards even before they were allowed to vote.[25]

School issues are often benign at town meeting. For instance, my students reported that the following discussion (reported in the minutes of the

23. Weather conditions had no special impact on women's attendance at town meetings at night or during the day.

24. Barry Bozeman, Sandra Thornton, and Michael McKinney, "Continuity and Change in Opinions on Sex Roles," in *A Portrait of Marginality: The Political Behavior of the American Woman*, ed. Marianne Githens and Jewel Limar Prestage (New York: David McKay, 1977), 38–65. See also Janet L. Bokemeier and John L. Tait, "Women as Power Actors: A Comparative Study of Rural Communities," *Rural Sociology* 45 (Summer 1980): 238–255.

25. Hallowell, "Women on the Threshold"; Bryan, "Comparative Town Meetings"; Bryan, "How Does Town Meeting Treat Women?"

school meeting in Warren in 1996) took only sixty seconds of deliberative time:[26]

> Article 7: To appropriate the sum of $16,000 to be added to the reserve
> fund for the purchase of a school bus.
>   Lori Klein moved that the $16,000 be added to the reserve fund for
> the purpose of purchasing a school bus. Motion Seconded. Balance of
> fund is $17,000. Plans are to purchase new bus in 1999–2000 estimated
> cost of $80,000. Article 7 approved by a voice vote in the affirmative.[27]

Sometimes school matters are more contentious. Consider the following from the minutes of the 1996 meeting in Danville. It represents a typical account of what often happens when school budgets are brought before a town meeting:

> Gerard DeLisle moved to suspend the rules to take up Article 6
> out-of-order. The motion was seconded. A request for a paper ballot was
> approved. Results: Yes—141; No—68. The motion was so voted.[28]
>   Article 6. To see what sum of money the School District will vote to
> raise in taxes for the support of the school for current expenses, capital
> improvements and debt service.
>   Tim Ide moved to raise $1,579,660. As presented in the school
> budget. Seconded. Chairman DeLisle explained in detail the expenditure
> and revenue figures and that Danville was a "maximum loss" town
> regarding state aid.
>   Associate Principal Miriam Benson showed charts and statistics
> regarding students' performance standings.
>   Alan Parker, negotiator for teacher contracts, explained the 18-month
> process and that the board voted 4–1 in favor of the 3.5 percent salary
> increase for three years.

26. Benjamin Cooper, Grant Hansel, and Sarah Leib, "The 1996 Comparative Town Meeting Study: Town of Warren," Burlington, University of Vermont, Real Democracy Data Base, March 1996. Benjamin Cooper points out in his essay: "The majority of the people at the school meeting were women, whereas at town meeting it was men." But he is hard on the officers of the town and school district for hurrying the completion of the town meeting before lunch. The school meeting was "warned" for 1:00 p.m. This meant that if the town meeting was not completed by that time it would have to reconvene *after* the school meeting was over. Cooper suspected that the town meeting was hurried to prevent this from happening. "Having the town meeting before the school meeting is a poor system. Issues that residents are concerned with should be dealt with no matter how long it takes." Benjamin Cooper, "1996 Warren Town Meeting," Burlington, University of Vermont, March 1996), 10.

27. Town of Warren, *Town Report*, year ending December 1996.

28. A request for a "paper ballot" is a signal. It is in effect a request for anonymity.

Tim Ide stated that this budget would raise the tax rate from 1.84 to 2.01 if the grand list increases by 1.

Bert Frye moved to amend the motion for a zero increase, to raise the same as last year–$1,409,089. The motion was seconded. Judge Springer moved that the budget at least be increased by the cost of living or 2.5 percent.

Toby Balivet moved to create a blank and insert a figure that the voters agree on. Amendment to create a blank was defeated by a 76–128 ballot vote.

Bert Frye proposed a substitute amendment for a 2.5 maximum increase over last year's school tax amount. Substitution was made without objection. Amendment was defeated by a voice vote. Motion to call the question was sustained by a 2/3 standing vote. The main motion to raise $1,579,660 in taxes was approved by a ballot vote.[29]

The Danville town meeting in 1996 lasted 400 minutes.[30] In that time thirty-eight warning items were considered. Article 6 of the school meeting took 154 minutes (38 percent) of this time.[31]

Overall I expected that the 1,092 meetings held in towns that deal with issues like these on town meeting day as Danville did[32] would have a higher percentage of women in attendance than the 217 meetings held in towns that have their town and school meetings on different days. More specifically, in the now familiar hierarchy of town/school meeting types, I further expected that those meetings where school items are mixed in with

29. Town of Danville, *Town Report*, year ending December 1996, 49.

30. Women made up only 39.1 percent of the voters attending Danville's 1996 meeting. Danville's high school was in my high school's "league," the Hilldale League. We competed with Danville in sports, public speaking, drama, and so forth. None of the seven schools in the league had more than one hundred students. Most had far fewer. Later in life, I spoke at their Honors Day banquet and once gave the graduation address in their excellent little high school, the only one of the old Hilldale League schools still alive.

31. One of my students said the following (in part) about article 6 in his essay: "This is where the meeting got ugly (or political). During this time there were several heated arguments back and forth between the people and the school board as well as between the people." Robert Kaplan, "Democracy in Danville," Burlington, University of Vermont, March 1996.

32. One of the issues of particular importance in recent years has been the opening of school facilities for use by the townspeople. Many local school establishments are not happy with the notion that regular citizens ought to be able to use school facilities. Here is a typical warning item: "To authorize the Board of School Directors to make available school facilities and equipment for specified public purposes if they appear to be in the best interest of the residents of the District, due consideration being given to efficient, economical, and appropriate use of the facilities and equipment." Town of Charlotte, *Town Report*, year ending December 1995, 113.

other articles on the town meeting warning would have a stronger feminine attendance than those where separate school meetings are held either before the town meeting begins or after it ends. My expectations were misplaced. The data did not indicate that school issues draw more women to town meeting.[33] When school issues were on the warning, fully integrated into the business of town meeting day, 46.8 percent of the attenders were women. When school issues were resolved at a meeting held on another day altogether, 46.4 percent were women.

The Australian Ballot

The presence or nonpresence of the Australian ballot is an important variable because it marks a distinction between liberal and communitarian politics. Indeed, it can be seen as a liberal hedge on the communitarian bet that real democracy will work in practice. By now you know that the Australian ballot provides a way for people to vote in private and to make decisions "on the edge" of town meeting. It can involve going into the town hall at some time during the day on Tuesday (town meeting may or may not be in session, depending on the time you arrive), entering a polling booth, voting for town officers and perhaps a few other special issues, and then leaving without participating in the discussion. Or it could involve going to town meeting Monday night and voting by ballot on officers and issues the next day at the town hall.

We might hypothesize that women would prefer this more anonymous form of democracy, since the psychic costs of open participation have traditionally been higher for them than for men. Women would in effect choose the protections of liberal processes. Or perhaps people feel that if one member of the family ought to "stay for the discussion," it is the man. Clearly, if traditional family responsibilities are significant determinants of women's ability to participate in communal variants of political participation, an ability to "vote and go home" would likely decrease the percentage of women at town meetings where that option was available.[34] In both cases we would expect lower attendance at town meeting for women where the Australian ballot option is available.

To test this notion I compared women's attendance at meetings where the Australian ballot was available with meetings where it was not used at all. But since all but thirty-five of the meetings held at night use the Australian ballot and night meetings are associated with decreased attendance by women,

33. For further discussion of this relation see chapter 10.
34. See Phillips, *Democracy and Difference*, 109–113.

it was difficult to disentangle the effects of the Australian ballot and of holding meetings at night. Nevertheless, separating out those meetings held during the day shows that women's attendance is a little better where the ballot is available. Women do not seem to take advantage of the Australian ballot (any more than do men) to vote and go home.

Predicting Women's Attendance: The Context of Community

Any observer traveling in Vermont who is trained to expect a relation between the context of community and the character of politics could not help but exclaim from time to time, "This is just the kind of town I would expect [whatever]." Pass from the perfectly manicured tourist towns to the upscale professional suburbs near Vermont's half dozen little cities to the hardscrabble, gasoline-culture towns of farm and forest, and one cannot help but be sure that variants of community life must matter to politics. More to the point, I could drive social scientists trained in modernization theory through towns that would make them conclude without reservation that women's attendance at the town meetings held there would most likely be abysmal.

Socioeconomic Status

Almost everything we have learned about how women break into the political process tells us that socioeconomic status is intimately involved. In fact, the connection between SES factors and women's tendency to participate in politics is as strong in the literature as the connection between SES and participation in general.[35] If the SES paradigm is applicable to real democracy, it is almost unimaginable that one could walk into a town meeting in some of Vermont's quintessential upscale communities and not see more women than, for instance, one would see in the tough dirt-road towns of the outback.

Education level is the key component of the status variable. Studies show that education builds confidence, improves efficacy, and increases commitment to the public weal. In a unique study of the contextual influences on pro-feminist attitudes at the individual level, for instance, Banazak and

35. Val Burris, "Who Opposed the ERA? An Analysis of the Social Bases of Antifeminism," *Social Science Quarterly* 64 (June 1983): 305–17; Sandra K. Gill, "Attitudes toward the Equal Rights Amendment," *Sociological Perspectives* 28 (October 1985): 441–62; Karen Oppenheim Mason, John L. Czajka, and Sara Arber, "Change in U.S. Women's Sex-Role Attitudes, 1964–1974," *American Sociological Review* 41 (August 1976): 573–96; Wilbur J. Scott, "The Equal Rights Amendment as Status Politics," *Social Forces* 64 (December 1985): 499–506; Arland Thornton, Duane F. Alwin, and Donald Camburn, "Causes and Consequences of Sex-Role Attitudes and Attitude Change," *American Sociological Review* 48 (April 1983): 211–227.

Plutzer, while not sure about some of the connector variables, are not hesitant about the impact of education. "It is clear at both the individual and aggregate level that women's access to higher education is the most important structural variable related to pro-feminism support by men and women. It establishes the psychic capital especially needed to enter the political marketplace. The education variable is, of course, connected at the hip to income."[36]

Integral to the arguments for the SES connection between women and participation is the finding that while higher SES levels are connected to higher participation for both men and women,[37] the connection may be stronger for women. Jane Mansbridge, in the best analysis of a single town meeting democracy ever published, notes: "Many, especially the women, view their lack of influence as an appropriate result of their lack of education."[38]

On the other hand, and more to the point in a book focusing on communities rather than individuals, upscale communities often demonstrate a commitment to women's participation of whatever social rank. At the town level in Vermont, for instance, support for women's participation in public life and educational achievement are clearly related. In fact the association produces the strongest statistical linkage between two variables I have been able to produce in over thirty years of research on Vermont elections. The R^2 between the percentage of college graduates in town and the yes vote on Vermont's equal rights amendment to its own constitution was .42, under controls for the Democratic base vote in the towns. Towns with larger cohorts of the college-educated certainly had electorates that were much more apt to vote for women's rights than towns that did not.

Consider the town of Lunenburg. Here is a town high on the upper Connecticut River, knee deep in the north woods. A town honeycombed with little brooks and laced with bog and marsh and edged by broad farmers' fields

36. Lee Ann Banazak and Eric Plutzer, "Contextual Determinants of Feminist Attitudes: National and Subnational Influences in Western Europe," *American Political Science Review* 87 (March 1993): 147–157.

37. Merritt, "Winners and Losers," 732. Susan Welch, "Women as Political Animals? A Test of Some Explanations for Male-Female Political Participation Differences," *American Journal of Political Science* 21 (November 1977): 711–730. Welch put it this way: "Women participate in the aggregate less than men not because of some belief that they hold about the role of women in politics, but largely because they are less likely to be found in those categories of people who participate in politics: the employed and highly educated in particular." Welch, "Women as Political Animals?" 726, 728. Education was also found to be an important criterion for recruitment to political office for women in state legislatures and may be critical if a woman has not achieved a party leadership position. Paula J. Dubeck, "Women and Access to Political Office: A Comparison of Female and Male State Legislators," *Sociological Quarterly* 17 (Winter 1976): 42–52.

38. Jane J. Mansbridge, "Town Meeting Democracy," *Working Papers for a New Society* 1 (Summer 1973): 7.

along the river. A town where the beaver and the fisher cats and the moose and the people all live together—if not in harmony, at least together. Here is a town casting a hefty majority of its votes for Ronald Reagan in 1980 and 1984 and ranking in the bottom 5 of the 210 towns in the sample on the liberal factor score. It is a town with one of the very lowest educational levels of the 210 towns in the sample (an average of 8 percent college graduates) for 1980 and 1990. Yet the percentage of women attending Lunenburg's seven town meetings in the sample was exactly 50 percent.

Recall Newark, the wild little town in the Northeast Kingdom and upscale Shelburne in the Burlington/Chittenden County SMSA. The percentage of college graduates in Shelburne was double that of Newark. But the percentage of women at Shelburne's ten town meetings in the sample was below average for the period, 41 percent, while the percentage of women at Newark's ten meetings was exactly average, 46 percent. Women's share of town meeting attendance for the full sample (beginning in 1977 when Census data became more trustworthy) explained only 1 percent of the variance in the more sensitive "education index" introduced earlier.

Expanding the analysis to other socioeconomic variables added little. Neither median family income nor percentage professional in the workforce was able to clear a very low bar of statistical significance. Expectedly, the combined SES index I created from these three variables also failed. But the upscale factor score built on a wider spectrum of variables (it was influenced positively by socioeconomic diversity and negatively by native Vermonters, for instance) did produce a significant but weak correlation of .12. Socioeconomic diversity also managed to stand alone with a coefficient of .11.

The overwhelming weight of the "thick" evidence supports the notion that SES is not an important filter for women's attendance at town meeting. The SES relation does not appear in the popular literature on town meeting or in press accounts. It has not shown up in the thousands of essays my students have submitted to me. I have attended over sixty meetings myself and have not seen it. One notices more upscale women at Shelburne's town meeting and fewer in Kirby's. That is because Shelburne has more upscale women than Kirby does. In short, when you look around inside a Vermont town meeting hall you are not struck by the lack of women, nor do you sense that their class identity is out of synch with the town's population. They seem to be like the men.[39]

---

39. In another context (city councils in 264 American cities of over 25,000 population), Welch and Karnig found SES factors were, although statistically significant, "tepidly related to the equitability of female representation on the council, and much less related to the presence of

PRESTON RIDGE LIBRARY
COLLIN COLLEGE
FRISCO, TX 75035

WITNESS

Archie Bunker would love this town. I counted 146 people at the town meeting, and only 59 of them were women. Most of them were with their husbands, and those that were not had probably outlived their husbands because they seemed very old. If the ladies cooking the lunch meal downstairs had come up there would have been a few more, but frankly I'm glad they didn't. The lunch was excellent! My girl friend is always complaining about women's rights, and I'm glad she didn't come here with me today because she would have been raising hell. My figures show only 40 percent of the people here are women. What kind of a democracy is that? But what can you expect from a hick town like this? I bet half the men around here haven't been told women can vote yet! When we drove into town I knew we were in trouble. No restaurants, and all the cars were as old as the people. Dirty snowbanks, stray dogs, and overweight people. Doesn't anyone around here work out? If women are to ever get their rights in Vermont someone had better tell this state about the twentieth century! The only positive thing I can think of is to say that the women at town meeting didn't seem any more destitute than the men. And they weighed about the same too. (Sorry, Professor Bryan, but you told us to tell it like it is.)

Richard Bellamy[40]

Other Socioeconomic Correlates

I first looked at the relation between population dynamics and women's attendance. This variable is in some sense a surrogate for cosmopolitanism, which is itself part of the SES paradigm. Still, my inclination was to believe that meetings in growing towns would exceed the norm for political involvement by women. Yet no community dynamics measure explained even half of 1 percent of the variation in women's attendance. Increases in population, native Vermonters in the population, the percentage living in the same house for five years before the Census count, and the percentage moving into town in the past five years all failed to even nudge women's share of town meeting attendance one way or the other.[41]

women in the mayor's seat." Susan Welch and Albert K. Karnig, "Correlates of Female Office Holding in City Politics," *Journal of Politics* 41 (May 1979): 478–491.

40. Richard Bellamy, "The 1977 Comparative Town Meeting Study [I've withheld the name of the town because I have too many friends there]," Burlington, University of Vermont, March 1977).

41. Timpone, however, found that women who had moved in the past two years were *less* apt to register to vote than men. Richard J. Timpone, "Structure, Behavior, and Voter Turnout in

Community boundedness contains elements of the cosmopolitan-upscale thesis as well. Communities ranking high on rural isolation, where people are less apt to work out of town, might be less influenced by forces of modernism, which, it is said, are supportive of an expanded vision for women in public life. But rural isolation by itself turned up nothing. Nor did workplace measures (out of town or in town) or how long it takes to get to work. The factor score that summarizes this concept, "rural isolation," failed to make a peep. The correlation coefficient was .03. If interaction with large-town life promotes women's involvement in politics, one would expect stronger ratios of women to men at town meeting in places like Underhill, Williston, and St. George, all within the Chittenden County SMSA. Weaker ratios would be expected in Kingdom towns like Canaan and Bloomfield and in towns like Granville, deep in the central range of the Green Mountains. But such a relation was nowhere to be found.

Two hardship variables seemed especially relevant. Population density as I measured it (population per road mile) identifies those towns where people are spread out. In Vermont this means living on a back road, almost always gravel. In towns where the number of people for every mile of road is low, getting to and from town meeting will be more difficult for more people. I hypothesized that this would be especially true for women because the difficulty of mixing distance with children or a job (or both) is more pronounced for women than for men. But towns where miles of back roads separate the citizens had no fewer women at town meeting than towns where citizens are more clustered.[42]

Towns with higher percentages of dependent citizens in the population might have lower women's attendance at town meeting. I looked at meetings in towns with relatively more children and meetings in towns with relatively more senior citizens. Both of these groups are more apt to need the care of an adult from time to time. Overwhelmingly, women are the adults who provide such care. But this did not interfere with attendance at town meeting. I then

---

the United States," *American Political Science Review* 92 (March 1998): 145–158. This seems reasonable, since "home duties" in a domestic relocation have traditionally fallen more to women than to men.

42. Some evidence from state legislative races suggests that the population density of the city districts helps women conduct campaigns. When voters are scattered over hill and dale in rural districts, women participate in campaigns less. Darcy, Welch, and Clark conclude, however, that "size is not an important factor" in women's attaining legislative seats. But they do not address population density. Darcy, Welch, and Clark, *Women, Elections, and Representations*, 60. Moreover, shorter distances to the state capital *from* city districts also attract women candidates. Carol Nechemias, "Geographic Mobility and Women's Access to State Legislatures," *Western Political Quarterly* 38 (March 1985): 119–131.

combined these individual statistics into a single variable I labeled "dependent population." Nothing happened.

In the 1980s Vermont towns began providing day care at town meeting. By 1995 it became apparent that enough towns had done so to warrant a measurement. The results show that child care does make a difference. Of the 210 meetings studied between 1995 and 1998, 44 were held during the day with child care provided. They averaged 49.5 percent female attendance. The 99 meetings held during the day without day care averaged 48.4 percent. At night the difference was greater. The eight meetings with day care averaged 46.2 percent female attendance, and the 59 meetings that did not averaged 44.3 percent. A percentage point here and a percentage point there add up to real equality.

Political Culture

Studies show that a town's political culture (indicators of electoral commitment, partisan balance, ideological posture) might provide clues to why women's attendance at town meeting is high in some towns and low in others.[43] The expectations are straightforward. First, women's issues in Vermont, as elsewhere, were historically more apt to be championed by the Democrats than by the Republicans. The "gender gap" in electoral politics generally favors Democrats. Perhaps towns where Democratic candidates receive a higher percentage of the vote have politically active women who expand women's attendance at town meeting. Second, the liberalism index might be associated with increased percentages of women at town meeting, not only because activism occupies a more elevated position in liberal strategies but because supporting women's rights does as well. Third, the vote for Socialist congressman Bernie Sanders, whose campaigns are popularly perceived to be associated with women's issues, could identify towns where women are more involved in local politics. Finally, it was reasonable to surmise that towns more strongly supporting an equal rights amendment to the Vermont constitution would have more equal ratios of women to men at town meeting.

43. Women's representation in state legislatures may be influenced by a state's long-term political folkways. Using Daniel Elazar's "moralistic" culture scores in combination with a state's "tradition of female representation" (going back to the 1930s), David B. Hill was able to explain 40 percent of the variance in women's representation in state legislatures in 1973 after considering structural variables, which explained 8 percent. David B. Hill, "Political Culture and Female Political Representation," *Journal of Politics* 43 (February 1981): 159–168.

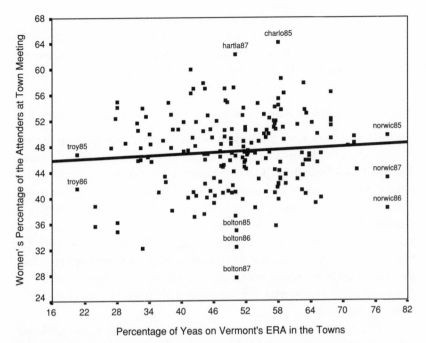

Figure 8.3. Women's attendance and Vermont's 1966 ERA vote (191 meetings, 1985–1987).

For the most part these hypotheses failed. The Democratic Party vote, liberalism, and the Sanders electorate all failed tests of their association with women's attendance at town meeting. So did the ERA vote. Figure 8.3 shows that among the 191 meetings we studied in 1985, 1986, and 1987 (the ERA referendum was held in 1986), Norwich's 80 percent of yes votes was best. But two of its three meetings fell below the statewide average for women at town meeting. Up north on the Canadian border, the town of Troy was at the very bottom of the ERA voting but matched Norwich on women's town meeting attendance. Bolton, the little town on the Winooski River where a lack of ramps leading on and off the interstate provides a shield of sorts from Burlington's magnetic forces, had the lowest percentage of women at town meeting over the period. Its percentage for the ERA, however, was 48 (almost the statewide average). Hartland, which also produced an average ERA vote, had the second highest town meeting attendance score for women. Charlotte, which was by no means among the ERA leaders, had the highest percentage of women at town meeting.

The relation between the ERA vote and women's attendance is so weak ($r = .09$) that the view from the very lowest point on the slope is almost the same as the view from the very highest point. And what we see all along the way is made uncertain by great cloudbanks of variation.[44]

Predicting Women's Attendance: The Variables in Combination

The analytical steps made throughout this chapter were retraced and summarized by way of a multiple regression equation. I experimented with various combinations of variables. The conclusion: the ratio of women to men at town meeting is nearly impossible to predict. There was wide variation in women's attendance from town to town, and within towns from meeting to meeting. But I was unable to detect any robust, systemic reason for these variations in women's attendance at town meeting within the socioeconomic or political culture of the towns where they were held. In an atmosphere where the percentage of women at town meeting is closing in on equality with men, I take this to be a good sign. We may be at a point where gender itself may become a nonissue.

The most potent arrangement of indicators features a structural indicator: when the meeting is held, day or night. It accounts for about 7 percent of the variance in women's attendance. Upscale communities and small towns added another 1.2 percent each. The entire equation fell short of explaining even 10 percent of the variance in the ratios of women to men at town meeting. Yet it may be important that upscale finished the exercise in second place and that it was strengthened a bit when town size was controlled. At the margin (a very narrow margin), the best environment for women's attendance is a meeting held during the day in an upscale small town with day care provided (see table 8.1).

In the meetings studied between 1995 and 1998, however (when data on day care were available), time of day when the meeting was held became the only variable that survived the regression equation. It alone accounted for nearly as much variation (9 percent) as the three variables that survived (eight were entered) the full sample equation for the meetings of 1977–1998.[45] Part of the "nighttime" effect is due to the lack of child care provided at night, when it is especially needed. Only eight of the sixty-seven meetings in the

44. The two factor scores used to reduce the political data to a pair of single components, one called "Sanders" and the other called "liberal," were also sent into the analysis without success.

45. Meetings held before 1977, remember, were omitted from the analysis because of unreliable Census data.

Table 8.1. Correlates of Women's Attendance: The Final Equation

Variable	r	R^2	Improvement in R^2	Beta
Night meetings	.262	.069	—	−.248
Upscale factor score	.284	.081	.012	.142
Log of town size	.305	.093	.012	−.116

Note: Dependent variable = women's percentage of the attenders; all coefficients are significant at the .001 level.

sample held at night had child care. It is worth repeating. The best thing Vermont could do to equalize attendance for women is the least theoretically complicated and the most practical. Meet during the day and provide child care. Although we will need more data to be sure, if this was done it seems likely Vermont could announce that its town meetings had virtually eliminated all attendance bias against women. How many legislative institutions in the world can make that claim?

Into their 40's they shared their last born babies, . . . forgetting afterward the worry of yet another child born to raise in hard times. They would sit nursing them in the back of the Town Hall at all the public gatherings they could get to, diapers modestly draped across their bosoms as they rocked and commented on local politics and social affairs with a fine mixture of sharp perception and grim humor—and always laughter.

Esther Titcomb McLean

The epigraph is from Esther Titcomb McLean, "Give My Regards to Deering," *Yankee* 39 (February 1975): 86–93. Even today the nursing of babies at town meeting never ceases to interest those "from away." Reporters from big-city newspapers always seem to report it when they see it. Women knitting are also a favorite observation. I suspect it adds the requisite old-time flavor that reporters want to portray. But it also suggests that while women may *attend* town meeting, they bring their "womanly duties" with them and are therefore less likely to participate in the business of the meeting. In 1987 Susan Levine, a staff writer from the *Philadelphia Inquirer,* went to the town meeting in Guilford, Vermont. "In the end, the people spoke—128 of them agreed with former Highway Commissioner Harvey Cutting that the 1987 road budget should be slashed by $40,000; there were 63 opposed. *As several women knitted and one or two nursed babies* [emphasis mine], Cutting rose from his chair and, notebook in hand, presented alternative figures." Susan Levine, "Town Meeting: A Cherished, but Troubled, Institution," *Philadelphia Inquirer,* March 8, 1987, 27A.

9

The Question of Equality

Women's Participation

Esther McLean was talking about her mother and other women and men of the Depression living in the small town of Deering, New Hampshire, across the river and a few miles south of Windsor, Vermont, where my own mother was raised in similarly hard times. Women of course "had the vote" in those days. But it is a long, long way from the vote to equality. It is a long way from the back of the hall to the front, just as it has been a long way from the back to the front of the bus.

The heart of town meeting is public talk. Yet speaking in public often tops the list of human fears. If this is especially true for minority groups and women (as many say it is),[1] doesn't it compromise real democracy's pretension to equality? We know that "feeling conspicuous" contributes importantly to speech anxiety. Men may feel conspicuous when they stand to speak at a town meeting, but not because they are men. For women, however, gender has provided an additional reason to feel conspicuous.

1. Behnke and Sawyer found, for instance, that in a two-week period before an oral presentation, female speakers demonstrated higher anxiety patterns. Ralph R. Behnke and Chris R. Sawyer, "Anticipatory Anxiety Patterns for Male and Female Public Speakers," *Communication Education* 49 (April 2000): 187–195. Others have found that "females generally report more communication anxiety than males" and that "boys are more comfortable speaking in class than girls." Myron W. Lustig and Peter A. Anderson, "Generalizing about Communication Apprehension and Avoidance: Multiple Replication and Meta-analysis," special issue, *Journal of Social Behavior and Personality* 5 (1990): 309–340, and John A. Daly, Pamela O. Kreiser, and Lisa A. Roghaar, "Question-Asking Comfort: Explorations of the Demography of Communication in the Eighth Grade Classroom," *Communication Education* 43 (January 1994): 27–41. The intervening variable between "minority status" and fear of public speaking may be conspicuousness. See the references in chapter 6.

Even more than attendance at town meeting, therefore, verbal participation offers a poignant test of the degree to which real, face-to-face talk democracy discriminates against American democracy's most wronged groups—women and (by extension) minorities.

In chapter 8 I touted town meeting's relatively high percentage of women attending. Alas, women's verbal participation in the discussion and debate of town meeting does not match their presence in the meeting place. On average women made up 46 percent of the attendance at the town meetings we studied between 1970 and 1998.[2] But they constituted only 36 percent of the citizens who spoke out at town meeting (what I call "speech") and were responsible for only 28 percent of the acts of speech (what I call "talk"). True, some of the deficit in women's speech reflects their lower attendance, and even more of the deficit in women's talk reflects their lower speech. You cannot speak if you are not present, and you cannot repeat acts of speech (talk) if you decide not to speak at all. The evidence, however, is clear. The public character of verbal participation has seriously inhibited women's role in the real democracy of town meeting.

The good news, as we shall see, is that this discrimination is ending. Women's verbal participation in town meeting (speech and talk combined) has increased dramatically since 1970. We will also see that women's total involvement in town meeting (attendance and verbal participation combined) is easier to predict than their attendance alone. This will make it easier to identify the conditions under which women's role in town meeting will become equal to men's. These findings will suggest in still another way that small settings are better for women than large ones. To get a flavor of the dimensions of how, when, and how much women speak out at town meeting, let us focus on one of Vermont's smallest towns, where women's involvement is perfectly visible to the naked eye, even though (in this case) it is far from good.

Mount Tabor

In 1990 the census takers could find only 214 people living in Mount Tabor, Vermont, and local people did the counting. Mount Tabor is one of the very few towns that report in the minutes the names of the people who attended town meeting. Because of the reasonably good minutes in the town report,

---

2. Rosner found the same thing happening in the Israeli kibbutz. One of the reasons he gave for this was the lack of women officeholders, since officeholders generally spoke more often than rank-and-file attenders. Menahem Rosner, *Participatory Political and Organizational Democracy and the Experience of the Israeli Kibbutz* (Haifa: University of Haifa, 1981), 13–14. My strong suspicion is that the same correlation obtains in town meeting. I am currently working on this question. See www.uvm.edu/~fbryan.

the work of Andrew Tufts (the student who went to Mount Tabor that year), and the fact that I know the town well, I was able to compile the names of everyone who participated in the meeting in 1987.[3]

Although it is the former home and headquarters of the state's first millionaire, lumber king Silas L. Griffith, in 1990 Mount Tabor had only one manufacturer, which made wreaths. The town also had a service station, a landscaper, three contractors, an electrician, and a cemetery. In 1988 voter turnout was 76 percent. Two years earlier in the off-year election it was 57 percent. In between these two elections the town held its annual town meeting on Monday night, March 2, 1987. There were 28 citizens in attendance, 21 percent of the town's 135 registered voters. A town with 135 registered voters was expected to turn out 36 percent of them at town meeting.

The school meeting began at 7:30 p.m. The first participation was by an officer of the school district, Hedvig E. Gaiotti. She participated six times on article 3, the school budget.[4] Next to speak was a town lister, Olaf Nielsen. He was followed by one of the town auditors, Anne Crosby. Five more men followed her. Then came a third woman, Bea Olsen. Robert Gasperetti followed her and was the last new person to speak during the school meeting. During the town meeting four other people joined the discussion. One of these was the last woman on the list of participators, Mabel Gaiotti. In all, four of the sixteen participators were women.

These four women participated 36 times, 9 times during the school meeting and 27 times during the town meeting. Twelve men at the meeting spoke 150 times, 28 times during the school meeting and 122 times during the town meeting. Thus women made up only 39 percent (11 of 28) of those in attendance and 25 percent (4 of 16) of the group that participated, and they accounted for 19 percent (36 of 186) of the participations. Few of the 1,388 meetings in the sample did worse than this one on women's verbal participation.[5]

Women's Participation: Walking the Bounds

On average women contributed sixteen speakers to each town meeting in the sample and were responsible for forty-nine "acts of speech" per meeting. As in

3. Andrew Tufts, "The 1987 Comparative Town Meeting Study: Town of Mt. Tabor," Burlington, University of Vermont, Real Democracy Data Base, March, 1987; Town of Mt. Tabor, Edward D. Risdon, Town Clerk, "Proceedings Mt. Tabor Town and Town School District Meeting, March 2 and 3, 1987," mimeograph, 1987.
4. The first two warning items were for election of town officers that would take place the next day by Australian ballot.
5. Forty-seven meetings had incomplete data.

chapters 6 and 7, I call the number (or percentage) of those in attendance who speak out at least once "speech" and the number of different acts of speech made by those who participate "talk." Thus in the average town meeting the total speech for women was 16 and the total talk was 49.

Women's verbal participation (speech and talk) compared with men's, however, is the more important comparison. Are the numbers low for women in some meetings and high in others because participation in general is low on the one hand and high on the other? To answer this question we need to compare the number of women participating at least once with the number of men participating at least once (speech) and the number of women's participations with the number of men's participations (talk). When this is done it is clear that both women's speech and women's talk at town meeting increase with men's. But the relationship contains a lot of slack. Variations in men's speech from meeting to meeting explain only 20 percent of the variance in women's speech, and variations in men's talk explain only 24 percent of the variance in women's talk.

Figure 9.1 puts a face on the distribution of speech by gender and makes clear the substantial gap between the verbal participation of women and men at town meeting. The steep diagonal represents the line of perfect equality between the sexes. Meetings falling above this line, like Plainfield and Worcester in 1997 and Holland and Elmore in 1998, had more women than men speaking out at least once. But most meetings fall below the line of equality. Some, like Wilmington in 1970 and 1971, fall dramatically below the line. The gap between the sexes is greater for talk than it is for speech.[6] Women's speech exceeded men's speech in 105 meetings; women's talk exceeded men's talk in 73.

These fundamental speech and talk statistics from nearly 1,388 meetings are normally distributed. They represent the world's first summary measures of women's participation in a large number of instances of open, face-to-face, legislative democracy in general purpose governments. Civilization has evolved dramatically since the days of early Athens when women were not even considered citizens. Now we have an accurate measure of how far we've come. Not far enough. Not yet.

A part of women's inequality in speech, of course, reflects their inequality in attendance, and a part of their inequality in talk reflects their inequality

6. In a study of over four hundred respondents in Madison, Wisconsin, Jack M. McLeod and his colleagues discovered that while anticipated attendance at public issues forums in the Madison area showed no gender bias, willingness to speak out at such a forum was higher among men than among women. Jack M. McLeod, Dietram A. Scheufele, Patricia Moy, Edward M. Horowitz, R. Lance Holbert, Weiwu Zhang, Stephen Zubric, and Jessica Zubric, "Understanding Deliberation: The Effects of Discussion Networks on Participation in a Public Forum," *Communication Research* 26 (December 1999): 743–774.

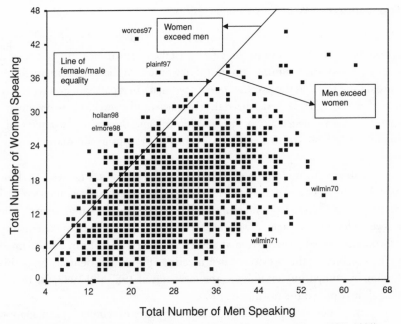

Figure 9.1. Women don't speak as much as men (1,389 town meetings, 1970–1998).

in speech. To take women's attendance out of the equation (for speech) and their speech out of the equation (for talk), I calculated two ratios: the ratio of the percentage of female attenders who speak to the percentage of male attenders who speak, and the ratio of the average talk of the females who speak to the average talk of the males who speak. These ratios compare the willingness of women and men attending the same town meeting to speak out at least once, and the willingness of women and men who do speak out at least once to speak out in total.

What we find is that on average 34 percent of the women in attendance speak out at least once, as do 52 percent of the men. The average ratio of women attenders who speak to men attenders who speak is 0.68, where 1.00 equals equality between the sexes. On the other hand, those women who speak out do so 3.1 times over the course of the meeting, and those men who speak out do so 4.4 times. The average ratio of women's talk to men's is 0.75. In short, the participatory gap between women and men at town meeting is wider for speech than it is for talk.[7]

7. For distributions, histograms, and other statistics for these and other variables in this chapter, see www.uvm.edu/~fbryan.

The Context of Women's Participation

To make judgments on the kinds of meetings and the kinds of towns that encourage women to join in the give-and-take of town meeting debate and discussion requires a summary indicator of women's verbal involvement. Since the data suggest that the psychic cost of a woman's first participation is greater than that of a man's, I standardized the two ratios and gave the ratio of women's speech to men's speech a two-thirds weighting and the ratio of women's talk to men's talk a one-third weighting. I called the resulting summary measure femindex.

Armed with this summary measure, we may now ask (as we asked for overall attendance and overall participation), How much does women's verbal participation change from meeting to meeting within the same town?[8] The answer: a lot. On average only about 20 percent of the variance in the equality of women's verbal participation at any given town meeting can be explained by its equality in the previous town meeting. Figure 9.2 demonstrates this finding by comparing femindex in the meetings of 1987 and 1988, the match that approximated the normal relation.

Town meetings producing the same equality of women's participation in 1988 as they did in 1987 would fall on the diagonal line on figure 9.2. However, few towns behaved like Cabot, where the femindex was low (but similar) in each year, or Panton, where the femindex was higher (but similar) in each. Although a number of other towns are on or near the line of perfect match (Newbury, Sharon, Starksboro, and a few others), the overall pattern is scattered. Whatever it was that caused women to participate more, for instance, in Charleston[9] in 1988 than in 1987 or less in Brownington[10] in

8. Although their groups are small, these kinds of questions are addressed in Renée A. Meyers, Dale E. Brashers, Latonia Winston, and Lindsay Grob, "Sex Differences and Group Argument: A Theoretical Framework and Empirical Investigation," *Communication Studies* 48 (Spring 1997): 19–41.

9. Charleston is a wild Kingdom town where you can still advertise to swap a '92 John Deer snowmobile and a 12-gauge shotgun for a 1987 Cadillac Riviera "parts" car. In the summer of 1998 I picked up a nice little 1987 Chevy Chevette for parts up there for $250. Melissa and I managed to drive it the 125 miles down to Starksboro in the dark and the rain. As this book goes to print, it still sits in my yard. I have eleven Chevettes on my place, two for the road and the rest for parts. When the pretty people who care more about cosmetics than serious recycling go by, it drives them nuts.

10. I lived for a year (1984–1985) in Brownington while I taught in the high school one town over in Orleans, a village in the town of Barton. In a class called Problems of American Democracy in the fall of 1964 I conducted a schoolwide mock presidential election (much to the consternation of several of the teachers). It was then I learned that Vermont was about to vote for the Democratic presidential candidate for the first time in over a century. Thirty-nine winters have

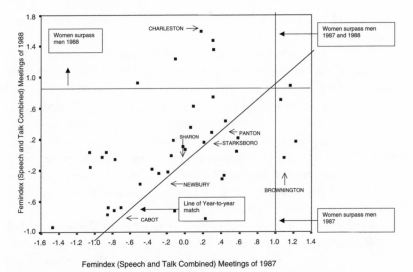

Femindex (Speech and Talk Combined) Meetings of 1987

Figure 9.2. Women's speech and talk combined (39 towns, 1987 and 1988).

1988 than in 1987, it is unlikely that the character of the towns or the structure of their meetings—the context of what happens—changed enough in those twelve months to generate the changes that took place in women's verbal participation.

The Architecture of Women's Verbal Participation

We found in chapter 8 that a structural variable—when town meeting was held—was the best of the three variables that in the end helped explain why women were more apt to be present at some town meetings than others. Day meetings turned out more women than night meetings. But structural variables did little to predict levels of verbal participation. As one might guess, whether a meeting was held at night or during the day had nothing to do with women's inclination to speak out. Women did significantly better on verbal participation when the Australian ballot was not in use, but this association disappeared when town size was controlled. Australian ballots are more likely to be used in larger towns, and larger towns, as we are about to discover, share

---

come and gone, and still I remember those rugged, beautiful kids of the Kingdom even better than I remember my students from last semester. I was twenty-three, and they were only a few years younger. Now, suddenly, when we cross paths they are as knotty and as old as I am.

an important but negative association with our summary measure of women's verbal participation, femindex.

Studies of both individual citizens and legislators show that women take a special interest in the politics of education.[11] On the other hand, our findings in the previous chapter show that the presence of education issues on the warning was not incentive enough to swell women's attendance at town meeting. Moreover, despite its impressive theoretical credentials, this variable behaves precisely as it should not when it comes to women's verbal participation. When school issues are being discussed at some point during the proceedings on town meeting day, women participate significantly less than if they are not on the agenda at all. Femindex is −0.02 when educational issues are present and 0.15 when they are not.

But this association too disappears when another variable is controlled: the passage of time. As I suggested earlier, women have made dramatic improvements in speech and talk over the past thirty years. The combination of increasing women's participation between 1970 and 1998 and the separation of education from town meeting warnings over the same period means that towns discussing education issues on town meeting day are more apt to fall in the earlier years of the sample, when participation was generally lower for women.[12]

Finally, I checked for crowdedness in the meeting hall, since scholars have found that women react more positively to crowding than men do.[13] I hypothesized that crowded meeting halls might be associated with more verbal participation by the women in attendance. They were not. No relation appeared between the measure of empty seats per attender (as I defined crowdedness) and femindex.

---

11. Rosner found that women were clearly more apt to participate verbally in the discussion at assembly meetings in the Israeli kibbutz when the topic was education. Menahem Rosner, *Democracy, Equality and Change: The Kibbutz and Social Theory* (Darby, PA: Norwood Editions, 1982), 53.

12. When dummy variables for educational issues and ballot type are correlated under controls, the following results occur. The correlation between femindex and use of the Australian ballot (controlling for town size) is reduced from −.14 to zero. The correlation between femindex and educational issues increases from −.08 to −.12 when town size is controlled. But controlling the year the meeting is held decreases it to −.02.

13. Y. M. Epstein and R. A. Karlin, "Effects of Acute Experimental Crowding," *Journal of Social Psychology* 5 (January–March 1936): 34–53; Bruce Layton, Bonnie Erickson, and John Schopler, "Affect, Facial Regard and Reactions to Crowding," *Journal of Personality and Social Psychology* 28 (October 1973): 69–76; and Daniel Stokols et al., "Physical, Social and Personal Determinants of the Perception of Crowding," *Environment and Behavior* 5 (March 1973): 87–115.

Peer Influence

Consider the following situations.

Hartland, Vermont, had the highest score for women's attendance in 1987 and the second lowest score for women's speech. Hartland is a traditional Connecticut River valley town. Its history and culture bespeak the river's flowing waters and broad meadows edged by the contours of rising plateaus leading to the foothills of the mountains. In the town's historic Damon Hall at 11:00 a.m. (one hour and fifteen minutes after the town meeting began), 58 women and 34 men were in attendance. Yet only 13 of the 58 women present (22 percent) participated verbally compared with 29 (85 percent) of the 34 men. This was a meeting where women strongly outnumbered men, but they tended to remain silent.[14]

Farther north in the town of Eden, the opposite happened. There women's attendance was low, their participation high. The moderator opened the meeting at 10:00 a.m. Mary Adams, the town clerk, then spent five minutes reading the warning. The next four new participators were men. Jackie Longly was the sixth person to participate when she nominated Haven Bullard for selectman. Another man participated, and then, after Carol Burnor was reelected lister, Donna Whitcomb (assistant town clerk) nominated Gloria Daige (an incumbent) for auditor. "So voted." By the end of the meeting 68 percent of the women at the meeting in the Eden Central School had participated at least once, while only 54 percent of the men had.[15]

14. Barbara Carney, Paul Carney, and Suzanne Betz, "The 1987 Comparative Town Meeting Study: Town of Hartland," Burlington, University of Vermont, Real Democracy Data Base, March 1987. Paul Carney and his sister Barbara (Suzanne Betz's roommate) lived in Hartland. That day Paul and Barbara's Aunt Mona (Ramona Lasure) defeated Miles Mushlin for school director by an Australian ballot vote of 250 to 190. Thus 440 (378 percent) more people chose representative democracy in Hartland in 1987 than chose real democracy. Had Paul attended the Hartland town meeting a year earlier in 1986, however, he might have written differently about citizen apathy. For that year he would have seen 351 people pack themselves into Damon Hall to vote 190 to 161 (after a "lengthy discussion") to reconsider an earlier vote to renovate space in the elementary school. Thus the attendance at town meeting in Hartland in 1986 was 281 percent higher than it was in 1987. In 1986 the Hartford town meeting lasted 285 minutes. In 1987 it lasted only 144 minutes. The people of Hartland talked almost 100 percent more than they did in 1987. This is why it is essential to look at hundreds and hundreds of town meetings. Although our sample did not pick up this particular variation, it did pick up similar ones in the meetings we studied over the three decades. Town of Hartland, "Abstract of Minutes Town and Town School District Annual Meeting March 4, 1986," *Town Report*, year ending December 1986.

15. Ed Canaday, Chris Pokorski, and Steve Krupkin, "The 1987 Comparative Town Meeting Study: Town of Eden," Burlington, University of Vermont, Real Democracy Data Base, March 1987. Town of Eden, Mary Adams, Town Clerk, "Minutes of the Annual Town Meeting, Tuesday, March 3rd, 1987," mimeograph, 1987.

In the town meeting in Hinesburg in 1978, 106 women and 100 men were in attendance. In the town meeting in Stowe a few years earlier in 1971, about the same number of men (100) were in attendance, but only 54 women were present. Any woman looking over the audience for peer support in Hinesburg was surely more apt to find it there than in Stowe.[16] But the actual number of female speakers was exactly the same: 12 in both meetings. Thus 22 percent of the women present in Stowe spoke, but only 11 percent of the women in Hinesburg did so. The peer influence model not only failed in these two meetings, it was reversed.

The full sample of town meetings extends and verifies the findings from individual meetings. The correlation coefficient for the relation between women's inclination to speak (the ratio of the percentage of women present at a town meeting who speak at least once to the percentage of men who do so) and the percentage of the attenders at the meeting who were women is $-.26$. This coefficient is statistically significant and explains 7 percent of the variance in women's speech at town meeting. The surprise is that the finding is negative. Having more women in attendance at town meeting (in comparison with men) does not embolden women to speak. On the contrary, women tend to speak more (in relation to men) as the ratio of women to men in the town hall declines.

By contrast, women's willingness to speak a second time (and perhaps again and again) improves slightly as the likelihood of seeing other women in the town hall rises. Here the variable I call women's "talk" (the ratio of the acts of speech per female participator to the acts of speech per male participator) demonstrates a weak ($r = .08$) but statistically significant and positive association with women's attendance. When weighted and combined with speech (to form femindex), however, the positive influence of increasing female attendance on talk cancels out very little of the negative influence of increasing female attendance on speech. The correlation between femindex and the percentage of attenders who are women is still negative ($r = -.20$).[17]

---

16. Banazak and Plutzer found that women with lower education levels have stronger pro-feminist attitudes in communities having more women with strong educational backgrounds. The context of the community, however, is unrelated to women who have higher levels of education. Lee Ann Banazak and Eric Plutzer, "Contextual Determinants of Feminist Attitudes: National and Subnational Influences in Western Europe," *American Political Science Review* 87 (March 1993): 147–157.

17. This is partly because speech accounts for two-thirds of femindex and talk accounts for only one-third. But even if we weighted the willingness to repeat the act of speaking equally with the willingness to speak at all, the association between femindex and women's attendance, while weakened, would still be negative.

These findings present an interesting puzzle. Increased equality of women's attendance at town meeting seems to mean a decline in women's equality in the discussion at town meeting—and this problem seems to be growing with time. The correlation between women's attendance and femindex was −.10 in the first five years of the study and −.33 in the last five. Since women's attendance has gone up over the years, women's verbal participation, which has gone up at the same time, has done so in the face of a growing tendency for the increasing women's percentage of the attendance to stymie verbal participation. With the dual impacts of the passage of time and women's attendance at odds with each other,[18] the modest increases in participation between 1970 and 1998 that we observed earlier seem more impressive.[19]

The Cost of Participation

The cost of a social action in diverse settings usually weighs disproportionately on minorities. In meetings, verbal participation grows dear as attendance grows larger. Having more people on hand who might wish to speak may make women more hesitant than men. Similarly, a sense that time is limited also may make speech more expensive. We might wonder if women will be more apt than men to "wait their turn" when the time available for discussion is limited.[20] At town meeting, however, the number present in the meeting place matters for women's participation more than the time the meeting lasts. Under controls, the correlation between femindex and the total number of people present is −.22, and the correlation between femindex and the time the meeting lasts is .04.

Socioeconomic Status

Most social scientists would assume that the socioeconomic context of a town correlates in some way with the distribution of verbal participation between men and women in an open forum like town meeting.

18. The correlation coefficient between femindex and the percentage of women in attendance when the year of the meeting was controlled increased to −.23, and the correlation between femindex and year the meeting was held increased to .29 when the percentage of women in attendance was controlled.

19. The standardized slope (beta) for the passage of time was .29. It was −.22 for the percentage of the attenders who were women.

20. Another possibility is that as women observe other women speaking, their fears of participating *as women* may be reduced. As the meeting lasts longer and the number of women participators grows, additional women will be more apt to join in.

Yet a bird's-eye view of the connection between a town's SES characteristics and women's verbal participation in town meeting debate shows a
stone-dead relation. When the SES factor score upscale, which combines an
array of variables such as income, occupation, and education, is matched with
femindex, the regression line lies flat and quiet across the relation like a fly
line on a twilit trout pond. This is hardly surprising given what the data have
so far revealed about the importance of SES in the contextual environment
of real democracy in general. Disaggregated measures like percentages of
managers and professionals in the workforce were ambiguous as well. Both
education variables were asleep. The percentage of working women and the
SES diversity index also refused to perform. A pair of weak negative associations between income and femindex suggest only that, if anything, women's
participation in direct democracy may trend in the opposite direction from
that predicted by the SES model.[21]

WITNESS

I'm interested in the women's study program at UVM, so this town meeting
field trip was very useful for me. I went to town meeting thinking that I would
find women in a minority like they are everywhere else. But it wasn't the case.
Almost half the people at town meeting were women, and my information
shows that there were actually a few more speakers that were women than
were men. Not only that, but they didn't seem to care about what they spoke
on, either. One woman (I call her Minnie Red Dress) spoke out on almost
everything. People were actually getting irritated with her. As a feminist I think
that is a good thing. Most of the women didn't seem awed about what they
were doing, either. Maybe it helped that two of the officers up front were
women. One was the town clerk and I don't know about the other. There was
some sexism of course! I saw two women actually urging their husbands to
get up and say something. Why couldn't they speak for themselves? But all
in all I was pleasantly surprised. Sex just didn't seem to matter at all in this
form of democracy. What was also nice is that these women didn't seem
especially well educated or huffy-puffy. They seemed to be just ordinary like
their men counterparts.

Stephanie Van DeWeld[22]

21. In a town-based analysis of these same variables (meeting data are aggregated for towns
for which I had at least ten meetings in the sample), I found a slight tendency for town size to
specify the relation. Women's involvement tended to suffer as communities got larger, *especially* if
they were downscale communities. This relation is developed in www.uvm.edu/~fbryan.

22. Stephanie Van DeWeld [a pseudonym], "Town Meeting Essay, Huntington 1986,"
Burlington, University of Vermont, March 1986.

Community Dynamics and Boundedness

The methodological design of this book is what I call creative description. For women's participation in town meeting, much of the requisite theoretical energy for creative description is found in modernization literature. We are told that a fair share of political activity for women and minorities awaits the breakdown of traditional social systems. As localism weakens, more cosmopolitan attitudes diversify the mix of acceptable behavior and free women to act openly in the political process. Now we compare those communities that have undergone the most demographic change—where new people and new behaviors are ascendant—with those places where the pulse of rural life hangs on stubbornly like the autumn rust of high ridge oak.

Modernization literature suggests that women will be most active in towns where population growth is highest, where the percentage of native Vermonters in the population is lowest, where the loss of the traditional agricultural lifestyle is most pronounced, where the population is less isolated from the influences of larger towns, and where the sense of the community as a bounded place is less rigid. Since these variables are not closely associated with traditional measures of socioeconomic status in Vermont's towns,[23] it is easier to judge the independent effect of community dynamics and boundedness variables on women's participation.

Only two of these variables exhibit statistically significant relations with women's verbal participation in town meeting, and these carry little authority. The percentage of the workforce employed outside town and the time it takes them to get to work both vary positively with women's increased verbal participation at town meeting. But the coefficients are only .22 and .12, respectively, explaining less than 5 percent of the variance in either case. Only out-of-town employment survives when controls are applied for the other eight measures. All in all, if my measures of community boundedness and dynamics are proper indicators of modernization, then modernization in a community is a poor predictor of just how egalitarian its town meeting will be on the question of women's involvement.

The Political Environment

Women's participation in direct democracy is also estranged from the political character of the community. Theoretically the expectations were the

---

23. The factor score upscale and another factor score I named stable community (summarizing the nine community dynamics and community boundedness variables) correlated at −.01.

same as those used in the analysis of women's attendance at town meeting. The hypothesized links they generated between community politics and verbal participation were as theoretically thin as they were for attendance. By now these variables are familiar. They are the turnout base for electoral politics in presidential and "off" years, the liberalism factor score, the vote for Socialist congressman Bernie Sanders, the Democratic base vote (the average percentage of the vote cast for Democratic candidates for governor in the three elections held closest to the year the town meeting was held), the percentage yes vote for the equal rights amendment to the Vermont constitution, and the intensity of the town's liberal/conservative ideological posture. Except with the Sanders vote, the attempt to establish a connection between these political characteristics and women's verbal involvement at town meeting was a wash. The Sanders factor score correlated at .20 with femindex. This seemed to make sense. But as we are about to discover, it was weakened considerably when the passage of the years was controlled.

The Passage of Time

Just as women's presence at town meeting increased over the course of this study (from an average of 44 percent of the total attendance in 1970 and 1971 to 48 percent in 1997 and 1998), so we would expect women's verbal participation to increase. And it did. Dramatically. Whereas in 1970, on the average, for every ten men speaking at town meeting only five women spoke (a ratio of 0.50), by 1998 for every ten men speaking an average of eight to nine women spoke (a ratio of 0.86). By 1998 the ratio of acts of speech (what I call "talk") between men and women had improved from 6.9 participations by women for every ten by men in 1970 to (again) 8.6 by women for every ten by men (see fig. 9.3). Femindex, which combines speech and talk, weighting the more difficult act of "speech" (speaking at least once) more than "talk" (speaking twice or more) into a standardized measure improved from −0.31 to 0.33 between 1970 and 1998.

Small Town, Big Town

Small towns are good for women's verbal participation in town meeting. Breaking down overall women's participation (femindex) into its components reveals a substantial improvement for women in the very smallest towns. In these towns the women present at town meeting are almost as apt to speak as the men. On average, for every ten men who speak at town meetings in towns of 250 registered voters or fewer, eight to nine women also speak. Moreover,

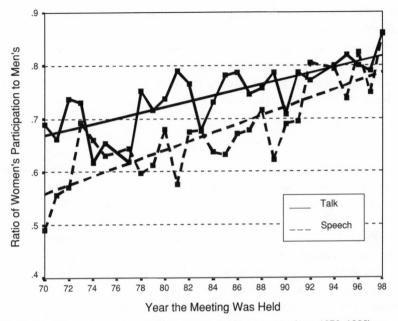

Figure 9.3. Women's speech and talk over time (1,389 town meetings, 1970–1998).

the women who do speak at these meetings in the very smallest towns are apt to speak as much as the men. For every ten acts of speech by the male participators, the female participators perform about 8.8 acts of speech. In towns of 2,500 registered voters or more, however, these ratios are much less favorable for women, especially the ratio for speech. The ratio of men speaking to women speaking drops from 0.85 to 0.59, and the ratio of male acts of speech to female acts of speech drops from to 0.88 to 0.73.

The greatest negative impact of town size on women's speech and talk combined (femindex) occurs as towns increase in size from fewer than 250 registered voters to between 250 and 500. After this point similar increases in town size continue to hurt women's speech, but not their talk. At these higher ranges of town size, the most important effect of increasing community size on women's participation is that it weakens their willingness to speak at all. Once they make their first participation (their speech), however, women's willingness to join in the discussion again is affected very little by the size of the community.

As attendance at town meeting increases for both sexes, participation goes down significantly more for women than for men. Town size is positively associated with total absolute attendance ($r = .67$), and both town size and attendance are negatively associated with women's participation. While both variables matter, however, town size matters more than meeting size. The simple correlation coefficient between town size and femindex is reduced from −.30 to −.20 when meeting size is controlled. But the simple correlation coefficient between meeting size and femindex is reduced from −.25 to −.06 when town size is controlled.

Putting the Variables Together

To review, three of the perplexing associations found between individual variables and women's speech and talk at town meeting were resolved when town size and the passage of time were controlled. The weak negative association between the Australian ballot and femindex fell when confronted with town size, because femindex goes down as town size goes up and big towns are more apt to use the Australian ballot. A second conundrum was the weak (−.08) correlation between towns that include educational matters on the town meeting day agenda and lower feminine participation.[24] But towns discussing educational matters on town meeting day were more apt to occur early in the sample, when women's participation was much lower. The passage of time also explained the positive association between the vote for Bernie Sanders and women's verbal participation at town meeting. Sanders's percentages at the polls increased with the passing years along with women's participation. With time controlled, the Sanders correlation coefficient was reduced from .20 to .06.

After experimenting with several additional models designed to filter out statistical overlaps, I developed a stepwise multiple regression routine

24. I explored several models of verbal participation of women that included the availability of day care in the post-1994 set of meetings. While day care did improve women attendance somewhat, I discovered no context in which it was significant for verbal participation. In the 1998 meeting in the town of Washington (one of the five meetings for which I recorded the data that year), a man brought two of his own kids and two of their playmates into town meeting and sat them down in the very front row. I sensed trouble immediately. These were five-to-eight-year-old boys. They'd raise hell for sure. But for close to an hour they sat like little angels; a bit of fidgeting now and then, but that was about all. At the right moment (when it seemed the boys' attention spans had about had it), the father leaned over and whispered to them. They got up and marched out in unison to play in the schoolyard. Two of them were suppressing grins on the way out. I interviewed the father after the meeting. "How'd you do it?" I wanted to know. "Home schooling," he said. Their mother worked in the afternoon. He was the teacher, and he had brought these kids to school—literally, and in a more profound way as well. A lot of children were at the meeting, which was held in the "all purpose room" of the K-6 schoolhouse. Tocqueville and Jefferson would have been pleased. Frank and Melissa Bryan, "The 1998 Comparative Town Meeting Study: Town of Washington," Burlington, University of Vermont, Real Democracy Data Base, March 1998.

Table 9.1. Correlates of Women's Verbal Participation: The Final Equation

Variable	r	R^2	Improvement in R^2	Beta
Log of town size	.270	.073	—	−.309
Passage of time	.381	.145	.072	.256
Percentage attenders women	.429	.184	.039	−.228
Out-of-town workers	.453	.206	.022	.157

Note: Dependent variable = women's combined participation (speech and talk); all coefficients are significant at the .001 level.

to help summarize the findings. The results are reported in table 9.1. The logged size of the town in registered voters and the passage of time were the most important predictors of women's participation. In combination they explain about 14 percent of the variance in women's verbal participation. Within the context of an overall increase in femindex over time, small-town women are more apt to have a say in direct democratic settings than women who live in larger towns. The annoying tendency for meetings where the ratio of women to men in attendance is more equal to undermine feminine verbal participation remains intact and jacks up the explained variance from 14.5 to 18.4 percent. Finally, the positive association between femindex and the percentage of workers employed out of town, which would not go away (despite my persistent efforts), added another perplexing 2 percent of variance explained.

"Involvement": Combining Attendance with Participation

Real democracy, of course, entails both presence and participation in combination. The ideal situation occurs when both are as natural for women as they are for men. So far women's attendance at town meeting and their participation in town meetings have been treated as separate indicators of real democracy's capacity to integrate traditional minority groups into the political process. We discovered that women's share of the attendance at town meeting was (strangely) negatively associated with their share of participation in town meeting. Participation was defined as women's share of the speakers (the variable called speech) in combination with their share of the participations (the variable called talk). The mildness of the connection between attendance and participation, however, ($r = −.13$) allows us to create a combination variable for attendance and participation by standardizing each and then combining the two.

The Parameters of the Combined Variable

The combined variable is called "involvement," and it gives attendance at town meeting and participation in town meeting equal weight. Its statistical parameters are healthy.[25] To judge the possibility that involvement might be predictable from the kind of community where the town meeting was held, I returned to the fourteen instances in the sample when at least twenty towns had back-to-back yearly meetings. In each of these instances the involvement score in a town's meeting for one year was matched with its involvement score for the following year. Overall, the linkages between meetings in back-to-back years within the same town are tighter for involvement than they were for either variable that went to make it up. The average correlation was .40 for the attendance measure, .45 for verbal participation, and .57 for the combination, involvement. This means that the possibility of identifying reasons for women's activity in the nature of the towns themselves or in the structure of the meetings these towns hold is better for our overall measure than it was for its components. On average, close to one-third of the variance in women's involvement in town meeting can be explained by what their involvement was the previous year. Evidently some towns' meetings have been consistently more friendly to women than others'.[26]

The Correlates of Women's Involvement

Chapter 8 told us that only a single variable, holding meetings during the day rather than in the evening, importantly improved women's attendance. It explained 7 percent of the variance. Women's attendance was about 3.7 percentage points lower at evening meetings. Beyond that, upscale towns accounted for another 1 percent improvement in prediction (increasing women's attendance a tad), and larger towns added a final 1 percent by lowering attendance a fraction. The entire equation reduced the uncertainty about what women's attendance will be in any given town in any given meeting by only 9.3 percent.

Participation, as we just discussed, was far more predictable than attendance. In the equation using meetings studied after 1976, four variables accounted for 20.6 percent of the variance. Three of these, the size of the town (negative), the passage of time (positive), and the percentage of women in attendance (negative) contributed almost all (18.8 percent) of the explanatory

---

25. For the parameters of this variable see www.uvm.edu/~fbryan.

26. This relation may be disappearing, however. The correlation coefficients seem to trend downward. Before 1985 the average was .67. After 1985 it was .47. In the last three cases where I had at least twenty towns having meetings in the sample on back-to-back years (1996–1998), it averaged only .38.

Table 9.2. Correlates of Women's Total Involvement: The Final Equation

Variable	r	R^2	Improvement in R^2	Beta
Log of town size	.274	.075	—	−.301
Passage of time	.390	.152	.077	.235
Night meetings	.434	.189	.037	−.203
Out-of-town workers	.463	.214	.025	.145
Upscale	.470	.221	.007	.088

Note: Dependent variable = women's involvement (verbal participation combined with attendance); all coefficients are significant at the .001 level.

power. Since attendance and participation were assigned equal weight in the combined variable, the variables associated with participation take the lead in predicting involvement. In the final stepwise multiple regression model, town size and the passage of time led with 15.2 percent of the variance explained. When the meeting was held (day or night) added 3.7 percentage points (this is where attendance mattered), the percentage employed out of town added 2.5, and upscale tiptoed past the test for statistical significance to add another 0.07 percentage points. (A summary of the model is found in table 9.2.)

Thus nearly all of the capacity of the context of community to explain variations in women's involvement in real democracy is reduced to three factors: the passing of the years, the size of the community, and when the meetings are held. Many fine variables died on the trail to this discovery. Unfortunately for women's involvement in town meeting, the surviving variables do not share a positive alliance. As time has passed, involvement has increased independent of the fact that town size has grown. This product of the years—bigger communities—has had its own negative, independent, and therefore countervailing effect on women's involvement. Meanwhile the people of Vermont have voted to hold more and more of their meetings in the evening, which has had its own independent and negative impact.

In short, both night meetings and larger towns depress women's attendance, and both have increased over time. But despite this, women's overall involvement has managed to grow steadily. A lot of this growth is most likely due to public acceptance of women's role in governance, which has improved steadily since the 1960s. Because the upscale factor did appear last in the final regression equation, it is worth speculating at least that a small (very small) portion of the causation may be tied to increasing levels of socioeconomic status in the towns. Be that as it may, however, we can hopefully report that in small towns that hold traditional town meetings during the day, women's and men's involvement in town meeting is nearly identical.

When citizens know the issues to be dealt with [at town meeting] are trivial or uncontroversial, they choose to stay home—and why not? But controversial issues bring them out.

Robert Dahl

Citizens are not likely to "fly to the assemblies" [Rousseau] when the decisions they make in those assemblies are trivial.

Jane Mansbridge

The epigraphs are from Robert A. Dahl, *On Democracy* (New Haven: Yale University Press, 1998), 111, and Jane Mansbridge, *Beyond Adversary Democracy* (New York: Basic Books, 1980), 130.

10

If You Build It, Let Them Play

Over the years I have often asked my colleagues "from away":
"What do you think would cause variations in turnout at town
meeting?" Or "What stimulates people to speak at town meeting?" Seldom is the answer like the one a Vermonter would give:
"They had a big fight over road salt." Or "School taxes went
up 15 percent this year and the wages around here went up only
3 percent." Or "The town is getting ready to reappraise property."
Every year I deal with reporters who call me (often from out of
state) looking for a "good" town meeting to attend. They seem
surprised when I suggest that issues matter. Practicing democrats
in Vermont take it as a given.

Mark this. Beyond town size, issues are the single most
important variable that draws citizens to town meeting. Beyond
meeting size, issues are the most important determinant of discussion at town meeting. Moreover, it is a principal finding of
this book that (voluminous and respected studies notwithstanding) contentious issues and the conflict they often produce are
not subdued by small-town life.[1] Indeed, the evidence is quite to
the contrary. Open conflict over issues seems more likely in the
smaller towns. It is time to explore these issues (conflict and all)
that add so much zest (and participation) to the practice of real
democracy.

To do this, I let the measurable attributes of town size,
meeting structure, community life variables, and so on rate each

1. The best summary of the literature on size and conflict is still
Mansbridge, *Beyond Adversary Democracy*, 374–375.

meeting in the database on the degree to which it met expectations on each of the components of real democracy covered in the preceding chapters (attendance, participation, and women's involvement). For each of these components I then selected the fifty best and fifty worst of these meetings for further study. From the fifty-five towns for which I had at least ten meetings in the sample, I also selected the best and worst meeting for each town (if it was not one of the original top fifty meetings). This identified meetings with abnormal performances for the particular town where they were held.

I next sought to determine what was happening in each meeting—minute by minute, issue by issue, and vote by vote. In addition to my own data on vote margins, time spent discussing particular issues, and the amount of discussion on warning items, I used state and local newspapers (Vermont has an amazing network of local papers), minutes of the meetings when available, my own familiarity with the towns and the issues, personal interviews, and (especially) the students' essays and reports.[2]

Attendance

Conflict draws people to town meeting. The opportunity to have an impact on things that matter overcomes the potential distaste for open face-to-face disagreement with people we know and like (such as our hunting buddies) or people we may fear (such as our employers) or officials who have the discretionary power to make our lives more pleasant or less pleasant (like the tax collector or road commissioner). Moreover, citizens in the smallest towns, where human-scale costs of conflict are dearest (buffers between individuals are thin), are as willing to pay the price of face-to-face conflict (and often more willing) as citizens of larger towns, where size provides thicker buffers between individuals. What follows is a brief account of the six meetings that most exceeded predictions of their attendance when town size and other causes of high attendance identified in chapters 4 and 5 are held constant.

North Hero

The little town of North Hero up in the Lake Champlain islands opened its town meeting at 6:09 p.m. at the end of a weather-perfect Tuesday, March 1,

---

2. The following is typical of hundreds of such remarks found in my students' essays: "In an interview with a member of the town after the meeting it was stated that the attendance was particularly high due to the controversial tax issues." David Smith, "Report on the Town Meeting of Highgate," Colchester, VT, St. Michael's College, May 1970.

1994. At 6:23 my student Alex Wilcox (aided by his parents) took the first attendance count. At that time 268 citizens were on hand. At 7:40 the Wilcoxes counted 315 citizens of the town in attendance, 65 percent of the registered voters.[3] Controlling for its size and other variables associated with variations in attendance, North Hero's performance was about 2.7 times higher than expected. Of the meetings we studied between 1970 and 1998, none exceed its predicted attendance more than North Hero's meeting in 1994, including of course the other ten town meetings we studied there. What was going on?

Two of the issues before the townspeople involved the kind of situations that make face-to-democracy difficult—gains and losses for particular individuals. The first (article 7) was taken up at 7:11 and debated for an hour and nine minutes: "Will the legal voters authorize the Board of Selectmen to enter into a contract with the Howard O'Neils for a period of 25 years at the cost of $2,500 per year in lieu of payment for the right of way on West Shore Road."[4] Twenty-six people spoke on the issue for a total of sixty-seven individual acts of participation. The details were complex, involving deeds, rights-of-way, access to lake frontage, and promises made and deferred. Wilcox summed up the result: "The question to this year's voters was, essentially, would they keep the promise of the selectman, and pay the O'Neils $2,500 per year for 25 years for the right of way and eventual deed transfer of the property in question, thereby effecting the promised tax break?"[5] The town did so by secret ballot, 170 to 75.

The second issue involved the job of Jean Hutchins, who had been town clerk and treasurer for over two decades. Criticism of her performance had been circulating in town, and Barbara St. Gelais was running against her. Wilcox summarized their "campaign speeches": "Jean said she wanted the job and liked the town. Barbara said she wanted it too, she had degrees in accounting and understood computers, and she explained that the only reason she spent part of her life outside North Hero was to be with her husband while he served in the U.S. Army in North Carolina." The subtext of the contest was that, if elected for only one more term, Jean Hutchins would be eligible for

3. Alexander Wilcox, Aince Rousseau, Bert Wilcox, and Catherine Wilcox, "The 1994 Comparative Town Meeting Study: Town of North Hero," Burlington, University of Vermont, Real Democracy Data Base, March 1994.

4. "Official Warning Annual Meeting Town of North Hero" and "Official Warning Annual Meeting of North Hero School District," *Town Report*, year ending June 30, 1993, 67–68. The abstracts of the North Hero town meetings (no minutes are available) report the fate of each article in simple one-liners. From the town reports, these meetings appear absolutely conflictless.

5. Alexander Wilcox, "Town Meeting Essay, North Hero 1994," Burlington, University of Vermont, March 1994.

retirement benefits. After thirty minutes of debate the town voted by a margin of thirty-six votes (again by secret ballot) to return Hutchins to her job.

Jean Hutchins had successfully stood for election as town clerk in North Hero for twenty-seven years in a row. Her previous year's salary was $20,143.63. She asked for just one more year to secure her retirement benefits. Forty percent of the townspeople sitting with her in the town hall that day voted to deny them to her. That is why I call the subject of this book real democracy.

The O'Neils West Shore Road case had been festering for several years, and it involved the very heart of the town—access to lake frontage. The town clerk is the single most important officer in Vermont's towns. The clerk (even more than the road crew) is the "face" of the town—the officer most citizens are most likely to deal with. Both of these issues involved friends and neighbors in a town of fewer than 500 voters. The debate involved their personal finances, their integrity, and their futures. These are the issues that test real democracy. No hidden elite decided these matters. They were not resolved in lawyers' offices or by a personnel board. They were debated openly (and I suspect in some measure painfully) before the town. Most important, these issues did not keep the people from town meeting. They drew them there.

WITNESS

The most important issue in Marshfield was whether or not to give the owners of new houses a tax break for a few years. The town was so divided on this issue and people being people and families being families that even a brother and sister found themselves speaking on opposite sides of the heated discussion. Many who spoke in favor of the tax exemption were young people who owned trailers on top of "Sloppy Hill," a name thrown out by one of this hill's residents. After much debate, a vote was taken and counted and the exemption was granted, much to the delight of the crew from "Sloppy Hill."

Jerry Flanagan[6]

Victory

Vermont's smallest town had the second best attended town meeting in the sample. It was not pretty. Victory's size alone in 1997 (77 registered voters

---

6. Jerry Flanagan, "Grassroots Democracy in Marshfield," Colchester, St. Michael's College, March, 1969.

in a town of about 100 residents) predicted that 35 of the registered voters (46 percent) would turn out. But the actual turnout in 1997 was 54 (70 percent), the second highest (uncontrolled) percentage turnout of any meeting we studied over twenty-eight years.

The trouble had started in Victory a year earlier at the meeting of 1996,[7] a meeting so rowdy that two special meetings had to be called in the summer and fall of 1996 to repair the damage.[8] Unless my student was guilty of grotesque exaggeration (and my research, subsequent events, and press reports indicate he was not), the 1996 meeting in Victory was far more ugly than any of the other 1,434 we studied. A clique had developed that challenged the town officers on just about everything. In his essay, Dan Mezzalingua called its leader "Mr. Black Hat," a foul-mouthed bully utterly contemptuous of *Robert's Rules of Order*.[9] Black hat "was supported by 'the four evils'—a younger guy who laughed at everything he (Black hat) said and three middle-aged women." The issues ranged from rubbish removal to a selectman "hiring himself" to do roadwork to the accuracy of the town reports.[10]

When Victory met a year later in 1997 the conflict was gavel to gavel, and it featured a full-scale attack on the town's elected officials. Nearly every officer was challenged, beginning with the moderator, a post rarely contested at town meeting. The incumbent, Janet Copp, won reelection by only two votes, 26 to 24. Seven of the next ten town officers were also contested. The

---

7. The meeting of 1996 was itself one of the best attended in the sample. It ranked ninety-first out of 1,435 meetings.

8. The town report that featured the Witness on page ••• was in the hands of the townspeople at the 1996 meeting. The juxtaposition of the words in this passage (which bespeak the human bonds of small-town life) with what happened at the town meeting is a testimony to the resiliency of community.

9. This meeting was far worse than any town meeting I have ever even heard about in Vermont in the forty years I have been paying close attention to them. Dan Mezzalingua's essay was (as is often the case with human tragedy) wildly funny and totally depressing. To wit: "A little old lady who must have been in her late eighties voiced an opinion. Another woman made a remark implying that she (the little old lady) never helped out on any committees. To this the cute little old lady yelled, "you're a fucking liar!" Still, Mezzalingua finishes his essay as follows: "The town meeting displayed how some of the citizens of Victory used this time to vent their personal feelings towards other townspeople. However, despite the problems, this was still a democratic process. 'Black Hat and the Evils' were intimidating, but because of secret ballots, the other townspeople could vote comfortably and confidentially [Mansbridge's important point in *Beyond Adversary Democracy*]. Only a handful [were disruptive], and most were quiet and respectful of others. I could see that the people not engaged in verbal battles would listen to issues debated and decide how to vote. Forget all the bickering and arguing, Victory's town meeting reflected the voice of the people, and they decided issues that reflected the town's will." Dan Mezzalingua, "Town Meeting Essay, Victory 1996," Burlington, University of Vermont, March 1996.

10. Town of Victory, *Town Report*, year ending December 1995.

average margin of victory was six votes. The town also voted on whether to elect or appoint a road commissioner. A standing vote (28 to 18) showed they preferred an election. The incumbent road commissioner, Tony Spera, then defeated Walt Neborsky by five votes. Administration of highway funds had been at the center of the town's troubles for several years. All of the votes for town officers were by secret ballot.[11] In these elections, eight incumbents won and three lost.[12]

Still, the 1997 town meeting was much more civil than the 1996 meeting. The memory of the 1996 meeting and the two special meetings in the summer and fall just past (the town's politics had been covered extensively in the region's chief daily newspaper, the *Caledonia Record*) did not cause Victory's townspeople to shy away from their democracy. All the bitterness and hostility and even shame did not dissuade them. They took a deep breath and attended still another meeting, this time in record numbers.

The following year's meeting in Victory, the meeting of 1998, was the third best on attendance (with all variables controlled) of the 1,435 meetings we studied, just behind North Hero in 1994 and the Victory meeting a year earlier in 1997. Sixty-eight percent of the voters were in attendance in 1998. The meeting began with the town's voting 40 to 3 not to elect the road commissioner, but rather to have the office filled by the selectmen. This was a vote of confidence for the selectmen and the incumbent road commissioner. It meant the highway crisis was over. No incumbent officers were challenged, and the winners of the two open contests won handily. No significant new issues appeared. The town's final decision of the evening was to start a town newsletter on current issues.[13] The near record attendance performance by the 1998 town meeting in Victory is best understood in the context of the town's dramatic and controversial meetings of the preceding

---

11. Jeremy Spaulding and Joe Spaulding, "The 1997 Comparative Town Meeting Study: Town of Victory," Burlington, University of Vermont, Real Democracy Data Base, March 1997). See also Town of Victory, *Town Report*, year ending December 1996.

12. Unlike the situation in North Hero, the conflict in Victory was revealed in the minutes of the meeting. Town of Victory, Janet Copp, Town Clerk, "Town Meeting March 4, 1997," *Town Report*, February 1998), 4–7.

13. John Carolan, Scott Gannon, Brian Slack, and Leila Zeppelin, "The 1998 Comparative Town Meeting Study: Town of Victory" Burlington, University of Vermont, Real Democracy Data Base, March 1998. Carolan and Gannon report: "The election of town officers came first. Residents made motions to place their neighbors' names in nomination. Motions were accepted silently or declined courteously, and when more than one resident was suggested the dispute was settled by ballot. . . . The town officials were elected in an orderly, systematic way, electing thirteen officials in just over 45 minutes." John Carolan and Scott Gannon, "Town Meeting in Victory, Vermont," Burlington, University of Vermont, April 1998.

two years—difficult, face-to-face meetings that stimulated rather than re-
tarded civic engagement.[14]

Holland

In 1880, 913 people lived in the town of Holland. A century later that number
had been nearly cut in half to 473. In 1982, 250 of these citizens were registered to vote. A Canadian border town, Holland (as Ansel Adams once said
of American cowboys) has "the bark still on." My student Steve Farrow, who
grew up in Holland, describes his hometown as follows: "The Swede Eric
Lindhorn said of his native land, 'In birth we are pitched against the north,
our wilderness looks to the wind and to death.' It is not an overstatement
to compare this town, which the state tried commendably to name Elysiana,
with the cold northern lands."[15]

The meeting opened at 10:10 a.m. It was snowing, Farrow reported,
but the plows were "out" (which means they were still plowing) and the
hills were sanded. At 11:45 a.m. Farrow counted 150 people in attendance,
60 percent of the registered voters—exactly twice as many as Holland's size
predicted. It was the fourth best attendance in the full sample of meetings
studied. The reason for the high turnout that snowy morning was remarkably
different from the personalized issues in North Hero and the raucous, polis-
threatening conflicts in Victory. Roads. Holland is a big town geographically,
with only ten people for every mile of usable roads in the town. The average
town in the sample contained twenty-six people per road mile.

Some years earlier Holland had entrusted its roads to the three-member
Selectboard that would appoint a road foreman. Critics of road maintenance
in Holland either had to persuade the town to vote to elect a road commissioner and then persuade it to choose their candidate, or they had to
replace members of the Selectboard with their own candidates who would
then presumably appoint a road foreman to their liking. Both approaches
were tried. Both failed. At 10:50 the town allowed the selectmen to continue

14. Just how difficult the 1996 meeting was for most of the citizens who were present can
be seen in Dan Mezzalingua's essay. At one point he described attenders' "putting lowered heads in
their hands" in embarrassment. At the end of the meeting the town clerk apologized to
Mezzalingua for the town's behavior. On the way to his car another couple "apologized for the 'bad
behavior of a few' and asked me if I wanted to stay overnight at their house since the weather was
so bad." Mezzalingua, "Town Meeting Essay, Victory 1996," Burlington, University of Vermont,
March 1996.

15. Steve Farrow, "On New Vermonters at Town Meeting," Burlington, University of
Vermont, March 1982.

to appoint the road commissioner, 67 to 48. The vote for a new selectman was even closer, but the incumbent, Augustin Patenaud, defeated the challenger, Harley Sykes, 55 to 51.[16]

Two other issues may have produced additional attendance in 1982. The first was a proposal to increase funding for the county sheriff's department. The town took three votes, one by voice, one by a show of hands (both were ruled too close to call by the moderator), and finally a paper ballot. The final vote was no. The other issue, the famous Vermont nuclear weapons freeze resolution, may have boosted attendance also. But by the time it came up for a vote (it was the twenty-fifth of twenty-seven articles) only sixty-five people remained at the meeting. Two citizens spoke, and it passed by a voice vote. The two highway issues took up the most time, accounted for most of the participation, and caused the closest votes. In short, Holland is an example of a meeting centered on a single critical issue—a question of administrative efficiency on a matter of great importance to the town.

Thetford

A completely different kind of issue filled the Thetford meeting hall on February 29, 1988, and produced the fifth of the six best-attended meetings based on size-controlled attendance. Article 10 of the warning (supported by the American Legion) read: "To see if the voters will appropriate $2,000 toward the cost of a bronze plaque listing the names of Thetford's Korean and Vietnam veterans to be attached to the front of the town hall."[17]

A week before town meeting day Peter Blodgett, a citizen of Thetford, had let it be known he intended to offer an amendment to article 10 requiring that the names of Thetford's conscientious objectors to the Vietnam War be listed on the plaque alongside the names of the veterans. Well, you can imagine.

The meeting (scheduled for 7:30 p.m.) began late in order to seat the largest crowd that any of my students ever counted at a town meeting. The gavel came down at 7:45 after Bertha Brown offered the opening prayer. At 8:10, 547 of the town's 1,535 registered voters were in the Thetford Academy

16. Steve Farrow, "The 1982 Comparative Town Meeting Study: Town of Holland," Burlington, University of Vermont, Real Democracy Data Base, March 1982). Note that (as is often the case) a considerable number of people in both elections did not vote. I have watched this happen quite often myself. It is a secret ballot, but some people, for whatever reason, simply do not leave their seats and go up to drop their slips of paper in the ballot box.

17. "Warning Town of Thetford, Vermont Thetford School District 1988," *Town Report*, year ending December 1987, 8–13.

gymnasium.[18] Thetford's meeting of 1988, like the meeting of 1974 when the town became the first legal entity in America to call for the impeachment of Richard Nixon (see above, page ●●●), underscored the institutional fiber of town meeting democracy. Passion was in the air. But there was work to be done.

The "town meeting" began with the school meeting, which adjourned after a procedural discussion. Then the town meeting was opened. The townspeople approved the reports of the officers (article 1), decided how and when to raise taxes and established a penalty for late payment (article 2), appropriated $184,107.27 for the Highway Department (article 3), and likewise agreed to tax themselves $148,169.38 for the town's general fund (article 4). Next they took up whether to "vote on [the] town and highway budget by Australian Ballot" and discussed it for twenty-two minutes. Thirteen people spoke seventeen times before the town voted nay, four to one. After this the town temporarily adjourned the town meeting and reconvened the school meeting. Thetford would not be hurried.

The first thing the citizens of Thetford did during the reconvened school portion of town meeting was to tax themselves $1,636,794.53 for "the support of public schools and public education." This was well over four times as much as the amount for all other town services combined. Next they voted to keep the school budget vote a part of the town meeting process by rejecting the Australian ballot. A spirited debate followed over whether teachers' salaries should be published in the town report. No, said the people.[19]

The "town meeting" then reopened, and Gary Bahlkov presented a slide show on the role of the Planning Commission and Conservation Commission in development. Late at night on a weekday, with both sides of the war memorial issue waiting to have at it and members of the press anxiously looking at their watches and thinking about deadlines, the announcement that a slide show conducted by a member of the planning board was about to commence had to be one of the most delicious moments in the modern history of town meeting.

At last (10:29 p.m.) article 10, the request for $2,000 to help the American Legion prepare a bronze plaque honoring Korean and Vietnam War veterans, to be placed on the town hall, arrived on the floor. The proposal was made and seconded, and Peter Blodgett, the man who earlier in the

18. Kimberly Crossley and Katherine Glendenning, "The 1988 Comparative Town Meeting Study: Town of Thetford," Burlington, University of Vermont, Real Democracy Data Base, March 1988.

19. Emily E. Hood, "Minutes of the Annual Town and School District Meeting—February 29, 1988," Town of Thetford, *Town Report*, February 1989, 86.

week insisted that names of conscientious objectors be placed on the memorial along with the names of veterans, rose to speak. His amendment to the
motion on the floor (to approve article 10) would cut the appropriation in
half and limit the names on the plaque to Korean War veterans. A committee
would be established consisting of Vietnam veterans and nonveterans to work
out a compromise to be presented at next year's town meeting. Blodgett had
waffled.

Still, the discussion lasted fifty-five minutes. Sixteen people spoke a
total of nineteen times. Howard Knight of Thetford Center, wearing his
American Legion uniform, read a seven-page statement calling those who
opposed the plaque "chicken-track traitors and lame-brained idiots."[20] But
most of the debate was civil. In the end the town (or better put, what was
left of the town at 11:20 p.m.) rejected Blodgett's amendment 127 to 68 and
then voted down the entire article 104 to 88 before going back to work on
the remaining articles and adjourning just after midnight. There would be
no war memorial of any kind that year.

A year later at the 1989 town meeting the town considered the following
article: "Article IV. To see if the voters will adopt the following resolution: The
Town of Thetford supports the placement of a granite monument in front of
the town hall to commemorate the sacrifices of our veterans in service to our
country. (The monument shall list the dates of all conflicts from the war for
independence to the present.)"[21]

No names were to be listed. The town would bear no cost. Only two
people spoke on the issue. The town clerk, Emily E. Hood, reported in the
minutes: "Motion carried by unanimous voice vote."[22]

Madison would have been pleased.

Newark

The Newark meeting of 1982 was the last of the six best-attended. One of
my three students at the meeting wrote, "Right before the meeting was called

20. Bob Hookway, "Thetford Shoots down War Memorial," *Valley News*, March 1, 1998,
1, 16.

21. "Warning," Town of Thetford, Vermont Thetford School District 1989, *Town Report*,
year ending December 1988, 8–14.

22. Two other articles, one for a plaque for Vietnam War veterans and another for a plaque
for Korean War veterans, were subsequently "tabled" (it takes a two-thirds vote to table an issue)
by "a strong" voice vote in the first case and a unanimous voice vote in the second case. I had no
students at this meeting, but we know from the minutes that at least 305 citizens were in
attendance for one of the votes taken. This would have placed Thetford's 1989 meeting (the one
held in the aftermath of its record-breaking 1988 meeting), if not in the top fifty meetings on
attendance, at least in the top one hundred. "Emily E. Hood, "Minutes of the Annual Town
Meeting, March 6, 1989," *Thetford Town Report*, year ending December 1989, 124–131.

to order, the town's only selectwoman came over and crouched down beside our chairs. As if she was releasing the information contained in a top-secret document, she briefed us on the new contests for local office (the fight for road commissioner was going to be a 'biggie' this year!) and some of the local gossip that would fuel the fires of debate later on."[23]

Newark's town meeting had conflict almost from the beginning. Another student, Holly Hackman, began her essay: "The school house where the meeting was held was situated on the top of a hill overlooking a small cluster of buildings. As the meeting began, the snow flurries ended and the sun broke through the clouds. A church could be seen from the picture window as the sun shone into the room." But then: "The first heated debate was over the smoking issue. It was proposed that smoking not be allowed at any town meetings. A vote was taken in which the nonsmokers won. With the decision, an elderly couple got up and left, ironically complaining that their rights were being violated. Even in this citadel of democracy all was not well."[24]

Seldom is the election of the moderator of a town meeting contested. But it was in Newark in 1982. The incumbent, Alfred Cole, was defeated. Four other town offices were challenged that day, all by secret ballot. This is a lot of contests for a town meeting, and they all were close. Carol Ketcham (see note 23) kept her selectman position by defeating two challengers with a bare majority of the votes (53 of 99 cast) on the first ballot. It took Ellen Chase two ballots to defeat Barry Moore and Charlie Cole in an election for lister. An incumbent auditor, Mary Channon, who had been appointed earlier to fill a vacancy, faced two challengers and was defeated on the first ballot.

23. Jennifer March, "Town Meeting in Newark—Again," Burlington, University of Vermont, March 1982. Being elected a selectman as a woman in 1982 was an accomplishment. This one's name was Carol Ketcham. In 1998, the last year of the sample used for this book, Ketcham was still a town officer in Newark (justice of the peace). In 1982, for the second year in a row, Jennifer March (and Holly Hackman) had driven the 120 miles deep into the Kingdom from Burlington to attend the Newark town meeting. March ended her 1981 essay as follows: "Once inside the community, it seems as though the outside world is standing still. Everyone will be happy tomorrow doing what they did today, and nothing outside their little town will bother them. It made me laugh to think that for all these years, I thought it was the other way around." Jennifer March, "Town Meeting in Newark," Burlington, University of Vermont, March 1981. Hackman wrote in 1981: "I have lived all my life in Warwick, Rhode Island. Warwick has about 100,000 residents. I wish every resident from Warwick could spend a day in Newark." H. Holly Hackman, "Town Meeting Essay, Town of Newark," Burlington, University of Vermont, March 1981. Twenty years have passed. (Their essays are in boxes down in the barn in the loft over the oxen.) Hackman and March must be looking middle age right in the face. I often wonder about these students of old and the dreams they must have had so long ago and if they still remember Newark. I cannot recall their faces. Yet their words, like the words of thousands of other students who drove off to a strange place to study town meeting when I too was young, always make me lonely.

24. H. Holly Hackman, "Town Meeting Essay, Town of Newark," Burlington, University of Vermont, March 1982.

Eight of the citizens at the meeting (nearly 10 percent of the assembly) were now sitting among the other 90 percent of the assembly that had just rejected them as town officers.[25]

But the "biggie" came up after lunch. The question was whether to keep the current road commissioner Stuart Cole—a blue-collar worker who needed the job. This was to be a public assessment of his job performance. No sugarcoating here. No golden parachute. No parachute at all.[26] Ten people (four women and six men) participated a total of eighteen times on article 4, "To elect a Road Commissioner." Nominations from the floor began at 1:20 p.m. and resulted in a three-way race between Jerry Bailey, Stuart Cole, and Richard Rogers. Thirty minutes later the town fired Stuart Cole and hired Richard Rogers: 101 people voted, 60 percent of the town's registered voters. Stuart Cole got 34 votes, Jerry Bailey, 8, and Richard Rogers, 59.

Other significant issues appeared that town meeting day in Newark. The nuclear freeze moratorium (article 22) was debated for twenty-six minutes and passed 38 to 22. (When the article came up at 2:52 only 74 citizens were left at town meeting.) Six members of the town heatedly debated a leash law proposal for ten minutes. Student Holly Hackman reported in her essay, "The first raised voices were heard. The debate ended with a statement from a man: 'No matter if the law is passed or not, I'm going to shoot the next dog that tears apart my rubbish, and the owner can pick up the dog where it lays.'" The leash law passed on a standing vote.[27]

Issues like those found in North Hero, Victory, Holland, Thetford, and Newark appear in the remaining top forty-four best-attended meetings. They also show up in the best-attended meetings in those towns that had at least ten meetings in the sample but none in the top fifty meetings overall. Quantification is risky in this kind of analysis and more work needs to be done, but

25. Kathy Allard, Holly Hackman, and Jennifer March, "The 1982 Comparative Town Meeting Study: Town of Newark," Burlington, University of Vermont, Real Democracy Data Base, March 1982).

26. It has been my observation over the years that newcomers (especially upscale newcomers) to Vermont and town meeting are much less willing to vote against local officers like town clerks and road commissioners (more or less full-time jobs) because they can't handle the pain, even though they agree the person ought to be removed. I think some guilt is involved—and ideology. Longtime Vermonters are more used to dealing with this kind of thing. Many have suffered similar trauma themselves. All know someone who has.

27. Like many of these issues, the leash law debate in Newark had gone on for some time. A year earlier when Holly Hackman had reported on the 1981 Newark town meeting she wrote: "One of the big issues of the day was whether to have a leash law. To me, this seemed rather funny, because in a town that size, with large plots of land, it would seem hardly necessary. One man brought up the question of who was going to enforce the law if it was passed. It all seemed rather satirical to us "flatlanders." H. Holly Hackman, "Town Meeting Report," Burlington, University of Vermont, March, 1981.

I can say that of the other ninety-four meetings in the combined categories, only seven remain on my "mystery list." The other eighty-seven meetings dealt with a wide variety of issues that for one reason or another sparked conflict—often dramatic conflict—within the towns holding them. Significantly, those meetings that had the least attendance (again, under controls) almost universally lacked any "defining issues." Of the eighty-two meetings[28] with the poorest showing on attendance, I have only five that, looking at the issues on the warning for the meeting, I would have bet would have scored higher.

It was impossible to establish more than a rudimentary classification of the kinds of issues bringing people to town meeting. "Rogue" issues like the veteran's memorial in Thetford were rare. Events that involved individual citizens as in North Hero, or a "blowup situation" as in Victory, occurred more often but were still in the minority. Most of the issues that drew people to town meetings in numbers that substantially exceeded expectations can be loosely described as policy based, like those in Holland and Newark. Roads, taxes, the election of town officers, zoning, and development were often found in this category. Education was the only surprise. Although education issues failed to significantly influence attendance in the aggregate, they cropped up as important influences several times in the list of best-attended meetings. The word that best describes issues drawing people to town meeting is variety. Life in small towns and the politics it spawns are less simple than is often believed.

WITNESS

I've seen men almost come to blows at town meeting. Personalities would crop up and wounding remarks be made. They hurt, and may hurt for a long time, but the rule is to forgive and forget quickly, for we small-towners live so close together that we are sure to come face-to-face almost every day, and after town meeting and an occasional blizzard, spring begins to suggest itself, and hard feelings melt.

Charles Edward Crane[29]

28. This is a shorter list because in several towns several meetings tied for "worst meeting" on attendance.

29. Charles Edward Crane, *Winter in Vermont* (New York: Alfred A. Knopf, 1942), 296. The story is told of the town meeting in northern Vermont in which someone placed the following resolution on the floor during the "new business" article: "The town wishes to extend its sympathy to Wayne Wheeler, whose barn recently burned only three weeks after Skidway Brook flooded and destroyed his corn piece. Wayne continued to perform his duties as selectman during this severe personal crisis, and for that the town is deeply grateful." Whereupon someone yelled out from the back of the hall, "Call for a secret ballot!"

Studying these meetings is pure joy. Not because the outcomes are always "correct." Not because the process is always (or even often) "pretty." These meetings are a joy to behold because they suggest that common people can and will engage in the ancient dream of public, face-to-face decision making, especially when the issues are difficult and the process is challenging. Beyond the constraints and opportunities I have discussed throughout this book, people come to town meetings to govern themselves. What could be more joyful to a democrat?

Participation

"I have never seen so much plaid in my life." This is how Shawn Anderson described the town meeting in Marshfield, Vermont, on a "miserable, rainy" Tuesday in March 1991.[30] After a postponement of fifteen minutes because of the icy roads, the meeting began at 9:17 a.m. When it adjourned at 3:41 p.m., it had become the most participatory of the 1,174 meetings in the sample.[31] The Gini index for Marshfield's 1991 meeting, controlling for the size of the meeting and the other factors contributing strong participation (see chapter 7), was 3.2 standard deviations above the mean. Of the 159 citizens in attendance, 68 produced 211 acts of speech.[32]

The Marshfield town meeting of 1991 demonstrates how some meetings generate traditions of talk that may escape "thin" statistical analysis. The people at Marshfield's town meeting seemed "participation conscious."[33] Anderson points this out in his essay. The moderator had just been elected when two men in "almost matching suits," representatives of Marshfield's district in the state legislature, "beckoned the moderator to make a motion to allow them to address the meeting. Gaynland [the moderator] made the motion and a woman in the front row rose to her feet and said, 'I'd like to amend it to a limit of 15 minutes.' Another man yelled, 'No—10.' Someone else lowered

30. Shawn Anderson, "Marshfield Calls the Question," Burlington, University of Vermont, April 1991.

31. Remember that since Census data by town became available only in 1980 (the counts for 1970 and earlier sampled too few to be useful for most Vermont towns), only meetings held from 1977 on entered the regression equations requiring Census data to control data like (for verbal participation) SES diversity.

32. Shawn Anderson and Jon Moore, "The 1991 Comparative Town Meeting Study: Town of Marshfield," Burlington, University of Vermont, Real Democracy Data Base, March 1991.

33. Unfortunately, I have only four town meetings in Marshfield in the sample since 1977. But in these four meetings Marshfield ranked first on participation for the 129 towns that had at least four meetings in the sample after 1976.

it to 5 and it was voted on. 'Well, thank you for the five minutes folks!' one of the well-dressed representatives sarcastically said. But the townspeople held them to their five minutes."[34]

The people of Marshfield guard their speaking time jealously. But they do more. Tradition requires that a funny story be told in memory of a past moderator, Joe Silversteen. Two women told stories that day. According to Anderson, Adele Dawson said: "Back in the olden days, I used to come to town meeting when Joe used to moderate. One meeting I stood up and said, 'Joe, why can't the women ever participate?' and he said, 'Why Adele, you can participate, you are always welcome to second anything I say!'" When Dawson finished her story, writes Anderson, "The room burst into laughter. This ritual really loosened up the meeting and maybe even attributed to higher participation."[35]

Beyond the flavor of this town meeting, a flavor no regression equation can taste, Marshfield's meeting also demonstrated that electing officers from the floor may not lower participation at a town meeting even though it uses up a lot of time. Marshfield spent three hours of a meeting lasting five hours and thirty-eight minutes electing town officers in 1991 and still had the best participation of all the meetings. While electing officers, the townspeople averaged about seven speakers and eighteen acts of speech per hour. During the rest of the meeting they averaged about seventeen speakers and fifty-nine acts of speech per hour.

Finally, Marshfield's meeting underscores the principal difference between the effects of issues on drawing citizens to town meeting and on stimulating them to speak once they arrive. In Marshfield, for instance, electing town officers, the Australian ballot, a plow for a town truck, and the town budget (especially as it pertained to roads) generated the most talk. But verbal participation in town meeting has a dynamic of its own that is difficult to gauge and nearly impossible to predict. Discussion sometimes triggers meetings to "take off" on unpredictable subjects. Issues that seem cut-and-dried when they appear in the warning of the town report may still spark drawn-out discussion at the town meeting.

In Marshfield, the abnormal number of ballots needed to elect the town officers, for instance, stimulated an additional "twenty minutes of heated discussion"[36] during the "new business" article on the need for the Australian

34. Shawn Anderson, "Marshfield Calls the Question."
35. Shawn Anderson, "Marshfield Calls the Question."
36. Shawn Anderson, "Marshfield Calls the Question."

ballot to "speed things up" at future meetings.[37] The budget debate turned
to a long discussion about a snowplow. This debate is a good example of
a common criticism of town meeting that goes something like this: "How
can they spend two minutes discussing a $700,000 school budget and forty-
five minutes on a $5,000 snowplow?" Anderson responded in his report:
"The beauty of the system was not based on how consistent or gracefully
the meeting process flowed, but, when someone had something to say, they
said it. Some might think it ridiculous that a group of people could breeze
over their budget to argue over the practicality of a snowplow. But isn't that
beautiful?"[38]

   Indeed, it is hard to imagine a single object more important to rural
people in Vermont than a snowplow. At highly participatory meetings townspeople often tended to talk at length about "little," understandable things.
At the second best meeting on participation (Fletcher in 1983), the election of second constable (which usually takes less than a minute and a single
participation—the nominator's) evolved into a long discussion of the "role"
of the town constable. Before it left the floor, twenty-seven people had participated fifty-seven times in thirty-two minutes:[39]

WITNESS

One problem that came up was filling the position of Second Constable.
Nobody wanted the job. Someone asked the First Constable what the
Second Constable did. He felt that maybe this would arouse some interest.
The reply was that the First Constable didn't know exactly what the lower
position entailed; didn't know exactly when he worked but he did know the
Second Constable was responsible for catching stray or bothersome dogs.
Basically the Second Constable is a dogcatcher. The next question was why
not change the name of Second Constable to Dog Catcher. This was
debated for a while. But then someone wondered what would happen if the
town really needed the assistance of a Second Constable (to do whatever it
was besides catch dogs that Second Constables normally did). The idea of
switching names was dismissed, yet the need for a Second Constable was

37. The vote was overwhelmingly against adopting the Australian ballot. One of my
students heard several whispered complaints about the time electing the officers took and
concluded it was the most interesting question of the day. Jon Moore, "Town Meeting Supported
in Marshfield, Vermont," Burlington, University of Vermont, April 1991. Shawn Anderson wrote
that a woman sitting in front of them ("who had been knitting all morning") talked to him and
Moore at lunch saying, "We have to speed up the system. It is not very efficient." Anderson agreed.
Shawn Anderson, "Marshfield Calls the Question."
   38. Shawn Anderson, "Marshfield Calls the Question."
   39. Lesley Kachadorian and Lisa Brest, "The 1983 Comparative Town Meeting Study:
Town of Fletcher," Burlington, University of Vermont, Real Democracy Data Base, March 1983.

still there. Finally one man said he would accept the position if he got paid
minimum wage and reimbursed for his gas money. That was fine with the
townspeople, and at last the position was filled.

Lisa Brest[40]

Issues matter for healthy verbal participation at a town meeting, but in ways
far subtler than the way they matter for attendance.

Basically, however, the issues associated with more egalitarian participation are similar to those associated with higher attendance. While trucks,
leash laws, zoning ordinances, taxes, school budgets, road salt, and so on do
not guarantee a lot of talk spread out over the assembly, when such participation occurs it often involves these kinds of issues. That they may arise from
the chemistry of the meeting itself and not from the community at large helps
explain why it is difficult to predict participation. Conversely, the chemistry
of the meeting may defuse issues that drew people to town meeting in the
first place. Many times I have heard comments like "Well, that was easy!" at
the end of a town meeting. Often students have returned from town meetings disappointed because what seemed like a "hot" issue failed to stir up
controversy.

Women's Involvement

For the life of me and after thirty years of research, I remain stumped when it
comes to predicting women's involvement—with two exceptions. First, men
usually dominate discussion of plows, loaders, graders, and trucks. This is
not an insignificant bias in the democratic give-and-take of important policy
decisions at town meeting. Yet even this certitude is on the wane. Women's
participation on these issues has picked up over the years. I suspect this is
partly due to the bureaucratizing of highway policy. More and more the
discussion is about how and when to purchase a road grader, not what kind
of road grader to purchase.

40. Lisa Brest, "Town Meeting in Fletcher, Vermont," Burlington, University of Vermont,
April 1983. Lisa Brest was sympathetic: "When I first heard these discussions I was amazed that
these were the most important things these people think about. I just felt there are so many other
issues that have more importance. Then I realized that in places like Fletcher these are the issues of
most importance. In Sociology I learned that cultural relativism is the characteristics acceptable
and relative to everything in a particular culture. At town meeting I could really see what that
meant." Brest's partner at the Fletcher town meeting said she (Brest) walked into the meeting that
day wearing a sweatshirt that said, "It's Better in the Bahamas." My guess is that most of the people
on that cold, rainy day in Vermont agreed.

Plus, men in the aggregate know less and less about road equipment themselves and therefore spend less time demonstrating their familiarity with this or that kind of gearbox. Finally, as women participate more often at town meeting and on a wider range of issues, and as women are here and there elected to the post of selectman (whose primary duty is to keep the roads well tended), eyebrows are less apt to be lifted when a woman rises to make a point about rear end differentials (or whatever).

The second issue area that seems to affect women's participation is a caveat to our earlier finding that the presence of education issues on town meeting agendas does little to increase women's involvement. Even though the overall association with women's involvement remains essentially ambiguous in the full sample of meetings, education issues are more apt to be absent in those meetings where women's involvement (measured as a combination of attendance and verbal participation) is most tepid, while issues involving schools are more apt to be present when women's involvement is most robust.

Controlling for town size (small is better), the year the meeting was held (later years are better), day/night (day is better), and two SES variables of lesser importance,[41] the 1998 meeting in the town of Hyde Park led the list of 1,174 meetings on women's involvement in town meeting. Although overall women's attendance throughout both the town and school meetings was slightly below average, a significant number of men did not return for the school meeting, which began after lunch, while women's attendance improved during the school meeting. While women's verbal participation throughout the entire day exceeded men's, the ratio of women speakers to men speakers was much higher when education issues were on the floor.

Overall the ratio of women's speech to men's was 1.5 to 1 in favor of women. Similarly, for every act of speech made by men, women made 1.65. However, on issues not involving the schools, the ratio of women to men speakers was exactly equal, 1.00, and the ratio of women's to men's acts of speech was nearly equal, 0.95. But on school issues the ratio of women to men speakers favored women 2 to 1, and the ratio of women's to men's acts of speech favored women 3.25 to 1. Women's intensified participation in the school meeting made the Hyde Park meeting of 1998 the best town meeting for women's involvement that we studied.

The town of Holland's meeting the same year was the second best for women's involvement, and education was important there also. The meeting

41. These variables are the percentage of the total workforce employed out of town (more is better), which remains a conundrum variable for me, and the upscale factor score, which adds less than 1 percent variance explained to the equation.

featured a highly competitive race for school director among two women and two men. Since a majority is required to win, three ballots were necessary. Both men withdrew after the second ballot, and the final vote between the two women was 61 to 24. Overall, six school items were on the town meeting warning. On these six articles female participators exceeded male participators 2 to 1, and female participations exceeded male participations 1.67 to 1.

But unlike the situation in Hyde Park, where women's overall advantage in involvement was built on especially high participation on education issues, in Holland women's speech (the ratio of women to men participators) was about equal on school and nonschool matters, and women's acts of speech (the ratio of women's to men's participations) was actually higher on non-school issues than on school issues. All the while on both kinds of issues, women outparticipated men on speech and talk. Meanwhile, unlike the situation in Hyde Park, women outnumbered men in attendance. One might venture a guess that the race for school director drew women to Holland's 1998 meeting. This may have helped spark high verbal participation for women overall, but women's verbal participation was not higher on education articles per se.

In the other meetings where women did especially well on involvement in town meeting, the evidence is mixed. In Worcester in 1997 (as in Hyde Park), the school meeting was held after lunch and the town meeting was held before lunch. As in Hyde Park, women's attendance was higher during the school meeting than during the town meeting. But (unlike Hyde Park) here women's attendance was higher than men's throughout the day, improving from 55 percent of the total in the morning to 61 percent in the afternoon. But (unlike Holland, where a competitive election on the floor for school director may have caused higher attendance), here the school director's election was by Australian ballot and uncontested.

While some conflict arose on the school budget in Worcester (the discussion lasted one hour and fourteen minutes and its resolution required a secret ballot, passing 58 to 25), women participated significantly less on the school budget and other school issues than they did on nonschool issues even though, as in Holland and Hyde Park, they outparticipated men overall and (as in Holland) did so on both kinds of issues. In short, Worcester seemed to have no hot school issues to draw women out on town meeting day, but they came out anyway. When they got there they did not seem particularly interested in education, but they participated anyway, outdoing men on speech 2.67 to 1 on nonschool issues but only 1.22 to 1 on school issues. On acts of speech they outdid men 1.45 to 1 on nonschool issues and fell below men on school issues 0.75 to 1.

Creeping ambiguity on the education hypothesis continues as we go down the list from the best of the very best meetings on women's involvement to the worst of the very best. Continuing the search through the very worst meetings for women, my best guess is that education matters considerably to women's overall involvement in town meeting, even though it (by and large) failed to penetrate the earlier regression equations. We can imagine many explanations for this, both statistical and substantive. Still, my research suggests that to the extent that we remove decisions about education from local democracy, we may be hurting women's equal participation in the democratic process.

Beyond road equipment and possibly education, however, women's involvement (attendance and participation combined) goes up and down with the same kinds of issues as men's involvement does. Moreover, women do not shy away from participating in high-conflict meetings. They become more involved in high-conflict meetings and less involved in low-conflict meetings to the same degree as men. While issues therefore do much to increase levels of attendance and debate, they do much less to close the equality gap that remains between men's and women's involvement in town meeting democracy.

A Final Word on Conflict and Issues

Over the years I have given hundreds of talks to civic groups in Vermont on the subject of local government and town meeting. Often I am asked to suggest ways to improve attendance at and verbal participation in town meeting. There always seems to be general approval of my suggestions until I get to the matter of local empowerment. At that point the mood often changes. Some nod their heads approvingly. "So what else is new?" their eyes seem to say. But others are not especially happy. Their eyes seem to narrow and say: "Here we go again with all that old 'local control' business." When I speak to professional audiences (especially academic audiences) the dissonance is magnified.

Small-town people are not afraid of dealing face-to-face with difficult issues and the open conflict and even hostility they sometimes produce. Charles Crane (see Witness above) was right. Bitterness occurs. People get over it. Life goes on. Community continues. Why are so many democrats so gloriously committed to statistical democracy (increasing numerical involvement in all manner of "input" mechanisms) yet so hesitant to let people participate to an immediate end they can see and feel? Why are we so willing to let the people watch the game (and even umpire from time to time) and so unwilling to let them join in the conflict itself?

Beyond the unwillingness (for whatever reason) of many to entrust local people with conducting their own business, and beyond the recommendations of an entire generation of sociologists who have concluded that small-town people will not handle conflict fairly or (even worse) will stifle it to protect their peace of mind, I believe there is something more fundamental at work, something that strikes at the heart.

I see it across the pond in the late October hills that flank Big Hollow Road where I live. Only a few colors remain; the yellow green of the poplar leaves, and here and there a clump of rusty oak. These are but patches on the prevailing gray of the ascendant season, a gray that will soon consume everything but the green of the hemlocks and then will itself disappear under a blanket of white. In many ways I dread the cold and the snow. Winter so exacerbates the struggle and pain of outside work.

And yet there is hope in winter's premonition, much as in the anticipation of a good sleep there resides the promise of a new day. So too, I believe, does the promise of an enduring democracy reside in significant measure in the struggle over things that matter to common people. It is a mark of the fundamental humanity of democrats, is it not, that we long to avoid the anguish of face-to-face conflict and dream instead of a better governance where the sins of the garden are put behind us? My findings suggest, however, that as long as politics is a part of human nature, conflict is as necessary to democracy as winter is to spring.

No one pretends that democracy is perfect or all-wise. Indeed, it has been said that democracy is the worst form of government except all those other forms that have been tried from time to time.

Winston Churchill

This epigraph was issued in the House of Commons on November 11, 1947. Churchill may have been paraphrasing the American Radical William Godwin from his *Enquiry concerning Political Justice*, published in 1793: "Supposing that we should even be obliged to take democracy with all the disadvantages that were ever annexed to it, and that no remedy could be discovered for any of its defects, it would still be greatly preferable to the exclusive system of other forms."

11

The Best Democracy, the Worst Democracy

All things considered—from attendance levels to the length of the meeting—what does real democracy look like at its very best? What does it look like at its very worst? Real democracy demands first the presence of citizens. Then comes deliberation. Third, real democracy requires that no cohort of society be excluded. Finally, the amount of time devoted to deliberation needs to be sufficient. We have established the parameters of these components and discussed how they are related (or not related) to the contexts in which they are practiced. But to understand and judge real democracy thoroughly, we must consider how well town meetings accomplish all of these goals in concert.

Since the components of real democracy are not systematically related, a simple additive summary of the standardized values of each component provides an appropriate summary measure of a meeting's overall performance. I weighted these components as follows: attendance (40 percent), participation (25 percent), women's involvement (25 percent), and time (10 percent). I called the result the raw best democracy index (RBDI). Weighting the components was difficult. Should we penalize a meeting more for poor discussion or for poor women's involvement? The literature provides few clues. I therefore sought the counsel of four theorists in my department, combined it with my own instincts, and concluded, first, that attendance at town meeting should have priority.[1] Second, equality for women in both presence and talk

---

1. As my colleague Alan Wertheimer reminded me, this paradigm has the support of Woody Allen, who once said that 80 percent of life is showing up.

(our women's involvement measure) ought to weigh equally with the equality of overall deliberative discussion. These two decisions left time the meeting lasted as the weakest component.

Comparing attendance at town meetings in the little town of Newark with attendance in the much larger town of Shelburne, when we know that attendance declines as town size increases (something the citizens of Shelburne can do nothing about), doesn't seem "fair." Nor does it seem fair to compare women's participation at meetings held in the early 1970s with meetings held in the late 1990s when we know that women's participation increased substantially over time (something citizens of the 1970s could do nothing about). Should participation equality in a meeting of 200 be compared with that in a meeting of 100, when larger meetings depress participation equality (something those in attendance cannot control)?

It depends. In making a recommendation to a friend who wants to visit a town meeting and observe real democracy in its fullest form, send her to a town that typically ranks high on a measure that takes no causal factors into account, the raw best democracy index (RBDI). But if she wants to visit a place where citizens work harder at real democracy than their circumstances predict, then you need a measure that controls for causal factors. While the first measure gauges democratic performance, the second gauges democratic achievement. This latter is called the controlled best democracy index (CBDI).

Accordingly, the RBDI does not adjust attendance for town size, participation for meeting size, women's equality for the year the meeting was held, or length of the meeting for participation. In fact, all the variables associated with increases or decreases in any of the components in the raw best democracy index are ignored. The RBDI makes no excuses and asks no questions. It says, "This is what the best (or the worst) democratic meetings look like. Take it or leave it."

The second measure, the controlled best democracy index, takes into account the fundamental qualifiers of real democracy. It says, "These meetings measure best (or worst) on real democracy given the conditions in which they operate." Thus, if the percentage of a town's registered voters who attend town meeting is lower in a big town than in a small town, the CBDI is sympathetic and responds by scoring the meeting's attendance in light of the level of attendance expected for towns of similar size. Similarly, for women's attendance the CBDI will "curve" the grade of the meetings depending on whether they are held at night, when women's attendance is generally lower. This measure tells us in which meetings a town's citizens have overcome systemic handicaps to democratic achievement.

The Best (and Worst) Town Meetings in the Raw

This is democracy from the citizens' point of view. Live in these communities, and the probability that you and your neighbors will participate in the practice of real democracy improves by definition. The raw best democracy index doesn't care what kind of town has the largest or smallest proportion of its citizens in attendance at town meeting. What matters for the RBDI is that a greater proportion of the citizens practice democracy more completely in (for instance) Belvidere than in Richford.

Belvidere

Belvidere is a wild, tough little town. Over the millennia the north branch of the Lamoille River cut an east-west trough between the Cold Hollow Mountains to the north and the Butternut and Bowen Mountains to the south. A decent blacktop road now angles along the river most of the way through town. This is where most of Belvidere's 218 people lived in 1980. Seventy-seven percent of the town's citizens were born in Vermont. Only 57 percent of the citizens of the average town in the database were born in Vermont. Sixteen percent of Belvidere's citizens over twenty-five years old had college degrees, 20 percent below the average town. The per capita income in Belvidere in 1980 was $4,637, 21 percent below the average. In the general election of 1980, 62 percent of the registered voters turned out. Reagan got 48 votes, Carter 24, John Anderson 8, Barry Commoner 1, and the Libertarian candidate, Ed Clark, 3.

The people had been warned to attend the 1980 town meeting as follows: "The inhabitants of the Town of Belvidere, who are legal voters in Town Meeting and Town School District Meeting of said Belvidere, respectively, are hereby notified and warned to meet in Town Meeting and Town School District Meeting at the Town Hall in said Belvidere on Tuesday, March 4, 1980 at ten o'clock in the forenoon, to transact the following articles of business."[2]

When students Janice Rubin and Pat Watkins counted attendance at 10:20 a.m. 61 people occupied the 63 chairs that had been set up for the meeting. This was the highest count of the four taken that day. The average attendance was 48, 21 women and 27 men. The meeting lasted three hours and fifteen minutes not including a ninety-minute break for lunch. In that time 44 people spoke a total of 166 times on the seventeen articles on the

2. Town of Belvidere, *Town Report*, year ending December 1979, 3.

warning. A majority of the speakers (52 percent) were women. They were responsible for 58 percent of the individual acts of participation.[3]

By the time the moderator, Richard Spaulding, gaveled the meeting to a close at 2:55 p.m., Steven Locke had turned out one of the three incumbent selectmen (and chairman of the Selectboard), Mark Schroeder. Locke's wife, Penny, had won the seat on the school board vacated by twenty-one-year incumbent Joycelyn Adams, defeating Beverly Bennett and Kathy Hobart, whose spouse Geoffrey was reelected second constable without opposition. In the closest race of the day the moderator's wife, Charlene Spaulding, defeated Warren Thomas 25 to 20 for the office of auditor. The town and school budgets were approved. The selectmen were authorized to buy land to establish a town forest. Town officers' salaries were set at $3.25 an hour. After ten minutes of debate (2:43 p.m. to 2:53 p.m.) the town rejected the following: "Article 16: Will the town vote to install and maintain a uniform system of accounting as established by the auditor of accounts under 32 V.S.A. Section 163 (1)?"

WITNESS

THE COST OF BUREAUCRACY IN THE TOWN OF BELVIDERE

Town Expenditures
Selectmen's Account
  Administration:
  Town Officers:
  Town Clerk & Treasurers:

Larry Brown, Salary	$300.00	
Larry Brown, Civil Board & Selectmen's Meetings	25.00	325.00
Listers:		
James Bennett	286.76	
Geoffrey Hobart	178.75	
James Adams	66.63	532.14
Selectmen:		
Mark Schroeder	178.50	
Kenneth Tallman	64.50	
Glenn Davis	71.00	314.00
Auditors:		
Michael Coccoli	163.25	
James Bennett	59.25	
Earl Domina	97.50	320.00

3. Janice Rubin and Pat Watkins, "The 1980 Comparative Town Meeting Study: Town of Belvidere," Burlington, University of Vermont, Real Democracy Data Base, March 1980.

Board of Civil Authority:		
Amsden Brown	10.00	
Maefred Barry	10.00	
Mark Schroeder	10.00	
Hugh Tallman	<u>10.00</u>	40.00
Town Meeting Expenses:		
Town Report	341.20	
Larry Brown, Clerk of Meeting	16.25	
Richard Spaulding, Moderator	16.25	
Maefred Barry, Ballot Clerk	16.25	
Hersa Eldred, "	16.25	
Winnie Lanpher, "	16.25	
Mary Tallman, "	<u>16.25</u>	438.70
School Bond Issue:		
Maefred Barry, "	29.25	
Hersa Eldred, "	29.25	
Lena Rich, "	29.25	
Mary Tallman, "	29.25	
Larry Brown, "	<u>29.25</u>	<u>146.25</u>
Total Administrative Expense	$2,116.09	
(for the year 1979)		

Belvidere Town Report[4]

The Belvidere meeting of 1980 scored highest of the 1,435 in the database on the four-item, no-strings-attached democratic indicator, the raw best democracy index. On attendance Belvidere ranked 32 overall. Its Gini index of participation equality placed it thirteenth among the 1,435 meetings. Its strong showing on women's involvement left it ninth from the top on that indicator. The length of the meeting, however (three hours and fifteen minutes), was slightly below average, ranking Belvidere number 736. Here then is a statistical snapshot of the best real democracy.

61 of 136 registered voters were present
44 of 61 attenders spoke at least once
166 acts of speech were made
More of the attenders were men; more of the talk was by women
Deliberation lasted three hours and fifteen minutes

We studied 1,435 town meetings between 1970 and 1998. This was as good as it got.

4. Town of Belvidere, *Town Report*, year ending December 1979, 9.

Richford

Exactly 19 hours and 23 minutes before the gavel fell on the best meeting of
the full sample studied between 1970 and 1998, the worst meeting was gaveled
to order about twenty miles (as the crow flies) due north of Belvidere in the
Richford village town hall. Richford was built where the hard ridges of the
Green Mountains join the flowering pastures of the Champlain valley. The
glacier that once covered Vermont had twitched ever so slightly and carved
out a soft hollow interrupting the Missisquoi River's southwestern journey
to Lake Champlain. The river flowed north for a bit as if to return home
to Canada, but it soon changed its mind and meandered southward, building
topsoil for thousands of years. It is the kind of river that brings joy to Vermont
farm girls and boys on dreamy June days. Missisquoi is an Abenaki word for
"great grassy meadows." The Abenakis knew how to name their rivers.

Near the river's hairpin turnabout, the people built a town. The streets
still bespeak the compromise fashioned between citizens and land: Elm Street
and Maple Street, Sweat Street, and streets named Church, School, and
Home.[5] In 1878 a village was incorporated on the river's bend so that these
clustered residents of Richford town could tax themselves for the kinds of
services villagers need but dwellers in the rest of a town's "outback" do not.

As the twentieth century progressed, the trains and the farms began to
leave the valley of the Missisquoi,[6] and like other New England town centers,
Richford's "downtown" (the old village) began to fade like the great elms that
once brought majesty to Yankee thoroughfares. In 1950 the population of the
town was 2,643. By 1980 it was down to 2,206.[7] But the village lost population
much faster than the town, and in 1990 it disappeared as a legal entity when
the town and village reincorporated as one.

5. As a boy of seventeen I hired out for the summer working for the state geologist
mapping green stone outcroppings in northern Vermont. Our wanderings brought us through the
mountains on several occasions, following the Missisquoi's cuts in the summer landscape. I
remember lunches under the elms of Richford with sandwich and soda and the company of Lance
Meade and our boss, Jason Wark. This was the summer of 1958. In the two years I lived and
worked with Jason he (unknown to him, I suspect) did much to father my life. Then, in the dusk of
a late August evening he dropped me off in front of my mother's place in Newbury 150 miles to the
southeast and drove away down the street, the little red taillights of his 1951 Studebaker
disappearing under the elms like fireflies over a misty midnight meadow. Although for thirty years
we worked within a half-mile of each other (he became an orthodontist in downtown Burlington),
I never saw him again.

6. Richford was once the home of a "station" for Chinese immigrants who came to help
build the railroads. Close observers of Vermont history and in fact of rural life in many places know
that cultural diversity was never as weak as the stereotypes (penned assiduously by urban scholars
in the first two-thirds of this century) portray it.

7. Richford, unlike the vast majority of Vermont towns, did not experience a population
renaissance in the postwar period.

In 1980 an even larger proportion of Richford's population (87 percent) were born in Vermont than was the case in Belvidere. While Belvidere was below average on college graduates with 16.5 percent, Richford had one of the lowest percentages of all, 5.7 percent. (In only 4 of the 210 towns in the sample was it lower.) Richford's per capita income was almost exactly the same as Belvidere's, 21 percent below the average of the towns in the sample. Richford gave Ronald Reagan and John Anderson fewer votes and Jimmy Carter more votes in 1980 than Belvidere did. Turnout in the 1980 general election was a bit higher (69 percent) than in Belvidere (62 percent) but lower than the average town in the sample (74 percent).

The people of Richford attended their 1980 town meeting in what my students described as "a small auditorium" on the second floor of the town hall in Richford village. The meeting began at 7:32 p.m. At 7:45, there were 117 in attendance. This increased to 135 at 8:15. At 8:22 the school district meeting began and, as the students put it, "several people left." By 8:40 attendance was down to 111. At 8:57, an hour and twenty-five minutes after it started, the meeting ended. Throughout, more seats went unfilled (an average of 159) than were filled.[8] The town warning contained ten articles (not including the "new business" article), and the school warning contained six. No votes at all were taken on any of these during the meeting. All came the next day by Australian ballot.

At the highest attendance count, men outnumbered women 3.5 to 1. Only 24 people participated in the meeting. Two of these were women, and they both spoke on educational issues.[9] Only 88 participations were made in all. The issue that received the most attention was warned as follows: "To see if the Town will vote to authorize the selectmen to purchase a new gas truck at a cost not to exceed $21,000 to be paid for from Revenue Sharing Funds."[10] Of the 88 participations, 21 occurred on this issue. The bottom line? Richford's meeting ranked number 1,234 on the percentage of registered voters attending town meeting out of the 1,435 meetings for which data were available. It ranked 1,300 out of 1,375 on the Gini index of participation

8. David Dumont and Carl Johnson, "The 1980 Comparative Town Meeting Study: Town of Richford," Burlington, University of Vermont, Real Democracy Data Base, March 1980.

9. One of the two women on the five-member school board spoke four times, once on the budget (article 4) and three times on new business. The other, the school accountant, spoke twice on new business. Ibid.

10. Town of Richford, *Town Report*, year ending December 1979, 5. Critics of town meeting often deride town truck debates. Many of my students react similarly. But then the Vermont legislature was also called down for its "raccoon debates," especially the issue of shooting does in deer season or how long a trout must be before it becomes a "keeper." I view these debates as a glorious manifestation of democracy.

equality, 1,372 out of 1,413 on time the meeting lasted, and dead last on women's participation—1,374. This was as bad as town meeting democracy got.

The Best (and Worst) Town Meetings in Context

Although the town of Belvidere produced the most democratic town meeting, some of the reasons may be more or less givens and not directly related to its people's democratic effort. In Belvidere, for instance, the town's tiny population strengthened the percentage of registered voters in attendance. Verbal participation was enhanced because the actual number of persons at the meeting is lower in a small town. On the other hand, women's attendance would most likely have been higher had the meeting been held, for instance, in 1998 rather than 1980. The time spent in discussion would have been longer had the total attendance and number of persons who spoke been greater. Similar factors might explain Richford's dismal meeting.

The controlled best democracy index (CBDI), however, considers attendance as if every meeting were held in the same-sized town. It measures participation as if the actual number of attenders at each meeting were equal. Similarly, it standardizes the year each meeting was held (for women's equality) and the number of attenders and participators involved (for time spent in discussion). Other variables of lesser importance that helped account for the variance in each of the four requirements of real democracy are similarly controlled. This process identifies the most democratic meetings given the conditions under which they occur—meetings like the one in North Hero in 1994.

North Hero

According to the controlled best democracy index, in 1994 the town of North Hero held the most democratic meeting we found in twenty-eight years of research. I discussed the issues treated at this meeting in chapter 10 because (under controls) it was the best-attended meeting in the sample. Alexander Wilcox, the student who studied North Hero in 1994, described the town as follows: "As the pamphlet in North Hero's general store 'The Hero's Welcome,' announces, North Hero is the middle town on the middle island in the very middle of the lake. The position of the town is indeed central, and North Hero is officially described as both the Shire Town and the county seat of Grand Isle County. The words North Hero describe both an Island (more accurately two islands with a link no wider than Route #2) and a town.

(The words island and town are used interchangeably in the vernacular. North Hero is named, along with South Hero, after Ethan and Ira Allen, also known as the 'two heroes.')"[11]

Wilcox continues with Samuel de Champlain's description of the area in 1609: "There are also several rivers that flow into the lake that is bordered by many fine trees of the same sorts that we have in France, with a quality of vines more beautiful than many I had seen in any other place, many chestnut trees, and I have not seen any at all before, except on the shore of the lake, where there is a great abundance of fish of a great many varieties . . . beautiful valleys and open stretches fertile in grain, such as I had eaten in this country with a great many other fruits."[12]

The 1990 Census counted a population of 546 in North Hero. Sixty-three percent of these were born in Vermont. Of North Hero's population over twenty-five years of age, 30 percent had college degrees. The average for the towns where meetings were held was 24 percent. North Hero's per capita income was also slightly higher than for the average town in the sample. On all these measures North Hero scored higher than either Belvidere or Richford. At the same time, North Hero seems to be more conservative than the average town. In the presidential election of 1996, North Hero's votes for Bill Clinton and Socialist Bernie Sanders were well below the sample average and also below the results in Belvidere and Richford. In 1986 its vote for Vermont's equal rights amendment was likewise below the sample average. Sixty-nine percent of North Hero's voters went to the polls in the 1996 general election, while 71 percent did in the average town in the sample.

We know from chapter 10 that with all the variables that matter taken into account, North Hero's 1994 meeting ranked the best of our 1,357 meetings on attendance.[13] But it also ranked in the top 25 percent on participation, above average on women's equality, and in the top third on time the meeting lasted. With attendance accounting for 40 percent of the controlled best democracy index, these variables combined to make North Hero's meeting of 1980 the most democratic town meeting we studied, given the constraints it labored under and the opportunities it enjoyed. North Hero's meeting achieved this best of the best because its citizens outperformed expectations.

11. Ethan Allen was to Vermont what Sam Houston was to Texas. Ira Allen founded the University of Vermont.

12. Allen L. Stratton, *History of the South Hero Island* (Burlington, VT: Queen City Printers, 1980), 10, quoted in Alexander D. Wilcox, "North Hero 1994," Burlington, University of Vermont, March 1994. After quoting Champlain's description Wilcox, a full-time resident of the islands, wrote dryly: "It is obvious that Champlain spent time in the islands only in the summer."

13. The number of meetings is reduced because meetings held before 1977, when town-level Census data was unavailable, are removed from the analysis.

Not only did the dramatic issues resolved that evening draw many more people to the meeting, they did not do so at the expense of the other values that make for good real democracy: strong verbal participation, women's involvement, and time spent discussing the issues.

Swanton

Swanton, which has the very worst CBDI, and Richford, which has the very worst RBDI, are only a few miles apart on the Canadian border in Franklin County. This accentuates the difficulty of using community context variables to predict variations in democratic performance. Northwest Vermont is known for its more homogeneous culture (French Canadian and Catholic) and, not surprisingly, its politics (Democratic). Although Swanton has twice the population of Richford (5,887 to 2,253 in 1990), both towns are in the top twentieth percentile of the sample on town population. Belvidere and North Hero, with meetings that occupy the very top positions on the RBDI and CBDI, respectively, are a little farther south in the same region, much smaller and more isolated—Belvidere by the ridges of the mountains and North Hero by the waters of the lake. Belvidere has about half the population (228) of North Hero.

Swanton is the last place that might be called a commercial center before you leave Vermont for Quebec. It has the regional high school for the area (Missisquoi Valley Union), and Interstate 89 goes through Swanton on its way to Montreal. The exit off the interstate in Swanton features a small Montana-like truck stop where you can buy county music cassettes along with cheap gas and all manner of sticky buns. It also offers the last chance to go west along around over through into New York on the marshside roads and bridges of the northern Lake Champlain basin. It is here that the Abenakis still lay claim to the lands of their ancestors. As the first residents of Swanton, they are also most likely the first human beings ever to live in Vermont.

This is a working-class, conservative town. Its citizens have fewer college degrees, lower incomes, and more Vermont birth certificates than the average town. In politics it votes for Democratic candidates when they are not running against Bernie Sanders. Then Swanton votes for Sanders. Swanton ranked near the bottom on the liberalism factor score, helped by its very low yes vote on Vermont's ERA. The town has a heavy French Canadian flavor, and French Canadians in Swanton are apt to have more impressive Vermont pedigrees than most citizens of the state. Voter turnout at the polls is consistently well below average for the towns in the sample.

At 8:10 p.m. on March 3, 1997, at the town meeting held at the Swanton Central School, 54 people (41 men and 13 women) occupied the 226 seats available. Of these, 20 participated in the discussion. The accountant for Missisquoi Valley Rescue, Inc., a woman, participated the most. But only 3 other women participated at all, and these spoke only a single time each. Of the total participations, 54 percent came from the 10 percent of the attenders who spoke the most. The meeting adjourned at 9:07, one hour and twenty-eight minutes after it had begun.

Like Richford, Swanton held its town meeting on Monday night. The Australian ballot was used to vote on the nine warning articles on Tuesday. The actual town meeting was billed "informational only" and was not even mentioned in the formal warning:

WARNING

TOWN OF SWANTON ANNUAL MEETING

The legal voters of the Town of Swanton, who are legal voters of the
Town Meeting, are hereby identified and warned to meet at the Swanton
Municipal Complex, First and Elm Streets, Swanton on March 4th 1997
at 7:00 a.m. to vote on all the articles herein set forth. All articles are to be
voted on by the Australian system. The polls open at 7:00 a.m., and close
at 7:00 p.m.

Thus the people were not "warned" to meet, they were warned to vote. The announcement of the Monday night meeting appeared on the warning after article 9: "The legal voters of the Town of Swanton are further notified that an informational meeting will be held at the Swanton Central School on Monday, March 3, 1997 at 7:30 p.m. for the purpose of explaining all budget items to the voters."

The citizens were not invited to deliberate and make decisions. They were invited to listen and (presumably) to ask questions. But they did talk, they did ask questions, and they did deliberate. This willingness to participate is demonstrated in that even though no "new business" article was presented to them on the warning, they spent more time discussing issues not on the warning (under "new business") than the nine "warned" articles they would be voting on the next day. They spent almost as much time listening to and questioning their state legislator from Montpelier (who spoke at the end of the meeting) as they spent on the town's agenda. In fact, half of the participations came at the end of the meeting on new business and state legislative matters.

The 1997 meeting in Swanton ranked 1,435 on attendance, 1,285 on participation, 1,370 on women's equality, and 1,072 on time spent in discussion. The combination of these scores placed it dead last on the CBDI. Bear in mind, Swanton scored low on these measures even when all the negative factors that tended to influence them were controlled. For instance, the controlled measure of real democracy gives Swanton slack for its large size and slack for its use of the Australian ballot when it considers its attendance level. The CBDI knows that women attend less at night and takes that into account when it considers Swanton's score on women's involvement. Still, with all extenuating circumstances considered, real democracy didn't get any worse than it was in Swanton's meeting of 1997.

The Best (and Worst) Democracy in the Towns

This book was built on a set of 1,435 town meetings held in 210 different towns. Fifty-five of these towns contributed ten or more meetings to the sample. By aggregating their data, we are able to bring fullness to the democratic portraits of towns we have come to recognize from individual visits to their town meetings between 1970 and 1998. Here we sacrifice precision for perspective, science for artistry. We leave the certitude of moments in time and seek to add to what we know about real democracy from the loftier perspective of a town's experience over several decades.

Newark, Vermont, has remained a small town using a traditional town meeting over the life of my project, and Shelburne has remained a large town holding its meeting at night and using the Australian ballot for elections. For each of the meetings we studied between 1970 and 1998, a town's meeting type and its community life characteristics were matched to the time and place of the meeting. Thus it is no surprise that the factors discovered to be associated with levels of real democracy based on fifty-five town-level aggregations of this data are roughly equivalent to those generated by the 1,435 individual meetings in the sample.[14] We need not visit them again.

But we can take a brief town's-eye view of the combined components of real democracy in the aggregate. In short, after collapsing the dependent variables of attendance, participation, women's involvement, and time the meeting lasted into a more holistic index of real democracy, we now collapse all the contextual (meeting-based and town-based) independent variables we have used throughout this book into the towns they came from. Which towns

14. Parallel analyses based on the town-level aggregates were conducted for each of the variable sets in the central chapters of the book. For results, see www.uvm.edu/~fbryan.

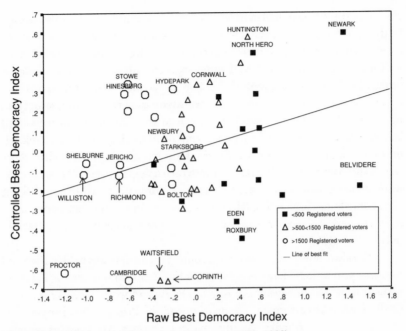

Figure 11.1. The best real democracies (55 towns, 1970–1998).

(as towns) were the best real democracies (all four components of real democracy considered) over the twenty-eight-year life of the study, and which ones were not? Which towns, while not the best democracies in fact, tried the hardest to be better than their circumstances predicted, and which ones did not? Answers to these questions will test our sense of the foregoing description and analysis of real democracy.

I arranged these fifty-five towns in a scatterplot in which the horizontal axis shows each town's score on the raw best democracy index and the vertical axis shows each town's score on the controlled best democracy index. These towns are also marked by their size. The regression line indicates that a town's score on the CBDI improves somewhat as its original RBDI improves. This is to be expected, since far from all of the reasons a town did better or worse on the RBDI were explained by the variables controlled in the CBDI. Having a higher RBDI produces a residual benefit in the CBDI. Towns falling below the regression line did relatively worse when variables associated with the ups and downs of real democracy were controlled with the CBDI, and towns falling above the line did relatively better. (See fig. 11.1.)

We know that the very best town meeting on the RBDI was held in Belvidere in 1980, see page 257). This meeting was not a fluke. In the other eleven meetings we studied in Belvidere, democracy in the raw was also strong. In the end Belvidere was the best of the fifty-five towns that had at least ten meetings in the sample. When the data for its twelve meetings were averaged for each component of the RBDI and compared with similar averages for the other fifty-four towns, it ranked third on attendance, first on participation, first on women's involvement, and sixteenth on time the meeting lasted (see fig. 11.1). What about Newark, the town in the Kingdom that we visited briefly at the beginning of chapter 3 and again in chapter 10? Its rankings on each component aggregated for the fourteen meetings we studied there were as follows: first on attendance, ninth on participation equality, second on women's involvement, and twenty-seventh on time the meeting lasted. Since time contributed least to the RBDI (10 percent) and attendance contributed most (40 percent), Newark's overall score on raw real democracy was second only to Belvidere's.

We also know that the worst meeting in the sample was held in Richford the same year as Belvidere's best meeting. But Richford was not studied often enough to make averages meaningful. The second worst meeting was held in the conservative former "company town" of Proctor, and Proctor had enough meetings to make the fifty-five-town subset. My students traveled there in ten different years beginning in 1971 and ending in 1998. Proctor's real democracy measures were consistently low, and as a town it scored dead last on the raw best democracy index (see fig. 11.1). It ranked 55 on women's involvement and time the meeting lasted, 52 on participation equality, and 50 on attendance.

Next to the bottom of the RBDI rankings were two upscale bedroom towns in the suburbs of Burlington; Williston and Shelburne. Williston ranked 52 on attendance, 50 on participation equality and women's involvement, and 47 on time the meeting lasted. Shelburne, the town I compared with Newark early in this book, scored dead last on attendance, 49 of 55 towns on participation, 40 on women's involvement, and 53 on time the meeting lasted.

These town performances make sense. The best two towns, Belvidere and Newark, had great advantages. They held their meetings during the day (helpful for women's involvement and for time the meeting lasts), they did not use the Australian ballot (which improves attendance), and they have many more dirt roads to support (also good for attendance). Most important of all, however, they are very small. Small size dramatically boosts the percentage of a town's registered voters in attendance at its town meetings. Small town size also reduces meeting size in absolute numbers, and this increases the likelihood that more people will speak more often. Finally, we know that small-town women are somewhat more involved in town meeting democracy than women in the larger towns.

Proctor, Williston, and Shelburne have none of these advantages. They met at night. They used Australian ballots. They are bigger, much bigger, than Belvidere and Newark. Proctor is nine times as big as Belvidere and six and a half times as big as Newark. Double these ratios for Williston, which is twice as big as Proctor. Shelburne is three times as big as Proctor. Larger size drives attendance down in percentage terms but up in its totality, which in turn depresses participation equality. Proctor, Williston, and Shelburne also share influences that drew less attention from the statistical routines used throughout our meeting-based analysis. The town-based approach shows that the three very lowest towns on the RBDI have half as many miles of road to service per capita (which reduces the reason to attend town meeting) and are close to much larger cities, which may threaten the community "boundedness" that many believe is essential to real democracy practiced well.

The controlled best democracy index can go a long way to level the playing field for towns like Proctor, Williston, and Shelburne, by controlling the negative effects of their larger size, and size defines the biggest chunk (40 percent) of both indexes of good democracy. The CBDI is forgiving to meetings when the towns where they are held are big (for attendance), when attendance is large (for participation), and so forth. On the other hand, it expects more from meetings that are not burdened by these factors. Given these adjustments, how do the best towns on the raw best democracy index— Belvidere and Newark—fare on the controlled best democracy index? How do Proctor and Williston and Shelburne, the worst towns on raw democracy, do on controlled democracy?

Belvidere and Newark, the little towns that did the best when their meetings were considered without controls, went their separate ways under controls. Newark improved its ranking from second to first, and Belvidere plummeted from first to forty-first. On the other end of the scale, Williston and Shelburne improved their positions substantially under controls. On the RBDI they shared fifty-third place. On the CBDI they improved in tandem to share twenty-eighth place. Proctor, on the other hand, hardly budged, moving from fifty-fifth place to fifty-second. Considered from the point of view of both indexes, Proctor's ten town meetings—based on their combined scores for attendance, verbal participation, women's involvement, and time the meeting lasted—produced far and away the worst real democracy scores of the fifty-five towns we studied over nearly thirty years. By the same token, Newark's ten meetings produced far and away the best real democracy scores.

Figure 11.1 cries out for a comparison of Newark and Proctor and demonstrates the value of combining thick and thin analysis. Statistical routines, laden with data and precise computer-produced calculations, did the heavy lifting necessary to test models built for the most part on deductive reasoning. Much was discovered and even more was verified about real democracy in the process—a process that could have been conducted in no other way. But by clearing away the brush and successfully isolating towns like Proctor and Newark on the opposite ends of indexes that rationalize and summarize these data, this "thin" approach has proved even more valuable by setting the direction for thick, on-the-ground research.

Proctor

Proctor is a medium-sized town in southwestern Vermont, only a stone's throw from Rutland, Vermont's second largest city. For a century it was the bailiwick of the most powerful political dynasty in Vermont. In 1880 Redfield Proctor, the first of four Proctors to become governor, formed the Vermont Marble Company, which soon became the largest in the world. This happened the year he completed his first term as governor. Two years later they named the village where he lived after him. Four years after that the state of Vermont added another two thousand acres to the village and incorporated it as a full-fledged town. The Proctor name went with it. After World War II and the coming of the Democrats, the Proctor influence disappeared. The Proctor Marble Company changed hands, and the family faded from public view with the death of Mortimer Proctor, the last Proctor governor.

Proctor has a "company town" legacy, complete with urban-type disputes between union and management. In 1935 the marble workers struck the Proctor Marble Company. What followed was one of Vermont's most bitter and violent labor disputes. Vermont writer and historian Peter S. Jennison says that the Proctor "company's feudal structure was severely shaken" and that the "bitter strike polarized the Rutland area and drew an unusual degree of national attention, partly because labor strife contrasted sharply with Vermont's pastoral image, and because several prominent left wing activists made it a cause."[15] Another "urban" trait, ethnicity, was also involved. Striking workers tended to be Italian and nonstriking workers Swedish. Thus Proctor became in reputation and lore Vermont's "company town," and this

15. Peter S. Jennison, *Roadside History of Vermont* (Missoula, MT: Mountain Press, 1989), 186–188.

image (and the accompanying rhetoric from Left and Right) stuck like glue for decades.

Throughout the period of this study, Proctor tended to vote for Republican candidates more than for Democrats. But many towns (twelve) in the sample of fifty-five were more Republican than Proctor. By my index of political conservatism, Proctor was more conservative than most of the towns. But ten were more conservative than Proctor. Proctor was hostile to Vermont's ERA. Still, nine of the fifty-five towns were more so. Moreover, Proctor is clearly not a wealthy town, and its voters have supported Bernie Sanders at a higher rate than the average town in the sample. Its upscale factor score was below average, and its population is more evenly split than the average town between managers and professionals on the one hand and working-class people on the other. Finally, Proctor's participation at the polls in fall statewide elections also dips below the mean.

Two statistics clearly distinguish Proctor from the other towns on the list of fifty-five with at least ten meetings in the sample: the density and the stability of its population. It has more people per road mile than any but two of the other towns, Shelburne and St. George. This is because Proctor is above the mean on population size and at the same time is the second smallest town geographically, only 4,800 acres. It is also the only town of the fifty-five that on average actually lost population in the twenty-year period that preceded the year when each town meeting we studied in Proctor was held. In short, Proctor seems to be blandly conservative, populated by a bimodal middle class, and tired. Its support for Sanders is in part a residue of its union days. Its moderate support for Republicans is most likely a residue of the Proctor dynasty.

One of the principal reasons Proctor scores so low on real democracy is its failure to involve women equally in town meeting. Bigger than average on population size (which hurts a lot) and lower than average on status (which hurts only a little), it also holds its meetings at night (which hurts more than a little). But the most important reason Proctor does so poorly on real democracy may be its history. Proctor's government was family based and supported by a network of intelligent and public-spirited men. The antithesis was blue-collar, union-based, often ethnic, and socially conservative. The men of the quarries had their own government—the union. Few towns in Vermont possessed such powerful male-dominated institutions, the family business and the union, sucking up energy from the commonweal.[16]

---

16. The last time Proctor made the sample was 1998. On that occasion one student reported in part: "The town meeting in Proctor was discouraging. It took only one hour for the

If you asked Vermont historians to name the most conservative town in Vermont, I suspect most would put Proctor high on the list. I would have. But Proctor's conservatism is subtle, a lingering ambiance of the old company town days mixed with a continuing class dichotomy. I have attended several town meetings there and have been struck by the efficiency with which the meeting is conducted. Proctor seems to be a model for what the traditional community power theorists and reform-minded progressives who influenced so much of the negative literature on small-town governance before 1970 were talking about. If so, there is nothing to do but agree that the reformers had a point—for this kind of town.

Newark

Proctor, if not a "eureka" moment for me as a social scientist, at least elicited a "well, whattaya know!" This was not the case for Newark, the best democracy I have studied over the past thirty years. I chose the 1992 meeting in Newark to lead the attendance chapter of this book not because I knew what was going on there at the time, but because I wanted to introduce a town deep in the Northeast Kingdom that would counterpoint an upscale, professional, suburban Burlington satellite town like Shelburne. You think of Newark as a wild place with a tiny population far from urban influences—a place of deer rifles and snowmobiles, a place poet Bill Jackson says was "passed over as if it were the back end of nowhere."[17] But many towns in the sample conjure up similar visions. What is it about Newark that produced such good real democracy? The honest answer is, I'm not sure.

My best guess is that the answer may be found in the way its newcomers mixed with its natives during and after the 1960s. I have seen similar chemistry appear in bits and pieces here and there all over Vermont in the past thirty years, but seldom with the fullness and clarity it has achieved in Newark. Newark's mix features "flatlanders" (as we call them) who came looking to

---

town and school meetings to do their business. The Pledge of Allegiance began at seven o'clock. . . . After the moderator announced the resignation of Charles Nichols, Jr., the 80-year-old selectman who had been active in Proctor for many years was given a round of applause for his contributions to the town. Ironically, he responded by putting down the community for its lack of political interest. His spirited speech was the highlight of the evening. . . . The Proctor town meeting was a joke." "Town Meeting in Proctor 1998," Burlington, University of Vermont, March 1998. I have omitted the names of students when some of their remarks might prove controversial.

17. There is no history of Newark, but there is a remarkable collection of historical notations and interviews. See Bill Jackson, *Walk through a Hill Town: Being a Walk through Newark, Vermont; a Northeast Kingdom Hill Town, or, A Poet's Rambling Account of an American Village* (West Burke, VT: Northern Lights Books, 1990).

downscale their lives and "woodchucks" (as they call native Vermonters) who were confident enough in their own status to see the possibilities the new-comers presented.[18]

Several commonalities are at work. The first is the willingness of the newcomers to take Vermont (and more especially the Kingdom) on its merits—to live in common with the land and the people they found there. But taking the Kingdom on its merits requires cooperation, for the mix of cultures (in a very small pot) was bound to spark conflict—snowmobiles versus cross-country skis comes to mind. This need to cooperate was the second commonality. The third was an appreciation for craft, technology, and education. Many newcomers to Vermont (especially in the 1970s) were influenced by the national energy crisis and the inflation accompanying it during that period. They came committed to human-scale technology applied so as to further sustainable living—brainy living in a tough spot. This fit well with the sensibilities of native Vermonters. Working smart has always been a necessity in rural places like Vermont, where the economy is thin. This kind of new-comer understands why the sound of a chain saw starting on the first pull is as sweet as the chirp of April's first robin.[19] Lots of small Vermont towns have lots of people with these sensibilities. From my wanderings about Newark and conversations with people from Newark, I got the sense that they had more than their share.

For the "Newark" kind of flatlander, town meeting was ideology. For the locals it was habit. In Proctor neither habit nor ideology supported town meeting democracy. In Newark a fundamental clash of cultures produced an abundance of public conflict, and town meeting was the only game in town. In Proctor the company and the union gobbled up public conflict and weakened the town meeting tradition. In any event, those who know Vermont best would agree that it would be difficult to find two towns in the state as dissimilar as Proctor and Newark.

---

18. A retired Newark farmer told Bill Jackson: "They were lined up years ago to get out of here, go to the cities: now they're coming back. Good. Let 'em I say.... I'm land poor." Jackson, *Walk through a Hill Town*, 62.

19. Throughout this period Newark was a much more Democratic and liberal town than Proctor. Newark ranked 26 among the 55 towns on the Democratic base vote, while Proctor ranked 42. Newark ranked 23 on liberalism while Proctor ranked 44. Still, Newark was close to the mean of the sample on both indicators. But Newark's support for Bernie Sanders was very low (47 on the list of 55 towns). This dissonance between Sanders and liberalism, which reflects his old-style, lunch-pail socialism, is found in many Vermont towns. For Proctor, where union/management conflict was once a way of life, the rank for Sanders was twenty slots *higher* than it was for the liberalism factor score. For Newark, the rank for Sanders was twenty-four slots *lower* than it was for the liberalism factor score.

These differences matter. In Newark on average 43 percent of the registered voters went to town meeting. In Proctor 11 percent did. In Newark on average 53 percent of those in attendance spoke out at least once, and the Gini index of participation was 28. In Proctor 22 percent spoke, and the Gini index was 15. Forty-six percent of the attenders in Newark were women. Forty percent of the attenders in Proctor were women. In Newark the ratio of women in attendance who spoke out at least once to men who did was 1.16 to 1 in favor of women. In Proctor the same ratio dropped to 0.39 to 1. Finally, the citizens of Newark practiced their democracy for an average of three hours and forty-two minutes each meeting, and the citizens of Proctor practiced theirs for one hour and thirty-eight minutes.

Importantly, when we make excuses for Proctor by controlling those variables we know may cause these low numbers, the town's relative scores on real democracy hardly budge. Meanwhile, towns like Williston and Shelburne, which also scored very low on real democracy indicators, improved their positions dramatically under controls. On the other hand, when we penalize Newark for possessing the variables that generally predict high real democracy scores, Newark maintains its lofty position while other towns with high numbers like Belvidere and Panton tumble considerably.[20]

Other Patterns in the Towns

Figure 11.1 provokes other notations that suggest at least three potential adjustments to my work in this book. The first recommends more analysis of suburbanization. The cluster of Burlington satellite towns—Shelburne, Williston, Jericho, and Richmond—that appear in the center left of the scatterplot shared very low and perfectly adjacent (54 to 51) rankings among the fifty-five towns on the raw real democracy measure, and they improved these rankings almost in unison (36 to 29) under controls. Both Williston and Shelburne are so closely attached to Burlington that the main highways south and east out of Burlington are commonly known as "Williston Road" and "Shelburne Road." Jericho and Richmond are "farther out" from Burlington and more "rural" in character.

---

20. It is tempting to make something of the differences between hills and valleys. In my last visit to Newark I was again struck (perhaps more so because the leaves were off the trees) by the expanse of sky visible from so many places in town, which can't be seen in Belvidere's valley. Newark stretches over a wide ridge, and there is a sense of freedom and loneliness about it reminiscent of the big skies of Montana. But if there is a causation in this observation it escapes me.

The scatterplot (fig. 11.1) also indicates that my failure to develop a measure of community cohesiveness (gauging centripetal community forces) to combine with my measure of community "boundedness" (which gauged centrifugal community forces) may be an important omission.[21] Cambridge, Waitsfield, and Corinth were the three worst towns (ranking 55 to 53) on the controlled best democracy index, and they ranked only 47, 40, and 38, respectively, on the raw best democracy index. You could make a case that each suffers a lack of internal cohesiveness. Cambridge is the best example, because the town includes the incorporated village of Jeffersonville, with Smuggler's Notch ski area and all its attendant economic influences. Cambridge is one of Vermont's largest town's geographically, containing several "places" (other than Jeffersonville) such as the town center itself, North Cambridge, and Cambridge Junction. The towns of Corinth and Waitsfield also have unique characteristics that may impede community cohesion.

Finally, figure 11.1 demonstrates that not paying more attention to issues and conflict may have been a mistake. Many of the towns that improve their positions the most under controls are towns that have dealt with a series of contentious issues over the years. Towns like Stowe, Hyde Park, Huntington, and Newark lead the list, but you could make the case for Cornwall and North Hero as well. In comparing town meetings in my town of Starksboro with those in our neighboring town of Huntington, for instance, the major explanation I see for Huntington's better performance (other than its greater geographical unity) is the highly contentious issues that have struck the town over the years. Stowe has the advantage of clear boundedness, but it also has had to resolve far more than its share of local conflicts. In Vermont both Huntington and Stowe are known for the political conflicts they have had to deal with.

With town size and other variables controlled for each of the four components of real democracy, with these components summarized for each meeting, and with each meeting then averaged for each town in the scatterplot, the variance in democratic performance from town to town is profoundly reduced. Still, the caveats that emerge are important, and they bring us full circle.

This book attempts to create the baseline record I wish we had for the demes of ancient Greece—to describe what real democracy in the New

21. I began to develop such an indicator in 1992 but found it very difficult and immensely time consuming (even though it is fun for a Vermont buff like me). Now that I have a better idea of which towns to concentrate on and can narrow the project from about two hundred towns to about seventy, I'll begin the process anew.

England town meeting looks like and how it works in the context of community. The "thin" data the bulk of this effort was based on now bid us to refocus the microscope, to draw our sights downward and inward, to peer still deeper into the thicker, richer inner life of real democracy—to go home to the towns. Figure 11.1 provides a rough map for such a journey.

We do not learn to read or write, ride or swim, by merely being told how to do it, but by doing it, so it is only by practicing popular government on a limited scale that the people will ever learn how to exercise it on a larger scale.

Carole Pateman

12

Conclusion

A Lovers' Quarrel

The words on Robert Frost's gravestone in Bennington, Vermont, read simply: "I had a lover's quarrel with the world." So too, it seems to me, has political science (and indeed, America as well) been haunted by a lovers' quarrel with democracy, the real democracy I have tried to describe in this book. My parting hope is that I have somehow touched the heart with distant memory, a memory beginning in ancient Athens twenty-five hundred years ago, a memory still cherished and preserved for the world in little towns that practice town meeting. I hope I have freshened that memory, sharpened it, and made clearer its romance, the passion of possibility that marked its early moments.

> Let the quarrel begin anew.
> The love is worth it.

This book was designed to describe real democracy in clear-eyed detail. At a minimum I sought to set right our age-old perceptions about real democracy. This alone, I reasoned, might prove useful for those who seek to preserve the representative democracy we have and prescribe new forms of democracy for the future. Beyond this modest goal, I fantasized that trustworthy reporting of real democracy's empirical parameters might in turn tease us into new quarrels about what I believe is our most compelling enterprise—to save the American republic by showing its leaders how to repair its underpinning, a citizenry acquainted with democracy. Such a fantasy requires brief (dangerously brief) answers to three questions. Each answer in turn might trigger a quarrel—a fantasy-fulfilling quarrel. How does town meeting democracy stack up against representative democracy? How does town meeting contribute to civic capability? Are town meetings realistic options for the future?

Quarrel 1: A Paragon of Participatory Democracy?

"Town meetings, it appears, are not exactly paragons of participatory democracy," wrote Robert Dahl (with droll understatement) after reviewing some of my findings published in 1995.[1] He has a point. When I review turnout levels at town meeting in my classes, for instance, dead (almost disbelieving) silence fills the room. The silence often becomes embarrassment (for me and town meeting) when I speak to larger audiences. During my limited appearances at professional meetings, in my colleagues' eyes I see knives being sharpened.

And why not? On average only 20 percent of a town's registered voters attended their yearly town meeting between 1970 and 1998, and only 7 percent of them spoke out. This, mind you, in the very places one would expect real democracy to work the best—small towns with over two hundred years of democratic tradition behind them. If town meetings can do no better than this under optimal conditions, one can only imagine with trepidation what their performance might be elsewhere. Besides, even this record of low town meeting attendance is in decline. Paragon indeed.

A response to Dahl might take several forms. First is concession. If by "paragon" he means the exaggerations that defenders of town meeting democracy are wont to make (and I think this is precisely what he means), then town meeting is indeed a failure. But it is a failure in a way that is essentially meaningless. I have been continually amused at the way critics of town meeting, with perfectly straight faces, take aim and fire away at the nonsense perpetrated by the romantics.[2] In short, without a more realistic definition of "paragon," to take on Dahl would be silly.

Or we might sidestep and suggest that the quality of the experience for those who attend town meeting compensates for the quantity of people who do not attend at all. Does this qualitative gain for the few "make up" for the quantitative loss for the many? Who knows? Worse, to my knowledge

---

1. Robert A. Dahl, *On Democracy* (New Haven: Yale University Press, 1998), 110–111. Frank Bryan, "Direct Democracy and Civic Competence," *Good Society* 5 (Fall 1995): 36–44.

2. Dahl is aware of this syndrome as it applies to classical Greek democracy: "It would scarcely be necessary [to point out that Greek democracy was not all it was cracked up to be] if it were not for the influence of the view of some classical historians that in his unswerving devotion to the public good the Athenian citizen set a standard for all time." Robert A. Dahl, *Democracy and Its Critics* (New Haven: Yale University Press 1989), 20.

no empirical work demonstrates that town-meeting-like participation is far better for the individual than voting in private, although my experience urges me to assert vigorously that it is. But you do not confront Robert Dahl with assertions.

Third, we can find excuses. Commuter-based lifestyles and other demographic and institutional dislocations have raised havoc with Vermont's town-based society,[3] much as they have throughout the rest of America. Vermont has experienced in full measure the negative forces for civic engagement so eloquently cataloged by Robert D. Putnam.[4] Also, attendance at town meeting would be significantly higher without the dramatic increases in town populations that the townspeople had no control over. Such excuses are important. They do not suffice.

The best way to deal with Dahl's observation is to reset our expectations,[5] and the best way to do that is to emphasize the costs of town meeting participation in the context of benchmark data on representative democracy's quintessential act of participation—voting. For the costs of town meeting are more severe—dramatically more severe—than the costs of voting,[6] and political scientists tout costs as one of the most important explanations for low participation. The cost hypothesis has roots in ancient Greece. Some classical scholars claim that without slave labor to free up time for citizenship, the Greeks could not have conducted real democracy in Athens. The modern

3. My favorite example of the erosion of town government is the decision by the business manager of Vermont's Department of Fish and Wildlife to discourage town clerks from selling fishing and hunting licenses. "Generations of young Vermonters who trooped into town clerk's offices to buy their first fishing and hunting licenses may be losing that tradition as the state takes a more profit-oriented approach to licensing." Monica Allen, "Town Clerks Discouraged from Selling Licenses," *Burlington Free Press*, January 31, 1988, 5. My first formal encounter with town government was when I was twelve years old and purchased my first hunting license from "Lil" Knight, Newbury's town clerk. I still mark the moment, that very moment, of walking home from the town clerk's office with my first hunting license as a wonderful and defining transition in my life. I was now a licensed hunter. Government, my government, was intimately involved with this passage from youth to adulthood, from private to public life. If I've got her right, Nancy Rosenblum might even call this my own personal "Hegelian moment." Nancy L. Rosenblum, *Membership and Morals: The Personal Uses of Pluralism in America* (Princeton: Princeton University Press, 1998), 25–29.

4. Robert D. Putnam, *Bowling Alone: The Collapse and Revival of American Community* (New York: Simon and Schuster, 2000).

5. Indeed, this was the advice given by the authors of *The Rebirth of Urban Democracy*, which contains more findings per page on the potential for face-to-face politics than any other book since Mansbridge's *Beyond Adversary Democracy*. Jane Mansbridge, *Beyond Adversary Democracy* (New York: Basic Books, 1980). See Jeffrey M. Berry, Kent E. Portney, and Ken Thomson, *The Rebirth of Urban Democracy*, (Washington, DC: Brookings Institution, 1993), 292.

6. John H. Aldrich, "Rational Choice and Turnout," *American Journal of Political Science* 37 (February 1993): 246–278. Aldrich says the low cost (and low benefit) of voting precludes its being considered a collective action problem.

"voter fatigue" explanation has been carefully demonstrated by Richard Boyd and others.[7] It helped persuade the president of the American Political Science Association to (in an eerie "Vietnam village" type of metaphor) call for saving voter turnout by limiting the number of elections and the number of officers elected at each.[8]

It takes close to three and a half hours to attend an average town meeting, not including a lunch break. If it is not held at night (and three-quarters of them are not), this means that attendance costs a day's pay or a vacation day (which is the same thing) for citizens with jobs.[9] When held at night, town meeting consumes the whole evening. For those with young children, it may mean the expense (and hassle) of getting a babysitter. Also, nearly all night meetings require citizens to go to the polls the next day to vote for local town officers. Town meeting "uses up" a day or an evening. It is almost impossible to fit it in with other activities.[10]

Compare the 20 percent turnout at town meeting with the turnout for the presidential election in America. After all the hoopla is over, all the money is spent, the last campaign ad is aired, the last interest group's mobilization team has gone home, the last political party's "get out the vote" apparatus closes down, and the last national news network airs its last prognostication, America has difficulty drawing even 50 percent of its eligible citizens to the polls once every four years to elect its president—a person who can do more harm or good in an single day than Genghis Khan or Mother Teresa in a hundred lifetimes.

During this same election Americans also elect members of the House of Representatives, one-third of the senators, governors of several states, state legislators, and countless other local officers. Would voter turnout in presidential years even reach town meeting's 20 percent level if presidential

7. Richard W. Boyd, "Decline in U.S. Voter Turnout: Structural Explanations," *American Politics Quarterly* 9 (April 1981): 133–159; Richard W. Boyd, "The Effects of Primaries and Statewide Races on Voter Turnout," *Journal of Politics* 51 (August 1989): 730–739. Robert W. Jackman and Ross A. Miller, "Voter Turnout in the Industrial Democracies during the 1980's," *Comparative Political Studies* 27 (January 1995): 467–492.

8. Arend Lijphart, "Unequal Participation: Democracy's Unresolved Dilemma," *American Political Science Review* 91 (March 1997): 1–14.

9. As early as 1962 Robert S. Babcock, a former professor of political science at the University of Vermont, wrote that "turnout (at town meeting) has fallen off considerably in recent years, for the very real economic reason that many wage earners cannot afford to take the day off for the business of the community." Robert S. Babcock, *State and Local Government and Politics* (New York: Random House, 1962), 96.

10. As Anne Phillips reminds us, there is a high cost associated with political meetings: "From Oscar Wilde through to Michael Walzer, people have recurrently worried that activism involves too many meetings." Anne Phillips, *Democracy and Difference* (University Park: Pennsylvania State University Press, 1993), 111.

elections occurred alone, were held every year, used up a full day in a citizen's life, and cost three-quarters of the voters the equivalent of one-fifth their weekly salary?

Finally, town meeting attendance looks better still when compared with local elections. At this level town meeting attendance figures begin to stand on their own even though the costs of voting in local elections (even more than in national elections) pale beside the costs of attending a town meeting. Voter turnout in local elections held alone seldom reaches 25 percent and often dips into the single digits.[11] Remember too that throughout this period variables positively associated with voter turnout like education levels and access to the polls have been improving while positive variables associated with town meeting attendance like small town sizes and town decision-making authority have been in decline.

Moreover, the "costs" side of the equation involves much more than time and money. Town meetings are mostly work. The romantics cast them in the rosy glow of "neighbor meeting neighbor," and there is plenty of that. But town meeting is not, as some suggest, primarily a social event. The chairs are hard, the hours can drag on.[12] Humor is nearly always present, but only in bits and pieces. Plus, one has to pay attention—keep up with the warning articles, understand what the vote means. People don't always speak clearly, the person sitting next to you is fidgety, a baby is crying in the back, the bathroom is sometimes (how shall I say it?) "problematical" or, as in Strafford, Vermont (see page 23), across the street in someone's house.

Because the towns are so small, huge per capita public responsibility costs inflate the costs of town meeting. The average town elects over a dozen officers and appoints at least a dozen more. Planning boards (and meetings), zoning boards (and meetings), and library boards (and meetings) are examples. The chances are high that any given citizen of a Vermont town could (with perfect justification) say something like "I've done enough for the town this year. I guess they can handle town meeting well enough without me." My old hometown of Newbury has twenty-four officers listed in the town report for 2000, and my current hometown of Starksboro has thirty-two.

Then come the psychic costs. Last town meeting you ended up sitting next to someone who smelled like celery. If you have to listen to another

11. See, for instance, Jacques Steinberg, "Boards and Minds Are Little Changed by School Elections," *New York Times*, June 14, 1996, B2, cited in Lijphart, "Unequal Participation," 8. Turnout in these elections was only 5 percent.

12. My students' essays are full of comments like, "As we left the meeting I was tired and sore. It was a very long day." Scott Denham, "Bakersfield Town Meeting," Colchester, VT, St. Michael's College, 1974.

impassioned plea for property tax relief you'll go nuts. It is always painful to see Jim, and he may be there. The Smiths will want to sit near you, and they are the most boring couple you know. Or you may get steamed when (as you know they will) those new people over on West Hill in their trophy house ask to have the West Hill Road paved. Last year you agonized (found your hands shaking) trying to get up your nerve to speak but failed. Two years earlier it took you ten minutes to calm down after you did get up your nerve to speak but your voice cracked and everyone heard it.

Attendance aside, other kinds of town meeting involvement compare remarkably well with institutions of representative government. At the average town meeting 44 percent of those in attendance speak out. I have yet to find evidence that state legislative assemblies, for instance, seem more like a parliament (a place for speaking) than does a Vermont town meeting. Nor do I have evidence that percentages of citizens speaking out at public hearings equal or surpass those at a town meeting. Finally, I'd wager my colleagues around the country would agree that verbal participation in meetings of equal size they have attended throughout their careers does not equal the levels achieved in town meeting as discussed in chapters 6 and 7.[13]

As for women's participation, the Vermont town meeting has not achieved parity. But where in the representative institutions of American democracy is it better? Where is it even close? Between 1970 and 1998 women constituted an average of 46 percent of those in attendance at town meeting. City councils cannot match this figure. State legislatures fall far behind. The American Congress isn't remotely close. Women at town meeting do not speak out as much as men do. But try as I might, I have not found comparative data suggesting they participate less at town meeting than they do in other venues.

My impressionistic conclusion that town meeting has failed to integrate the deeply disadvantaged into the process must be compared with voting behavior studies that have found the very same thing for the electoral process. Among this cohort of society, the contextual nature of town meeting democracy may make participation even more problematic than we know it is for the simple act of voting. That said, of this I am perfectly sure: step into the average town meeting in Vermont and you will see before you an approximation of the ranges of status groups in the community that is remarkably accurate.

---

13. In this case it is important to remember that we did not count "seconding a motion" as an act of participation, although it clearly is. Seconds were not counted because it was difficult to count them accurately. But they add to the overall participatory level of the meetings.

Finally, two contextual considerations: First, a key finding of this study is that issues matter, especially in the most important component of real democracy—presence at the assembly. More than any other variable (beyond size), issues are the most important explanation for turnout at town meeting. Yet in the second half of the twentieth century Vermont towns have steadily been losing the authority to deal with controversial issues. Unlike many states, Vermont has no home rule provision in its constitution to protect its localities' decision-making authority. In 1974 G. Ross Stephens found that between 1957 and 1971 (about the time this study began) no state's local governments had lost power as swiftly as Vermont's.[14] A few years later Jane Mansbridge referenced several policy areas exempted from town prerogatives, writing: "The diminishing power of the town has inevitably had an effect on town meeting attendance.... The surprise is that the effect of declining town powers on attendance has not been greater."[15]

In the twenty years since Mansbridge published *Beyond Adversary Democracy* this process has continued, as important elements of local discretion have been taken (or given) away. These have been replaced with ever increasing layers of administrative complexity as the state tries to ensure (correctly) that those policies it seeks to control are properly delivered. Meanwhile a burgeoning apparatus of regional nonprofit organizations has sprung up to help the towns deliver services. It is becoming more and more unlikely that important matters that once were the object of a town's commonweal can be framed in ways that allow deliberation and decisions by town meetings.

The second contextual consideration is the heavy democratic infrastructure that exists in Vermont's towns and competes with town meeting for civic capital. As my mother grew old in Newbury, her "local" property taxes went to four incorporated "governments": the village of Newbury (for streetlights, plowing the sidewalks, and providing water—not inconsequential services), the town of Newbury's school district (kindergarten through the sixth grade), the Oxbow Union High School District that Newbury shared with the towns of Bradford and Corinth (two-thirds of her taxes went there), and the town of Newbury itself, which provided all other local government services. Each one of these four entities had a yearly "town meeting." Thus, besides the real town meeting, my mother would have had to attend three other more issue-specific town meetings each year in order to fulfill her role as a citizen-legislator practicing real democracy in the town of Newbury.

14. G. Ross Stephens, "State Centralization and the Erosion of Local Autonomy," *Journal of Politics* 36 (February 1974): 44–76.

15. Mansbridge, *Beyond Adversary Democracy*, 130.

Newbury's citizens who live in Wells River village also pay taxes to their village (Wells River), their town (Newbury), and a couple of school districts. But the school districts are different from those used by citizens of Newbury village. Thus the Newbury town meeting is competing with several other little governments, each a real democracy where citizens set tax rates and make law in face-to-face assemblies. Fewer than 1,500 voters support all this democracy. Although these other meetings are held on different days of the year, they siphon off a considerable share of public concerns held by the town's citizens.

Paragons, it seems to me, are related to possibility. I am not about to suggest that town meetings are "pure" democracy if what we mean by pure is complete participation. Majorities, large majorities, of the citizens of Vermont's towns do not participate regularly in town meetings. But I do claim that, given the burdens under which they operate, town meetings come about as close to paragon status as reasonable people would agree is possible within the limits of human nature. More. All things considered, I claim that the record town meetings have established in Vermont in the past thirty years demonstrates that ordinary citizens are far more willing to expend the energy to practice real democracy in their towns than the ordinary American is to expend the energy to vote in representative democracy at any level in the United States of America.[16]

Quarrel 2: A Gentler Kind of Tutelage?

No description of how town meeting contributes to civic education surpasses that written by Michael J. Sandel:

> Benjamin Rush, a signer of the Declaration of Independence, wanted
> to ... teach each citizen "that he does not belong to himself, but that he is
> public property." But civic education need not take so harsh a form. In
> practice, successful republican soulcraft involves a gentler kind of

---

16. This claim and the following claim by Robert Dahl probably cannot coexist: "The smaller the unit, the greater the opportunity for citizens to participate in the decisions of their government, yet the less of the environment they can control. Thus for most citizens, participation in very large units becomes minimal and in very small units it becomes trivial." Robert Dahl, "The City in the Future of Democracy," *American Political Science Review* 61 (December 1967): 97. To political scientists who are working hard to figure out a way to keep the Republic functioning democratically, I suppose leash laws may seem trivial. To the nice man who likes to jog on Big Hollow Road in Starksboro and was accosted on several occasions by Mr. Jones, my black Lab/Chesapeake Bay retriever, leash laws are far from trivial—as witnessed by the language he used in describing Mr. Jones's behavior.

tutelage. For example, the political economy of citizenship that informed nineteenth-century American life sought to cultivate not only commonality but also the independence and judgment to deliberate well about the common good. It worked not by coercion but by a complex mixture of persuasion and habituation—what Alexis de Tocqueville called "the slow and quiet action of society upon itself."[17]

Town meeting differs from other options considered by social capital theorists in that it is in effect on-the-job training. Nancy Rosenblum casts these other options in two categories. The first group, "congruence" associations, emphasize "rights and due process." These associations fit Michael Walzer's dicta that "only a democratic state can create a democratic civil society" and "only a democratic civil society can sustain a democratic state."[18] I claim that town meetings possess the fundamental characteristics of "congruence" associations.

Rosenblum's second category comprises "mediating" associations. Groups in this category "orient us *away*" (emphasis in the original), says Rosenblum, "from civic and politically inspired" goals and emphasize instead generic values that "inculcate civility, sociability, responsibility and cooperation" along a wide "range of moral dispositions." Mediating associations are not designed to teach specific civic skills related to such liberal notions as due process. Town meeting provides both "congruent" and "mediating" influences.[19]

Town meeting is different from both types of associations because it is not an association at all. It is a branch, the legislative branch, of a general-purpose government. Thus its agenda is eclectic and places a greater premium on both civic skills and generic values associated with common enterprise—values like cooperation, sociability, responsibility, and (most of all) civility. On the other hand, civic associations, either congruent or mediating, by definition possess a certain unity of purpose generally held by people with

17. Michael J. Sandel, "America's Search for a Public Philosophy," *Atlantic Monthly* 277 (March 1996): 57, reprinted from Michael J. Sandel, *Democracy's Discontent: America in Search of a Public Philosophy* (Cambridge: Harvard University Press, 1996).

18. Michael Walzer, "The Idea of a Civil Society," *Dissent* 38 (Spring 1991): 302; cited in Nancy Rosenblum, *Membership and Morals: The Personal Uses of Pluralism in America* (Princeton: Princeton University Press, 1998).

19. Participation at town meeting can take many forms. I have seen hundreds of them. But the following, reported by one of my students, has haunted me for over a quarter of a century: "Lastly, there was an old man (let's call him Gramps) who could barely walk. He just sat on the aisle calmly and patiently throughout the meeting, staring at nothing, tapping his cane. He had made his annual appearance as he had for the last fifty years." Peter Lefeber, "Brighton, 1974," Colchester, St. Michael's College, March, 1974.

similar backgrounds and therefore mute the difficulties related to becoming both real citizens and good citizens.

Town meeting's capacity for tutelage is linked as much to its performance as a liberal institution supported by republican values as to its performance as a republican institution utilizing liberal means. The fundamental purpose of town meeting is to make decisions for the commonweal based on principles of due process and equal protection—but on a human scale. Consequently it establishes and nurtures by necessity the republican principles required to sustain an incessant, year-in, year-out series of face-to-face collective action decisions. What better way to train democratic citizens without intending to? In this lack of intention, town meeting avoids a critical liberal critique of republicanism—the forced adherence to ideals that abhor force.

The teaching of civic skills, specifically *Robert's Rules of Order*, is a fundamental element of (liberal) "congruence" provided by town meeting. How well do people at town meeting know *Robert's Rules*? Not well. Do they get confused with their application? All the time. But the degree to which town meeting orders talk, applies procedure, sticks to its guns on issues of due process, and bends over backward to ensure that minority rights are observed is perhaps the biggest surprise that newcomers to town meeting experience. Many of them are put off by the tedium of it. They come to town meeting expecting communalism, and they get liberalism. They say it with their eyes: "Do we have to go through all this?" The answer is yes. People growing up in the town meeting tradition know how to conduct public meetings.

What about town meeting as a tutor for "mediating values"? The playwright Jonathan Miller once said that in order for a relationship to be humane it must be complicated and dutiful. Complication and duty are products of intimacy, and intimacy is a product of small size, and small size gives birth to the critical human virtue of forbearance. If town meeting teaches anything, it is how to suffer damn fools and to appreciate the fact that from time to time you too may look like a damn fool in the eyes of people as good as yourself. Here I recommend the insight of Russell L. Hanson in his critique of the claim that deliberation has a depressing effect on tolerance. Forbearance, says Hanson, is a more important concept than tolerance. While we cannot exorcise intolerance from the human soul, we can create institutions that ensure forbearance in the face of intolerance.[20]

---

20. Russell L. Hanson, "Deliberation, Tolerance and Democracy," in *Reconsidering the Democratic Public*, ed. George E. Marcus and Russell L. Hanson (University Park: Pennsylvania State University Press, 1993).

Such an institution is town meeting, a place where people of their own volition (Hanson's term) tend not to act on their "intolerant orientations." Attend a town meeting with any consistency, and you cannot help but learn forbearance in the face of others' intolerance toward you and, conversely, your own intolerance toward others. As the ruler of Germany, someone once said, Adolf Hitler was a horror. At a New England town meeting he would have at once been recognized as a flaming jackass and subtly ostracized into impotence. This is the kind of learned "gentler tutelage" that town meeting offers.

Such learning takes time, and exceptions exist. "Black Hat and the Four Evils" of Victory certainly do not fit the model, nor do Jane Mansbridge's farmer Clayton Bedell and the lawyer who threatened to sue him.[21] These exceptions are to be expected. Still, Black Hat was "tolerated." His right to act like a damn fool in the context of public deliberation was preserved intact. Most important, the people of Victory learned from it. Many were ashamed for the town. Liberal critics of republicanism rightly fear for the rights of people like Black Hat and the Four Evils, but the town meeting experience tells us that this fear may better be directed at institutions of systems scale, where distance from personal contact may make intolerance less visible, easier, and thus profoundly more dangerous.

What evidence do we have that this kind of town meeting tutelage works?[22] The data show no significant association at the town level between turnout at town meeting and turnout at biennial state and national elections. But a strong association does exist in the aggregate between town meeting culture at the local level and an advanced civic culture at the state level. In *Bowling Alone*, Robert D. Putnam scores Vermont first among the fifty states on his tolerance index (gender/racial and civil liberties) and third on his

21. Mansbridge, *Beyond Adversary Democracy*, 59–65. Mansbridge's description of the farmer put down by a lawyer at town meeting was so real that it still makes me cringe when I think about it. This certainly did not seem like "gentle" tutelage. Yet in the fullness of time these occurrences are in my view an unavoidable (perhaps even a necessary) part of a fundamentally gentle process. Visible intolerance may be harder on the senses, but I judge it is far less egregious in quality and quantity than invisible intolerance. Meanwhile, clear and intentional acts of human kindness are continually displayed at town meeting at a measure dramatically exceeding acts of intolerance.

22. In an important return to Tocqueville's empirical roots in the American township, Robert T. Gannett Jr. claims it was the township's political and institutional life (not simply Americans' habit of associational participation) that spawned the "participatory vector" that was then "disseminated" (along with the "bracing vitality" of the township itself) to "civil society as a whole." Robert T. Gannett Jr., "Bowling Ninepins in Tocqueville's Township," *American Political Science Review* 97 (February 2003): 1. This is the dynamic I have seen at work throughout my lifetime in Vermont.

social capital index, below only North and South Dakota.[23] Tom W. Rice and Alexander F. Sumberg rank Vermont first on their measure of civic culture.[24]

Moreover, by the Rice-Sumberg measure Vermont is by far the strongest American state on civil society. This score is 1.52 (these are Z-scores that begin at −1.53), while the next closest state (Massachusetts) scores only 1.05. This forty-seven-point gap is far and away the largest between any two states on the scale. Finally, three of the six New England states (the only place in America where town meeting is practiced) finish in the top five states, and five of the six New England states finish in the top ten states on civil society. These findings establish no clinical causality between the tutelage of town meeting and civil society. Nor can I.[25] But the circumstantial evidence is overwhelming.[26]

While no state has stronger real democracy than Vermont, few if any have stronger representative democracy. Vermonters are voters. Historically they have participated more fully in their representative democracy at the state level than the great majority of Americans in other states.[27] Most important, Vermont's electoral participation in presidential politics has traditionally been far better than that of most American states. Vermont's elections in off years follow suit. Vermont is one of only two states to insist on electing its governor and other statewide officers every two years. Our state ballot is a long one, including a lieutenant governor, secretary of state, auditor of accounts,

23. Putnam, *Bowling Alone*, 298.

24. Tom W. Rice and Alexander F. Sumberg, "Civic Culture and Government Performance in the American States," *Publius: The Journal of Federalism* 27 (Winter 1977): 114.

25. To specify the direction of the relation between civil society and town meeting is difficult. Moreover, several American states with no hint of a town meeting tradition score higher than the New England states on social capital. Putnam, *Bowling Alone*, 298. Still, Vermont's system of what Hannah Arendt called "elementary republics" is in my view a near perfect replica of democratic institutions that "radiate" (Vaclav Havel's term) on their surroundings "by the force of their example, by the embarrassment felt by those who failed to act, by the indirect moral pressure exerted on the regime." This has been as true for the town's historical influence on Vermont's centralized government in Montpelier as it is beginning to be for Vermont's growing radiant impulses on the American nation—from pathbreaking environmental legislation in the late 1960s to the nuclear freeze referenda in the early 1980s to civil unions for gays and lesbians as the century closed. See Jeffrey C. Isaac, "Oases in the Desert: Hannah Arendt on Democratic Politics," *American Political Science Review* 88 (March 1994): 156–168.

26. In her comparison of a Michigan city council town and a Vermont town meeting town (matched on size and socioeconomic variables) Vivian Scott Hixson found that citizens of the Vermont town possessed dramatic advantages over citizens of the Michigan town in the kinds of civic capacities and skills that typically find their way into social capital indexes. Vivian Scott Hixson, "The New Town Meeting Democracy: A Study of Matched Towns" (Ph.D. diss., Michigan State University, 1974).

27. In recent years Vermont's position in the national rankings on these measures has slipped.

attorney general, and treasurer. No state save New Hampshire elects more state legislators per capita than Vermont.

Beyond its record in electoral arenas, Vermont's history has continually reflected liberal principles. From the very beginning, when the towns met in convention and established a new North American republic based on the first American constitution to outlaw slavery and offer the rights of freemen to those who were not property holders, to its outcry against secrecy (Vermont was the strongest anti-Mason state in America), to its nearly fanatical involvement in the Civil War (Lincoln fought the war more to save the Union than to free the slaves; Vermont did the opposite), to its leading role in the fight against McCarthyism, Vermont has demonstrated the politics of a liberal government comprising republican parts.[28]

The Vermont legislature that so overwhelmingly rejected McCarthyism in the 1950s was elected one member from each town, no matter its size, and was in every sense a statewide assembly of town officers and town meeting goers.[29] The state that elected the first female lieutenant governor (and the second female speaker of a house of representatives), that established the first school of higher education for women, that produced the first woman to argue a case before the Supreme Court, that elected the first African American to its state legislature, that graduated the first African American from college, that passed the first absentee voting law, that first adopted one of the most progressive state campaign finance reform laws in the nation, and that first bestowed the rights and privileges of marriage on gay and lesbian couples is more firmly rooted in town meeting politics than any state in the Union.

Vermont is a state that abhors negative campaigning, whose drivers are so polite that some say they cause traffic accidents, where the communal ethic worked out in its localities under the auspices of liberal codes of political process has produced a representative democracy that, while never perfect and sometimes blemished, seems to have become an object of national envy. Writing on the defection of Senator Jim Jeffords from the Republican Party in the spring of 2001, Jon Margolis said it about as well as it can be said. Jeffords's action, says Margolis, should be seen not as a measure of how much the typical Vermonter cherishes *autonomy* (emphasis mine) but rather "as evidence of the persistence of an old tradition and of how much Jeffords and Vermont

28. For an extended essay on the historical origins of town meeting in Vermont and its role in the development of Vermont's political culture, see www.uvm.edu/~fbryan.

29. In 1953 someone introduced a bill in the Vermont House of Representatives that would establish a board to review books used in the public schools to make sure they were free of subversive, pro-communist content. The bill was killed 202 to 11. It was a Vermont senator, Ralph Flanders, who led the fight against McCarthyism in Congress.

still depend on it, [an] attitude that cherishes restraint, civility, tolerance, and compromise." In New England, says Margolis, one finds an "implicit acknowledgment that one *might be wrong*" (emphasis mine).[30] No other place better teaches the virtue of humility—or its corollary, forbearance—than a New England town meeting. Of this I am sure.[31]

Quarrel 3: A Future for Town Meeting?

I am not altogether certain town meeting will survive the coming half-century even in Vermont, to say nothing of having a renewed future elsewhere in America. Still, my reasoning leads me beyond hope to possibility and even (on a good day) expectation. All are grounded in several axioms. (1) Real democracy must be limited to extremely small units. Stretching it over larger wholes is fatal. (2) To work well, town meetings must serve general-purpose governments that have complete authority (from taxation to assessing re-sults) over some areas of governance. (3) Town meeting—like control over all or even most of the services Americans expect from government is neither practical nor desirable. (4) Real democracies must be free to make mistakes. (5) Consequently, hard thinking about the division of powers is mandatory. (6) Deconcentrated government must not mean less government. It must mean better government more equally distributed. (7) The conservative/ liberal dichotomy and the partisan split on the decentralism issue are dead. They are what Robert Putnam calls "false debates."[32]

In *The Vermont Papers: Recreating Democracy on a Human Scale* (if one scrapes away our lapses into utopian rhapsody) John McClaughry and I suggested how such axioms might frame a plan for sustained town meet-ing democracy in postmodern societies.[33] To believe this is possible, you must accept two propositions. First, Vermont is (despite its bucolic image) more a "postmodern" society than the great majority of American states. Second, the postmodern world will become as decentralist in character as the urban-industrial world was centralist. The first proposition is defended

---

30. Jon Margolis, "As Vermont Goes, So Goes...Vermont," *U.S. News and World Report*, June 4, 2001, 21.

31. Of course, I could be wrong.

32. Putnam, *Bowling Alone*, 413. When Democratic senator Joseph Lieberman and Republican president George W. Bush agree that national educational standards should be placed on local schools and that schools not meeting these standards should be closed down, it is time to redraw the battle lines or (better) forget about them.

33. Frank Bryan and John McClaughry, *The Vermont Papers: Recreating Democracy on a Human Scale* (Chelsea, VT: Chelsea Green Press, 1989).

in *The Vermont Papers* and in the extended essay on Vermont available on the Web site.[34]

The intellectual infrastructure for the second dynamic, while clearly not prevailing, is nevertheless ascendant.[35] I see the argument as follows: Under an information age umbrella of centralized structural cooperation (the European Union being a model to watch), new decentralist opportunities (the Committee for the Regions within the European Union is an example) are being framed. With nationalist loyalties on the wane,[36] new smaller unions (often bioregional) are emerging. The work of nation-states will shift toward their roles as part of larger, transnational structures, and their attention will be siphoned away from the micromanagement of their own societies. In this vacuum lies the future of democracy.

This is the model suggested by Dahl and Tufte in 1973. Giant transnational organizations will necessitate "very small units" to "provide a place where ordinary people can acquire ... the reality of moral responsibility and political effectiveness."[37] Daniel Bell has added to this thesis by suggesting that domestic politics will gravitate toward the states and localities on domestic issues and outward toward transnational organizations on economic, diplomatic, and military issues. Evidence of this is already apparent in the United States Congress, says Alan Ehrenhalt. Congress's contemporary malaise can be explained as the beginnings of a search for ways to understand its role in operating within a new transnational framework that features both localism and globalism.[38]

About the time Dahl and Tufte published *Size and Democracy*, Robert J. Pranger published a prescient essay in *Publius: The Journal of Federalism* titled "The Decline of the American National Government." "The redemptive nature of broad national politics," he warned, "has been replaced by localism writ large." Because of this America is failing at its most fundamental

---

34. Www.uvm.edu/~fbryan.

35. For starters I suggest the symposium Alexandra Kogl, ed., "The Politics of Place in a Globalizing Era," *Good Society* 10, 2 (2001): 4–35.

36. As an extreme example I cite America's hostility to the metric system. Every time I have to go to the toolbox to substitute a 13-mm wrench for a 5/8-inch wrench I curse nationalism and capitalism. My instincts tell me the human race is unwilling—in the long run—to put up with inefficiencies like this. Let a global state secure human rights, prevent nuclear holocaust, and make up its mind on wrenches. My bet is that localities will flourish under such a system, especially if information continues to be democratized as it has been in the United States over the past several decades.

37. Robert A. Dahl and Edward Tufte, *Size and Democracy* (Stanford: Stanford University Press, 1973), 140.

38. Alan Ehrenhalt, "Demanding the Right Size Government," *New York Times*, October 4, 1999, 27.

task—being a nation that provides "a base for the broad general will" and a "system of national unity" that couples "liberty and safety."[39]

John McClaughry and I used this platform in 1989 to call for strengthening the federal government to do those things a nation must do. We said the loss of civic attachment to the center was caused by Americans' "lost faith in the things they have always expected from the nation: security and a sense of wholeness with the fundamentals of public life. They miss the sense of national well-being." Public work abounds for everyone, we claimed, and if the federal government insists on performing a wide range of tasks better done locally, "it will fail at its most important task, the maintenance of the context for a democratic civil order. And in heart and mind Americans will continue to drift away from the center."[40]

The future of town meeting resides in this charge: Let the Republic be a nation and lead us securely into a world of increasing political cooperation. In the meantime let the nation's people begin the process of learning to take care of themselves and each other once again—but now in their communities assembled under a new national framework that ensures in broad context the fundamentals of the post-Roosevelt agreement.[41] This is no call for a radical decentralism; rather, it asks for a careful reassessment of possibilities unbridled by the demons of doubt and fear. Let the following be heard more often: "This government is too big." And let us hear less often that "this government is too small." Hillary Clinton was right. In so many ways it does indeed take a village.

Real democracy requires, first, governments small enough to give a significant number of citizens a significant chance to make a significant difference on a significant number of issues. Second, real democracy requires larger governments that trust their citizens enough to let them make mistakes on matters of importance. Not all important matters. Not most important matters, but some important matters.[42] Decentralism and empowerment; put

39. Robert J. Pranger, "The Decline of the American National Government," *Publius: The Journal of Federalism* 3 (Fall 1973): 11–28. The events following September 11, 2001, and the formation of a new Department of Homeland Security are clearly within the purview cast by Pranger.

40. Bryan and McClaughry, *Vermont Papers.*

41. As Tocqueville put it, "What I want is a central government energetic in its own sphere of action." Quoted in Gannett, "Bowling Ninepins in Tocqueville's Township."

42. Tocqueville noted this critical element of democratic possibility when he said of the New England town, "Its sphere is limited, indeed; but *within this sphere, its action is unrestrained* [emphasis my own]. This independence alone gives it real importance, which its extent and population would not insure." For a model for such a distribution of powers with specific examples see Bryan and McClaughry, *Vermont Papers,* chapter 11 ("Education on a Human Scale") and chapter 12 ("The Compassionate Community").

these two requirements together and citizens will participate in governance to a degree that will dramatically transcend expectations. Real democracy not only will live, it will flourish. Take either away and it will die.

My claim is simply that history is moving slowly toward a time when the first requirement (smaller communities) will be satisfied, when we will come to understand that the term "global village" was a silly oxymoron born of our exuberance over third-generation (but still embryonic) computer technology. This leaves the second requirement—creative localism and empowerment. This one is up to us. Will we consider it? Will we plan for it? Or will we continue to so distrust our neighbors that we are unwilling to cast our lot with them in hopeful common enterprise?[43] Will we condemn ourselves to unyielding conservatism (cowering under the paradigms of past generations), or will we develop the intellectual infrastructure to help our leaders refit America with a new commonwealth—democratic in its parts, the heartland, and liberal at the center, its nationhood—a commonwealth in which real democracy therefore is an important component?

WITNESS

The culture shock I felt when we moved from outside Boston to West Windsor, Vermont (at age 10) was non-existent when I returned to town for the 1982 town meeting. I was thrilled to receive the special attention of my teacher who had taught me in grades 5 and 6. It had been quite easy to learn the names of all eleven of my classmates!

On the first Tuesday of March our principal would lead us down to the Story Memorial Hall, where we would sit up in the balcony and distract our parents, who were engaged in something we didn't understand.

Now, when I sit up in the balcony and look down on the people in my town I realize the faces really haven't changed much since I sat there seven years ago. A few new outsiders stand to speak, voice their opinions, and sit down. Someone in the back whispers to his friend, "Who's that?" and is informed, "He lives up on the Brook Road near the Ely place." Mr. Denyon, a life-long resident of the town, asks thirty questions ranging from the new grader to the mini-computer for the grade school. Selectman Ed Cyr answers each question patiently. The town speeds through the big money items and spends half an hour trying to decide whether to buy a smoke or heat detector for the school. It decides it definitely needs something to protect "our kids."

Perhaps the most important question raised was nuclear disarmament. Rev. Gottenburg, a retired Lutheran minister, began passing out literature

43. In his inspiring final chapter of *Bowling Alone*, Robert Putnam calls for "decentralism of government resources and authority" downward. As I awaited the publication of his book I anticipated (with pleasure) that he would use the term government "resources." But I prayed he would use the term government "authority."

during the town meeting. He spent his entire lunch hour asking for support of the question. The nuclear question was the last to be discussed, and after ten minutes it was passed unanimously.

The Rev. felt so moved by this that he stood up and began singing "God Bless America." The entire floor stood up and sang along. At first I thought that the act was silly and senseless, something I could not and would not take part in.

Reflecting on that past moment, I can honestly say that I am disappointed in myself for not joining in and professing my love for my country. Our society has become apathetic in dealing with government duties. We rarely vote, and when we do we don't know the candidate or what he stands for.

Vicki Johnson[44]

A Final Word

Liberalism has achieved its greatest enterprise. It has created the world's best continental (and therefore necessarily) representative democracy. Madison's classic admonition that we should organize ourselves against one another has worked out well enough. Liberalism was correct for the Republic.

It still is. But in our own times liberalism seems to run amok. The imperialism of liberalism inward, downward into the national heart is infesting the very soul liberalism depends on—a citizenry that knows self-government. Interest groups can give us participation. Elections can give us the vote. Involvement in governance is what is needed. The heart of democracy is found in our localities: our towns, counties, parishes, and boroughs.

It is liberalism by which the nation lives. It is communitarianism by which it dreams. And as life without dreams is unsustainable, so too is liberalism. Because living a dream is impossible, let the nation be liberal. But let the nation set free the times and places where living and dreaming are joined, where communitarian impulses and liberal requirements are mixed, where real democracy is learned and practiced and developed. We have always known that the nation's parts could not survive without the nation's whole. The time has come to understand that the reverse is equally so.

I have watched real democracy in all its goods and ills for nearly half a century, and this I know to be true: if given a chance, the people can govern themselves. I've seen them do it.

Moreover, I believe they must do so again—and soon. For there is a second requirement for controlling the passions of self-interest beyond

44. Vicki Johnson, "1982 West Windsor Town Meeting," Burlington, University of Vermont, March 1982.

Madison's cure of setting ourselves one against the other. In its absence the center will continue to fester, and our most cherished enterprise, our national, representative democracy—our glorious Republic—will continue to slip into atrophy and decline.

This requirement is to come together again. We are required to ensure that we see, that we feel, up close and face to face, what happens to each other when we do each other harm. We are required to allow ourselves no escape from our common humanity. We are required to mark together the renderings of our collective actions—the joy and satisfaction that come when we find the common good, the pain in each other's eyes when we ignore, as we will often do, what Lincoln called "the better angels of our natures."

To recreate the conditions for such a governance, limited in its breadth but sovereign in its depth, will be no easy task. But there are Madisons and Jeffersons among us. It is our calling as political scientists, is it not, to find them and inform their judgment? This is the calling Jane Mansbridge referred to in her classic *Beyond Adversary Democracy*. We should proceed, she said, past the democracy of balanced self-interest toward a balance of self-interest and common interest: not without liberalism, not in spite of liberalism.

The fulcrum of this balance,[45] I believe, is scale. The objects of this balance are town and nation, the instrumentalities are citizen and representative, and the processes are communal and liberal. More than anything else, therefore, I hope my work is an invitation for political scientists, as political scientists, to explore this paradigm and lead America back to the pasture springs in the high hills of home. Let the watersheds that sustain our nationhood be refreshed by our efforts. It will be a challenge, but we are up to it.

This task, I now realize, is to what Mansbridge referred in 1972 when she said to me with a patient smile (after enduring a particularly emotional outburst on the beauty of town meeting), "Actually, Frank, I suspect it's a little more complicated than that." And so I end where I began: on the banks of a little Vermont stream by a covered bridge in the hardwood hills of northern New England.

45. Mansbridge describes a "classic balance" between adversary and unitary democracy in Athens and opts for a similar balance in town-meeting-like structures. This balance makes town meeting possible. But the balance I am referring to here is between large representative systems where liberalism is the prevailing thesis and small communitarian systems where unitary values prevail.

Washington, VT, 103
Waterbury, CT, 32
Waterville, VT, 86
Watkins, Pat, 257
weather: coding severity of, 88; impact on
    attendance, 86–89; impact on verbal
    participation, 175–76; and women's
    attendance, 199n23
Webb Estate, 60
Webster, Clarence M., 36n35
Weir, Margaret, 52
Weissberg, Robert, 45n80
Welch, Barbara, 93n11
Welch, Susan, 52n101, 194n11, 204n37,
    205–6n39, 207n42
Wells River, VT, 286
Wertheimer, Alan, 255n1
West Braintree town hall, 103
Westbrook, Perry D., 32n25, 36n37
West Haven, VT, 173
Westminster, VT, 174
Weybridge, VT, 126
Wheeler, John, 151n25
White, E. B., 36
White, Edgar N., 157n35
White, Robert, 48n93
Whitehead, David, 9
White Mountains of New Hampshire,
    87
Whiting, VT, 122
Wiencke, Matthew, 48
Wierznski, Gregory, 46n84
Wilcox, Alexander, 235n3, 263n12
Wilcox, Bert, 235n3
Wilcox, Catherine, 235n3
Wilcox, Delos F., 30n17
Wildavsky, Aaron, 44
Wilder, Roger, 37n39
Wilder, Thornton, 36
Williams, Bruce A., 52n100
Williston, VT, 182, 274; town score on
    RBDI, 268–69
Wilmington, VT, 216
Wilson, Harold Fisher, 33n26,
    111n7
Wilson, James Q., 52n101
Wilson, Stanley T., 10n26

Wilson, Thomas C., 122n36
Wilson, William Julius, 181
Winston, Latonia, 218n8
Winters, Richard, 3, 42n63
Wirth, Louis, 122n36
Wise, David, 52n102
Wittebols, James H., 157n35
Wolfinger, Raymond E., 124n39
Wolfson, Tana, 61n13
Wolin, Sheldon S., 2
women's attendance: and Australian ballot,
    202; basic statistics on, 192–93; peer
    influence on, 196–97; related to
    men's, 193–94; over time (1970–98),
    194
women's attendance, correlates of: day vs.
    night meetings, 195–99; dependent
    population, 207–11; native
    Vermonters, 206; political culture,
    207–11; population density, 207–11;
    rural isolation, 207; school issues,
    199–202; socioeconomic status,
    203–6; town size, 194–95;
    Vermont's ERA vote, 207–11
women's issues, 249–52; examples, 249–51;
    similar to men's, 252
women's total involvement: combining
    attendance and verbal participation,
    229; correlates of, 230–31; from
    meeting to meeting, 230
women's verbal participation: and
    Australian ballot, 219; basic data,
    215–16; compared with men's,
    216–17; meeting-to-meeting
    variation, 218–19; as ratio of men's,
    217; as weighted combination of
    "speech" and "talk," 218
women's verbal participation, correlates of:
    conspicuousness, 213–14;
    crowdedness, 220; passage of time,
    214, 223, 226–28; peer influence,
    221; political culture, 225–26;
    school issues, 220, 250–52;
    socioeconomic status, 223–24; town
    size, 226–27
Wood, Joseph S., 33n27
Wood, Robert C., 43